THE SWALLOW CHECKLISTS
OF CRITICISM AND EXPLICATION

POETRY EXPLICATION
by Joseph M. Kuntz

THE ENGLISH NOVEL: 1578-1956
by Inglis Bell and Donald Baird

SHORT FICTION CRITICISM
by Jarvis Thurston, O. B. Emerson, Carl Hartman, and Elizabeth V. Wright

THE AMERICAN NOVEL
by Donna Gerstenberger and George Hendrick

THE AMERICAN NOVEL 1789-1959

A Checklist of Twentieth-Century Criticism

by

DONNA GERSTENBERGER
and
GEORGE HENDRICK

ALAN SWALLOW, *Denver*

Copyright 1961 by
Donna Gerstenberger and George Hendrick

Library of Congress Catalog Card Number: 61-9356

Second edition

INTRODUCTION

Criticism of the American novel has grown to such an extent over the last forty years that a checklist of twentieth-century criticism of the American novel has become desirable. The amount of critical work in this area is so extensive that any checklist is admittedly incomplete, but we have attempted to cover the standard sources and have added notations of individual bibliographies so that a scholar doing intensive work may be able to trace additional material.

The checklist is divided into two sections: criticism of individual authors and criticism of the American novel as a genre. In the first section we list criticism under three categories: (1) individual novels, (2) general studies, (3) bibliographies. The limitations of space have made it necessary for us to list most articles dealing with more than one novel under the category, *general*. We have not ordinarily attempted to list multiple reviews, reviews of secondary studies, or reviews of a single work which seem to contain no significant contribution to criticism. Authors studied primarily *as novelists* have received more complete treatment than authors who worked primarily in some other form. Thus, under *Melville* will be listed studies which cannot be called criticism in the strictest sense of the word but which contribute to an understanding of the canon of the novels. Under *Poe,* on the other hand, will be listed only studies dealing with his single novel, *The Narrative of A. Gordon Pym.* Short fiction not ordinarily classified as novels is excluded.

The second major section of the checklist lists general studies of the American novel, divided, as far as possible, into centuries. Studies which span centuries are classified under the category, *general*. Complete bibliographic entries for individual books may be found in the master list at the end of the volume, where collections of essays by different authors are indexed by the title of the volume rather than by the name of the editor.

Because of the large number of general histories of American literature, we have not usually attempted to survey what is, in many cases, repetitious material, although we have included histories of the American novel. Six basic sources which are not included but which should be consulted by anyone working on the American novel are Spiller, *The Literary History of the United States;* Millett, *Contemporary American Authors;* Blanck, *Bibliography of American Literature; The Cambridge History of American Literature;* Leary, *Articles on American Literature 1900-1950;* and Parrington, *Main Currents in American Thought.*

In preparation of this checklist, we wish to acknowledge the support given us by the Council on Research and Creative Work, by Dean Dayton D. McKean of the Graduate School and by the University of Colorado Library, especially Marjorie Stephenson of the Humanities Division of the Library. Special assistance has been rendered by John Edward Schamberger, Edwin Johson, Louise Duus, and Willene Hendrick.

GEORGE HENDRICK
Johann Wolfgang Goethe University
Frankfurt/Main, Germany

DONNA GERSTENBERGER
University of Washington
Seattle, Washington

ADAMS, HENRY

DEMOCRACY
Beaty, Richmond C. "Henry Adams and American Democracy," *Georgia Review* IV (Fall 1950), 147-156.
Canby, Henry Seidel. "Democracy," *Saturday Review of Literature* II (Oct 17, 1925), 205, 213.
Himmelfarb, Gertrude. "Henry Adams' Skeptic Faith in Democracy: What if it should succeed...!" *Commentary* XIV (Dec 1952), 598-602.
Howe, Irving. *Politics and the Novel*, 175-182.
Hume, Robert A. *Runaway Star*, 131-142.
Levenson, J. C. *The Mind and Art of Henry Adams*, 85-97.
Stevenson, Elizabeth. *Henry Adams*, 169-173.

ESTHER
Hume, Robert A. *Runaway Star*, 142-150.
Levenson, J. C. *The Mind and Art of Henry Adams*, 199-204.
Spiller, Robert E. Introduction, *Esther* (Gainesville, 1938), pp. xxv.
Stevenson, Elizabeth. *Henry Adams*, 176-185.

GENERAL
Blackmur, R. P. "The Expense of Greatness: Three Emphases on Henry Adams," *The Expense of Greatness*, 253-276.
——————. "Henry Adams: Three Late Moments," *Kenyon Review* II (Winter 1940), 7-29.
——————. "The Novels of Henry Adams," *Sewanee Review* LI (Apr-Jun 1943), 281-304.
Brooks, Van Wyck. *New England: Indian Summer*.
Cargill, Oscar. "The Freudians," *Intellectual America*, 551-569.
Gohdes, Clarence. "A Challenge of Social Problems and of Science," *The Literature of the American People*, 782-789.
Morris, Lloyd. *Postscript to Yesterday*, 379-401.
Samuels, Ernest. *Henry Adams: The Middle Years*.
Saveth, Edward N. "The Heroines of Henry Adams," *American Quarterly* VIII (Fall 1956), 231-242.
Speare, Morris Edmund. "The Pioneer American Political Novel of Henry Adams," *The Political Novel*, 287-305.
Whipple, T. K. "Henry Adams," *Spokesmen*, 23-44.

ADAMS, SAMUEL HOPKINS

REVELRY
Blotner, Joseph L. *The Political Novel*, 38.
GENERAL
Baldwin, Charles C. "Samuel Hopkins Adams," *The Men Who Made Our Novels*, 10-16.

AGEE, JAMES

GENERAL
Frohock, W. M. "James Agee: The Question of Unkept Promise," *Southwest Review* XLII (Summer 1957), 221-229.

AIKEN, CONRAD

GENERAL
Hatcher, Harlan. "Eroticism and the Psychological Novel: Conrad Aiken," *Creating the Modern American Novel*, 183-187.
Rein, David M. "Conrad Aiken and Psychoanalysis," *Psychoanalytic Review* 42 (Oct 1955), 402-411.
Whicher, George F. "Impressionists and Experimenters," *The Literature of the American People*, 867.

ALCOTT, LOUISA MAY

LITTLE WOMEN
Morse, Katherine. Introduction, *Little Women* (New York, 1926; 1934), pp. xvi.
Stern, Madeleine B. "The First Appearance of a 'Little Women' Incident," *American Notes & Queries* III (Oct 1943), 99-100.
Warner, Frances Lester. Introduction, *Little Women* (New York, 1928), pp. xviii.
GENERAL
Anthony, Katharine. *Louisa May Alcott*.
Bradford, Gamaliel. "Louisa May Alcott," *Portraits of American Women*, 167-194.
Meigs, Cornelia. *Invincible Louisa*.
Perényi, Eleanor. "Dear Louisa," *Harper's* CCXI (Oct 1955), 69-72.

ALCOTT, LOUISA MAY, Continued

Roller, Bert. "When Jo Died," *Sewanee Review* XXXVI (Apr-Jun 1928),164-170.
Stern, Madeleine B. *Louisa May Alcott.*
──────────────. "Louisa M. Alcott: An Appraisal," *New England Quarterly* XXII (Dec 1949), 475-498.
Worthington, Marjorie. *Miss Alcott of Concord.*
BIBLIOGRAPHY
Gulliver, Lucile. *Louisa May Alcott: A Bibliography.*

ALDRICH, BESS STREETER

GENERAL
Rosse, James C. "Bess Streeter Aldrich," *Prairie Schooner* III (Summer 1929), 226-229.

ALDRICH, THOMAS BAILEY

GENERAL
Brooks, Van Wyck. "Writers of the Eighties," *Saturday Review of Literature* XXII (Jun 8, 1940), 18-19.
Cowie, Alexander. "Indian Summer Novelist," *New England Quarterly* XV (Dec 1942), 608-621.
──────────────. "Local-Color, Frontier, and Regional Fiction: Thomas Bailey Aldrich (1836-1907)," *The Rise of the American Novel,* 579-591.
Grattan, C. Hartley. "Thomas Bailey Aldrich," *American Mercury* V (May 1925), 41-45.
Greenslet, Ferris. *The Life of Thomas Bailey Aldrich.*
Perry, Bliss. "Thomas Bailey Aldrich," *Park-Street Papers,* 141-170.

ALGER, HORATIO, JR.

JED, THE POOR HOUSE BOY
Wimberly, Lowry C. "Hemingway and Horatio Alger, Jr.," *Prairie Schooner* X (Fall 1936), 208-211.
GENERAL
Allen, Frederick Lewis. "Horatio Alger, Jr.," *Saturday Review of Literature* XVIII (Sept 17, 1938), 3-4; 16-17.

ALGER, HORATIO, J., Continued

Holland, Norman N. "Hobbling with Horatio, or the Uses of Literature," *Hudson Review* XII (Winter 1959-60), 549-557.
Mayes, Herbert R. *Alger: A Biography Without a Hero.*

ALGREN, NELSON

GENERAL
Anderson, Alston and Terry Southern. "Nelson Algren," *Writers at Work,* 231-249.
Bluestone, George. "Nelson Algren," *Western Review* XXII (Autumn 1957), 27-44.
Breit, Harvey. *The Writer Observed,* 85-87.
Geismar, Maxwell. "Nelson Algren: The Iron Sanctuary," *College English* XIV (Mar 1953), 311-315; *American Moderns,* 187-194.

ALLEN, HERVEY

ACTION AT AQUILA
Daniels, Jonathan. "Escape from a Legend," *Saturday Review of Literature* XVII (Mar 5, 1938), 3-4; 16; 18.
ANTHONY ADVERSE
Allen, Hervey. "The Sources of *Anthony Adverse*," *Saturday Review of Literature* X (Jan 13, 1934), 401; 408-410.
THE FOREST AND THE FORT
Burt, Struthers. "Hervey Allen's Cornerstone: The First Block in a Six-Story Structure," *Saturday Review of Literature* XXVI (Apr 17, 1943), 13-14.
GENERAL
Clark, Emily. "Hervey Allen," *Saturday Review of Literature* X (Dec 9, 1933), 323.

ALLEN, JAMES LANE

GENERAL
Knight, Grant C. *James Lane Allen and the Genteel Tradition.*
Quinn, Arthur Hobson. "James Lane Allen and the Novel of the Spirit," *American Fiction,* 472-483.
Toulmin, Harry Aubrey. *Social Historians,* 101-130.

ALLEN, JAMES LANE, Continued

Wagenknecht, Edward. "Some Southern Novelists of the 'Nineties and After: The Finely-Wrought Art of James Lane Allen," *Cavalcade of the American Novel*, 186-191.

ANDERSON, SHERWOOD

BEYOND DESIRE
Whipple, T. K. "Sherwood Anderson," *Saturday Review of Literature* IX (Dec 10, 1932), 305.
DARK LAUGHTER
Chase, Cleveland B. *Sherwood Anderson*, 56-60.
KIT BRANDON: A PORTRAIT
Van Doren, Mark. *The Private Reader*, 247-251.
MANY MARRIAGES
Wilson, Edmund. *The Shores of Light*, 91-93.
MARCHING MEN
Chase, Cleveland B. *Sherwood Anderson*, 27-31.
WINDY McPHERSON'S SON
Chase, Cleveland B. *Sherwood Anderson*, 16-27.
WINESBURG, OHIO
Budd, Louis J. "The Grotesques of Anderson and Wolfe," *Modern Fiction Studies* V (Winter 1959-1960), 304-310.
Chase, Cleveland B. *Sherwood Anderson*, 31-40.
Gold, Herbert. *Twelve Original Essays on Great American Novels*, 196-209.
Howe, Irving. "The Book of the Grotesque," *Partisan Review* XVIII (Jan-Feb 1951), 32-40.
Phillips, William L. "The First Printing of Sherwood Anderson's *Winesburg, Ohio*," *Studies in Bibliography* IV (1951-52), 211-213.
——————. "How Sherwood Anderson Wrote *Winesburg, Ohio*," *American Literature* XXIII (Mar 1951), 7-30.
Schevill, James. *Sherwood Anderson*, 93-108.
Thurston, Jarvis. "Anderson and 'Winesburg': Mysticism and Craft," *Accent* XVI (Spring 1956), 107-128.
GENERAL
Almy, Robert F. "Sherwood Anderson—The Non-Conforming Rediscoverer," *Saturday Review of Literature* XXVIII (Jan 6, 1945), 17-18.

ANDERSON, SHERWOOD, Continued

Anderson, Karl James. "My Brother, Sherwood Anderson," *Saturday Review of Literature* XXXI (Sept 4, 1948), 6-7; 26-27.

Anderson, Sherwood. "So You Want to Be a Writer?" *Saturday Review of Literature* XXI (Dec 9, 1939), 13-14.

Baldwin, Charles C. "Sherwood Anderson," *The Men Who Make Our Novels*, 26-33.

Berland, Alwyn. "Sherwood Anderson and the Pathetic Grotesque," *Western Review* XV (Winter 1951), 135-138.

Boynton, Percy H. "Sherwood Anderson," *America in Contemporary Fiction*, 113-130; *More Contemporary Americans*, 157-177.

Calverton, V. F. "Sherwood Anderson: A Study in Sociological Criticism," *The Newer Spirit*, 52-118.

Canby, Henry Seidel. "Sherwood Anderson," *Saturday Review of Literature* XXIII (Mar 22, 1941), 10.

Cargill, Oscar. "The Primitivists," *Intellectual America*, 322-331; 677-685.

Chapman, Arnold. "Sherwood Anderson and Eduardo Mallea," *PMLA* LXIX (Mar 1954), 34-45.

Chase, Cleveland B. *Sherwood Anderson*.

——————. "Sherwood Anderson," *Saturday Review of Literature* IV (Sept 24, 1927), 129-130.

Duffey, Bernard. "The Struggle for Affirmation—Anderson, Sandburg, Lindsay," *The Chicago Renaissance in American Letters*, 194-238.

Eliason, Norman W. "Sherwood Anderson," *Prairie Schooner* IV (Winter 1930), 52-59.

Fagin, Nathan Bryllion. *The Phenomenon of Sherwood Anderson*.

——————. "Sherwood Anderson," *South Atlantic Quarterly* XLIII (Jul 1944), 256-262.

Farrell, James T. "A Memoir on Sherwood Anderson," *Perspective* VII (Summer 1954), 83-88.

——————. "A Note on Sherwood Anderson," *Reflections at Fifty*, 164-168.

Faulkner, William. "Sherwood Anderson," *Atlantic Monthly* CXCI (Jun 1953), 27-29.

——————. "Sherwood Anderson," *Princeton University Library Chronicle* XVIII (Spring 1957), 89-94.

ANDERSON, SHERWOOD, Continued

Flanagan, John T. "Hemingway's Debt to Sherwood Anderson," *Journal of English and Germanic Philology* LIV (Oct 1955), 507-520.

──────────. "The Permanence of Sherwood Anderson," *Southwest Review* XXXV (Summer 1950), 170-177.

Geismar, Maxwell. "Sherwood Anderson: Last of the Townsmen," *The Last of the Provincials*, 223-284.

Gelfant, Blanche Housman. *The American City Novel*, 99-106.

Gold, Herbert. "The Purity and Cunning of Sherwood Anderson," *Hudson Review* X (Winter 1957-58), 548-557.

Gregory, Alyse. "Sherwood Anderson," *Dial* LXXV (Sept 1923), 243-246.

Hansen, Harry. "Sherwood Anderson, Corn-fed Mystic, Historian of the Middle Age of Man," *Midwest Portraits*, 109-179.

──────────. "Sherwood Anderson's Story," *Saturday Review of Literature* XXV (Apr 11, 1942), 5-6.

Hartwick, Harry. "Broken Face Gargoyles," *The Foreground of American Fiction*, 111-142.

Hatcher, Harlan. "Sherwood Anderson," *Creating the Modern American Novel*, 155-171.

Hoffman, Frederick J. *Freudianism and the Literary Mind*, 229-250.

──────────. "Sherwood Anderson: A 'Groping, Artistic, Sincere Personality,'" *Western Review* XVIII (Winter 1954), 159-162.

Howe, Irving. *Sherwood Anderson*.

──────────. "Sherwood Anderson: An American as Artist," *Kenyon Review* XIII (Spring 1951), 193-203.

──────────. "Sherwood Anderson and the Power Urge: A Note on Populism in American Literature," *Commentary* X (Jul 1950), 78-80.

Jones, Howard Mumford and Walter B. Rideout (eds.). *Letters of Sherwood Anderson*.

Kazin, Alfred. "The New Realism: Sherwood Anderson and Sinclair Lewis," *On Native Grounds*, 205-217.

Lovett, Robert Morss. "Sherwood Anderson," *After the Genteel Tradition*, 88-99.

──────────. "Sherwood Anderson, American," *Virginia Quarterly Review* XVII (Summer 1941), 379-388.

ANDERSON, SHERWOOD, Continued

Macafee, Helen. "Some Novelists in Mid-Stream," *Yale Review* XV (Jan 1926), 349-351.

McCole, John. *Lucifer at Large,* 125-150.

Michaud, Régis. *The American Novel To-Day,* 154-199.

——————. "Sherwood Anderson," *Panorama de la Litterature Americaine Contemporaine,* 170-173.

Morris, Lloyd. *Postscript to Yesterday,* 145-148.

Quinn, Arthur Hobson. "Critics and Satirists—The Radicals," *American Fiction,* 656-661.

Raymund, Bernard. "The Grammar of Not-Reason: Sherwood Anderson," *Arizona Quarterly* XII (Spring 1956), 48-60.

Rosenfeld, Paul. Introduction, *The Sherwood Anderson Reader* (Boston 1947). viii-xxx.

——————. "Sherwood Anderson," *Dial* LXXII (Jan 1922), 29-42; *Port of New York,* 175-198.

Schevill, James. *Sherwood Anderson.*

Sherman, Stuart. "Sherwood Anderson's Tales of the New Life," *Critical Woodcuts,* 3-17.

Smith, Rachel. "Sherwood Anderson: Some Entirely Arbitrary Reactions," *Sewanee Review* XXXVII (Apr-Jun 1929), 159-163.

Trilling, Lionel. "Sherwood Anderson," *Kenyon Review* III (Summer 1941), 293-302; *The Liberal Imagination,* 22-23; *Critiques and Essays on Modern Fiction,* 319-327.

Van Doren, Carl. *Contemporary American Novelists,* 153-157.

Wagenknecht, Edward. "In the Second Decade: Sherwood Anderson: The *Cri de Coeur* as Novel," *Cavalcade of the American Novel,* 311-318.

Walcutt, Charles Child. "Sherwood Anderson: Impressionism and the Buried Life," *Sewanee Review* LX (Jan-Mar 1952), 28-47; *American Literary Naturalism,* 222-239.

West, Rebecca. "Sherwood Anderson, Poet," *The Strange Necessity,* 309-320.

Whicher, George F. "Analysts of Decay," *The Literature of the American People,* 871-873.

Whipple, T. K. "Sherwood Anderson," *Spokesmen,* 115-138.

Wickham, Harvey. "Laughter and Sherwood Anderson," *The Impuritans,* 268-282.

ANDERSON, SHERWOOD, Continued

Winther, S. K. "The Aura of Loneliness in Sherwood Anderson," *Modern Fiction Studies* V (Summer 1959), 145-152.

ARTHUR, TIMOTHY SHAY

GENERAL

Cowie, Alexander. "The Domestic Sentimentalists and Other Popular Writers (1850-1870): Timothy Shay Arthur (1809-1885)," *The Rise of the American Novel*, 436-438.

French, Warren. "Timothy Shay Arthur's Divorce Fiction," *Texas Studies in English* XXXIII (1954), 90-96.

──────────. "Timothy Shay Arthur: Pioneer Business Novelist," *American Quarterly* X (Spring 1958), 55-65.

ATHERTON, GERTRUDE

GENERAL

Sinclair, Upton. "Incense to Mammon," *Money Writes!* 78-84.

Underwood, John Curtis. *Literature and Insurgency*, 391-446.

AUSTIN, MARY

GENERAL

DuBois, Arthur E. "Mary Hunter Austin: 1868-1934," *Southwest Review* XX (Apr 1935), 231-275.

Mary Austin: A Memorial.

Overton, Grant. "Mary Austin," *The Women Who Make Our Novels*, 8-22.

Pearce, T. M. "Mary Austin and the Patterns of New Mexico," *Southwest Review* XXII (Jan 1937), 140-148.

Sergeant, Elizabeth Shepley. "Mary Austin: A Portrait," *Saturday Review of Literature* XI (Sept 8, 1934), 96.

Van Doren, Carl. *Contemporary American Novelists*, 140-143.

Wagenknecht, Edward. "Voices of the New Century: Mary Austin, Sybil," *Cavalcade of the American Novel*, 230-235.

Wynn, Dudley Taylor. *A Critical Study of the Writings of Mary Hunter Austin.*

──────────. "Mary Austin, Woman Alone," *Virginia Quarterly Review* XIII (Spring 1937), 243-256.

AUSTIN, MARY, Continued

Young, Vernon. "Mary Austin and the Earth Performance," *Southwest Review* XXXV (Summer 1959), 153-163.

BASSO, HAMILTON

THE LIGHT INFANTRY BALL

Hicks, Granville. "Pompey's Head," *Saturday Review* XLII (Jun 6, 1959), 16.

SUN IN CAPRICORN

Rubin, Louis D., Jr. "All the King's Meanings," *Georgia Review* VIII (Winter 1954), 422-434.

BEER, THOMAS

GENERAL

Baldwin, Charles C. "Thomas Beer," *The Men Who Make Our Novels,* 42-45.

Kazin, Alfred. "The Exquisites," *On Native Grounds,* 238-242.

Mumford, Lewis. "Thomas Beer: Aristocrat of Letters," *Saturday Review of Literature* XXII (Apr 27, 1940), 3-4; 17.

Sherman, Stuart. "Thomas Beer: Our Own Petronius at Last," *The Main Stream,* 157-167.

Woolley, Monty and Cary Abbott. "Thomas Beer As Remembered by Two Classmates," *Saturday Review of Literature* XIV (Sept 13, 1941), 12-13.

BELLAMY, EDWARD

EQUALITY

Bowman, Sylvia E. "Bellamy's Missing Chapter," *New England Quarterly* XXXI (Mar 1958), 47-65.

LOOKING BACKWARD

Baxter, Sylvester. Introduction, *Looking Backward* (New York, 1920), pp. xxi.

Becker, George J. "Edward Bellamy: Utopia, American Plan," *Antioch Review* XIV (Jun 1954), 181-194.

Bellamy, Paul. Introduction, *Looking Backward* (Cleveland, 1945; 1950).

BELLAMY, EDWARD, Continued

Broun, Heywood. Introduction, *Looking Backward* (New York, 1942), pp x.
Franklin, John Hope. "Edward Bellamy and the Nationalist Movement," *New England Quarterly* XI (Dec 1938), 739-772.
Morgan, Arthur E. *Edward Bellamy*, 204-244.
Sadler, Elizabeth. "One Book's Influence: Edward Bellamy's 'Looking Backward,'" *New England Quarterly* XVII (Dec 1944), 530-555.
Schiffman, Joseph. Introduction, *Looking Backward* (New York, 1959).
Shurter, Robert L. "The Writing of *Looking Backward*," *South Atlantic Quarterly* XXXVIII (1939), 255-261.
White, Frederic R. Introduction, *Looking Backward* (Chicago, 1946), pp. xxxviii.

GENERAL

Bowman, Sylvia E. *The Year 2000.*
Gohdes, Clarence. "A Challenge of Social Problems and of Science," *The Literature of the American People*, 767-769.
Hicks, Granville. *The Great Tradition*, 139-142.
Madison, Charles A. "Edward Bellamy, Social Dreamer," *New England Quarterly* XV (Sept 1942), 444-466.
Morgan, Arthur E. *Edward Bellamy.*
──────────. *The Philosophy of Edward Bellamy.*
Schiffman, Joseph. "Edward Bellamy's Altruistic Man," *American Quarterly* VI (Fall 1954), 195-209.
──────────. "Edward Bellamy's Religious Thought," *PMLA* LXVIII (Sept 1953), 716-732.
Shurter, Robert L. "The Literary Work of Edward Bellamy," *American Literature* V (Nov 1933), 229-234.
Taylor, Walter F. *The Economic Novel in America*, 184-213.

BELLOW, SAUL

THE ADVENTURES OF AUGIE MARCH

Aldridge, John W. *In Search of Heresy*, 126-148.
Bergler, Edmund. "Writers of Half-Talent," *American Imago* XIV (Summer 1957), 155-164.
Breit, Harvey. *The Writer Observed*, 271-274.

BELLOW, SAUL, Continued

Harwell, Meade. "Picaro from Chicago," *Southwest Review* XXXIX (Summer 1954), 273-276.

Popkin, Henry. "American Comedy," *Kenyon Review* XVI (Spring 1954), 329-334.

Webster, Harvey Curtis. "Quest Through the Modern World," *Saturday Review* XXXVI (Sept 19, 1953), 12-13.

DANGLING MAN

Rothman, Nathan L. "Introducing an Important New Writer," *Saturday Review of Literature* XXVII (Apr 15, 1944), 27.

HENDERSON THE RAIN KING

Chase, Richard. "The Adventures of Saul Bellow: Progress of a Novelist," *Commentary* XXVII (Apr 1959), 323-330.

Stern, Richard G. "Henderson's Bellow," *Kenyon Review* XXI (Autumn 1959), 655-656.

GENERAL

Eisinger, Chester E. "Saul Bellow: Love and Identity," *Accent* XVIII (Summer 1958), 179-203.

Fiedler, Leslie. "Saul Bellow," *Prairie Schooner* XXXI (Summer 1951), 103-110.

Frank, Rueben. "Saul Bellow: The Evolution of a Contemporary Novelist," *Western Review* XVIII (Winter 1954), 101-112.

Geismar, Maxwell. "Saul Bellow: Novelist of the Intellectuals," *American Moderns*, 210-224.

Levine, Paul. "Saul Bellow: The Affirmation of the Philosophical Fool," *Perspective* X (Winter 1959), 163-176.

Sanavio, Piero. "Il Romanzo Di Saul Bellow," *Studi Americani* II (1956), 261-283.

BIRD, ROBERT MONTGOMERY

NICK OF THE WOODS

Keiser, Albert. *The Indian in American Literature*, 144-153.

Williams, Cecil B. Introduction, *Nick of the Woods* (New York, 1939), pp. lxxv.

GENERAL

Cowie, Alexander. "Contemporaries and Immediate Followers of Cooper, II: Robert Montgomery Bird (1806-1845)," *The Rise of the American Novel*, 246-258.

BIRD, ROBERT MONTGOMERY, Continued

Lewis, R. W. B. "The Hero in Space: Brown, Cooper, Bird," *The American Adam*, 90-109.
Quinn, Arthur Hobson. "The Development of Idealistic Romance," *American Fiction*, 108-10.
——————. "The Romance of History and the Frontier," *The Literature of the American People*, 237-239.
Williams, Cecil B. "R. M. Bird's Plans for Novels of the Frontier," *American Literature* XXI (Nov 1949), 321-324.

BOURJAILY, VANCE

THE END OF MY LIFE
Aldridge, John W. *After the Lost Generation*, 117-132.
THE VIOLATED
Hicks, Granville. "The Maturity of Vance Bourjaily," *Saturday Review* XLI (Aug 23, 1958), 13.

BOWLES, PAUL

THE SHELTERING SKY
Aldridge, John W. *After the Lost Generation*, 184-193.
Prescott, Orville. *In My Opinion*, 116-117.
GENERAL
Evans, Oliver. "Paul Bowles and the 'Natural' Man," *Critique* III (Spring-Fall 1959), 43-59.
Hassan, Ihab H. "The Pilgrim as Prey: A Note on Paul Bowles," *Western Review* XIX (Autumn 1954), 23-36.

BOYD, JAMES

GENERAL
Meade, Julian R. "James Boyd," *Saturday Review of Literature* XII (Jun 29, 1935), 10-11.
Whicher, George F. "Loopholes of Retreat," *The Literature of the American People*, 890.

BOYESEN, HJALMAR HJORTH

GENERAL

Hicks, Granville. *The Great Tradition,* 156-158.

Turner, Arlin. "A Novelist Discovers A Novelist: The Correspondence of H. H. Boyesen and George W. Cable," *Western Humanities Review* V (Autumn 1951), 343-372.

White, George L., Jr. "H. H. Boyesen: A Note on Immigration," *American Literature* XIII (Jan 1942), 363-371.

BOYLE, KAY

AVALANCHE

Burt, Struthers. "Kay Boyle's Coincidence and Melodrama," *Saturday Review of Literature* XXVII (Jan 15, 1944), 6.

DEATH OF A MAN

Van Doren, Mark. *The Private Reader,* 241-244.

Carpenter, Richard C. "Kay Boyle," *College English* XV (Nov 1953), 81-87.

BRACE, GERALD WARNER

GENERAL

Harris, Arthur S., Jr. "Gerald Warner Brace: Teacher-Novelist," *College English* XVIII (Dec 1956), 157-160.

BRACKENRIDGE, HUGH HENRY

MODERN CHIVALRY

Brennecke, Ernest. Introduction, *Modern Chivalry* (New York, 1926), pp. xviii.

Newlin, Claude M. Introduction, *Modern Chivalry* (New York, 1937), pp. xliv.

Wagenknecht, Edward. *Cavalcade of the American Novel,* 6-9.

GENERAL

Cowie, Alexander. "Early Satire and Realism: Hugh Henry Brackenridge (1748-1816)," *The Rise of the American Novel,* 43-60.

Newlin, Claude Milton. *The Life and Writings of Hugh Henry Brackenridge.*

BROMFIELD, LOUIS

MR. SMITH

Smith, Harrison. "Babbitt of a New Generation," *Saturday Review of Literature* XXXIV (Aug 25, 1951), 12-13.

WHAT BECAME OF ANNA BOLTON?

Wilson, Edmund. *A Literary Chronicle*, 271-278.

GENERAL

Baldwin, Charles C. "Louis Bromfield," *The Men Who Make Our Novels*, 46-51.

Bromfield, Mary. "The Writer I Live With," *Atlantic Monthly* CLXXXVI (Aug 1950), 77-79.

Inescort, Frieda. "Louis Bromfield of Mansfield," *Saturday Review of Literature* X (Apr 14, 1934), 629.

Whicher, George F. "Spokesmen of the Plain People," *The Literature of the American People*, 839-840.

BIBLIOGRAPHY

Derrenbacher, Merle. "Louis Bromfield: A Bibliography," *Bulletin of Bibliography* XVII (Sept-Dec 1941), 112; (Jan-Apr 1942), 141-145.

BROWN, CHARLES BROCKDEN

ALCUIN

Kimball, LeRoy Elwood. Introduction, *Alcuin* (New Haven, Conn., 1935), pp. xxi.

ARTHUR MERVYN

Vilas, Martin S. *Charles Brockden Brown*, 31-33.

Warfel, Harry R. *Charles Brockden Brown*, 141-148.

Wiley, Lulu Rumsey. *The Sources and Influence of the Novels of Charles Brockden Brown*, 141-154.

CLARA HOWARD

Vilas, Martin S. *Charles Brockden Brown*, 40-43.

Warfel, Harry R. *Charles Brockden Brown*, 141-148.

Wiley, Lulu Rumsey. *The Sources and Influence of the Novels of Charles Brockden Brown*, 172-176.

EDGAR HUNTLY

Carter, Boyd. "Poe's Debt to Charles Brockden Brown," *Prairie Schooner* XXVII (Summer 1953), 190-196.

Chase, Richard. *The American Novel and Its Tradition*, 35-37.

BROWN, CHARLES BROCKDEN, Continued

Clark, David Lee. Introduction, *Edgar Huntly* (New York, 1928), pp. xxiii.
Vilas, Martin S. *Charles Brockden Brown*, 34-39.
Warfel, Harry R. *Charles Brockden Brown*, 149-164.
Wiley, Lulu Rumsey. *The Sources and Influence of the Novels of Charles Brockden Brown*, 155-171.

JANE TALBOT
Vilas, Martin S. *Charles Brockden Brown*, 44-46.
Warfel, Harry R. *Charles Brockden Brown*, 182-202.
Wiley, Lulu Rumsey. *The Sources and Influence of the Novels of Charles Brockden Brown*, 176-188.

ORMOND
Marchand, Ernest. Introduction, *Ormond* (New York, 1937), pp. li.
Vilas, Martin S. *Charles Brockden Brown*, 27-30.
Warfel, Harry R. *Charles Brockden Brown*, 125-140.
Wiley, Lulu Rumsey. *The Sources and Influence of the Novels of Charles Brockden Brown*, 122-141.

WIELAND
Chase, Richard. *The American Novel and Its Tradition*, 29-35.
Kerlin, R. T. "*Wieland* and *The Raven*," *Modern Language Notes* XXXI (Dec 1916), 503-505.
Pattee, Fred Lewis. Introduction, *Wieland* (New York, 1926; 1959).
Prescott, F. C. "*Wieland* and *Frankenstein*," *American Literature* II (May 1930), 172-173.
Vilas, Martin S. *Charles Brockden Brown*, 19-26.
Warfel, Harry R. *Charles Brockden Brown*, 96-115.
Wiley, Lulu Rumsey. *The Sources and Influence of the Novels of Charles Brockden Brown*, 96-121.

GENERAL
Berthoff, W. B. "Adventures of the Young Man: An Approach to Charles Brockden Brown," *American Quarterly* IX (Winter 1957), 421-434.
──────. "'A Lesson on Concealment': Brockden Brown's Method in Fiction," *Philological Quarterly* XXXVII (Jan 1958), 45-57.
Blake, Warren Barton. "Brockden Brown and the Novel," *Sewanee Review* XVIII (Oct 1910), 431-443.

BROWN, CHARLES BROCKDEN, Continued

Chase, Richard. "A Note on Melodrama," *The American Novel and Its Tradition*, 37-41.
Clark, David Lee. *Charles Brockden Brown*.
——————————. "Unpublished Letters of Charles Brockden Brown and W. W. Wilkins," *Texas Studies in English* XXVII (1948), 75-107.
Cowie, Alexander. "Vaulting Ambition: Brockden Brown and Others," *The Rise of the American Novel*, 69-104.
Erskine, John. "Charles Brockden Brown," *Leading American Novelists*, 3-49.
Haviland, Thomas P. "Precosité Crosses the Atlantic," *PMLA* LIX (Mar 1944), 131-141.
Hintz, Howard W. "Charles Brockden Brown," *The Quaker Influence in American Literature*, 34-40.
Lewis, R. W. B. "The Hero in Space: Brown, Cooper, Bird," *The American Adam*, 90-109.
Loshe, Lillie Deming. *The Early American Novel*, 29-58.
Marble, Annie Russell. "Charles Brockden Brown and Pioneers in Fiction," *Heralds of American Literature*, 279-318.
Marchand, Ernest C. "The Literary Opinions of Charles Brockden Brown," *Studies in Philology* XXXI (Oct 1934), 541-566.
McDowell, Tremaine. "Scott on Cooper and Brockden Brown," *Modern Language Notes* XLV (Jan 1930), 18-20.
Morris, Mabel. "Charles Brockden Brown and the American Indian," *American Literature* XVIII (Nov 1946), 244-247.
Pattee, Fred Lewis. "Charles Brockden Brown," *The First Century of American Literature*, 96-106.
Quinn, Arthur Hobson. "Charles Brockden Brown and the Establishment of Romance," *American Fiction*, 25-39.
Sickels, Eleanor. "Shelley and Charles Brockden Brown," *PMLA* XLV (1930), 1116-1128.
Snell, George. "Charles Brockden Brown," *The Shapers of American Fiction*, 32-45.
——————————. "Charles Brockden Brown: Apocalypticalist," *University of Kansas City Review* XI (Winter 1944), 131-138.
Solve, Melvin T. "Shelley and the Novels of Brown," *Fred Newton Scott Anniversary Papers*, 141-156.
Wagenknecht, Edward. "The Author of Wieland," *Cavalcade of the American Novel*, 9-13.

BROWN, CHARLES BROCKDEN, Continued

Warfel, Harry R. "Charles Brockden Brown's German Sources," *Modern Language Quarterly* (Sept 1940), 357-365.

Wiley, Lulu Rumsey. *The Sources and Influence of the Novels of Charles Brockden Brown.*

BIBLIOGRAPHY

Wiley, Lulu Rumsey. *The Sources and Influence of the Novels of Charles Brockden Brown*, 371-381.

BROWN, WILLIAM HILL

IRA AND ISABELLA

Martin, Terence. "William Hill Brown's *Ira and Isabella*," *New England Quarterly* XXXII (Jun 1959), 238-242.

THE POWER OF SYMPATHY

Ellis, Milton. "The Author of the First American Novel," *American Literature* IV (Jan 1933), 359-368.

McDowell, Tremaine. "The First American Novel," *American Review* II (Nov 1933), 73-81.

Walser, Richard. "More about the First American Novel," *American Literature* XXIV (Nov 1952), 352-357.

BUCK, PEARL

THE GOOD EARTH

Canby, Henry Seidel. "The Good Earth: Pearl Buck and the Nobel Prize," *Saturday Review of Literature* XIX (Nov 19, 1938), 8.

IMPERIAL WOMAN

Schoyer, Preston. "*Imperial Woman*," *Saturday Review* XXXIX (Mar 31, 1956), 12.

GENERAL

Buck, Pearl S. "Advice to Unborn Novelists," *Saturday Review of Literature* XI (Mar 2, 1935), 513-514; 520-521.

Cargill, Oscar. "The Naturalists," *Intellectual America*, 146-154.

Catel, Jean. "Pearl Buck: Prix Nobel," *Etudes Anglaises* III (Jan-Mar 1939), 98-99.

Henchoz, Ami. "A Permanent Element in Pearl Buck's Novels," *English Studies* XXV (1943), 97-103.

BUCK, PEARL, Continued

Lee, Henry. "Pearl S. Buck—Spiritual Descendant of Tom Paine," *Saturday Review of Literature* XXV (Dec 5, 1942), 16-18.

Whicher, George F. "Spokesmen of the Plain People," *The Literature of American People,* 840.

BIBLIOGRAPHY

Brenni, Vito J. "Pearl Buck: A Selected Bibliography," *Bulletin of Bibliography* XXII (May-Aug 1957), 65-69; (Sept-Dec 1957), 94-96.

BUECHNER, FREDERICK

A LONG DAY'S DYING

Aldridge, John W. *After the Lost Generation,* 194-230.

Prescott, Orville. *In My Opinion,* 117-118.

CABELL, JAMES BRANCH

BEYOND LIFE

Holt, Guy. Introduction, *Beyond Life* (New York, 1919; 1923).

CHIVALRY

Rascoe, Burton. Introduction, *Chivalry* (New York, 1921).

CORDS OF VANITY

Follett, Wilson. Introduction, *Cords of Vanity* (New York, 1920), pp. ix.

THE CREAM OF THE JEST

Parks, Edd Winfield. "Cabell's *Cream of the Jest,*" *Modern Fiction Studies* II (May 1956), 68-70.

DOMNEI

Hergesheimer, Joseph. Introduction, *Domnei* (New York, 1920), pp. viii.

EAGLE'S SHADOW

Björkman, Edwin. Introduction, *Eagle's Shadow* (New York, 1923). pp. xl.

FIGURES OF EARTH

Brewster, Paul G. "*Jurgen* and *Figures of Earth* and the Russian Skazki," *American Literature* XIII (Jan 1942), 305-319.

GALLANTRY

Untermeyer, Louis. Introduction, *Gallantry* (New York, 1922), pp. xxii.

CABELL, JAMES BRANCH, Continued

HIGH PLACE
Papé, Frank G. Introduction, *High Place* (New York, 1923). pp. viii.

JURGEN
Aiken, Conrad. *A Reviewer's A B C,* 143-148.

Allen, Gay W. "Jurgen and Faust," *Sewanee Review* XXXIX (Oct-Dec 1931), 485-492.

Brewster, Paul G. *"Jurgen* and *Figures of Earth* and the Russian Skazki," *American Literature* XIII (Jan 1942), 305-319.

Loveman, Samuel. *A Round-Table in Poictesme,* 51-53.

Walpole, Hugh. Introduction, *Jurgen* (New York, 1932).

Zolla, Elémire. "Il 'Jurgen' Di Joseph [sic] Cabell," *Studi Americani* II (1956), 195-205.

SOMETHING ABOUT EVE
Canby, Henry Seidel. *American Estimates,* 70-79.

THERE WERE TWO PIRATES
Redman, Ben Ray. "A True 'Comedy of Diversion,'" *Saturday Review of Literature* XXIX (Aug 10, 1946), 7-8.

GENERAL
Baldwin, Charles C. "James Branch Cabell," *The Men Who Make Our Novels,* 74-88.

Boyd, Ernest. "Cabell versus Cabell and Others," *A Round-Table in Poictesme,* 21-28.

Boynton, Percy H. "James Branch Cabell," *America in Contemporary Fiction,* 73-90.

————. "Mr. Cabell Expounds Himself," *Some Contemporary Americans,* 145-161.

Bregenzer, Don. "A Practitioner in Perfection," *A Round-Table in Poictesme,* 31-47.

Cargill, Oscar. "The Intelligensia," *Intellectual America,* 495-503.

Clark, Emily. *Innocence Abroad,* 35-52.

Edgar, Pelham. *The Art of the Novel,* 261-267.

Follett, Wilson. "A Gossip on James Branch Cabell," *Dial* LXIV (Apr 25, 1918), 392-396.

Glasgow, Ellen. "The Biography of Manuel," *Saturday Review of Literature* VI (Jun 7, 1930), 1108-1109.

Hartwick, Harry. "The Journeys of Jurgen," *The Foreground of American Fiction,* 177-186.

CABELL, JAMES BRANCH, Continued

Hatcher, Harlan. "James Branch Cabell," *Creating the Modern American Novel*, 191-201.
Hergesheimer, Joseph. "James Branch Cabell," *American Mercury* XIII (Jan 1928), 38-47.
Hicks, Granville. *The Great Tradition*, 220-221.
Himelick, Raymond. "Cabell and the Modern Temper," *South Atlantic Quarterly* LXIII (Spring 1959), 176-184.
──────. "Cabell, Shelley, and the 'Incorrigible Flesh,' " *South Atlantic Quarterly* XLVII (Jan 1948), 88-95.
──────. "Figures of Cabell," *Modern Fiction Studies* II (Winter 1956-1957), 214-220.
Hooker, Edward Niles. "Something About Cabell," *Sewanee Review* XXXVII (Apr-Jun 1929), 193-203.
Howard, Leon. "Figures of Allegory: A Study of James Branch Cabell," *Sewanee Review* XLII (Jan-Mar 1934), 54-66.
Hubbell, Jay B. *The South in American Literature*, 845-846.
Jack, Peter Monro. "The James Branch Cabell Period," *After the Genteel Tradition*, 141-154.
Kazin, Alfred. "The Exquisites," *On Native Grounds*, 231-235.
McIntyre, Clara F. "Mr. Cabell's Cosmos," *Sewanee Review* XXXVIII (Jul-Sept 1930), 278-285.
McCole, John. *Lucifer at Large*, 57-69.
McNeill, Warren A. *Cabellian Harmonics*.
Mencken, H. L. *James Branch Cabell*.
──────. "The Style of Cabell," *A Round-Table in Poictesme*, 115-117.
Michaud, Régis. *The American Novel To-Day*, 200-237.
──────. "James Branch Cabell," *Panorama de la Littérature Américaine Contemporaine*, 177-180.
Minarik, Frank L. "Some Impressions of Cabell's Satire," *A Round-Table in Poictesme*, 57-60.
Mooney, M. P. "Some Rogueries of James Branch Cabell," *A Round-Table in Poictesme*, 77-89.
Morley, Christopher. "A Cabellian Comment," *A Round-Table in Poictesme*, 93-94.
Parks, Edd Winfield. James Branch Cabell," *Southern Renascence*, 251-261.
Redman, Ben Ray. "Bülg the Forgotten," *A Round-Table in Poictesme*, 63-73.

CABELL, JAMES BRANCH, Continued

Rubin, Louis D., Jr. "Part II. A Southerner in Poictesme," *No Place on Earth*, 50-81.

Van Doren, Carl. *Contemporary American Novelists*, 104-113.

——————. *James Branch Cabell*.

——————. "James Branch Cabell," *The American Novel 1789-1939*, 315-322.

Van Vechten, Carl. "Mr. Cabell of Lichfield and Poictesme," *Yale University Library Gazette* XXIII (Jul 1948), 1-7.

Wagenknecht, Edward. "James Branch Cabell: The Anatomy of Romanticism," *Cavalcade of the American Novel*, 339-353; first appeared in part as "Cabell: A Re-Consideration," *College English* IX (Feb 1948), 238-246.

Walpole, Hugh. *The Art of James Branch Cabell*.

——————. "The Art of James Branch Cabell," *Yale Review* IX (Jul 1920), 684-698.

Whicher, George F. "Loopholes of Retreat," *The Literature of the American People*, 889.

Wickham, Harvey. "The Tesam of the Crej," *The Impuritans*, 137-168.

Wolf, Howard. "James Branch Cabell and William Jennings Bryan," *A Round-Table in Poictesme*, 105-111.

BIBLIOGRAPHY

Brussel, I. R. *A Bibliography of the Writings of James Branch Cabell (A Revised Bibliography)*.

Holt, Guy. *A Bibliography of the Writings of James Branch Cabell*.

CABLE, GEORGE WASHINGTON

THE GRANDISSIMES

Arvin, Newton. Introduction, *The Grandissimes* (New York, 1957).

Chase, Richard. *The American Novel and Its Tradition*, 167-176.

——————. "Cable and His Grandissimes," *Kenyon Review* XVIII (Summer 1956), 373-383.

Fiske, Horace Spencer. *Provincial Types in American Fiction*, 118-132.

Howells, W. D. *Heroines of Fiction* II, 234-244.

Turner, Arlin. *George W. Cable*, 89-104.

CABLE, GEORGE WASHINGTON, Continued

JOHN MARCH, SOUTHERNER
Rubin, Louis D., Jr. "The Road to Yoknapatawpha," *Virginia Quarterly Review* XXXV (Winter 1959), 119-132.

GENERAL
Bikle, Lucy Leffingwell Cable. *George W. Cable.*
Bowen, Edwin W. "George Washington Cable: An Appreciation," *South Atlantic Quarterly* XVIII (Apr 1919), 145-155.
Brooks, Van Wyck. "The South: Miss Murfree and Cable," *The Times of Melville and Whitman,* 378-394.
Butcher, Philip. *George W. Cable: The Northampton Years.*
Cardwell, Guy A. *Twins of Genius.*
Cowie, Alexander. "Local-Color, Frontier, and Regional Fiction: George Washington Cable (1844-1925)," *The Rise of the American Novel,* 556-567.
Edison, John Olin. "George W. Cable's Philosophy of Progress," *Southwest Review* XXI (Jan 1936), 211-216.
Hicks, Granville. *The Great Tradition,* 49-57.
Hubbell, Jay B. *The South in American Literature,* 804-822.
Pugh, Griffith Thompson. *George Washington Cable.*
Quinn, Arthur Hobson. "Place and Race in American Fiction," *American Fiction,* 345-352.
Tinker, Edward Larocque. "Cable and the Creoles," *American Literature* V (Jan 1934), 313-326.
Toulmin, Harry Aubrey. *Social Historians,* 35-56.
Turner, Arlin. "George W. Cable, Novelist and Reformer," *South Atlantic Quarterly* XLVIII (Oct 1949), 539-545.
——————. "A Novelist Discovers A Novelist: The Correspondence of H. H. Boyesen and George W. Cable," *Western Humanities Review* V (Autumn 1951), 343-372.
Wilson, Edmund. "Citizen of the Union," *A Literary Chronicle,* 123-128.

CAIN, JAMES M.

MILDRED PIERCE
Farrell, James T. *Literature and Morality,* 79-89.

GENERAL
Frohock, W. M. "James M. Cain: Tabloid Tragedy," *The Novel of Violence in America,* 87-99.

CAIN, JAMES M., Continued

———————. "The Tabloid Tragedy of James M. Cain," *Southwest Review* XXXIV (Autumn 1949), 380-386.
Wilson, Edmund. "The Boys in the Back Room: James M. Cain," *Classics and Commercials*, 19-22; *A Literary Chronicle*, 216-219.

CALDWELL, ERSKINE

GOD'S LITTLE ACRE
Caldwell, Erskine. Introduction, *God's Little Acre* (New York, 1934), pp. xi.
Kubie, Lawrence S. " 'God's Little Acre': An Analysis," *Saturday Review of Literature* XI (Nov 24, 1934), 305-306; 312.
TRAGIC GROUND
Daniels, Jonathan. "American Lower Depths," *Saturday Review of Literature* XXVII (Oct 14, 1944), 46.
GENERAL
Beach, Joseph Warren. *American Fiction*, 219-231; 235-249.
Burke, Kenneth. "Caldwell: Maker of Grotesques," *The Philosophy of Literary Form*, 350-360.
Caldwell, Erskine. *Call It Experience*.
Cantwell, Robert. "Caldwell's Characters: Why Don't They Leave?" *Georgia Review* XI (Fall 1957), 252-264.
Cargill, Oscar. The Primitivists," *Intellectual America*, 386-396.
Frohock, W. M. "Erskine Caldwell: The Dangers of Ambiguity," *The Novel of Violence in America*, 127-145.
———————. "Erskine Caldwell: Sentimental Gentleman from Georgia," *Southwest Review* XXXI (Autumn 1946), 351-359.
Hazel, Robert. "Notes on Erskine Caldwell," *Southern Renascence*, 316-324.
Snell, George. "Erskine Caldwell and Vardis Fisher: The Nearly-Animal Kingdom," *The Shapers of American Fiction*, 263-276.
Wagenknecht, Edward. "Chamber of Horrors—Southern Exposure," *Cavalcade of the American Novel*, 415-417.
Whicher, George F. "Analysts of Decay," *The Literature of the American People*, 885-886.

CANFIELD, DOROTHY
(see FISHER, DOROTHY CANFIELD)

CAPOTE, TRUMAN
OTHER VOICES, OTHER ROOMS
Aldridge, John W. *After the Lost Generation,* 194-230.

Levine, Paul. "Truman Capote: The Revelation of the Broken Image," *Virginia Quarterly Review* XXXIV (Autumn 1958), 600-617.

Young, Marguerite. "Tiger Lilies," *Kenyon Review* X (Summer 1948), 516-518.

GENERAL
Aldridge, John W. "The Metaphorical World of Truman Capote," *Western Review* XV (Summer 1951), 247-260.

Baldanza, Frank. "Plato in Dixie," *Georgia Review* XII (Summer 1958), 150-167.

Breit, Harvey. *The Writer Observed,* 235-237.

Hill, Pati. "Truman Capote," *Writers at Work,* 283-299.

Prescott, Orville. *In My Opinion,* 114-116.

CARUTHERS, WILLIAM ALEXANDER
THE KNIGHTS OF THE HORSE-SHOE
Davis, Curtis Carroll. "The Virginia 'Knights' and their Golden Horseshoes: Dr. William A. Caruthers and an American Tradition," *Modern Language Quarterly* X (Dec 1959), 490-507.

GENERAL
Cowie, Alexander. "The Mixed Thirties: William Alexander Caruthers (1800[?]-1846)," *The Rise of the American Novel,* 276-284.

Davis, Curtis Carroll. "An Early Historical Novelist Goes to the Library: William A. Caruthers and His Reading, 1823-29," *Bulletin of The New York Public Library,* LII (Apr 1948), 159-169.

Hubbell, Jay B. "Cavalier and Indentured Servant in Virginia Fiction," *South Atlantic Quarterly* XXVI (Jan 1927), 22-39.

──────────. *The South in American Literature,* 495-502.

Quinn, Arthur Hobson. "The Romance of History and the Frontier," *The Literature of the American People,* 242.

CATHER, WILLA
ALEXANDER'S BRIDGE
Cather, Willa. *On Writing,* 91-93.

CATHER, WILLA, Continued

Hinz, John P. "The Real Alexander's Bridge," *American Literature* XXI (Jan 1950), 473-476.

DEATH COMES FOR THE ARCHBISHOP

Bloom, Edward A. and Lillian D. Bloom. "The Genesis of *Death Comes for the Archbishop*," *American Literature* XXVI (Jan 1955), 479-506.

Cather, Willa. *On Writing*, 3-13.

Greene, George. "*Death Comes for the Archbishop*," *New Mexico Quarterly* XXVII (Spring-Summer 1957), 69-82.

Rapin, René. *Willa Cather*, 69-71.

West, Rebecca. *The Strange Necessity*, 233-248.

A LOST LADY

Lasch, Robert N. "Willa Cather," *Prairie Schooner* I (Apr 1927), 166-169.

Rapin, René. *Willa Cather*, 69-71.

Ravitz, A. C. "Willa Cather Under Fire: Hamlin Garland Misreads *A Lost Lady*," *Western Humanities Review* IX (Spring 1955), 182-184.

Wilson, Edmund. *The Shores of Light*, 41-43.

LUCY GAYHEART

Jones, Howard Mumford. "Willa Cather Returns to the Middle West," *Saturday Review of Literature* XII (Aug 3, 1935), 7.

MY ÁNTONIA

A., G. W. "Cather's *My Ántonia*," *Explicator* V (Mar 1947), No. 35.

Dahl, Curtis. "An American *Georgic*: Willa Cather's *My Ántonia*," *Comparative Literature* VII (Winter 1955), 43-51.

Fiegenbaum, Martha. "Willa Cather as Local Colorist," *Prairie Schooner* III (Winter 1929), 65-68.

Havighurst, Walter. Introduction, *My Ántonia* (Boston, 1949), pp. xvi.

Hinz, John P. "Willa Cather—Prairie Spring," *Prairie Schooner* XXIII (Spring 1949), 86-88.

Miller, James E., Jr. "*My Ántonia*: A Frontier Drama of Time," *American Quarterly* X (Winter 1958), 476-484.

Rapin, René. *Willa Cather*, 47-51.

O PIONEERS!

Cather, Willa. *On Writing*, 93-97.

CATHER, WILLA, Continued

Fiegenbaum, Martha. "Willa Cather as Local Colorist," *Prairie Schooner* III (Winter 1929), 65-68.

Rapin, René. *Willa Cather*, 21-26.

ONE OF OURS

Rapin, René. *Willa Cather*, 55-68.

Wilson, Edmund. *The Shores of Light*, 39-41.

THE PROFESSOR'S HOUSE

Cather, Willa. *On Writing*, 30-32.

Fay, Eliot G. "Borrowings from Anatole France by Willa Cather and Robert Nathan," *Modern Language Notes* LVI (May 1941), 377.

Hinz, John. "A Lost Lady and 'The Professor's House,'" *Virginia Quarterly Review* XXIX (Winter 1953), 70-85.

Hoffman, Frederick J. *The Twenties*, 157-162.

Rapin, René. *Willa Cather*, 72-77.

SHADOWS ON THE ROCK

Bloom, E. A. and L. D. "*Shadows on the Rock*: Notes on the Composition of a Novel," *Twentieth Century Literature* II (Jul 1956), 70-85.

Brown, E. K. "Willa Cather's Canada," *University of Toronto Quarterly* XXII (Jan 1953), 184-196.

Cather, Willa. *On Writing*, 14-17.

THE SONG OF THE LARK

Rapin, René. *Willa Cather*, 27-46.

GENERAL

Baum, Bernard. "Willa Cather's Waste Land," *South Atlantic Quarterly* XLVIII (Oct 1949), 589-601.

Bennett, Mildred R. *The World of Willa Cather*.

Bloom, Edward A. and Lillian D. "Willa Cather's Novels of the Frontier: A Study in Thematic Symbolism," *American Literature* XXI (Mar 1949), 71-93.

_____. "Willa Cather's Novels of the Frontier: The Symbolic Function of 'Machine-Made Materialism,'" *University of Toronto Quarterly* XX (Oct 1950), 45-60.

_____. "Willa Cather's Portrait of the Artist," *University of Toronto Quarterly* XXVII (Apr 1958), 273-288.

Boynton, Percy H. "Willa Cather," *America in Contemporary Fiction*, 150-163.

CATHER, WILLA, Continued

──────────. "Willa Cather," *Some Contemporary Americans*, 162-177.
Brown, E. K. "Homage to Willa Cather," *Yale Review* XXXVI (Sept 1946), 77-92.
──────────. *Willa Cather: A Critical Biography*.
──────────. "Willa Cather and the West," *University of Toronto Quarterly* V (Jul 1936), 544-566.
Cabell, James Branch. "A Note as to Willa Cather," *Some of Us*, 43.
Canby, Henry Seidel. "Willa Cather (1876-1947)," *Saturday Review of Literature* XXX (May 10, 1947), 22-24.
Connolly, Francis X. "Willa Cather: Memory as Muse," *Fifty Years of the American Novel*, 69-87.
Daiches, David. *Willa Cather: A Critical Introduction*.
Edgar, Pelham. "Two Anti-Realists," *The Art of the Novel*, 255-261.
Footman, Robert H. "The Genius of Willa Cather," *American Literature* X (May 1938), 123-141.
Gale, Robert L. "Willa Cather and the Past," *Studi Americani* IV (1958), 209-222.
Geismar, Maxwell. "Willa Cather: Lady in the Wilderness," *The Last of the Provincials*, 153-220.
Gerber, Philip L. "Willa Cather and the Big Red Rock," *College English* XIX (Jan 1958), 152-157.
Hartwick, Harry. "Simplicity with Glory," *The Foreground of American Fiction*, 389-404.
Hatcher, Harlan. "Willa Cather and the Shifting Moods," *Creating the Modern American Novel*, 58-71.
Hicks, Granville. *The Great Tradition*, 221-226.
Hinz, John P. "Willa Cather—Prairie Spring," *Prairie Schooner* XXIII (Spring 1949), 82-88.
Hoffman, Frederick J. "The Text: Willa Cather's Two Worlds," *The Twenties*, 153-162.
──────────. "Willa Cather and Ellen Glasgow," *The Modern Novel in America*, 52-75.
Jacks, L. V. "Willa Cather and the Southwest," *New Mexico Quarterly* XXVII (Spring-Summer 1957), 83-87.
Jessup, Josephine Lurie. *The Faith of Our Feminists*.

CATHER, WILLA, Continued

Jones, Howard Mumford. "The Novels of Willa Cather," *Saturday Review of Literature* XVIII (Aug 6, 1938), 3-4; 16.

Kazin, Alfred. "Elegy and Satire: Willa Cather and Ellen Glasgow," *On Native Grounds*, 247-257.

King, Marion. "Willa Cather: The Sunlit Peak," *Saturday Review of Literature* XXXVII (May 8, 1954), 11.

Knight, Grant C. "Willa Cather," *American Literature and Culture*, 421-425.

Kohler, Dayton. "Willa Cather: 1876-1947," *College English* IX (Oct 1947), 8-18.

Lasch, Robert N. "Willa Cather," *Prairie Schooner* I (Apr 1927), 166-169.

Lewis, Edith. *Willa Cather Living.*

Macafee, Helen. "Some Novelists in Mid-Stream," *Yale Review* XV (Jan 1926), 343-344.

Michaud, Régis. "Reinforcements: Willa Cather, Zona Gale, Floyd Dell, Joseph Hergesheimer, Waldo Frank," *The American Novel To-Day*, 238-256.

Monroe, N. Elizabeth. "Trends of the Future in Willa Cather," *The Novel and Society*, 225-245.

Morris, Lloyd. *Postscript to Yesterday*, 130-133.

——————. "Willa Cather," *North American Review* 210 (May 1924), 641-652.

Overton, Grant. "Willa Cather," *The Women Who Make Our Novels*, 76-97.

Porter, Katherine Anne. "Reflections on Willa Cather," *The Days Before*, 61-73.

Porterfield, Alexander. "An English Opinion: Willa Cather," *Willa Cather: A Biographical Sketch, an English Opinion and an Abridged Bibliography*, 4-14.

Quinn, Arthur Hobson. *American Fiction*, 683-697.

Sergeant, Elizabeth Shepley. "The Roots of a Writer," *Saturday Review* XXXVI (Apr 11, 1953), 50; 72.

——————. *Willa Cather.*

Sherman, Stuart P. "Willa Cather and the Changing World," *Critical Woodcuts*, 32-48

Smith, Eleanor M. "The Literary Relationship of Sarah Orne Jewett and Willa Sibert Cather," *New England Quarterly* XXIX (Dec 1956), 472-492.

CATHER, WILLA, Continued

Snell, George. "The James Influence," *The Shapers of American Fiction*, 151-156.

Tennant, Stephen. "The Room Beyond," Foreward to Willa Cather, *On Writing*, v-xxiv.

Trilling, Lionel. "Willa Cather," *After the Genteel Tradition*, 52-63.

Van Doren, Carl. *Contemporary American Novelists*, 113-122.

——————. "Willa Cather," *The American Novel 1789-1939*, 281-293.

Wagenknecht, Edward. "Willa Cather," *Sewanee Review* XXXVII (Apr-Jun 1929), 221-239.

——————. "Willa Cather and the Lovely Past," *Cavalcade of the American Novel*, 319-338.

Whicher, George F. "In the American Grain," *The Literature of the American People*, 907-911.

Whipple, T. K. "Willa Cather," *Spokesmen*, 139-160.

White, George L., Jr. "Willa Cather," *Sewanee Review* L (Jan-Mar 1942), 18-25.

Zabel, Morton Dauwen. "Willa Cather: The Tone of Time," *Craft and Character*, 264-275.

BIBLIOGRAPHY

Hutchinson, Phyllis Martin. "The Writings of Willa Cather: A List of Works by and about Her," *Bulletin of The New York Public Library* LX (Jun 1956), 267-287; Part II (Jul 1956), 338-356; Part III (Aug 1956), 378-400.

CATHERWOOD, MARY HARTWELL

GENERAL

Price, Robert. "Mrs. Catherwood's Early Experiments with Critical Realism," *American Literature* XVII (May 1945), 140-151.

CHAMBERS, ROBERT W.

GENERAL

Underwood, John Curtis. "Robert W. Chambers and Commercialism," *Literature and Insurgency*, 447-480.

CHANDLER, RAYMOND

GENERAL
Flint, R. W. "A Cato of the Cruelties," *Partisan Review* XIV (May-Jun 1947), 328-330.

CHASE, MARY ELLEN

GENERAL
Boynton, Percy H. "Two New England Regionalists," *America in Contemporary Fiction*, 21-34.

CHILD, LYDIA M.

THE FRUGAL HOUSEWIFE
Edwards, Herbert. "Lydia M. Child's *The Frugal Housewife*," *New England Quarterly* XXVI (Jun 1953), 243-249.
PHILOTHEA
Streeter, Robert E. "Mrs. Child's 'Philothea' A Transcendentalist Novel?" *New England Quarterly* XVI (Dec 1943), 648-654.
GENERAL
Cowie, Alexander. "Contemporaries and Immediate Followers of Cooper, I: Lydia Maria (Francis) Child (1802-1880)," *The Rise of the American Novel*, 177-184.

CHOPIN, KATE

THE AWAKENING
Eble, Kenneth. "A Forgotten Novel: Kate Chopin's *The Awakening*," *Western Humanities Review* X (Summer 1956), 261-269.

CHURCHILL, WINSTON

CONISTON
Walcutt, Charles Child. *The Romantic Compromise in the Novels of Winston Churchill*, 11-13.
THE DWELLING-PLACE OF LIGHT
Walcutt, Charles Child. *The Romantic Compromise in the Novels of Winston Churchill*, 35-45.
A FAR COUNTRY
Walcutt, Charles Child. *The Romantic Compromise in the Novels of Winston Churchill*, 31-34.

CHURCHILL, WINSTON, Continued

THE INSIDE OF THE CUP
Walcutt, Charles Child. *The Romantic Compromise in the Novels of Winston Churchill,* 25-31.

A MODERN CHRONICLE
Walcutt, Charles Child. *The Romantic Compromise in the Novels of Winston Churchill,* 20-25.

MR. CREWE'S CAREER
Walcutt, Charles Child. *The Romantic Compromise in the Novels of Winston Churchill,* 14-20.

GENERAL
Baldwin, Charles C. "Winston Churchill," *The Men Who Make Our Novels,* 97-106.

Blotner, Joseph L. "Winston Churchill and David Phillips: Bosses and Lobbies," *The Political Novel,* 36-37.

Hofstadter, Richard and Beatrice. "Winston Churchill: A Study in the Popular Novel," *American Quarterly* II (Spring 1950), 12-28.

Speare, Morris Edmund. "Winston Churchill and the Novel of Political Reform," *The Political Novel,* 306-321.

Underwood, John Curtis. "Winston Churchill and Civic Righteousness," *Literature and Insurgency,* 299-345.

Van Doren, Carl. *Contemporary American Novelists,* 47-56.

Walcutt, Charles Child. *The Romantic Compromise in the Novels of Winston Churchill.*

——————. "The Romantic Compromise of Winston Churchill," *American Literary Naturalism,* 157-179.

Whicher, George F. "Loopholes of Retreat," *The Literature of the American People,* 890.

CLARK, WALTER VAN TILBURG

THE OX-BOW INCIDENT
Bluestone, George. *Novels into Film,* 170-196.

THE TRACK OF THE CAT
Young, Vernon. "An American Dream and Its Parody," *Arizona Quarterly* VI (Summer 1950), 112-123.

GENERAL
Carpenter, Frederic I. "The West of Walter Van Tilburg Clark," *College English* XIII (Feb 1952), 243-248.

CLARK, WALTER VAN TILBURG, Continued

Eisinger, Chester E. "The Fiction of Walter Van Tilburg Clark: Man and Nature in the West," *Southwest Review* XLIV (Summer 1959), 214-226.

Maxwell, William. "A Different Reno, Nevada," *Saturday Review of Literature* XXVIII (Jun 2, 1945), 13.

Milton, John R. "The Western Attitude: Walter Van Tilburg Clark," *Critique* II (Winter 1959), 57-73.

Portz, John. "Idea and Symbol in Walter Van Tilburg Clark," *Accent* XVII (Spring 1957), 112-128.

Swallow, Alan. "The Mavericks," *Critique* II (Winter 1959), 84-88.

Wilner, Herbert. "Walter Van Tilburg Clark," *Western Review* XX (Winter 1956), 103-122.

Young, Vernon. "Gods Without Heroes: The Tentative Myth of Van Tilburg Clark," *Arizona Quarterly* VII (Summer 1951), 110-119.

COOKE, JOHN ESTEN

GENERAL

Beaty, John O. *John Esten Cooke, Virginian.*

Cowie, Alexander. "Experiment and Tradition: John Esten Cooke (1830-1886)," *The Rise of the American Novel*, 463-472.

Holliday, Carl. "John Esten Cooke as a Novelist," *Sewanee Review* XIII (Apr 1905), 216-220.

Hubbell, Jay B. *The South in American Literature*, 511-521.

COOKE, ROSE TERRY

GENERAL

Westbrook, Percy D. *Acres of Flint*, 87-95.

BIBLIOGRAPHY

Downey, Jean. "Rose Terry Cooke: A Bibliography," *Bulletin of Bibliography* XXI (May-Aug 1955), 159-163; (Sept-Dec 1955), 191-192.

COOPER, JAMES FENIMORE

THE CHAINBEARER
Ellis, David M. *James Fenimore Cooper: A Re-Appraisal*, 412-422.

THE CRATER
Gates, W. B. "Cooper's *The Crater* and Two Explorers," *American Literature* XXIII (May 1951), 243-246.

---------------. "A Defense of the Ending of Cooper's *The Crater*," *Modern Language Notes* LXX (May 1955), 347-349.

---------------. "A Note on Cooper and *Robinson Crusoe*," *Modern Language Notes* LXVII (Jun 1952), 421-422.

Ringe, Donald A. "Cooper's *The Crater* and the Moral Basis of Society," *Papers of the Michigan Academy of Science, Arts, and Letters* XLIV (1959), 371-380.

Scudder, Harold H. "Cooper's *The Crater*," *American Literature* XIX (May 1947), 109-126.

THE DEERSLAYER
Davenport, Basil. Introduction, *The Deerslayer* (New York, 1952).

Davis, David Brion. *Twelve Original Essays on Great American Novels*, 1-22.

Paine, Gregory L. Introduction, *The Deerslayer* (New York, 1927), pp. xxxvi.

HOME AS FOUND
Outland, Ethel R. *The "Effingham" Libels on Cooper.*

HOMEWARD BOUND
Scudder, Harold H. "Cooper and the Barbary Coast," *PMLA* LXII (Sept 1947), 784-792.

Wright, Nathalia. "The Confidence Men of Melville and Cooper: an American Indictment," *American Quarterly* IV (Fall 1952), 266-268.

THE LAST OF THE MOHICANS
Angoff, Charles. Introduction, *The Last of the Mohicans* (1956).

Becker, May Lamberton. Introduction, *The Last of the Mohicans* (Cleveland, 1957).

Charvat, William. Introduction, *The Last of the Mohicans* (Boston, 1958), pp. xxii.

Cook, Agnes S. Introduction, *The Last of the Mohicans* (New York, 1901).

COOPER, JAMES FENIMORE, Continued

Cooper, James Fenimore. Introduction, *The Last of the Mohicans* (New York, 1959).

Cooper, Susan Fenimore. Introduction, *The Last of the Mohicans* (Boston, 1930), pp. lviii.

Davenport, Basil. Introduction, *The Last of the Mohicans* (New York, 1951), pp. vii.

Dunbar, John B. Introduction, *The Last of the Mohicans* (New York, 1924), pp. xxix.

Morris, Mowbray. Introduction, *The Last of the Mohicans* (New York, 1900; 1925).

Smith, E. Boyd. Introduction, *The Last of the Mohicans* (New York, 1910), pp. ix.

Wight, John G. Introduction, *The Last of the Mohicans* (Boston, 1932), pp. xxi.

MERCEDES OF CASTILE

Goodfellow, Donald M. "The Sources of *Mercedes of Castile*," *American Literature* XII (Nov 1940), 319-338.

THE PATHFINDER

Cooper, Susan Fenimore. Introduction, *The Pathfinder* (Boston, 1908), pp. xxxiii.

Pearson, Norman Holmes. Introduction, *The Pathfinder* (New York, 1952), pp. xi.

THE PIONEERS

Cooper, Susan Fenimore. Introduction, *The Pioneers* (Boston, 1908), pp. xxxii.

Howard, Leon. Introduction, *The Pioneers* (New York, 1959).

Nelson, Andrew. "James Cooper and George Croghan," *Philological Quarterly* XX (Jan 1941), 69-73.

THE PRAIRIE

Bewley, Marius. "The Cage and the Prairie: Two Notes on Symbolism," *Hudson Review* X (Autumn 1957), 408-413.

Chase, Richard. *The American Novel and Its Tradition*, 52-65.

Cooper, Susan Fenimore. Introduction, *The Prairie* (Boston, 1908), pp. xxviii.

Flanagan, John T. "The Authenticity of Cooper's *The Prairie*," *Modern Language Quarterly* II (Mar 1941), 99-104.

Hansen, Harry. Introduction, *The Prairie* (1940), pp. xv.

Muszynska-Wallace, E. Soteris. "The Sources of *The Prairie*," *American Literature* XXI (May 1949), 191-200.

COOPER, JAMES FENIMORE, Continued

Smith, Henry Nash. Introduction, *The Prairie* (New York, 1950), pp. xxv.

Vandiver, Edward P., Jr. "Cooper's *The Prairie* and Shakespeare," *PMLA* LXIX (Dec 1954), 1302-1304.

Wherry, George. "Col. Newcome's Death," *Notes and Queries* 11 S. IV (Sept 16, 1911), 225.

PRECAUTION

Scudder, Harold H. "What Mr. Cooper Read to His Wife," *Sewanee Review* XXXVI (Apr-Jun 1928), 177-194.

THE RED ROVER

Gordan, John D. *"The Red Rover* Takes the Boards," *American Literature* X (Mar 1938), 66-75.

THE REDSKINS

Ellis, David M. *James Fenimore Cooper: A Re-Appraisal,* 412-422.

SATANSTOE

Chase, Richard. *The American Novel and Its Tradition,* 47-52.

Dondore, Dorothy. "The Debt of Two Dyed-in-the-Wool Americans to Mrs. Grant's Memoirs: Cooper's *Satanstoe* and Paulding's *The Dutchman's Fireside," American Literature* XII (Mar 1940), 52-58.

Spiller, Robert E. and Joseph D. Coppock. Introduction, *Satanstoe* (New York, 1937), pp. xli.

THE SEA LIONS

Gates, W. B. "Cooper's *The Sea Lions* and Wilkes' *Narrative," PMLA* XLV (Dec 1950), 1069-1075.

THE SPY

Boynton, Percy H. Introduction, *The Spy* (New York, 1928), pp. xxxi.

Brenner, C. D. "The Influence of Cooper's *The Spy* on Hauff's *Lichtenstein," Modern Language Notes* XXX (Nov 1915), 207-210.

Canby, Henry Seidel. Introduction, *The Spy* (New York, 1929; London, 1930).

Diemer, James S. "A Model for Harvey Birch," *American Literature* XXVI (May 1954), 242-247.

Lane, M. A. L. Introduction, *The Spy* (New York, 1917).

McDowell, Tremaine. "The Identity of Harvey Birch," *American Literature* II (May 1930), 111-120.

COOPER, JAMES FENIMORE, Continued

──────────. Introduction, *The Spy* (New York, 1931), pp. xlvii.
Revel, E. Isabel. Introduction, *The Spy* (Chicago, 1914), pp. xii.
Thomas, Charles Swain. Introduction, *The Spy* (Boston, 1911).
Thurber, Samuel. Introduction, *The Spy* (New York, 1909).

THE TWO ADMIRALS

Ballinger, Richard H. "Origins of James Fenimore Cooper's *The Two Admirals*," *American Literature* XX (Mar 1948), 20-30.

GENERAL

Anderson, Charles. "Cooper's Sea Novels Spurned in the Maintop," *Modern Language Notes* LXVI (Jun 1951), 388-391.
Beard, James F., Jr. "Cooper and His Artistic Contemporaries," *James Fenimore Cooper: A Re-Appraisal*, 480-495.
Becker, George J. "James Fenimore Cooper and American Democracy," *College English* XVII (Mar 1956), 325-334.
Bewley, Marius. *The Eccentric Design*, 47-100.
──────────. "Fenimore Cooper and the Economic Age," *American Literature* XXVI (May 1954), 166-195.
──────────. "Revaluations (XVI): James Fenimore Cooper," *Scrutiny* XIX (Winter 1952-53), 98-125.
Bonner, Willard Hallam. "Cooper and Captain Kidd," *Modern Language Notes* LXI (Jan 1946), 21-27.
Boynton, Henry Walcott. *James Fenimore Cooper*.
Brady, Charles A. "Myth-Maker and Christian Romancer," *American Classics Reconsidered*, 59-97.
Brooks, Van Wyck. "Fenimore Cooper and Longfellow," *The Dream of Arcadia*, 55-68.
──────────. *The World of Washington Irving*, 167-182; 313-333.
Brownell, William C. *American Prose Masters*, 3-60.
Burton, Richard. "Cooper," *Literary Leaders of America*, 42-56.
Butterfield, L. H. "Cooper's Inheritance: The Ostego Country and Its Founders," *James Fenimore Cooper: A Re-Appraisal*, 374-411.
Cady, Edwin Harrison. *The Gentleman in America*, 103-145.
Canby, Henry Seidel. *Classic Americans*, 97-142.
──────────. "James Fenimore Cooper," *Saturday Review of Literature* III (Apr 23, 1927), 747-749.

COOPER, JAMES FENIMORE, Continued

Charvat, William. "Cooper as Professional Author," *James Fenimore Cooper: A Re-Appraisal*, 496-511.
Chase, Richard. "The Significance of Cooper," *The American Novel and Its Tradition*, 43-47.
Clymer, William Branford Shubrick. *James Fenimore Cooper*.
Conrad, Joseph. "Tales of the Sea," *Notes on Life and Letters*, 55-57.
Cooper, James Fenimore (ed.). *Correspondence of James Fenimore Cooper*.
——————. "Unpublished Letters of James Fenimore Cooper," *Yale Review* V (Jul 1916), 810-831.
——————. "Unpublished Letters of James Fenimore Cooper," *Yale Review* XI (Apr 1922), 449-466.
Cowie, Alexander. "James Fenimore Cooper and the Historical Romance." *The Rise of the American Novel*, 115-164.
Cunliffe, Marcus. "Independence—The First Fruits: James Fenimore Cooper," *The Literature of the United States*, 56-64.
Erskine, John. "James Fenimore Cooper," *Leading American Novelists*, 51-129.
Ferguson, John De Lancey. "James Fenimore Cooper," *American Literature in Spain*, 32-54.
Frederick, John T. "Cooper's Eloquent Indians," *PMLA* (Dec 1956), 1004-1017.
Gates, W. B. "Cooper's Indebtedness to Shakespeare," *PMLA* (Sept 1952), 716-731.
Griffin, Max L. "Cooper's Attitude Toward the South," *Studies in Philology* LXVIII (Jan 1951), 67-76.
Grossman, James. *James Fenimore Cooper*.
——————. "James Fenimore Cooper: An Uneasy American," *Yale Review* XL (Jun 1951), 696-709.
Haeuptner, Gerhard. "Der Jäger Natty Bumppo: Das Bild des Menschen in den Lederstrumpferzählunger James Fenimore Coopers," *Jahrbuch für Amerikastudien* II (1957), 181-196.
Hale, Edward Everett, Jr. "American Scenery in Cooper's Novels," *Sewanee Review* XVIII (Jul 1910), 317-332.
Hastings, George E. "How Cooper Became a Novelist," *American Literature* XII (Mar 1940), 20-51.

COOPER, JAMES FENIMORE, Continued

Hewett-Thayer, Harvey W. "The First Literary Invasion: Irving and Cooper," *American Literature as Viewed in Germany, 1818-1861*, 18-37.
Hintz, Howard W. "James Fenimore Cooper," *The Quaker Influence in American Literature*, 41-48.
Holman, C. Hugh. "The Influence of Scott and Cooper on Simms," *American Literature* XXIII (May 1951), 203-218.
Jones, Howard Mumford. "Prose and Pictures: James Fenimore Cooper," *Tulane Studies in English* III (1952), 133-154.
Keiser, Albert. "James Fenimore Cooper," *The Indian in American Literature*, 101-143.
Kirk, Russell. "Cooper and the European Puzzle," *College English* VII (Jan 1946), 198-205.
Knight, Grant C. "James Fenimore Cooper," *American Literature and Culture*, 113-126.
Lawrence, D. H. *Studies in Classic American Literature*, 43-73.
Lewis, R. W. B. "The Hero in Space: Brown, Cooper, Bird," *The American Adam*, 90-109.
Lüdeke, H., "James Fenimore Cooper and the Democracy of Switzerland," *English Studies* XXVII (1946), 33-44.
Macy, John. "Cooper," *The Spirit of American Literature*, 35-44.
McDowell, Tremaine. "James Fenimore Cooper As Self-Critic," *Studies in Philology* XXVII (Jul 1930), 508-516.
─────────. "Scott on Cooper and Brockden Brown," *Modern Language Notes* XLV (Jan 1930), 18-20.
Mills, Gordon. "The Symbolic Wilderness: James Fenimore Cooper and Jack London," *Nineteenth-Century Fiction* XIII (Mar 1959), 329-340.
Mott, Frank Luther. *Golden Multitudes*, 73-76.
Paine, Gregory. "Cooper and *The North American Review*," *Studies in Philology* XXVIII (Oct 1931), 267-277.
─────────. "The Indians of the Leather-Stocking Tales," *Studies in Philology* XXIII (Jan 1926), 16-39.
Parker, Arthur C. "Sources and Range of Cooper's Indian Lore," *James Fenimore Cooper: A Re-Appraisal*, 447-456.
Pattee, Fred Lewis. "Cooper," *The First Century of American Literature*, 314-345.
─────────. "James Fenimore Cooper," *American Mercury* IV (Mar 1925), 289-297.

COOPER, JAMES FENIMORE, Continued

Pearce, Roy Harvey. "The Leather-stocking Tales Re-examined," *South Atlantic Quarterly* XLVI (Oct 1947), 524-536.
Phillips, Mary E. *James Fenimore Cooper.*
Quinn, Arthur Hobson. *American Fiction,* 53-76.
——————. *The Literature of the American People,* 226-235; 428-432.
Ringe, Donald A. "James Fenimore Cooper and Thomas Cole: An Analogous Technique," *American Literature* XXX (Mar 1958), 26-36.
Ross, John F. "The Social Criticism of Fenimore Cooper," *University of California Publications in English* III, 17-118.
Routh, James. "The Model of the Leather-Stocking Tales," *Modern Language Notes* XXVIII (Mar 1913), 77-79.
Shulenberger, Arvid. *Cooper's Theory of Fiction.*
Smith, Henry Nash. *Virgin Land,* 59-70, 211-223; (Vintage) 64-76, 246-260.
Snell, George. "J. Fenimore Cooper: Shaper of American Romance," *The Shapers of American Fiction,* 15-27.
——————. "The Shaper of American Romance," *Yale Review* XXXIV (Mar 1954), 482-494.
Spiller, Robert E. *Fenimore Cooper: Critic of his Times.*
——————. *The Cycle of American Literature,* 39-46; (Mentor) 40-45.
——————. "Second Thoughts on Cooper as a Social Critic," *James Fenimore Cooper: A Re-Appraisal,* 540-557.
Sutton, Walter. "Cooper as Found—1949," *University of Kansas City Review* XVI (Autumn 1959), 3-10.
Thorp, Willard. "Cooper Beyond America," *James Fenimore Cooper: A Reappraisal,* 522-539.
Van Doren, Carl. "James Fenimore Cooper," *The American Novel 1789-1939,* 21-42.
Vandiver, Edward P., Jr. "Simms's Porgy and Cooper," *Modern Language Notes* LXX (Apr 1955), 272-274.
Wagenknecht, Edward. "The Novel Established: The Age of Cooper and Simms," *Cavalcade of the American Novel,* 14-29.
Walker, Warren. "Ames Vs. Cooper: The Case Re-Opened," *Modern Language Notes* LXX (Jan 1955), 27-32.
Walker, Warren S. "Elements of Folk Culture in Cooper's Novels," *James Fenimore Cooper: A Re-Appraisal,* 457-467.

COOPER, JAMES FENIMORE, Continued

Wallace, Paul A. W. "Cooper's Indians," *James Fenimore Cooper: A Re-Appraisal,* 423-446.

Waples, Dorothy. *The Whig Myth of James Fenimore Cooper.*

Whitehill, Walter Muir. "Cooper as a Naval Historian," *James Fenimore Cooper: A Re-Appraisal,* 468-479.

Winters, Yvor. "Fenimore Cooper or The Ruins of Time," *In Defense of Reason,* 176-199; *Maule's Curse,* 25-50.

BIBLIOGRAPHY

Spiller, Robert E. and Philip C. Blackburn. *A Descriptive Bibliography of the Writings of James Fenimore Cooper.*

COSTAIN, THOMAS B.

GENERAL

Frederick, John T. "Costain and Company: The Historical Novel Today," *College English* XV (Apr 1954), 373-379; Stedman, Jane W. "Letters to the Editor," *College English* XVI (Nov 1954), 130.

COZZENS, JAMES GOULD

BY LOVE POSSESSED

Garrett, George. "By Love Possessed: The Pattern and the Hero," *Critique* I (Winter 1958), 41-47.

Leonard, Frank G. "Cozzens without Sex: Steinbeck without Sin," *Antioch Review* XVIII (Summer 1958), 209-218.

Macdonald, Dwight. "By Cozzens Possessed: A Review of Reviews," *Commentary* XXV (Jan 1958), 36-47.

Powers, Richard H. "Praise the Mighty: Cozzens and the Critics," *Southwest Review* XLIII (Summer 1958), 263-270.

Stern, Richard G. "A Perverse Fiction," *Kenyon Review* XX (Winter 1958), 140-144.

THE JUST AND THE UNJUST

Farrell, James T. "Eternal Verities," *Kenyon Review* V (Winter 1943), 142-143.

Weimer, David R. "The Breath of Chaos in *The Just and the Unjust,*" *Critique* I (Winter 1958), 30-40.

MEN AND BRETHREN

Davies, Horton. *A Mirror of the Ministry in Modern Novels,* 153-164.

COZZENS, JAMES GOULD, Continued
GENERAL
Bracher, Frederick. "James Gould Cozzens: Humanist," *Critique* I (Winter 1958), 10-29.
──────────. *The Novels of James Gould Cozzens.*
Coxe, Louis O. "The Complex World of James Gould Cozzens," *American Literature* XXVII (May 1955), 157-171.
Coxe, Louis O. and others. "Comments on Cozzens," *Critique* I (Winter 1958), 48-56.
De Voto, Bernard. "The Easy Chair," *Harper's* CXCVIII (Feb 1949), 72-73.
Geismar, Maxwell. "By Cozzens Possessed," *American Moderns*, 145-150.
Hicks, Granville. "The Reputation of James Gould Cozzens," *College English* XI (Jan 1950), 177-183.
Hyman, Stanley Edgar. "James Gould Cozzens and the Art of the Possible," *New Mexico Quarterly* XIX (Winter 1949), 476-498.
Ludwig, Richard M. "A Reading of the James Gould Cozzens Manuscripts," *Princeton University Library Chronicle* XIX (Autumn 1957), 1-14.
Lydenberg, John. "Cozzens and the Conservatives," *Critique* I (Winter 1958), 3-9.
──────────. "Cozzens and the Critics," *College English* XIX (Dec 1957), 99-104; Frederick, John T. "Rebuttal: John Lydenberg's 'Cozzens and the Critics,'" *College English* XIX (Apr 1958), 313-316; Hermann, John. "Cozzens and A Critic," *College English* XIX (Apr 1958), 316-317; Frost, William. "Cozzens: Some Reservations about BLP," *College English* XIX (Apr 1958), 317-318.
Prescott, Orville. *In My Opinion.* 182-191.
Ward, John W. "James Gould Cozzens and the Conditions of Modern Man," *American Scholar* XXVII (Winter 1957-58), 92-99.
Watts, Harold H. "James Gould Cozzens and the Genteel Tradition," *Colorado Quarterly* VI (Winter 1958), 257-273.
BIBLIOGRAPHY
Ludwig, Richard M. "James Gould Cozzens: A Review of Research and Criticism," *Texas Studies in Literature and Language* I (Spring 1959), 123-136.

COZZENS, JAMES GOULD, Continued

Meriwether, James B. "A James Gould Cozzens Check List," *Critique* I (Winter 1958), 57-63.

CRADDOCK, CHARLES EGBERT
(see MURFREE, MARY NOAILLES)

CRANE, STEPHEN

MAGGIE: A GIRL OF THE STREETS

Beer, Thomas. *Hanna, Crane, and the Mauve Decade*, 267-288; *Stephen Crane*, 78-107.

Cunliffe, Marcus. "Stephen Crane and the American Background of *Maggie*," *American Quarterly* VII (Spring 1955), 31-44.

Gullason, Thomas Arthur. "The Sources of Stephen Crane's *Maggie*," *Philological Quarterly* XXXVIII (Oct 1959), 497-502.

Howells, William Dean. "An Appreciation," *Prefaces to Contemporaries*, 62-64.

Linson, Corwin K. *My Stephen Crane*, 12-24.

Stallman, R. W. "Crane's 'Maggie': A Reassessment," *Modern Fiction Studies* V (Autumn 1959), 251-259.

──────────. "Stephen Crane's Revision of *Maggie: A Girl of the Streets*," *American Literature* XXVI (Jan 1955), 528-536.

Stein, William Bysshe. "New Testament Inversions in Crane's *Maggie*," *Modern Language Notes* LXXIII (Apr 1958), 268-272.

THE RED BADGE OF COURAGE

Brereton, F. Introduction, *The Red Badge of Courage* (London, 1939).

Colvert, James B. "*The Red Badge of Courage* and a Review of Zola's *La Débâcle*," *Modern Language Notes* LXXI (Feb 1956), 98-100.

──────────. "Structure and Theme in Stephen Crane's Fiction," *Modern Fiction Studies* V (Autumn 1959), 204-208.

Conrad, Joseph. Introduction, *The Red Badge of Courage* (London, 1937).

Cox, James Trammell. "The Imagery of 'The Red Badge of Courage,'" *Modern Fiction Studies* V (Autumn 1959), 209-219.

CRANE, STEPHEN, Continued

Friedman, Norman. "Criticism and the Novel," *Antioch Review* XVIII (Fall 1958), 356-361.
Gibson, William M. Introduction, *The Red Badge of Courage and Selected Prose and Poetry* (New York, 1956), pp. xxi.
Gullason, Thomas A. "Additions to the Canon of Stephen Crane," *Nineteenth-Century Fiction* XII (Sept 1957), 157-160.
——————. "New Sources for Stephen Crane's War Motif," *Modern Language Notes* LXXII (Dec 1957), 572-575.
Hart, John E. "*The Red Badge of Courage* as Myth and Symbol," *University of Kansas City Review* XIX (Summer 1953), 249-256.
Hartwick, Harry. *The Foreground of American Fiction*, 21-44.
Herzberg, Max J. Introduction, *The Red Badge of Courage and Other Stories* (New York, 1957).
Hoffman, Daniel G. "Crane's Decoration Day Article and *The Red Badge of Courage*," *Nineteenth-Century Fiction* XIV (Jun 1959), 78-80.
——————. Introduction, *The Red Badge of Courage* (New York, 1957), pp. xxxi.
Klotz, Marvin. "Crane's *The Red Badge of Courage*," *Notes and Queries* 204 (Feb 1959), 68-69.
Linson, Corwin K. *My Stephen Crane*, 35-47.
Marcus, Mordecai and Erin. "Animal Imagery in *The Red Badge of Courage*," *Modern Language Notes* LXXIV (Feb 1959), 108-111.
O'Donnell, Thomas F. "Charles Dudley Warner on *The Red Badge of Courage*," *American Literature* XXV (Nov 1953), 363-365.
——————. "DeForest, Van Petten, and Stephen Crane," *American Literature* XXVII (Jan 1956), 578-580.
——————. "John B. Van Petten: Stephen Crane's History Teacher," *American Literature* XXVII (May 1955), 196-202.
Osborn, Scott C. "Stephen Crane's Imagery: 'Pasted Like A Wafer,'" *American Literature* XXIII (Nov 1951), 362.
Pratt, Lyndon Upson. "A Possible Source of *The Red Badge of Courage*," *American Literature* XI (Mar 1939), 1-10.
Sewall, R. B. "Crane's *The Red Badge of Courage*," *Explicator* III (May 1945), No. 55.

CRANE, STEPHEN, Continued

Solomon, Eric. "Another Analogue for The Red Badge of Courage,'" *Nineteenth-Century Fiction* XIII (Jun 1958), 63-67.

────────────. "The Structure of 'The Red Badge of Courage,'" *Modern Fiction Studies* V (Autumn 1959), 220-234.

Stallman, Robert Wooster. Introduction, *The Red Badge of Courage* (New York, 1951); *Critiques and Essays on Modern Fiction*, 244-269.

Stone, Edward. "The Many Suns of *The Red Badge of Courage*," *American Literature* XXIX (Nov 1957), 322-326.

Targ, William. Introduction, *The Red Badge of Courage* (Cleveland, 1951), pp. xvi.

Van Doren, Carl. Introduction, *The Red Badge of Courage* (New York, 1944; 1956). pp. xiii.

Webster, H. T. "Wilbur F. Hinman's *Corporal Si Klegg* and Stephen Crane's *The Red Badge of Courage*," *American Literature* XI (Nov 1939), 285-293.

Weisberger, Bernard. *Twelve Original Essays on Great American Novels*, 96-123.

Winterich, John T. Introduction, *The Red Badge of Courage* (New York, 1951; 1954).

GENERAL

Åhnebrink, Lars. *Beginnings of Naturalism in American Fiction.*

Ayers, Robert W. "W. D. Howells and Stephen Crane: Some Unpublished Letters," *American Literature* XXVIII (Jan 1957), 469-477.

Beer, Thomas. "Henry James and Stephen Crane," *The Question of Henry James*, 105-107.

────────────. "Stephen Crane: A Study in American Letters," *Hanna, Crane, and the Mauve Decade*, 211-391; *Stephen Crane.*

Berryman, John. *Stephen Crane.*

Cargill, Oscar. "The Naturalists," *Intellectual America*, 84-89.

Colvert, James B. "The Origins of Stephen Crane's Literary Creed," *Texas Studies in English* XXXIV (1954), 179-188.

────────────. "Structure and Theme in Stephen Crane's Fiction," *Modern Fiction Studies* V (Autumn 1959), 199-208.

Ford, Ford Madox. "Stephen Crane," *Portraits from Life*, 21-37.

CRANE, STEPHEN, Continued

Garland, Hamlin. "Stephen Crane," *Roadside Meetings*, 189-206.
──────. "Stephen Crane as I Knew Him," *Yale Review* III (Apr 1914), 494-506.
Geismar, Maxwell. "Stephen Crane: Halfway House," *Rebels and Ancestors*, 69-136.
Gohdes, Clarence. *The Literature of the American People*, 754-760.
Gordon, Caroline. "Stephen Crane," *Accent* IX (Spring 1949), 153-157.
Greenfield, Stanley B. "The Unmistakable Stephen Crane," *PMLA* LXXIII (Dec 1958), 562-572.
Gullason, Thomas Arthur. "New Light on the Crane-Howells Relationship," *New England Quarterly* XXX (Sept 1957), 389-392.
Hartwick, Harry. "The Red Badge of Nature," *The Foreground of American Fiction*, 21-44.
Hicks, Granville. *The Great Tradition*, 159-163.
Josephson, Matthew. "The Voyage of Stephen Crane," *Portrait of the Artist As American*, 232-264.
Knight, Grant C. "Stephen Crane," *American Literature and Culture*, 395-400.
Kwiat, Joseph J. "The Newspaper Experience: Crane, Norris, and Dreiser," *Nineteenth-Century Fiction* VIII (Sept 1953), 99-117.
Linson, Corwin K. *My Stephen Crane*.
Morris, Lloyd. *Postscript to Yesterday*, 107-110.
Osborn, Scott C. "The 'Rivalry-Chivalry' of Richard Harding Davis and Stephen Crane," *American Literature* XXVIII (Mar 1956), 50-61.
Pizer, Donald. "Crane Reports Garland on Howells," *Modern Language Notes* LXX (Jan 1955), 37-38.
──────. "Romantic Individualism in Garland, Norris and Crane," *American Quarterly* X (Winter 1958), 463-475.
Quinn, Arthur Hobson. "The Journalists," *American Fiction*, 532-538.
Raymond, Thomas L. *Stephen Crane*.
Snell, George. "Naturalism Nascent: Crane and Norris," *The Shapers of American Fiction*, 223-226.

CRANE, STEPHEN, Continued

Stallman, Robert Wooster. Introduction, *Omnibus* (New York, 1952), pp. xlv.

───────. "Stephen Crane's Letters to Ripley Hitchcock," *Bulletin of the New York Public Library* LX (Jul 1956), 319-332.

Starrett, Vincent. "An Estimate of Stephen Crane," *Sewanee Review* XXVIII (Jul 1920), 405-413.

Stevenson, John W. "The Literary Reputation of Stephen Crane," *South Atlantic Quarterly* LI (Apr 1952), 287-300.

Van Doren, Carl. "Stephen Crane," *American Mercury* I (Jan 1924), 11-14.

Van Doren, Mark. *The Private Reader*, 156-158.

Wagenknecht, Edward. "Towards Naturalism: Stephen Crane, Harbinger," *Cavalcade of the American Novel*, 212-216.

Walcutt, Charles Child. "Stephen Crane: Naturalist and Impressionist," *American Literary Naturalism*, 66-86.

Wells, H. G. "Stephen Crane from an English Standpoint," *North American Review* 171 (Jul 1900), 233-242.

Westbrook, Max. "Stephen Crane: The Pattern of Affirmation," *Nineteenth-Century Fiction* XIV (Dec 1959), 219-229.

Wilson, Edmund. "A Vortex in the Nineties: Stephen Crane," *The Shores of Light*, 109-114.

Winterich, John T. "Stephen Crane: Lost and Found," *Saturday Review of Literature* XXXIV (Feb 3, 1951), 21; 43.

BIBLIOGRAPHY

Beebe, Maurice and Thomas A. Gullason. "Criticism of Stephen Crane: A Selected Checklist with an Index to Studies of Separate Works," *Modern Fiction Studies* V (Autumn 1959), 282-291.

Starrett, Vincent. *Stephen Crane: A Bibliography.*

Stolper, Benjamin J. R. *Stephen Crane.*

West, Herbert Faulkner. *A Stephen Crane Collection.*

Williams, Ames W. and Vincent Starrett. *Stephen Crane: A Bibliography.*

CRAWFORD, MARION
GENERAL

Brooks, Van Wyck. "Writers of the Eighties," *Saturday Review of Literature* XXII (Jun 8, 1940), 3-4; 18-19.

CRAWFORD, MARION, Continued

Gohdes, Clarence. "Escape from the Commonplace," *The Literature of the American People*, 684-686.

Pilkington, John, Jr. "F. Marion Crawford: Italy in Fiction," *American Quarterly*, VI (Spring 1954), 59-65.

Quinn, Arthur Hobson. "Francis Marion Crawford and the Cosmopolitan Novel," *American Fiction*, 385-407.

Wagenknecht, Edward. "Novelists of the 'Eighties: The Far-Ranging Novels of Marion Crawford," *Cavalcade of the American Novel*, 166-171.

DANA, RICHARD HENRY

TWO YEARS BEFORE THE MAST

Becker, May Lamberton. Introduction, *Two Years Before the Mast* (Cleveland, 1946), pp. vii.

Bond, William H. "Melville and *Two Years Before the Mast*," *Harvard Library Bulletin* VII (Autumn 1953), 362-365.

Grenfell, Sir Wilfred. Introduction, *Two Years Before the Mast* (New York, 1919; 1949), pp. ix.

Hart, James D. "Melville and Dana," *American Literature* IX (Mar 1937), 49-55.

——————. "A Note on Sherman Kent's 'Russian Christmas Before the Mast,'" *American Literature* XIV (Nov 1942), 294-298.

Kent, Sherman. "Russian Christmas Before the Mast," *American Literature* XIII (Jan 1942), 395-398.

Keyes, Homer Eaton. Introduction, *Two Years Before the Mast* (New York, 1909).

Lawrence, D. H. *Studies in Classic American Literature*, 121-142.

Lucid, Robert F. "The Influence of *Two Years Before the Mast* on Herman Melville," *American Literature* XXXI (Nov 1959), 243-256.

Patterson, J. E. Introduction, *Two Years Before the Mast* (New York, 1912), pp. xii.

Welsh, Charles. Introduction, *Two Years Before the Mast* (New York, 1917), pp. xiii.

DAVIS, H. L.

GENERAL
Kohler, Dayton. "H. L. Davis: Writer in the West," *College English* XIV (Dec 1952), 133-140.

DAVIS, REBECCA HARDING

MARGARET HOWTH
Gohdes, Clarence. "Realism for the Middle Class," *The Literature of the American People*, 662-663.
GENERAL
Quinn, Arthur Hobson. "The Transition to Realism," *American Fiction*, 181-190.

DAVIS, RICHARD HARDING

GENERAL
Davis, Charles Belmont (ed.). *Adventures and Letters of Richard Harding Davis.*
Downey, Fairfax. *Richard Harding Davis: His Day.*
Gohdes, Clarence. "The Facts of Life *Versus* Pleasant Reading," *The Literature of the American People*, 760-761.
Osborn, Scott C. "The 'Rivalry-Chivalry' of Richard Harding Davis and Stephen Crane," *American Literature* XXVIII (Mar 1956), 50-61.
BIBLIOGRAPHY
Quinby, Henry Cole. *Richard Harding Davis: A Bibliography.*

DE FOREST, JOHN WILLIAM

KATE BEAUMONT
Howells, W. D. *Heroines of Fiction* II, 152-163.
MISS RAVENEL'S CONVERSION
Haight, Gordon S. Introduction, *Miss Ravenel's Conversion* (New York, 1939; 1955).
O'Donnell, Thomas F. "DeForest, Van Petten, and Stephen Crane," *American Literature* XXVII (Jan 1956), 578-580.
GENERAL
Blotner, Joseph L. "John W. DeForest: Post-War Corruption," *The Political Novel*, 35-36.

DE FOREST, JOHN WILLIAM, Continued

Cowie, Alexander. "Civil War and Reconstruction: J. W. DeForest (1826-1906)," *The Rise of the American Novel*, 505-520.

Gargano, James W. "A DeForest Interview," *American Literature* XXIX (Nov 1957), 320-322.

Gohdes, Clarence. "Realism for the Middle Class," *The Literature of the American People*, 663-665.

Haight, Gordon S. "The John William DeForest Collection," *Yale University Library Gazette* XIV (Jan 1940), 41-46.

Hubbell, Jay B. *The South in American Literature*, 393-400.

Quinn, Arthur Hobson. "The Transition to Realism," *American Fiction*, 166-174.

Wagenknecht, Edward. "[DeForest]." *Cavalcade of the American Novel*, 104-108.

BIBLIOGRAPHY

Hagemann, E. E. "A Checklist of the Writings of John William DeForest (1826-1906)," *Studies in Bibliography* VIII (1956), 185-194.

DELL, FLOYD

GENERAL

Baldwin, Charles C. "Floyd Dell," *The Men Who Make Our Novels*, 129-133.

Cargill, Oscar. "The Freudians," *Intellectual America*, 651-660.

Michaud, Régis. "Reinforcements: Willa Cather, Zona Gale, Floyd Dell, Joseph Hergesheimer, Waldo Frank," *The American Novel To-Day*, 238-256.

Sherman, Stuart. "Floyd Dell on the Coast of Bohemia," *Critical Woodcuts*, 49-62.

Van Doren, Carl. *Contemporary American Novelists*, 166-171.

DIGGES, THOMAS ATWOOD

ADVENTURES OF ALONSO

Elias, Robert H. "The First American Novel," *American Literature* XII (Jan 1941), 419-434.

DOS PASSOS, JOHN

ADVENTURES OF A YOUNG MAN
Blotner, Joseph L. *The Political Novel*, 39-40.
Chamberlain, John. "John Dos Passos," *Saturday Review of Literature* XX (Jun 3, 1939), 3-4; 14-15.

THE BIG MONEY
DeVoto, Bernard. "John Dos Passos: Anatomist of Our Time," *Saturday Review of Literature* XIV (Aug 8, 1936), 3-4; 12-13.
Geismar, Maxwell. Introduction, *The Big Money* (Pocket Books, 1955).

42ND PARALLEL
Dos Passos, John. Introduction, *42nd Parallel* (New York, 1937), pp. ix.
Geismar, Maxwell. Introduction, *42nd Parallel* (Pocket Books, 1952).
Wilson, Edmund. *A Literary Chronicle*, 142-145.

GRAND DESIGN
Blotner, Joseph L. *The Political Novel*, 40.

MANHATTAN TRANSFER
Arden, Eugene. "*Manhattan Transfer*: An Experiment in Technique," *University of Kansas City Review* XXII (Dec 1955), 153-158.
Canby, Henry Seidel. "Thunder in Manhattan," *Saturday Review of Literature* II (Jan 16, 1926), 489; 495.
Henderson, Philip. "Dos Passos," *The Novel Today*, 130-136.
Lewis, Sinclair. "Manhattan at Last!" *Saturday Review of Literature* II (Dec 5, 1925), 361.
"Manhattan Transfer," *American Writing Today*, 364-365.

1919
Geismar, Maxwell. Introduction, *1919* (Pocket Books, 1954).

NUMBER ONE
Jones, Howard Mumford. "Sound-Truck Caesar," *Saturday Review of Literature* XXVI (Mar 6, 1943), 7-8.
Rubin, Louis D., Jr. "All the King's Meanings," *Georgia Review* VIII (Winter 1954), 422-434.

THREE SOLDIERS
Dos Passos, John. Introduction, *Three Soldiers* (New York, 1932). pp. ix.

U. S. A.
Geismar, Maxwell. *American Moderns*, 65-76.

DOS PASSOS, JOHN, Continued

Kazin, Alfred. *The American Writer and the European Tradition*, 129-131.

Schwartz, Delmore. "John Dos Passos and the Whole Truth," *Southern Review* IV (Autumn 1938), 351-367.

Trilling, Lionel. "The America of John Dos Passos," *Partisan Review* IV (Apr 1938), 26-32.

GENERAL

Aldridge, John W. "Dos Passos: The Energy of Despair," *After the Lost Generation*, 59-81.

Baldwin, Charles C. "John Dos Passos," *The Men Who Make Our Novels*, 138-140.

Beach, Joseph Warren. *American Fiction*, 25-44; 47-66.

——————. "Dos Passos: 1947," *Sewanee Review* LV (Summer 1947), 406-418.

——————. *The Twentieth Century Novel*, 437-448, 501-511.

Blotner, Joseph L. "John Dos Passos and Ernest Hemingway: Liberal Causes Abroad," *The Political Novel*, 15-16.

Boynton, Percy H. "John Dos Passos," *America in Contemporary Fiction*, 185-203.

Bradford, Curtis B. "John Dos Passos—A Defense," *University of Kansas City Review* VIII (Summer 1942), 267-272.

Breit, Harvey. *The Writer Observed*, 143-145.

Brown, Deming. "Dos Passos in Soviet Criticism," *Comparative Literature* V (Fall 1953), 332-350.

Calmer, Alan. "John Dos Passos," *Sewanee Review* XL (Jul-Sept 1932), 341-349.

Cowley, Malcolm. "Dos Passos: Poet Against the World," *After the Genteel Tradition*, 168-185.

Dos Passos, John. "The Situation in American Writing," *Partisan Review* VI (Summer 1939), 26-27.

Footman, Robert H. "John Dos Passos," *Sewanee Review* XLVII (Jul-Sept 1939), 365-382.

Frohock, W. M. "John Dos Passos: Of Time and Frustration," *Southwest Review* XXXIII (Winter 1948), 71-80; Part II (Spring 1948), 170-179; *The Novel of Violence in America*, 17-45.

Geismar, Maxwell. *American Moderns*, 76-90.

Gelfant, Blanche Housman. "John Dos Passos: The Synoptic Novel," *The American City Novel*, 133-174.

DOS PASSOS, JOHN, Continued

Hartwick, Harry. "The Anarchist," *The Foreground of American Fiction*, 282-293.

Hatcher, Harlan. "The Critical Spirit: John Dos Passos," *Creating the Modern American Novel*, 132-139.

Hersey, John. "The Novel of Contemporary History," *Atlantic Monthly* CLXXXIV (Nov 1949), 80-82.

Hicks, Granville. *The Great Tradition*, 287-292.

——————. "The Politics of John Dos Passos," *Antioch Review* X (Mar 1950), 85-98.

Hoffman, Frederick J. *The Twenties*, 57-61.

John Dos Passos: An Appreciation.

Kallich, Martin. "John Dos Passos Fellow-Traveler: A Dossier with Commentary," *Twentieth Century Literature* I (Jan 1956), 173-190.

——————. "John Dos Passos: Liberty and the Father Image," *Antioch Review* X (Mar 1950), 99-106.

Kazin, Alfred. "All the Lost Generations," *On Native Grounds*, 341-359.

McCole, John. *Lucifer at Large*, 175-200.

McLuhan, Herbert Marshall. "John Dos Passos: Technique vs. Sensibility," *Fifty Years of the American Novel*, 151-164.

Mizener, Arthur. "The Gullivers of Dos Passos," *Saturday Review of Literature* XXXIV (Jun 30, 1951), 6-7; 34-36.

——————. "The Novel of Manners in America," *Kenyon Review* XII (Winter 1950), 1-19.

Rugoff, Milton. "Dos Passos, Novelist of Our Time," *Sewanee Review* XLIX (Oct-Dec 1941), 453-468.

Sartre, Jean-Paul. "American Novelists in French Eyes," *Atlantic Monthly* CLXXXVIII (Aug 1946), 114-118.

Schwartz, Delmore. "John Dos Passos and the Whole Truth," *Critiques and Essays on Modern Fiction*, 176-189.

Slochower, Harry. *No Voice Is Wholly Lost*, 69-75.

Smith, James Steel. "The Novelist of Discomfort: A Reconsideration of John Dos Passos." *College English* XIX (May 1958), 332-338.

Snell, George. "John Dos Passos: Literary Collectivist," *The Shapers of American Fiction*, 249-263.

Stovall, Floyd. *American Idealism*, 147-150.

DOS PASSOS, JOHN, Continued

Wade, Mason. "Novelist of America: John Dos Passos," *North American Review* 244 (Winter 1937-38), 349-367.

Wagenknecht, Edward. "Novelists of the 'Twenties: John Dos Passos: The Collectivist Novel," *Cavalcade of the American Novel*, 382-389.

Walcutt, Charles Child. "Later Trends in Form: Dos Passos," *American Literary Naturalism*, 280-289.

Whicher, George F. "Analysts of Decay," *The Literature of the American People*, 880-882.

Wilson, Edmund. "Dos Passos and the Social Revolution," *The Shores of Light*, 429-435; 442-450.

BIBLIOGRAPHY

Kallich, Martin. "A Bibliography of John Dos Passos," *Bulletin of Bibliography* XIX (May-Aug 1949), 231-235.

Potter, Jack. *A Bibliography of John Dos Passos.*

DOUGLAS, LLOYD C.

THE ROBE

Wilson, Edmund. *A Literary Chronicle*, 309-313.

GENERAL

Bode, Carl. "Lloyd Douglas: Loud Voice in the Wilderness." *American Quarterly* II (Winter 1950), 340-352.

DREISER, THEODORE

AN AMERICAN TRAGEDY

"An American Tragedy," *American Writing Today*, 362-364.

Canby, Henry Seidel. "An American Tragedy," *Saturday Review of Literature* II (Feb 20, 1926), 569-570.

Kazin, Alfred. Introduction, *An American Tragedy* (New York, 1959).

Matthiessen, F. O. *Theodore Dreiser*, 187-211; *The Stature of Theodore Dreiser*, 204-218.

Mencken, H. L. Introduction, *An American Tragedy* (Cleveland, 1946; 1947; 1948).

Shafer, Robert. *Humanism and America*, 149-169; *The Stature of Theodore Dreiser*, 113-126.

THE BULWARK

Friedrich, Gerhard. "A Major Influence on Theodore Dreiser's

DREISER, THEODORE, Continued

The Bulwark," American Literature XXIX (May 1957), 180-193.

Hicks, Granville. "Theodore Dreiser," *American Mercury* LXII (Jun 1946), 751-756; *The Stature of Theodore Dreiser,* 219-224.

THE "GENIUS"

Elias, Robert H. *Theodore Dreiser: Apostle of Nature,* 117-194.

Kwiat, Joseph J. "Dreiser's *The 'Genius'* and Everett Shinn, the 'Ash-Can' Painter," *PMLA* LXVII (Mar 1952), 15-31.

Matthiessen, F. O. *Theodore Dreiser,* 159-173.

JENNIE GERHARDT

Elias, Robert H. *Theodore Dreiser: Apostle of Nature,* 152-176; *The Stature of Theodore Dreiser,* 188-203.

Matthiessen, F. O. *Theodore Dreiser,* 109-125.

Rapin, René. "Dreiser's *Jennie Gerhardt,* Chapter LXII," *Explicator* XIV (May 1956), No. 54.

Shapiro, Charles. *Twelve Original Essays on Great American Novels,* 177-195.

SISTER CARRIE

Cowley, Malcolm. *The Stature of Theodore Dreiser,* 171-181.

"Early Newspaper Reviews," *The Stature of Theodore Dreiser,* 53-68.

Elias, Robert H. *Theodore Dreiser: Apostle of Nature,* 103-117.

Farrell, James T. Introduction, *Sister Carrie* (New York, 1957).

——————. *The Stature of Theodore Dreiser,* 182-187.

Geismar, Maxwell. "Jezebel on the Loop," *Saturday Review* XXXVI (Jul 4, 1953), 12.

——————. "Theodore Dreiser," *American Moderns,* 49-53; Introduction, *Sister Carrie* (Pocket Books, 1949).

Handy, William J. "A Re-examination of Dreiser's *Sister Carrie,*" *Texas Studies in Literature and Language* I (Autumn 1959), 381-393.

Kazin, Alfred. *The American Writer and the European Tradition,* 121-128.

Lynn, Kenneth S. Introduction, *Sister Carrie* (New York, 1957), pp. xx.

Matthiessen, F. O. *Theodore Dreiser,* 55-108.

Rascoe, Burton. Introduction, *Sister Carrie* (1939), pp. xiv.

Simpson, Claude. "*Sister Carrie* Reconsidered," *Southwest Review* XLIV (Winter 1959), 44-53.

DREISER, THEODORE, Continued

──────────. Introduction, *Sister Carrie* (Boston, 1959), pp. xxi.

Steinbrecher, George, Jr. "Inaccurate Accounts of *Sister Carrie*," *American Literature* XXIII (Jan 1952), 490-493.

THE TITAN

Matthiessen, F. O. *Theodore Dreiser*, 127-158.

GENERAL

Adams, Theodore. "The Heavy Hand of Dreiser," *The Shape of Books to Come*, 54-83.

Anderson, Carl. *The Swedish Acceptance of American Literature*, 75-82.

Anderson, Sherwood. "An Apology for Crudity," *The Stature of Theodore Dreiser*, 81-83.

Arnavon, Cyrille. "Theodore Dreiser and Painting," *American Literature* XVII (May 1945), 113-126.

Baldwin, Charles C. "Theodore Dreiser," *The Men Who Make Our Novels*, 141-153.

Beach, Joseph Warren. "The Realist Reaction: Dreiser," *The Twentieth Century Novel*, 321-331.

Becker, George J. "Theodore Dreiser: The Realist As Social Critic," *Twentieth Century Literature* I (Oct 1955), 117-127.

Bellow, Saul. "Dreiser and the Triumph of Art," *The Stature of Theodore Dreiser*, 146-148.

Berryman, John. "Dreiser's Imagination," *The Stature of Theodore Dreiser*, 149-153.

Bourne, Randolph. "The Art of Theodore Dreiser," *Dial* LXII (Jun 14, 1917), 507-509.

──────────. "The Art of Theodore Dreiser," *The History of a Literary Radical & Other Papers*, 124-131; *The Stature of Theodore Dreiser*, 92-95.

Boynton, Percy H. "Theodore Dreiser," *America in Contemporary Fiction*, 131-149.

──────────. "Theodore Dreiser," *Some Contemporary Americans*, 126-144.

Brooks, Van Wyck. "Theodore Dreiser," *The Confident Years*, 301-320.

──────────. "Theodore Dreiser," *University of Kansas City Review* XVI (Spring 1950), 187-197.

DREISER, THEODORE, Continued

Burgum, Edwin Berry. "Theodore Dreiser and the Ethics of American Life," *The Novel and the World's Dilemma*, 292-301.
Campbell, Louise. *Letters to Louise.*
Cargill, Oscar. "The Naturalists," *Intellectual America*, 107-127.
Chamberlain, John. "Theodore Dreiser," *After the Genteel Tradition*, 27-36; "Theodore Dreiser Remembered,'" *The Stature of Theodore Dreiser*, 127-131.
Cohen, Lester. "Theodore Dreiser: A Personal Memoir," *discovery* 4 (1954), 99-126.
Crawford, Bruce. "Theodore Dreiser: Letter-Writing Citizen," *South Atlantic Quarterly* LIII (Apr 1954), 231-237.
Davis, David Brion. "Dreiser and Naturalism Revisited," *The Stature of Theodore Dreiser*, 225-236.
Dreiser, Helen. *My Life with Dreiser.*
Dudley, Dorothy. *Forgotten Frontiers.*
Duffus, Robert L. "Dreiser," *American Criticism 1926*, 46-61.
——————. "Dreiser," *American Mercury* VII (Jan 1926), 71-76.
Drummond, Edward J. "Theodore Dreiser: Shifting Naturalism," *Fifty Years of the American Novel*, 33-47.
Edgar, Pelham. "American Realism, Sex, and Theodore Dreiser," *The Art of the Novel*, 244-254.
Elias, Robert H., (ed.). *Letters of Theodore Dreiser.*
——————. *Theodore Dreiser: Apostle of Nature.*
Farrell, James T. "Some Correspondence with Theodore Dreiser," *Reflections at Fifty*, 124-141; *The Stature of Theodore Dreiser*, 36-50.
——————. "Theodore Dreiser: In Memoriam," *Saturday Review of Literature* XXIX (Jan 12, 1946), 16-17, 27-28; *Literature and Morality*, 26-34.
Flanagan, John T. "Theodore Dreiser in Retrospect," *Southwest Review* XXXI (Autumn 1946), 408-411.
Ford, Ford Madox. "Portrait of Dreiser," *Portraits from Life*, 164-182; *The Stature of Theodore Dreiser*, 21-35.
Friedrich, Gerhard. "Theodore Dreiser's Debt to Woolman's Journal," *American Quarterly* VII (Winter 1955), 385-392.
Geismar, Maxwell. "Dreiser and the Dark Texture of Life," *American Scholar* XXII (Spring 1953), 215-221.

DREISER, THEODORE, Continued

———. "Theodore Dreiser: The Double Soul," *Rebels and Ancestors*, 287-379.

Gelfant, Blanche Housman. "Theodore Dreiser: The Portrait Novel," *The American City Novel*, 42-94.

Harris, Frank. "Theodore Dreiser," *Contemporary Portraits*, second series, 81-106.

Hartwick, Harry. "The Hindenburg of the Novel," *The Foregound of American Fiction*, 85-110.

Hatcher, Harlan. "Theodore Dreiser," *Creating the Modern American Novel*, 34-57.

Hicks, Granville. *The Great Tradition*, 227-230.

Kazin, Alfred. "Dreiser," *The Inmost Leaf*, 236-241.

———. Introduction, *The Stature of Theodore Dreiser*, 3-12.

———. "Two Educations: Edith Wharton and Theodore Dreiser," *On Native Grounds*, 82-90; "Theodore Dreiser: His Eductation and Ours," *The Stature of Theodore Dreiser*, 154-160.

Kern, Alexander. "Dreiser's Difficult Beauty," *Western Review* XVI (Winter 1952), 129-136; *The Stature of Theodore Dreiser*, 161-168.

Knight, Grant C. "Theodore Dreiser," *American Literature and Culture*, 400-413.

Kwiat, Joseph J. "Dreiser and the Graphic Artist," *American Quarterly* III (Summer 1951), 127-141.

———. "The Newspaper Experience: Crane, Norris, and Dreiser," *Ninetenth-Century Fiction* VIII (Sept 1953), 99-117.

Leaver, Florence. "Theodore Dreiser, Beyond Naturalism," *Mark Twain Quarterly* IX (Winter 1951), 5-9.

Lewis, Sinclair. "Our Formula for Fiction," *The Stature of Theodore Dreiser*, 111-112.

Lewisohn, Ludwig. "An American Memory," *The Stature of Theodore Dreiser*, 17-20.

Lord, David. "Dreiser Today," *Prairie Schooner* XV (Winter 1941), 230-239.

Lydenberg, John. "Theodore Dreiser: Ishmael in the Jungle, *American Radicals*, 37-52.

Lynn, Kenneth S. "Theodore Dreiser: The Man of Ice," *The Dream of Success*, 13-74.

DREISER, THEODORE, Continued

Lyon, Harris Merton. "What Manner of Man He Is," *Theodore Dreiser, America's Foremost Novelist*, 5-12.
Matthiessen, F. O. *Theodore Dreiser.*
McCole, John. *Lucifer at Large*, 17-54.
Mencken, H. L. "The Dreiser Bugaboo," *The Stature of Theodore Dreiser*, 84-91.
──────────. "Theodore Dreiser," *A Book of Prefaces*, 67-148; *The Vintage Mencken*, 35-56; *Critiques and Essays on Modern Fiction*, 388-401.
Michaud, Régis. *The American Novel To-Day*, 71-127.
──────────. "Theodore Dreiser," *Panorama de la Littérature Américaine Contemporaine*, 165-170.
Morris, Lloyd. *Postscript to Yesterday*, 121-131.
Mumford, Lewis. *The Golden Day*, 250-254; (Beacon Press edition) 127-130.
Munson, Gorham B. "The Motivation of Theodore Dreiser," *Destinations*, 41-56.
Powys, John Cowper. "The Writer and His Writings," *Theodore Dreiser, America's Foremost Novelist*, 16-23.
Quinn, Arthur Hobson. "Critics and Satirists—The Radicals," *American Fiction*, 645-652.
Rascoe, Burton. *Theodore Dreiser.*
Ross, Woodburn O. "Concerning Dreiser's Mind," *American Literature* XVIII (Nov 1946), 233-243.
Schneider, Isidor. "Theodore Dreiser," *Saturday Review of Literature* X (Mar 10, 1934), 533-535.
Sherman, Stuart P. "The Barbaric Naturalism of Theodore Dreiser," *On Contemporary Literature*, 85-101; *The Stature of Theodore Dreiser*, 71-80.
──────────. "Mr. Dreiser in Tragic Realism," *The Main Stream*, 134-144.
Snell, George. "Theodore Dreiser: Philosopher," *The Shapers of American Fiction*, 233-248.
Spiller, Robert. *The Cycle of American Literature*, 224-230; (Mentor) 171-176.
Stewart, Randall. "Dreiser and the Naturalistic Heresy," *Virginia Quarterly Review* XXXIV (Winter 1958), 100-116.
Stovall, Floyd. *American Idealism*, 131-138.

DREISER, THEODORE, Continued

Trilling, Lionel. "Reality in America," *The Liberal Imagination*, 3-21; *The Stature of Theodore Dreiser*, 132-145.
Van Doren, Carl. *Contemporary American Novelists*, 74-83.
──────────. "Theodore Dreiser," *The American Novel 1789-1939*, 245-259.
Van Vechten, Carl. "Theodore Dreiser As I Knew Him," *Yale University Libary Gazette* XXV (Jan 1951), 87-92.
Vivas, Eliseo. "Dreiser, An Inconsistent Mechanist," *The Stature of Theodore Dreiser*, 237-245.
Wagenknecht, Edward. "Theodore Dreiser, The Mystic Naturalist," *Cavalcade of the American Novel*, 281-293.
Walcutt, Charles Child. "Theodore Dreiser and the Divided Stream," *The Stature of Theodore Dreiser*, 246-269.
──────────. "Theodore Dreiser: The Wonder and Terror of Life," *American Literary Naturalism*, 180-221.
──────────. "The Three Stages of Theodore Dreiser's Naturalism," *PMLA* LV (1940), 266-289.
Whicher, George F. "Respectability Defied," *The Literature of the American People*, 847-851.
Whipple, T. K. "Theodore Dreiser," *Spokesmen*, 70-93; "Aspects of a Pathfinder," *The Stature of Theodore Dreiser*, 96-110.
Willen, Gerald. "Dreiser's Moral Seriousness," *University of Kansas City Review* XXIII (Spring 1957), 181-187.
Wirzberger, Karl-Heinz. "Das Leben und Schaffen Theodore Dreisers," *Zeitschrift für Anglistik und Amerikanistik* II (Heft 1 1954), 5-42.

BIBLIOGRAPHY

Birss, J. H. "A Bibliographical Note on Theodore Dreiser," *Notes and Queries* CLXV (1933), 266.
Kazin, Alfred and Charles Shapiro. "A Selected Bibliography of Dreiser Biography and Criticism," *The Stature of Theodore Dreiser*, 271-303.
McDonald, Edward D. *A Bibliography of the Writings of Theodore Dreiser*.
Miller, R. N. *A Preliminary Checklist of Books and Articles on Theodore Dreiser*.
Orton, Vrest. *Dreiserana*.

EDMONDS, WALTER

GENERAL

McCord, David. "Edmonds Country," *Saturday Review of Literature* XVII (Dec 11, 1937), 10-11.

Whicher, George F. "Loopholes of Retreat," *The Literature of the American People*, 890-891.

EGGLESTON, EDWARD

THE HOOSIER SCHOOL-MASTER

Fiske, Horace Spencer. *Provincial Types in American Fiction*, 167-178.

Holloway, Emory. Introduction, *Hoosier Schoolmaster* (New York, 1928). pp. xxviii.

Loggins, Vernon. Introduction, *Hoosier Schoolmaster* (New York, 1957; Gloucester, Mass., 1959).

Rawley, James A. "Some New Light on Edward Eggleston," *American Literature* XI (Jan 1940), 453-458.

GENERAL

Åhnebrink, Lars. "Realism in the Middle West: Edward Eggleston, Edgar Watson Howe, and Joseph Kirkland," *The Beginnings of Naturalism in American Fiction*, 50-59.

Cowie, Alexander. "Local-Color, Frontier, and Regional Fiction: Edward Eggleston (1837-1902)," *The Rise of the American Novel*, 538-556.

Flanagan, John T. "The Novels of Edward Eggleston," *College English* V (Feb 1944), 250-254.

Gohdes, Clarence. "Exploitation of the Provinces," *The Literature of the American People*, 646-648.

Hicks, Granville. *The Great Tradition*, 49-57.

Randel, William Peirce. *Edward Eggleston*.

Stone, Edward. "Edward Eggleston's Religious Transit," *Texas Studies in English* XIX (1939), 210-218.

BIBLIOGRAPHY

Randel, William Peirce. *Edward Eggleston*, 263-313.

ELLISON, RALPH

INVISIBLE MAN

Webster, Harvey Curtis. "Inside a Dark Shell," *Saturday Review of Literature* XXXV (Apr 2, 1952), 22-23.

ELLISON, RALPH, Continued

West, Anthony. *Principles and Persuasions*, 212-218.
GENERAL
Breit, Harvey. *The Writer Observed*, 243-245.
Glicksberg, Charles I. "The Symbolism of Vision," *Southwest Review* XXXIX (Summer 1954), 259-265.

EVANS, AUGUSTA JANE

GENERAL
Calkins, Earnest Elmo. "St. Elmo: or, Named for a Best Seller," *Saturday Review of Literature* XXI (Dec 16, 1939), 3-4, 14-17.
Hubbell, Jay B. *The South in American Literature*, 610-616.

FARRELL, JAMES T.

FATHER AND SON
Benét, Stephen Vincent. "Chicago's Danny O'Neill," *Saturday Review of Literature* XXII (Oct 12, 1940), 12.
Farrell, James T. Introduction, *Father and Son* (Cleveland, 1947), pp. xii.
JUDGMENT DAY
Farrell, James T. Introduction, *Judgment Day* (Cleveland, 1944).
MY DAYS OF ANGER
Burt, Struthers. "Realism and James Farrell," *Saturday Review of Literature* XXVI (Nov 27, 1943), 16-17.
Farrell, James T. Introduction, *My Days of Anger* (Cleveland, 1947), pp. xii.
NO STAR IS LOST
Stevens, George. "Life and Danny O'Neill," *Saturday Review of Literature* XVIII (Sept 17, 1938), 6.
STUDS LONIGAN
Beach, Joseph Warren. *American Fiction*, 273-283.
Canby, Henry Seidel. "James T. Farrell's Indelible Portraits," *Saturday Review of Literature* XIII (Dec 7, 1935), 7.
Farrell, James T. Introduction, *Studs Lonigan* (New York, 1938), pp. xxvii.
Gregory, Horace. *The Coming of Age of a Great Book*, 5-6.
Gurko, Leo. *The Angry Decade*, 119-125.
Kazin, Alfred. *The Coming of Age of a Great Book*, 5.

FARRELL, JAMES T., Continued

THIS MAN AND THIS WOMAN
Little, Carl Victor. "The Problem of Senescence," *Saturday Review of Literature* XXXIV (Oct 20, 1951), 18.

A WORLD I NEVER MADE
DeVoto, Bernard. "Beyond Studs Lonigan," *Saturday Review of Literature* XIV (Oct 24, 1936), 5-6.

Farrell, James T. Introduction, *A World I Never Made* (Cleveland, 1947), pp. xii.

YET OTHER WATERS
Blotner, Joseph L. *The Political Novel*, 39-40.

YOUNG LONIGAN
Farrell, James T. Introduction, *Young Lonigan* (Cleveland, 1943), pp. xi.

Thrasher, Frederic M. Introduction, *Young Lonigan* (New York, 1932), pp. xii.

YOUNG MANHOOD OF STUDS LONIGAN
Farrell, James T. Introduction, *The Young Manhood of Studs Lonigan* (Cleveland, 1944).

GENERAL
Aldridge, John W. "The Education of James T. Farrell," *In Search of Heresy*, 186-191.

Beach, Joseph Warren. "James T. Farrell: The Plight of the Children," *American Fiction*, 287-305; *Critiques and Essays on Modern Fiction*, 402-414.

Bettelheim, Bruno. *The Coming of Age of a Great Book*, 19.

Bradley, Van Allen. *The Coming of Age of a Great Book*, 7.

Cargill, Oscar. "The Naturalists," *Intellectual America*, 159-171.

Farrell, James T. "In Answer to a Young Man Who Wants to Become a Writer," *Saturday Review of Literature* XXI (Mar 23, 1940), 10.

——————. "The Author as Plaintiff: Testimony in a Censorship Case," *Reflections at Fifty*, 188-223.

——————. "My Beginnings as a Writer," *Reflections at Fifty*, 156-163.

——————. "A Novelist Begins," *Atlantic Monthly* CLXII (Sept 1938), 330-334.

——————. "The Situation in American Writing," *Partisan Review* VI (Summer 1939), 30-33.

FARRELL, JAMES T., Continued

Frohock, W. M. "James Farrell: The Precise Content," *The Novel of Violence in America*, 69-85.

——————. "James Farrell: The Precise Content," *Southwest Review* XXXV (Winter 1950), 39-48.

Gelfant, Blanche Housman. "James T. Farrell: The Ecological Novel," *The American City Novel*, 175-227.

Grattan, C. Harvey. "James T. Farrell: Moralist," *Harper's* CCIX (Oct 1954), 93-98.

Gregory, Horace. "James T. Farrell: Beyond the Provinces of Art," *New World Writing* 5 (1954), 52-65.

Hatfield, Ruth. "The Intellectual Honesty of James T. Farrell," *College English* III (Jan 1942), 337-346.

Kazin, Alfred. "The Revival of Naturalism," *On Native Grounds*, 380-385.

McCole, John. *Lucifer at Large*, 277-290.

Morris, Lloyd. *Postscript to Yesterday*, 162-166.

O'Malley, Frank. "James T. Farrell: Two Twilight Images," *Fifty Years of the American Novel*, 237-256.

Porter, Arabel J. *The Coming of Age of a Great Book*, 25-28.

Schlesinger, Arthur, Jr. *The Coming of Age of a Great Book*, 3.

Snell, George. "James T. Farrell and the Poverty of Spirit," *The Shapers of American Fiction*, 288-300; *The Coming of Age of a Great Book*, 9-15.

Targ, William. *The Coming of Age of a Great Book*, 21-22.

Walcutt, Charles Child. "James T. Farrell: Aspects of Telling the Whole Truth," *American Literary Naturalism*, 240-257.

——————. "James T. Farrell and the Reversible Topcoat," *Arizona Quarterly* VII (Winter 1951), 293-310.

Whicher, George F. "Respectability Defied," *The Literature of the American People*, 851.

White, Morton. *The Coming of Age of a Great Book*, 17.

BIBLIOGRAPHY

Branch, Edgar Marquess. *A Bibliography of James T. Farrell's Writings 1921-1957*.

FAST, HOWARD
GENERAL
Fast, Howard. "On Leaving the Communist Party," *Saturday Review* XLII (Nov 16, 1959), 15-17; 55-58.
Hicks, Granville. "Howard Fast's One-Man Reformation," *College English* VII (Oct 1945), 1-6.
Kopka, Hans W. K. "Howard Fasts Entwicklung als Mensch und Schriftsteller," *Zeitschrift für Anglistik und Amerikanistik* II (Heft 3 1954), 275-294.

FAULKNER, WILLIAM
ABSALOM, ABSALOM!
Breit, Harvey. Introduction, *Absalom, Absalom!* (New York, 1951), pp. xii.
Brooks, Cleanth. "*Absalom, Absalom*: The Definition of Innocence," *Sewanee Review* LIX (Oct-Dec 1951), 543-558.
Campbell, Harry Modean. "Faulkner's *Absalom, Absalom!*" *Explicator* VII (Dec 1948), No. 24.
Hoffman, A. C. "Faulkner's *Absalom, Absalom!*" *Explicator* X (Nov 1951), No. 12.
──────. "Point of View in *Absalom, Absalom!*" *University of Kansas City Review* XIX (Summer 1953), 233-239.
Howe, Irving. *William Faulkner*, 161-172.
Lind, Ilse Dusoir. "The Design and Meaning of *Absalom, Absalom!*" *PMLA* LXX (Dec 1955), 887-912.
O'Connor, William Van. *The Tangled Fire of William Faulkner*, 94-100.
Poirier, William R. " 'Strange Gods' in Jefferson, Mississippi: Analysis of *Absalom, Absalom!*" *Sewanee Review* LIII (Summer 1945), 343-361; *William Faulkner: Two Decades of Criticism*, 217-243.
Scott, Arthur L. "The Faulknerian Sentence," *Prairie Schooner* XXVII (Spring 1953), 91-98.
──────. "The Myriad Perspectives of *Absalom, Absalom!*" *American Quarterly*, VI (Fall 1954), 210-220.
Sullivan, Walter. "The Tragic Design of *Absalom, Absalom!*" *South Atlantic Quarterly* L (Oct 1951), 552-566.
Thomas, Douglas M. "Memory-Narrative in *Absalom, Absalom!*" *Faulkner Studies* II (Summer 1953), 19-22.

FAULKNER, WILLIAM, Continued

Vickery, Olga W. *The Novels of William Faulkner,* 84-102.
Waggoner, Hyatt H. *William Faulkner: From Jefferson to the World,* 148-169.
Whan, Edgar W. "*Absalom, Absalom!* as Gothic Myth." *Perspective* III (Autumn 1950), 192-201.
Zoellner, Robert H. "Faulkner's Prose Style in *Absalom, Absalom!*" *American Literature* XXX (Jan 1959), 486-502.

AS I LAY DYING

Blotner, Joseph L. "*As I Lay Dying*: Christian Lore and Irony," *Twentieth Century Literature* III (Apr 1957), 14-19.
Campbell, Harry M. "Experiment and Achievement: *As I Lay Dying* and *The Sound and The Fury,*" *Sewanee Review* LI (Apr-Jun 1943), 305-320.
Chase, Richard. *The American Novel and Its Tradition,* 207-210.
Collins, Carvel. "The Pairing of *The Sound and the Fury* and *As I Lay Dying,*" *Princeton University Library Chronicle* XVIII (Spring 1957), 114-123.
Douglas, Harold J. and Robert Daniel. "Faulkner and the Puritanism of the South," *Tennessee Studies in Literature* II (1957), 5-10.
Garrett, George Palmer. "Some Revisions in *As I Lay Dying,*" *Modern Language Notes* LXXIII (Jun 1958), 414-417.
Goellner, Jack Gordon. "A Closer Look at 'As I Lay Dying,'" *Perspective* VII (Spring 1954), 42-54.
Handy, William J. "*As I Lay Dying*: Faulkner's Inner Reporter," *Kenyon Review* XXI (Summer 1959), 437-451.
Howe, Irving. *William Faulkner,* 127-142.
King, Roma, Jr. "The Janus Symbol in *As I Lay Dying,*" *University of Kansas City Review* XXI (Jun 1955), 287-290.
O'Connor, William Van. *The Tangled Fire of William Faulkner,* 45-54.
Sawyer, Kenneth B. "Hero in *As I Lay Dying,*" *Faulkner Studies* III (Summer-Autumn 1954), 30-33.
Smith, Henry. "A Troubled Vision," *Southwest Review* XVI (Jan 1931), xvi-xvii.
Vickery, Olga [Westland]. "*As I Lay Dying,*" *Perspective* III (Autumn 1950), 179-191; *William Faulkner: Two Decades of Criticism,* 189-205.
―――――. *The Novels of William Faulkner,* 50-65.

FAULKNER, WILLIAM, Continued

Waggoner, Hyatt H. *William Faulkner: From Jefferson to the World,* 62-87.
Wasiolek, Edward. "*As I Lay Dying*: Distortion in the Slow Eddy of Current Opinion," *Critique* III (Spring-Fall 1959), 15-23.

A FABLE

Bartlett, Phyllis. "Other Countries, Other Wenches," *Modern Fiction Studies* III (Winter 1957-1958), 347-349.
Chametzky, Jules. "Some Remarks on *A Fable,*" *Faulkner Studies* III (Summer-Autumn 1954), 39-40.
Connolly, Thomas E. "Faulkner's *A Fable* in the Classroom," *College English* XXI (Dec 1959), 165-171.
Coughlan, Robert. *The Private World of William Faulkner,* 139-151.
Flint, R. W. "What Price Glory," *Hudson Review* VII (Winter 1955), 602-606.
Geismar, Maxwell. "Latter-Day Christ Story," *Saturday Review* XXXVII (Jul 31, 1954), 11-12; *American Moderns,* 97-101.
Hafley, James. "Faulkner's 'Fable': Dream and Transfiguration," *Accent* XVI (Winter 1956), 3-14.
Howe, Irving. "Thirteen Who Mutinied: Faulkner's First World War," *The Reporter* XI (Sept 14, 1954), 43-45.
King, Roma A., Jr. "Everyman's Warfare: A Study of Faulkner's 'Fable,'" *Modern Fiction Studies* II (Autumn 1956), 132-138.
Kohler, Dayton. "*A Fable*: The Novel as Myth," *College English* XVI (May 1955), 471-478.
Lewis, R. W. B. *The Picaresque Saint,* 209-219.
Lytle, Andrew. "The Son of Man: He Will Prevail," *Sewanee Review* LXII (Winter 1955), 114-137.
Podhoretz, Norman. "William Faulkner and the Problem of War," *Commentary* XVIII (Sept 1954), 227-232.
Rice, Philip Blair. "Faulkner's Crucifixion," *Kenyon Review* XVI (Autumn 1954), 661-670.
Stavrow, C. N. "William Faulkner's Apologia: Some Notes on 'A Fable,'" *Colorado Quarterly* III (Spring 1955), 432-439.
Taylor, Walter Fuller. "William Faulkner: The Faulkner Fable," *American Scholar* XXVI (Autumn 1957), 471-477.
Vickery, Olga W. *The Novels of William Faulkner,* 192-210.
Waggoner, Hyatt H. *William Faulkner: From Jefferson to the World,* 225-232.

FAULKNER, WILLIAM, Continued
THE HAMLET

Benét, Stephen Vincent. "Flem Snopes and His Kin," *Saturday Review of Literature* XXI (Apr 6, 1940), 7.

Greet, T. Y. "The Theme and Structure of Faulkner's *The Hamlet*," *PMLA* LXXII (Sept 1957), 775-790.

Hopkins, Viola. "William Faulkner's 'The Hamlet': A Study in Meaning and Form," *Accent* XV (Spring 1955), 125-144.

Howe, Irving. *William Faulkner*, 179-186.

Leaver, Florence. "The Structure of *The Hamlet*," *Twentieth Century Literature* I (Jul 1955), 77-84.

Lisca, Peter. "*The Hamlet*: Genesis and Revisions," *Faulkner Studies* III (Spring 1954), 5-13.

O'Connor, William Van. *The Tangled Fire of William Faulkner*, 111-124.

Stonesifer, Richard J. "Faulkner's *The Hamlet* in the Classroom," *College English* XX (Nov 1958), 71-77.

Vickery, Olga W. *The Novels of William Faulkner*, 167-181.

Waggoner, Hyatt H. *William Faulkner: From Jefferson to the World*, 170-193.

Warren, Robert Penn. "The Snopes World," *Kenyon Review* III (Spring 1941), 253-257.

Watkins, Floyd C. and Thomas Daniel Young. "Revisions of Style in Faulkner's 'The Hamlet,'" *Modern Fiction Studies* V (Winter 1959-1960), 327-336.

INTRUDER IN THE DUST

Elias, Robert H. "Gavin Stevens: Intruder?" *Faulkner Studies* III (Spring 1954), 1-4.

Geismar, Maxwell. "Ex-Aristocrat's Emotional Education," *Saturday Review of Literature* XXXI (Sept 25, 1948), 8-9; *American Moderns*, 91-93.

Glicksberg, Charles I. "*Intruder in the Dust*," *Arizona Quarterly* V (Spring 1949), 85-88.

Hardwick, Elizabeth. "Faulkner and the South Today," *Partisan Review* XV (Oct 1948), 1130-1135; *William Faulkner: Two Decades of Criticism*, 244-250.

Lytle, Andrew. "Regeneration for the Man," *Sewanee Review* LVII (Winter 1949), 120-127; *William Faulkner: Two Decades of Criticism*, 251-259.

FAULKNER, WILLIAM, Continued

Mizener, Arthur. "The Thin, Intelligent Face of American Fiction," *Kenyon Review* XVII (Autumn 1955), 507-524.
O'Connor, William Van. *The Tangled Fire of William Faulkner*, 136-142.
Vickery, Olga W. *The Novels of William Faulkner*, 134-144.
Waggoner, Hyatt H. *William Faulkner: From Jefferson to the World*, 214-219.
Welty, Eudora. "In Yoknapatawpha," *Hudson Review* I (Winter 1949), 596-598.
Wilson, Edmund. *A Literary Chronicle*, 422-431.

LIGHT IN AUGUST

Abel, Darrel. "Frozen Movement in *Light in August*," *Boston University Studies in English* III (Spring 1957), 32-44.
Benson, Carl. "Thematic Design in *Light in August*," *South Atlantic Quarterly* LIII (Oct 1954), 540-555.
Chase, Richard. *The American Novel and Its Tradition*, 210-219.
──────── "The Stone and The Crucifixion: Faulkner's *Light in August*," *Kenyon Review* X (Autumn 1948), 539-551; *William Faulkner: Two Decades of Criticism*, 205-217; *Critiques and Essays on Modern Fiction*, 190-199.
Cottrell, Beekman W. "Christian Symbols in 'Light in August,'" *Modern Fiction Studies* II (Winter 1956-1957), 207-213.
Frazier, David L. "Lucas Burch and the Polarity of *Light in August*," *Modern Language Notes* LXXIII (Jun 1958), 417-419.
Hirshleifer, Phyllis. "As Whirlwinds in the South: An Analysis of *Light in August*," *Perspective* II (Summer 1949), 225-238.
Holman, C. Hugh. "The Unity of Faulkner's *Light in August*," *PMLA* LXXIII (Mar 1958), 155-166.
Howe, Irving. *William Faulkner*, 147-157.
Kazin, Alfred. "The Stillness of 'Light in August,'" *Partisan Review* XXIV (Fall 1957), 519-538; *Twelve Original Essays on Great American Novels*, 257-283; *Interpretations of American Literature*, 349-368.
Lamont, William H. F. "The Chronology of 'Light in August,'" *Modern Fiction Studies* III (Winter 1957-1958), 360-361.
Lind, Ilse Dusoir. "The Calvinistic Burden of *Light in August*," *New England Quarterly* XXX (Sept 1957), 307-329.

FAULKNER, WILLIAM, Continued

Linn, James Weber and Houghton Wells Taylor. *A Foreword to Fiction*, 144-157.

Longley, John L., Jr. "Joe Christmas: The Hero in the Modern World," *Virginia Quarterly Review* XXXIII (Spring 1957), 233-249.

McElderry, B. R., Jr. "The Narrative Structure of *Light in August*," *College English* XIX (Feb 1958), 200-207.

O'Connor, William Van. *The Tangled Fire of William Faulkner*, 72-87.

Rovere, Richard H. Introduction, *Light in August* (New York, 1950), pp. xiv.

Vickery, Olga W. *The Novels of William Faulkner*, 66-83.

Waggoner, Hyatt H. *William Faulkner: From Jefferson to the World*, 88-120.

Zink, Karl E. "Faulkner's Garden: Woman and the Immemorial Earth," *Modern Fiction Studies* II (Autumn 1956), 146-149.

THE MANSION

Hicks, Granville. "The Last of the Snopeses," *Saturday Review* XLII (Nov 14, 1959), 20-21.

MOSQUITOES

Aiken, Conrad. *A Reviewer's A B C*, 197-200.

Vickery, Olga W. *The Novels of William Faulkner*, 8-14.

Waggoner, Hyatt H. *William Faulkner: From Jefferson to the World*, 1-19.

THE OLD MAN

Moses, W. R. "The Unity of 'The Wild Palms,'" *Modern Fiction Studies* II (Autumn 1956), 125-131.

————. "Water, Water Everywhere: 'Old Man' and 'A Farewell to Arms,'" *Modern Fiction Studies* V (Summer 1959), 172-174.

Stonesifer, Richard J. "Faulkner's *Old Man* in the Classroom," *College English* XVII (Feb 1956), 254-257.

PYLON

Howe, Irving. *William Faulkner*, 158-161.

Marvin, John R. "Pylon: The Definition of Sacrifice," *Faulkner Studies* I (Summer 1952), 20-23.

Monteiro, George. "Bankruptcy in Time: A Reading of William Faulkner's *Pylon*," *Twentieth Century Literature* IV (Apr-Jul 1958), 9-20.

FAULKNER, WILLIAM, Continued

Redman, Ben Ray. "Flights of Fancy," *Saturday Review of Literature* XI (Mar 30, 1935), 577; 581.

Torchiana, Donald T. "Faulkner's 'Pylon' and the Structure of Modernity," *Modern Fiction Studies* III (Winter 1957-1958), 291-308.

Vickery, John B. "William Faulkner and Sir Philip Sidney?" *Modern Language Notes* LXX (May 1955), 349-350.

Vickery, Olga W. *The Novels of William Faulkner*, 145-155.

Waggoner, Hyatt H. *William Faulkner: From Jefferson to the World*, 121-147.

REQUIEM FOR A NUN

Baker, James R. "Ideas and Queries," *Faulkner Studies* I (Spring 1952), 4-7.

Geismar, Maxwell. *American Moderns*, 93-95.

Smith, Harrison. "Purification by Sacrifice," *Saturday Review of Literature* XXXIV (Sept 29, 1951), 12.

Vickery, Olga W. *The Novels of William Faulkner*, 114-123.

Waggoner, Hyatt H. *William Faulkner: From Jefferson to the World*, 219-225.

SANCTUARY

Brown, James. "Shaping the World of Sanctuary," *University of Kansas City Review* XXV (Winter 1958), 137-142.

Canby, Henry Seidel. "The School of Cruelty," *Saturday Review of Literature* VII (Mar 21, 1931), 673-674.

Chase, Richard. *The American Novel and Its Tradition*, 237-241.

Collins, Carvel. "Nathanael West's *The Day of the Locust* and *Sanctuary*," *Faulkner Studies* II (Summer 1953), 23-24.

Eshelman, William R. "Faulkner's *Sanctuary*," *Explicator* IV (Nov 1945), Q8; Harry Modean Campbell, "Faulkner's *Sanctuary*," (Jun 1946), No. 61; Lienhard Bergel, "Faulkner's *Sanctuary*," VI (Dec 1947), No. 20.

Faulkner, William. Introduction, *Sanctuary* (New York, 1932), pp. vi.

Fowler, Albert. "Source Books of Violence," *Trace* No. 21 (Apr 1957), 11-18.

Frazier, David L. "Gothicism in 'Sanctuary': The Black Pall and the Crap Table," *Modern Fiction Studies* II (Autumn 1956), 114-124.

Howe, Irving. *William Faulkner*, 143-147.

FAULKNER, WILLIAM, Continued

Howell, Elmo. "The Quality of Evil in Faulkner's *Sanctuary*," *Tennessee Studies in Literature* IV (1959), 99-107.

Kubie, Lawrence S. "William Faulkner's 'Sanctuary,'" *Saturday Review of Literature* XI (Oct 20, 1934), 218; 224-226.

Lisca, Peter. "Some New Light on Faulkner's *Sanctuary*," *Faulkner Studies* II (Spring 1953), 5-9.

Massey, Linton. "Notes on the Unrevised Galleys of Faulkner's *Sanctuary*," *Studies in Bibliography* VIII (1956), 195-208.

Monteiro, George. "Initiation and Moral Sense in Faulkner's *Sanctuary*," *Modern Language Notes* LXXIII (Nov 1958), 500-504.

O'Connor, William Van. "A Short View of Faulkner's *Sanctuary*," *Faulkner Studies* I (Fall 1952), 33-39.

——————. *The Tangled Fire of William Faulkner*, 55-64.

Vickery, Olga W. *The Novels of William Faulkner*, 103-114.

Waggoner, Hyatt H. *William Faulkner: From Jefferson to the World*, 88-120.

SARTORIS

Backman, Melvin. "Faulkner's Sick Heroes: Bayard Sartoris and Quentin Compson," *Modern Fiction Studies* II (Autumn 1956), 95-108.

Carpenter, Richard C. "Faulkner's *Sartoris*," *Explicator* XIV (Apr 1956), No. 41.

Howell, Elmo. "Faulkner's *Sartoris*." *Explicator* XVII (Feb 1959), No. 33.

Vickery, Olga W. "The Making of a Myth: *Sartoris*," *Western Review* XXII (Spring 1958), 209-219.

——————. *The Novels of William Faulkner*, 15-27.

Waggoner, Hyatt H. *William Faulkner: From Jefferson to the World*, 20-33.

SOLDIER'S PAY

"Soldier's Pay," *American Writing Today*, 372-374.

Vickery, Olga W. "Faulkner's First Novel," *Western Humanities Review* XI (Summer 1957), 251-256.

——————. *The Novels of William Faulkner*, 1-8.

Waggoner, Hyatt H. *William Faulkner: From Jefferson to the World*, 1-19.

FAULKNER, WILLIAM, Continued

THE SOUND AND THE FURY

Adams, Robert M. "Poetry in the Novel: or, Faulkner Esemplastic," *Virginia Quarterly Review* XXIX (Summer 1953), 419-434.

Backman, Melvin. "Faulkner's Sick Heroes: Bayard Sartoris and Quentin Compson," *Modern Fiction Studies* II (Autumn 1956), 95-108.

Bowling, Lawrence E. "Faulkner and the Theme of Innocence," *Kenyon Review* XX (Summer 1958), 466-487.

——————. "Faulkner: Technique of *The Sound and the Fury*," *Kenyon Review* X (Autumn 1948), 552-566; *William Faulkner: Two Decades of Criticism*, 165-179.

Brooks, Cleanth. "Primitivism in *The Sound and the Fury*," *English Institute Essays* (1952), 5-28.

Campbell, Harry M. "Experiment and Achievement: *As I Lay Dying* and *The Sound and The Fury*," *Sewanee Review* LI (Apr-Jun 1943), 305-320.

Chase, Richard. *The American Novel and Its Tradition*, 219-236.

Collins, Carvel. "Faulkner's *The Sound and the Fury*," *Explicator* XVII (Dec 1958), No. 19.

——————. "The Interior Monologues of *The Sound and the Fury*," *English Institute Essays* (1952), 29-56.

——————. "The Pairing of *The Sound and the Fury* and *As I Lay Dying*," *Princeton University Library Chronicle* XVIII (Spring 1957), 114-123.

Edel, Leon. *The Psychological Novel*, 149-154.

England, Martha Winburn. "Teaching *The Sound and the Fury*," *College English* XVIII (Jan 1957), 221-224.

Gwynn, Frederick L. "Faulkner's Raskolnikov," *Modern Fiction Studies* IV (Summer 1958), 169-172.

Hoffman, Frederick J. *The Twenties*, 213-216.

Howe, Irving. *William Faulkner*, 109-127.

Hughes, Richard. Introduction, *The Sound and the Fury* (London, 1933; 1954).

Humphrey, Robert. "The Form and Function of Stream of Consciousness in William Faulkner's 'The Sound and the Fury,'" *University of Kansas City Review* XIX (Autumn 1952), 34-40.

Labor, Earle. "Faulkner's *The Sound and the Fury*," *Explicator* XVII (Jan 1959), No. 30.

FAULKNER, WILLIAM, Continued

Lee, Edwy B. "A Note on the Ordonnance of *The Sound and the Fury*," *Faulkner Studies* III (Summer-Autumn 1954), 37-39.

Lowrey, Perrin. "Concepts of Time in *The Sound and the Fury*," *English Institute Essays* (1952), 57-82.

Mueller, William R. *The Prophetic Voice of Modern Fiction*, 110-135.

O'Connor, William Van. *The Tangled Fire of William Faulkner*, 37-44.

Powell, Sumner C. "William Faulkner Celebrates Easter, 1928," *Perspective* II (Summer 1949), 195-218.

Ryan, Marjorie. "The Shakespearean Symbolism in *The Sound and the Fury*," *Faulkner Studies* II (Autumn 1953), 40-44.

Sartre, Jean-Paul. *William Faulkner: Two Decades of Criticism*, 180-187.

Smith, Henry. "*The Sound and the Fury*," *Southwest Review* XIV (Autumn 1929), iii-iv.

Stewart, George R. and Joseph M. Backus. "'Each in Its Ordered Place': Structure and Narrative in 'Benjy's Section' of *The Sound and the Fury*," *American Literature* XXIX (Jan 1958), 440-456.

Swiggart, Peter. "Moral & Temporal Order in *The Sound and the Fury*," *Sewanee Review* LXI (Spring 1953), 221-237.

Thompson, Lawrance. "Mirror Analogues in *The Sound and the Fury*," *English Institute Essays* (1952), 83-106.

Vickery, Olga W. *The Novels of William Faulkner*, 28-49.

―――――. "*The Sound and the Fury*: A Study in Perspective," *PMLA* LXIX (Dec 1954), 1017-1037.

Waggoner, Hyatt H. *William Faulkner: From Jefferson to the World*, 34-61.

Whicher, Stephen E. "The Compsons' Nancies—A Note on *The Sound and the Fury* and 'That Evening Sun,'" *American Literature* XXVI (May 1954), 253-255.

Wilder, Amos N. *Theology and Modern Literature*, 119-131.

THE TOWN

Lytle, Andrew, "*The Town*: Helen's Last Stand," *Sewanee Review* LXV (Jul-Sept 1957), 475-484.

Vickery, Olga W. *The Novels of William Faulkner*, 181-191.

Waggoner, Hyatt H. *William Faulkner: From Jefferson to the World*, 232-237.

FAULKNER, WILLIAM, Continued

THE UNVANQUISHED

DeVoto, Bernard. "Faulkner's South," *Saturday Review of Literature* XVII (Feb 19, 1938), 5.

Knoll, Robert E. *"The Unvanquished* for a Start," *College English* XIX (May 1958), 338-343.

Waggoner, Hyatt H. *William Faulkner: From Jefferson to the World,* 170-193.

THE WILD PALMS

Galharn, Carl. "Faulkner's Faith: Roots from *The Wild Palms," Twentieth Century Literature* I (Oct 1955), 139-160.

Howe, Irving. *William Faulkner,* 172-179.

Maxwell, Allen. *"The Wild Palms," Southwest Review* XXIV (Apr 1939), 357-360.

Moses, W. R. "The Unity of 'The Wild Palms,'" *Modern Fiction Studies* II (Autumn 1956), 125-131.

Redman, Ben Ray. "Faulkner's Double Novel," *Saturday Review of Literature* XIX (Jan 21, 1939), 5.

Richardson, H. Edward. "The 'Hemingwaves' in Faulkner's 'Wild Palms,'" *Modern Fiction Studies* IV (Winter 1958-1959), 357-360.

O'Connor, William Van. *The Tangled Fire of William Faulkner,* 104-110.

Stevens, George. "Wild Palms and Ripe Olives," *Saturday Review of Literature* XIX (Feb 11, 1939), 8.

Vickery, Olga W. *The Novels of William Faulkner,* 156-166.

Waggoner, Hyatt H. *William Faulkner: From Jefferson to the World,* 121-147.

GENERAL

Aiken, Conrad. *A Reviewer's A B C,* 200-207.

——————. "William Faulkner: the Novel as Form," *Atlantic Monthly* CLXIV (Nov 1939), 650-654; *William Faulkner: Two Decades of Criticism,* 139-147.

Anderson, Charles. "Faulkner's Moral Center," *Etudes Anglaises* VII (Jan 1954), 48-58.

Arthos, John. "Ritual and Humor in the Writing of William Faulkner," *Accent* IX (Autumn 1948), 17-30; *William Faulkner: Two Decades of Criticism,* 101-118.

FAULKNER, WILLIAM, Continued

Backman, Melvin. "Sickness and Primitivism: A Dominant Pattern in William Faulkner's Work," *Accent* XIV (Winter 1954), 61-73.

Baker, James R. "The Symbolic Extension of Yoknapatawpha County," *Arizona Quarterly* VIII (Autumn 1952), 223-228.

Beach, Joseph Warren. "William Faulkner: The Haunted South," *American Fiction*, 123-143; 147-169.

Beck, Warren. "Faulkner and the South," *Antioch Review* I (Mar 1941), 82-94.

──────────. "Faulkner's Point of View," *College English* II (May 1941), 736-749.

──────────. "A Note on Faulkner's Style," *Rocky Mountain Review* VI (Spring-Summer 1942), 5-6; 14.

──────────. "William Faulkner's Style," *William Faulkner: Two Decades of Criticism*, 147-164.

Bouvard, Loic. "Conversation with William Faulkner," *Modern Fiction Studies* V (Winter 1959-1960), 361-364.

Breaden, Dale G. "William Faulkner and the Land," *American Quarterly* X (Fall 1958), 344-357.

Breit, Harvey. "A Sense of Faulkner," *Partisan Review* XVIII (Jan-Feb 1951), 88-94.

──────────. "William Faulkner," *Atlantic Monthly* CLXXXVIII (Oct 1951), 53-56.

──────────. *The Writer Observed*, 281-284.

Brumm, Ursula. "Wilderness and Civilization: A Note on William Faulkner," *Partisan Review*, XXII (Summer 1955), 340-350.

Burgum, Edwin Berry. "William Faulkner's Patterns of American Decadence," *The Novel and the World's Dilemma*, 205-222.

Buttita, Anthony. "William Faulkner," *Saturday Review of Literature* XVIII (May 21, 1938), 6-8.

Campbell, Harry M. "Structural Devices in the Works of Faulkner," *Perspective* III (Autumn 1950), 209-226.

Campbell, Harry Modean and Ruel E. Foster. *William Faulkner*.

Cantwell, Robert. "The Faulkners: Recollections of a Gifted Family," *New World Writing* 2 (1952), 300-315.

Cargill, Oscar. "The Primitivists," *Intellectual America*, 370-386.

Carter, Hodding. "Faulkner and His Folk," *Princeton University Library Chronicle* XVIII (Spring 1957), 95-107.

FAULKNER, WILLIAM, Continued

Coindreau, Maurice Edgar. "On Translating Faulkner," *Princeton University Library Chronicle* XVIII (Spring 1957), 108-113.

Collins, Carvel. "Faulkner and Certain Earlier Southern Fiction," *College English* XVI (Nov 1954), 92-97.

Coughlan, Robert. *The Private World of William Faulkner*.

Cowley, Malcolm. Introduction, *The Portable Faulkner*, 1-24; *William Faulkner: Two Decades of Criticism*, 63-82; *Critiques and Essays on Modern Fiction*, 427-446.

——————. "William Faulkner's Legend of the South," *Sewanee Review* LIII (Jul-Sept 1945), 343-361; *A Southern Vanguard*, 13-27; *Essays in Modern Literary Criticism*, 513-526.

——————. "William Faulkner Revisited," *Saturday Review of Literature* XXVIII (Apr 14, 1945), 13-16.

D'Agostino, Nemi. "William Faulkner," *Studi Americani* I (1955), 257-308.

Dominicis, A. M. "An Interview with Faulkner," *Faulkner Studies* III (Summer-Autumn 1954), 33-37.

Douglas, Harold J. and Robert Daniel. "Faulkner and the Puritanism of the South," *Tennessee Studies in Literature* II (1957), 1-13.

Edgar, Pelham. *The Art of the Novel*, 338-351.

Edmonds, Irene C. "Faulkner and the Black Shadow," *Southern Renascence*, 192-206.

Fadiman, Clifton. "William Faulkner," *Party of One*, 98-125.

Faulkner, William. "Faith or Fear," *Atlantic Monthly* CXCII (Aug 1953), 53-55.

Fiedler, Leslie A. "William Faulkner: An American Dickens," *Commentary* X (Oct 1950), 384-387.

Flint, R. W. "Faulkner as Elegist," *Hudson Review* VII (Summer 1954), 246-257.

Foster, Ruel E. "Dream as Symbolic Act in Faulkner," *Perspective* II (Summer 1949), 179-194.

Frohock, W. M. "William Faulkner: The Private versus the Public Vision," *Southwest Review* XXXIV (Summer 1949), 281-294.

——————. "William Faulkner: The Private Vision," *The Novel of Violence in America*, 101-124.

FAULKNER, WILLIAM, Continued

Garrett, George. "Faulkner's Early Literary Criticism," *Texas Studies in Literature and Language* I (Spring 1959), 3-10.
Geismar, Maxwell. "William Faulkner: Before and After the Nobel Prize," *American Moderns*, 91-106.
────────. "William Faulkner: The Negro and the Female," *Writers in Crisis*, 143-183.
Gerard, Albert. "Justice in Yoknapatwpha County: Some Symbolic Motifs in Faulkner's Later Writing," *Faulkner Studies* II (Winter 1954), 49-57.
Glicksberg, Charles I. "The World of William Faulkner," *Arizona Quarterly* V (Spring 1949), 46-58.
Green, A. Wigfall. "William Faulkner at Home," *Sewanee Review* XL (Jul-Sept 1932), 294-306; *Willaim Faulkner: Two Decades of Criticism*, 33-47.
Grenier, Cynthia. "The Art of Fiction: An Interview with William Faulkner—September, 1955," *Accent* XVI (Summer 1956), 167-177.
Griffin, William J. "How to Misread Faulkner: A Powerful Plea for Ignorance," *Tennessee Studies in Literature* I (1956), 27-34.
Gurko, Leo. *The Angry Decade*, 117-119, 128-136.
Gwynn, Frederick L. "Faulkner's Prufrock—and Other Observations," *Journal of English and Germanic Philology* LII (Jan 1953), 63-70.
Gwynn, Frederick L. and Joseph L. Blotner (eds.). *Faulkner in the University*.
────────. "Faulkner in the University," *College English* XIX (Oct 1957), 1-6.
Hamilton, Edith. "Faulkner: Sorcerer or Slave?" *Saturday Review* XXXV (Jul 12, 1952), 8-10; 39-41.
Hartwick, Harry. "The Cult of Cruelty," *The Foreground of American Fiction*, 160-166.
Henderson, Philip. "William Faulkner," *The Novel Today*, 147-150.
Hicks, Granville. "Faulkner's South: A Northern Interpretation," *Georgia Review* V (Fall 1951), 269-284.
────────. *The Great Tradition*, 265-268.
Hopper, Vincent F. "Faulkner's Paradise Lost," *Virginia Quarterly Review* XXIII (Summer 1947), 405-420.

FAULKNER, WILLIAM, Continued

Hornberger, Theodore. "Faulkner's Reputation in Brazil," *Faulkner Studies* II (Spring 1953), 9-10.

Howe, Irving "The Southern Myth and William Faulkner," *American Quarterly* III (Winter 1951), 357-362.

──────────. *William Faulkner*.

──────────. "William Faulkner and the Negroes: A Vision of Lost Fraternity," *Commentary* XII (Oct 1951), 359-368.

Hudson, Tommy. "William Faulkner: Mystic and Traditionalist," *Perspective* III (Autumn 1950), 227-235.

Jackson, James Turner. "Delta Cycle: A Study of William Faulkner," *Chimera* V (Autumn 1946), 3-14.

Jacobs, Robert D. "Faulkner's Tragedy of Isolation," *Southern Renascence*, 170-191.

Jelliffe, Robert A. (ed.). *Faulkner at Nagano*.

Kazin, Alfred. "Faulkner in His Fury," *The Inmost Leaf*, 257-273.

──────────. "Faulkner: The Rhetoric and the Agony," *Virginia Quarterly Review* XVIII (Summer 1942), 389-402.

──────────. "The Rhetoric and the Agony," *On Native Grounds*, 453-465.

Kohler, Dayton. "William Faulkner and the Social Conscience," *College English* XI (Dec 1949), 119-127.

Leaver, Florence. "Faulkner: The Word as Principle and Power," *South Atlantic Quarterly* LVII (Autumn 1958), 464-476.

Le Breton, Maurice. "Technique et Psychologie chez William Faulkner," *Etudes Anglaises* I (Sept 1937), 418-438.

Lewis, R. W. B. "William Faulkner: The Hero in the New World," *The Picaresque Saint*, 179-219.

Lewis, Wyndham. "William Faulkner: The Moralist with the Corn-cob," *Men Without Art*, 42-64.

Lind, Isle Dusoir. "The Teachable Faulkner," *College English* XVI (Feb 1955), 284-287.

Litz, Walton. "William Faulkner's Moral Vision," *Southwest Review* XXXVII (Summer 1952), 200-209.

Maclachlan, John. "No Faulkner in Metropolis," *Southern Renascence*, 101-111.

MacLure, Millar. "William Faulkner," *Queen's Quarterly* LXII (Autumn 1956), 334-343.

Malin, Irving. *William Faulkner: An Interpretation*.

FAULKNER, WILLIAM, Continued

Mayoux, J. "La création au réel chez William Faulkner," *Etudes Anglaises* V (Feb 1952), 25-39.

McCole, John. *Lucifer at Large*, 203-228.

Miner, Ward L. *The World of William Faulkner*.

Morris, Lloyd. *Postscript to Yesterday*, 160-162.

Morris, Wright. "The Function of Rage," *The Territory Ahead*, 171-184.

O'Connor, William Van. "Faulkner's Legend of the Old South," *Western Humanities Review* VII (Summer 1953), 293-301.

——————. "Hawthorne and Faulkner: Some Common Ground," *Virginia Quarterly Review* XXXIII (Winter 1957) 105-123.

——————. "Protestantism in Yoknapatawpha County," *Southern Renascence*, 153-169.

——————. "Rhetoric in Southern Writing: Faulkner," *Georgia Review* XII (Spring 1958), 83-86.

——————. *The Tangled Fire of William Faulkner*.

——————. "William Faulkner's Apprenticeship," *Southwest Review* XXXVIII (Winter 1953), 1-14.

——————. *William Faulkner*, University of Minnesota Pamphlets on American Writers, No. 3.

O'Donnell, George Marion. "Faulkner's Mythology," *Kenyon Review* I (Summer 1939), 285-299; *William Faulkner: Two Decades of Criticism*, 49-62.

Prescott, Orville. *In My Opinion*, 84-91.

Rabi. "Faulkner and the Exiled Generation," *William Faulkner: Two Decades of Criticism*, 118-138.

Rascoe, Lavon. "An Interview with William Faulkner," *Western Review* XV (Summer 1951), 300-304.

Riedel, F. C. "Faulkner as Stylist," *South Atlantic Quarterly* LVI (Autumn 1957), 462-479.

Robb, Mary Cooper. *William Faulkner: An Estimate of his Contribution to the Modern American Novel*.

Roth, Russell. "The Centaur and the Pear Tree," *Western Review* XVI (Spring 1952), 199-205; Harry M. Campbell, "Mr. Roth's Centaur and Faulkner's Symbolism," (Summer 1952), 320-321.

——————. "Ideas and Queries," *Faulkner Studies* I (Summer 1952), 23-26.

FAULKNER, WILLIAM, Continued

——————. "William Faulkner: The Pattern of Pilgrimage," *Perspective* II (Summer 1949), 246-254.
Sandeen, Ernest. "William Faulkner: Tragedian of Yoknapatawpha," *Fifty Years of the American Novel*, 165-182.
Sartre, Jean-Paul. "American Novelists in French Eyes," *Atlantic Monthly* CLXXVIII (Aug 1946), 114-118.
Schwartz, Delmore. "The Fiction of William Faulkner," *Southern Review* VII (Summer 1941), 145-160.
Sherwood, John C. "The Traditional Element in Faulkner," *Faulkner Studies* III (Summer-Autumn 1954), 17-23.
Slatoff, Walter J. "The Edge of Order: The Pattern of Faulkner's Rhetoric," *Twentieth Century Literature* III (Oct 1957), 107-127.
Smith, Harrison. "The Nobel Winners," *Saturday Review of Literature* XXXIII (Nov 25, 1950), 20-21.
——————. "William Faulkner vs. the Literary Conference," *Saturday Review* XXXIX (Jul 7, 1956), 16.
Smith, Henry Nash. "William Faulkner and Reality," *Faulkner Studies* II (Summer 1953), 17-19.
Snell, George. "The Fury of Faulkner," *The Shapers of American Fiction*, 87-104.
——————. "The Fury of William Faulkner," *Western Review* XI (Autumn 1946), 29-40.
Spiller, Robert E. *The Cycle of American Literature*, 291-300; (Mentor) 220-226.
Stein, Jean. "William Faulkner," *Writers at Work*, 119-141.
Stewart, Randall. "Hawthorne and Faulkner," *College English* XVII (Feb 1956), 258-262.
Stone, Phil. "William Faulkner and His Neighbors," *Saturday Review of Literature* XXV (Sept 19, 1942), 12.
Swiggart, Peter. "Time in Faulkner's Novels," *Modern Fiction Studies* I (May 1955), 25-29.
Tritschler, Donald. "The Unity of Faulkner's Shaping Vision," *Modern Fiction Studies* V (Winter 1959-1960), 337-343.
Vickery, Olga W. "Faulkner and Time," *Georgia Review* XII (Summer 1958), 192-201.
——————. "Gavin Stevens: From Rhetoric to Dialectic," *Faulkner Studies* II (Spring 1953), 1-4.

FAULKNER, WILLIAM, Continued

Wagenknecht, Edward. "Chamber of Horrors—Southern Exposure," *Cavalcade of the American Novel,* 417-425.
Warren, Robert Penn. "William Faulkner," *Selected Essays,* 59-79; *William Faulkner: Two Decades of Criticism,* 82-101; *Forms of Modern Fiction,* 125-143.
Wheeler, Otis B. "Faulkner's Wilderness," *American Literature* XXXI (May 1959), 127-136.
Whicher, George F. "Analysts of Decay," *The Literature of the American People,* 884-885.
Wilder, Amos N. *Theology and Modern Literature,* 113-131.
Williams, Cecil B. "William Faulkner and the Nobel Prize Awards," *Faulkner Studies* I (Summer 1952), 17-19.
Zink, Karl E. "Faulkner's Garden: Woman and the Immemorial Earth," *Modern Fiction Studies* II (Autumn 1956), 139-149.
―――――――. "Flux and the Frozen Moment: The Imagery of Stasis in Faulkner's Prose," *PMLA* LXXI (Jun 1956), 285-301.
―――――――. "William Faulkner: Form as Experience," *South Atlantic Quarterly* LIII (Jul 1954), 385-403.

BIBLIOGRAPHY

Beebe, Maurice. "Criticism of William Faulkner: A Selected Checklist with an Index to Studies of Separate Works," *Modern Fiction Studies* II (Autumn 1956), 150-164.
"Bibliography," *Faulkner Studies* I (Spring 1952), 12-16; (Summer 1952), 29-32; (Fall 1952), 47-48; (Winter 1954), 62-66; II (Spring 1953), 11-16; (Summer 1953), 30-32; (Autumn 1953), 44-48; (Winter 1954), 60-67; (Summer-Autumn 1954), 43-45.
Critiques and Essays on Modern Fiction, 582-586.
Daniel, Robert W. *A Catalogue of the Writings of William Faulkner.*
Hoffman, Frederick J. and Olga W. Vickery. *William Faulkner: Two Decades of Criticism,* 269-280.
Longley, John L., Jr. and Robert Daniel. "Faulkner's Critics: A Selective Bibliography," *Perspective* III (Autumn 1950), 202-208.
Meriwether, James B. "William Faulkner: A Check List," *Princeton University Library Chronicle* XVIII (Spring 1957), 136-158.

FAULKNER, WILLIAM, Continued

Perry, Bradley T. "A Selected Bibliography of Critical Works on William Faulkner," *University of Kansas City Review* XVIII (Winter 1951), 159-164.
William Faulkner: Biography and Criticism, 1951-1954.

FERBER, EDNA

GENERAL

Bromfield, Lewis. "Edna Ferber," *Saturday Review of Literature* XII (Jun 15, 1935), 10-12.
Overton, Grant. "Edna Ferber," *The Women Who Make Our Novels*, 126-138.

FERN, FANNY

GENERAL

Cowie, Alexander. "The Domestic Sentimentalists and Other Popular Writers (1850-1870): Fanny Fern (Mrs. Sara Payson Willis Parton) (1811-1872)," *The Rise of the American Novel*, 427-429.
Schlesinger, Elizabeth Bancroft. "Proper Bostonians as Seen by Fanny Fern," *New England Quarterly* XXVII (Mar 1954), 97-102.

FISHER, DOROTHY CANFIELD

GENERAL

Boynton, Percy H. "Two New England Regionalists," *America in Contemporary Fiction*, 21-34.
Hartwick, Harry. *The Foreground of American Fiction*, 407-409.
Hatcher, Harlan. "Newer Arrivals," *Creating the Modern American Novel*, 99-106.
Overton, Grant. "Dorothy Canfield (Dorothy Canfield Fisher)," *The Women Who Make Our Novels*, 61-74.
Quinn, Arthur Hobson. "The Celebration of the Individual," *American Fiction*, 706-714.
Smith, Bradford. "Dorothy Canfield Fisher: A Presence Among Us," *Saturday Review* XLI (Nov 29, 1958), 13-14.
Van Doren, Carl. *Contemporary American Novelists*, 173-175.
Wagenknecht, Edward. "In the Second Decade: Dorothy Canfield: 'The Rhythm of the Permanent,'" *Cavalcade of the American Novel*, 294-299.

FISHER, DOROTHY CANFIELD, Continued

Whicher, George F. "In the American Grain," *The Literature of the American People*, 911-912.
Yates, Elizabeth. *Pebble in a Pool*.

FISHER, VARDIS

CHILDREN OF GOD
Long, Louise. "*Children of God*," *Southwest Review* XXV (Oct 1939), 102-108.

GENERAL
Bishop, John Peale. "The Strange Case of Vardis Fisher," *Collected Essays*, 56-65.
----------. "The Strange Case of Vardis Fisher," *Southern Review* III (Autumn 1937), 348-359.
Cargill, Oscar. "The Freudians," *Intellectual America*, 735-737.
Current-Garcia, E. "Writers in the 'Sticks,'" *Prairie Schooner* XII (Winter 1938), 301-304.
Snell, George. "Erskine Caldwell and Vardis Fisher: The Nearly-Animal Kingdom," *The Shapers of American Fiction*, 276-288.
Stegner, Wallace. "Forgive Us Our Neuroses," *Rocky Mountain Review* II (Spring 1938), 1-3.
Swallow, Alan. "The Mavericks," *Critique* II (Winter 1959), 79-84.

FITZGERALD, F. SCOTT

THE BEAUTIFUL AND DAMNED
Miller, James E., Jr. *The Fictional Technique of Scott Fitzgerald*, 39-66.

THE GREAT GATSBY
Aldridge, John W. *Twelve Original Essays on Great American Novels*, 210-237.
Bewley, Marius. "Scott Fitzgerald's Criticism of America," *Sewanee Review* LXII (Apr-Jun 1954), 223-246.
Burnam, Tom. "The Eyes of Dr. Eckleburg: A Re-examination of 'The Great Gatsby,'" *College English* XIV (Oct 1952), 7-12.
Chase, Richard. "The Great Gatsby," *The American Novel and Its Tradition*, 162-167.
Cowley, Malcolm. Introduction, *The Great Gatsby*, in *Three Novels* (New York, 1953), pp. xx.
Fitzgerald, F. Scott. Introduction, *The Great Gatsby* (New York, 1934), pp. xi.

FITZGERALD, F. SCOTT, Continued

Friedman, Norman. "Versions of Form in Fiction—'Great Expectations' and 'The Great Gatsby,'" *Accent* XIV (Autumn 1954), 246-264.

Fussell, Edwin F. "Fitzgerald's Brave New World," *ELH* XIX (Dec 1952), 291-306.

Hanzo, Thomas A. "The Theme and the Narrator of 'The Great Gatsby,'" *Modern Fiction Studies* II (Winter 1956-1957), 183-190.

Harvey, W. J. "Theme and Texture in *The Great Gatsby*," *English Studies* XXXVIII (Feb. 1957), 12-20.

Hindus, Milton. "F. Scott Fitzgerald and Literary Anti-Semitism: A Footnote to the Mind of the 20's," *Commentary* III (1947), 508-516.

——————————. "The Mysterious Eyes of Doctor T. J. Eckleburg," *Boston University Studies in English* III (Spring 1957), 22-31.

Hoffman, Frederick J. *The Twenties*, 111-119.

Mencken, H. L. *F. Scott Fitzgerald: The Man and His Work*, 88-92.

Miller, James E., Jr. *The Fictional Technique of Scott Fitzgerald*, 67-114.

Ornstein, Robert. "Scott Fitzgerald's Fable of East and West," *College English* XVIII (Dec 1956), 139-143.

Perkins, Maxwell E. *F. Scott Fitzgerald: The Man and His Work*, 84-87.

Raleigh, John Henry. "Fitzgerald's *The Great Gatsby*," *University of Kansas City Review* XXIII (Jun 1957), 283-291; XXIV (Oct 1957), 55-58.

Solomon, Eric. "A Source for Fitzgerald's *The Great Gatsby*," *Modern Language Notes* LXXIII (Mar 1958), 186-188.

Stallman, Robert Wooster. "Conrad and *The Great Gatsby*," *Twentieth Century Literature* I (Apr 1955), 5-12.

——————————. "Gatsby and the Hole in Time," *Modern Fiction Studies* I (Nov 1955), 2-16.

Taylor, Douglas. "*The Great Gatsby*: Style and Myth," *University of Kansas City Review* XX (Autumn 1953), 30-40.

Trilling, Lionel. Introduction, *The Great Gatsby* (New York, 1945), pp. xiv.

Watkins, Floyd C. "Fitzgerald's Jay Gatz and Young Ben Franklin," *New England Quarterly* XXVII (Jun 1954), 249-252.

FITZGERALD, F. SCOTT, Continued

THE LAST TYCOON

Benét, Stephen Vincent. "Fitzgerald's Unfinished Symphony," *Saturday Review of Literature* XIV (Dec 6, 1941), 10; *F. Scott Fitzgerald: The Man and His Work*, 130-132.

Dos Passos, John. "A Note on Fitzgerald," in F. Scott Fitzgerald, *The Crack-Up*, 338-343; *F. Scott Fitzgerald: The Man and His Work*, 154-159.

Mizener, Arthur. *The Far Side of Paradise*, 303-306.

──────────. "The Maturity of Scott Fitzgerald," *Sewanee Review* LXVIII (Oct-Dec 1959), 658-675.

Wilson, Edmund. Foreword, *The Last Tycoon*, in *Three Novels*, (New York, 1953), pp. iii-v.

──────────. Introduction, *The Last Tycoon* (London, 1949).

TENDER IS THE NIGHT

Chamberlain, John. *F. Scott Fitzgerald: The Man and His Work*, 95-99.

Cowley, Malcolm. Introduction, Appendix, and Notes, *Tender Is the Night*, in *Three Novels* (New York, 1953), iii-xii.

Fussell, Edward F. "Fitzgerald's Brave New World," *ELH* XIX (Dec 1952), 291-306.

Grattan, C. Hartley. *F. Scott Fitzgerald: The Man and His Work*, 104-107.

Harding, D. W. "Mechanisms of Misery," *F. Scott Fitzgerald: The Man and His Work*, 100-103.

Hoffman, Frederick J. *Freudianism and the Literary Mind*, 264-271.

Mizener, Arthur. *The Far Side of Paradise*, 307-314.

Stanton, Robert, "'Daddy's Girl': Symbol and Theme in 'Tender Is the Night,'" *Modern Fiction Studies* IV (Summer 1958), 136-142.

Steinberg, A. H. "Fitzgerald's Portrait of a Psychiatrist," *University of Kansas City Review* XXI (Mar 1955), 219-222.

THIS SIDE OF PARADISE

Broun, Heywood. *F. Scott Fitzgerald: The Man and His Work*, 50-52.

Brucolli, Matthew J. "A Collation of F. Scott Fitzgerald's *This Side of Paradise*," *Studies in Bibliography* IX (1957), 263-265.

Hoffman, Frederick J. *The Twenties*, 100-108.

FITZGERALD, F. SCOTT, Continued

Marquand, John P. "Looking Backwards—Fitzgerald: 'This Side of Paradise,'" *Saturday Review of Literature* XXXII (Aug 6, 1949), 30-31.

Miller, James E., Jr. *The Fictional Technique of Scott Fitzgerald*, 1-38.

R.V.A.S. *F. Scott Fitzgerald: The Man and His Work*, 48-49.

Wilson, Edmund. *F. Scott Fitzgerald: The Man and His Work*, 77-83.

GENERAL

Aldridge, John W. "Fitzgerald: The Horror and the Vision of Paradise," *After the Lost Generation*, 44-58.

Baldwin, Charles C. "F. Scott Fitzgerald," *The Men Who Make Our Novels*, 166-173.

Berryman, John. "F. Scott Fitzgerald," *Kenyon Review* VIII (Winter 1946), 103-112.

Bewley, Marius. "Scott Fitzgerald and the Collapse of the American Dream," *The Eccentric Design*, 259-287.

Bicknell, John W. "The Waste Land of F. Scott Fitzgerald," *Virginia Quarterly Review* XXX (Summer 1954), 556-572.

Bishop, John Peale. "Fitzgerald at Princeton," *Virginia Quarterly Review* XIII (Winter 1937), 106-121; *F. Scott Fitzgerald: The Man and His Work*, 45-47.

Cargill, Oscar. "The Primitivists," *Intellectual America*, 342-349.

Cowley, Malcolm. "Fitzgerald: The Double Man," *Saturday Review of Literature* XXXIV (Feb 24, 1951), 9-10; 42-44.

——————. "F. Scott Fitzgerald: The Romance of Money," *Western Review* XVII (Summer 1953), 245-255.

——————. "Third Act and Epilogue," *F. Scott Fitzgerald: The Man and His Work*, 146-153.

D'Agostino, Nemi. "F. Scott Fitzgerald," *Studi Americani* III (1957), 239-263.

Embler, Weller. "F. Scott Fitzgerald and the Future," *F. Scott Fitzgerald: The Man and His Work*, 212-219.

Farrelly, John. "Scott Fitzgerald; Another View," *Scrutiny* XVIII (Jun 1952), 266-272.

Fiedler, Leslie. "Some Notes on F. Scott Fitzgerald," *An End to Innocence*, 174-182.

Frohock, W. M. "Morals, Manners, and Scott Fitzgerald," *Southwest Review* XL (Summer 1955), 220-228.

FITZGERALD, F. SCOTT, Continued

Geismar, Maxwell. "Fitzgerald: Bard of the Jazz Age," *Saturday Review* XLI (Apr 26, 1958), 17-18.

──────────. "F. Scott Fitzgerald: Orestes at the Ritz," *The Last of the Provincials*, 287-352.

Gurko, Leo and Miriam Gurko. "The Essence of F. Scott Fitzgerald." *College English* V (Apr 1944), 372-376.

Harding, D. W. "Scott Fitzgerald," *Scrutiny* XVIII (Winter 1951-52), 166-174.

Häusermann, H. W. "Fitzgerald's Religious Sense: Note and Query," *Modern Fiction Studies* II (May 1956), 81-82.

Hoffman, Frederick J. "Points of Moral Reference: a Comparative Study of Edith Wharton and F. Scott Fitzgerald," *English Institute Essays* (1949), 147-176.

Hughes, Riley. "F. Scott Fitzgerald: The Touch of Disaster," *Fifty Years of the American Novel*, 135-149.

Ingrisano, Michael N., Jr. "A Note on A Critique of F. Scott Fitzgerald," *American Literature* XXIV (Jan 1953), 539-540.

Kallich, Martin. "F. Scott Fitzgerald: Money or Morals?" *University of Kansas City Review* XV (Summer 1949), 271-280.

Kazin, Alfred. "An American Confession," *F. Scott Fitzgerald: The Man and His Work*, 172-181.

──────────. "Into the Thirties: All the Lost Generations," *On Native Grounds*, 315-323.

──────────. Introduction, *F. Scott Fitzgerald: The Man and His Work*, 11-19.

Kuehl, John. "Scott Fitzgerald: Romantic and Realist," *Texas Studies in Literature and Language* I (Autumn 1959), 412-426.

Loveman, Amy. "Fitzgerald and the Jazz Age," *Saturday Review of Literature* XXIII (Jan 4, 1941), 8.

Lubell, Albert J. "The Fitzgerald Revival," *South Atlantic Quarterly* LIV (Jan 1955), 95-106.

Marshall, Margaret. "On Rereading Fitzgerald," *F. Scott Fitzgerald: The Man and His Work*, 113-115.

Mizener, Arthur. "F. Scott Fitzgerald: A Biography," *Atlantic Monthly* CLXXXVI (Dec 1950), 68-77; CLXXXVII (Jan 1951), 59-66; (Feb 1951), 72-80.

──────────. "F. Scott Fitzgerald 1896-1940: The Poet of Borrowed Time," *F. Scott Fitzgerald: The Man and His Work*, 23-44; *Critiques and Essays on Modern Fiction*, 286-302.

FITZGERALD, F. SCOTT, Continued

———————. "F. Scott Fitzgerald, The Poet of Borrowed Time," *Critiques and Essays on Modern Fiction*, 286-302.

———————. *The Far Side of Paradise*.

———————. "The Novel of Manners in America," *Kenyon Review* XII (Winter 1950), 1-19.

———————. "Scott Fitzgerald and the Imaginative Possession of American Life," *Sewanee Review* LIV (Jan-Mar 1946), 66-86.

Morris, Lloyd. *Postscript to Yesterday*, 149-153.

Morris, Wright. "The Ability to Function: A Reappraisal of Fitzgerald and Hemingway," *New World Writing* 13 (1958), 34-42.

———————. "The Function of Nostalgia," *The Territory Ahead*, 157-170.

Mosher, John Chapin. "That Sad Young Man," *F. Scott Fitzgerald: The Man and His Work*, 66-70.

Piper, Henry Dan. "Fitzgerald's Cult of Disillusion," *American Quarterly* III (Spring 1951), 69-80.

———————. "Frank Norris and Scott Fitzgerald," *Huntington Library Quarterly* XIX (Aug 1956), 393-400.

———————. "F. Scott Fitzgerald and the Image of His Father," *Princeton University Library Chronicle* XII (Summer 1951), 181-186.

"Power Without Glory," *F. Scott Fitzgerald: The Man and His Work*, 205-211.

Powers, J. F. "Dealer in Diamonds and Rhinestones," *F. Scott Fitzgerald: The Man and His Work*, 182-186.

Rosenfeld, Paul. "F. Scott Fitzgerald," *Men Seen*, 215-224; in *F. Scott Fitzgerald, The Crack-Up*, 317-322; *F. Scott Fitzgerald: The Man and His Work*, 71-76.

Savage, D. S. "The Significance of F. Scott Fitzgerald," *Arizona Quarterly* VIII (Autumn 1952), 197-210.

Schoenwald, Richard L. "F. Scott Fitzgerald as John Keats," *Boston University Studies in English* III (Spring 1957), 12-21.

Schulberg, Budd. "Fitzgerald in Hollywood," *F. Scott Fitzgerald: The Man and His Work*, 109-112.

Shockley, Martin Staples. "Harsh Will Be the Morning," *Arizona Quarterly* X (Summer 1954), 127-135.

FITZGERALD, F. SCOTT, Continued

Simon, J. "Francis Scott Key Fitzgerald, 1896-1940," *Etudes Anglaises* V (Nov 1952), 326-335.
Stewart, Lawrence D. "Scott Fitzgerald D'Invilliers," *American Literature* XXIX (May 1957), 212-213.
Taylor, Dwight. "Scott Fitzgerald in Hollywood," *Harper's Magazine* CCXVIII (Mar 1959), 67-71.
Trilling, Lionel. "F. Scott Fitzgerald," *The Liberal Imagination*, 243-254; *F. Scott Fitzgerald: The Man and His Work*, 194-204.
Troy, William. "Scott Fitzgerald—the Authority of Failure," *Accent* VI (Autumn 1945), 56-60; *F. Scott Fitzgerald: The Man and His Work*, 187-193; *Forms of Modern Fiction*, 80-86.
Van Doren, Carl. *Contemporary American Novelists*, 172-173.
Wanning, Andrews. "Fitzgerald and His Brethren," *F. Scott Fitzgerald: The Man and His Work*, 160-168.
Weir, Charles, J. "An Invite with Gilded Edges," *Virginia Quarterly Review* XX (Winter 1944), 100-113; *F. Scott Fitzgerald: The Man and His Work*, 133-145.
Wescott, Glenway. "The Moral of Scott Fitzgerald," in F. Scott Fitzgerald, *The Crack-Up*, 323-337; *F. Scott Fitzgerald: The Man and His Work*, 116-129.
Whicher, George F. "Loopholes of Retreat," *The Literature of the American People*, 888-889.
Wilson, Edmund. "F. Scott Fitzgerald," *The Shores of Light*, 27-35; *A Literary Chronicle*, 30-37.
——————. "A Weekend at Ellerslie," *The Shores of Light*, 373-383.
Wilson, Robert N. "Fitzgerald as Icarus," *Antioch Review* XVII (Dec 1957), 481-492.

BIBLIOGRAPHY

Mizener, Arthur. "The F. Scott Fitzgerald Papers," *Princeton University Library Chronicle* XII (Summer 1951), 190-195.
Piper, Henry Dan. "F. Scott Fitzgerald: A Check List," *Princeton University Library Chronicle* XII (Summer 1951), 196-208.

FLINT, TIMOTHY

THE LOST CHILD

Hamilton, John A. "Timothy Flint's 'Lost Novel,'" *American Literature* XXII (Mar 1950), 54-56.

FLINT, TIMOTHY, Continued
GENERAL
Cowie, Alexander. "Contemporaries and Immediate Followers of Cooper, I: Timothy Flint (1780-1840) and Early Western Fiction," *The Rise of the American Novel*, 212-227.
Kirkpatrick, John Ervin. *Timothy Flint*.
Quinn, Arthur Hobson. "The Romance of History and the Frontier," *The Literature of the American People*, 235-237.

FOSTER, HANNAH WEBSTER
GENERAL
Shurter, Robert L. "Mrs. Hannah Webster Foster and the Early American Novel," *American Literature* IV (Nov 1932), 306-308.

FRANK, WALDO
THE BRIDEGROOM COMETH
Bittner, William. *The Novels of Waldo Frank*, 149-166.
CHALK FACE
Bittner, William. *The Novels of Waldo Frank*, 104-116.
CITY BLOCK
Bittner, William. *The Novels of Waldo Frank*, 61-75.
THE DARK MOTHER
Bittner, William. *The Novels of Waldo Frank*, 42-55.
Rosenfeld, Paul. "The Novels of Waldo Frank," *Dial* LXX (Jan 1921), 95-105.
THE DEATH AND BIRTH OF DAVID MARKAND
Bittner, William. *The Novels of Waldo Frank*, 129-148.
HOLIDAY
Bittner, William. *The Novels of Waldo Frank*, 88-103.
THE INVADERS
Bittner, William. *The Novels of Waldo Frank*, 192-201.
ISLAND IN THE ATLANTIC
Bittner, William. *The Novels of Waldo Frank*, 180-191.
NOT HEAVEN
Bittner, William. *The Novels of Waldo Frank*, 202-215.
RAHAB
Bittner, William. *The Novels of Waldo Frank*, 76-87.
SUMMER NEVER ENDS
Bittner, William. *The Novels of Waldo Frank*, 167-179.

FRANK, WALDO, Continued

THE UNWELCOME MAN

Bittner, William. *The Novels of Waldo Frank*, 33-41.
Rosenfeld, Paul. "The Novels of Waldo Frank," *Dial* LXX (Jan 1921), 95-105.

GENERAL

Baldwin, Charles C. "Waldo Frank," *The Men Who Make Our Novels*, 174-179.
Bittner, William. *The Novels of Waldo Frank*.
Cargill, Oscar. "The Freudians," *Intellectual America*, 662-676.
Hatcher, Harlan. "Eroticism and the Psychological Novel: Waldo Frank," *Creating the Modern American Novel*, 173-179.
Hoffman, Frederick J. *Freudianism and the Literary Mind*, 250-263.
Jocelyn, John. "Getting at Waldo Frank," *Sewanee Review* XL (Oct-Dec 1932), 405-414.
Michaud, Régis. "Reinforcements: Willa Cather, Zona Gale, Floyd Dell, Joseph Hergesheimer, Waldo Frank," *The American Novel To-Day*, 238-256.
Rosenfeld, Paul. "Waldo Frank," *Men Seen*, 89-109.

FREDERIC, HAROLD

THE DAMNATION OF THERON WARE

Davies, Horton. *A Mirror of the Ministry in Modern Novels*, 71-78.
Lovett, Robert Morss. Introduction, *Damnation of Theron Ware* (New York, 1924).
Raleigh, John Henry. "The Damnation of Theron Ware," *American Literature* XXX (May 1958), 210-227.

GENERAL

Gohdes, Clarence. "The Facts of Life *Versus* Pleasant Reading," *The Literature of the American People*, 742-746.
Walcutt, Charles Child. "Adumbrations: Harold Frederic," *American Literary Naturalism*, 45-53.
——————. "Harold Frederic and American Naturalism," *American Literature* XI (Mar 1939), 11-22.

FREEMAN, MARY WILKINS

JANE FIELD

Howells, W. D. *Heroines of Fiction* II, 253-259.

FREEMAN, MARY WILKINS, Continued

PEMBROKE
Fiske, Horace Spencer. *Provincial Types in American Fiction,* 43-63.

GENERAL
Foster, Edward. *Mary E. Wilkins.*

Pattee, Fred Lewis. *Side-Lights on American Literature,* 175-209.

Quinn, Arthur Hobson. "The Development of Realism," *American Fiction,* 433-440.

Westbrook, Percy D. *Acres of Flint,* 96-106.

FULLER, HENRY BLAKE

GENERAL
Duffey, Bernard. "Henry Fuller," *The Chicago Renaissance in American Letters,* 27-50.

Garland, Hamlin. "Henry B. Fuller," *Roadside Meetings,* 262-275.

Gohdes, Clarence. "The Facts of Life *Versus* Pleasant Reading," *The Literature of the American People,* 746-749.

Murray, Donald M. "Henry B. Fuller: Friend of Howells," *South Atlantic Quarterly* LII (Jul 1953), 431-444.

Quinn, Arthur Hobson. "The Urbane Note in American Fiction," *American Fiction,* 424-432.

Van Doren, Carl. *Contemporary American Novelists,* 138-140.

GALE, ZONA

GENERAL
Michaud, Régis. "Reinforcements: Willa Cather, Zona Gale, Floyd Dell, Joseph Hergesheimer, Waldo Frank," *The American Novel To-Day,* 238-256.

Overton, Grant. "Zona Gale," *The Women Who Make Our Novels,* 143-156.

Quinn, Arthur Hobson. "The Celebration of the Individual," *American Fiction,* 700-706.

Van Doren, Carl. *Contemporary American Novelists,* 164-166.

Whicher, George F. "Analysts of Decay," *The Literature of the American People,* 870-871.

GARLAND, HAMLIN

SON OF THE MIDDLE BORDER
McComb, E. H. Kemper. Introduction, *Son of the Middle Border* (New York, 1927; 1935).

A SPOIL OF OFFICE
Blotner, Joseph L. *The Political Novel*, 36.

GENERAL
Åhnebrink, Lars. *The Beginnings of Naturalism in American Fiction*, 63-89; 135-150; 233-249; 317-328; 363-378.

Cargill, Oscar. "The Naturalists," *Intellectual America*, 82-84.

Duffey, Bernard. "Hamlin Garland," *The Chicago Renaissance in American Letters*, 75-89.

——————. "Hamlin Garland's 'Decline from Realism,'" *American Literature* XXV (Mar 1953), 69-74.

Edwards, Herbert. "Herne, Garland, and Henry George," *American Literature* XXVIII (Nov 1956), 359-367.

Flanagan, John T. "Hamlin Garland Writes to His Chicago Publishers," *American Literature* XXIII (Jan 1952), 447-457.

Gohdes, Clarence. "Exploitation of the Provinces," *The Literature of the American People*, 648-651.

Goldstein, Jesse Sidney. "Two Literary Radicals: Garland and Markham in Chicago, 1893," *American Literature* XVII (May 1945), 152-160.

"Hamlin Garland: 1860-1940," *Mark Twain Quarterly* IV (Summer 1940), 1.

Henson, Clyde E. "Joseph Kirkland's Influence on Hamlin Garland," *American Literature* XXIII (Jan 1952), 458-463.

Hicks, Granville. *The Great Tradition*, 142-148.

Howells, William Dean. "Mr. Garland's Books," *North American Review* 196 (Oct 1912), 523-528.

Keiser, Albert. "Traveling the White Man's Road," *The Indian in American Literature*, 279-292.

Koerner, James D. "Comment on 'Hamlin Garland's "Decline from Realism,"'" *American Literature* XXVI (Nov 1954), 427-432; Bernard I. Duffey. "Mr. Koerner's Reply Considered," *American Literature* XXVI (Nov 1954), 432-435.

McElderry, B. R., Jr. "Hamlin Garland and Henry James," *American Literature* XXIII (Jan 1952), 433-446.

GARLAND, HAMLIN, Continued

Pizer, Donald. "Romantic Individualism in Garland, Norris and Crane," *American Quarterly* X (Winter 1958), 463-475.

Quinn, Arthur Hobson. "The Development of Realism," *American Fiction*, 454-459.

Ravitz, A. C. "Willa Cather Under Fire: Hamlin Garland Misreads *A Lost Lady*," *Western Humanities Review* IX (Spring 1955), 182-184.

Raw, Ruth M. "Hamlin Garland, the Romanticist," *Sewanee Review* XXXVI (Apr-Jun 1928), 202-210.

Simpson, Claude. "Hamlin Garland's Decline," *Southwest Review* XXVI (Winter 1941), 223-234.

Van Doren, Carl. *Contemporary American Novelists*, 38-47.

Wagenknecht, Edward. "Towards Naturalism: Hamlin Garland: 'Veritism' and After," *Cavalcade of the American Novel*, 205-212.

Walcutt, Charles Child. "Adumbrations: Hamlin Garland," *American Literary Naturalism*, 53-65.

GLASGOW, ELLEN

BARREN GROUND
Glasgow, Ellen. *A Certain Measure*, 152-164.

THE BATTLE-GROUND
Glasgow, Ellen. *A Certain Measure*, 3-25.

THE DELIVERANCE
Glasgow, Ellen. *A Certain Measure*, 26-47.

McDowell, Frederick P. W. "'The Old Pagan Scorn of Everlasting Mercy'—Ellen Glasgow's *The Deliverance*," *Twentieth Century Literature* IV (Jan 1959), 135-142.

IN THIS OUR LIFE
Glasgow, Ellen. *A Certain Measure*, 246-264.

LIFE AND GABRIELLA
Glasgow, Ellen. *A Certain Measure*, 97-123.

THE MILLER OF OLD CHURCH
Glasgow, Ellen. *A Certain Measure*, 127-151.

ROMANCE OF A PLAIN MAN
Glasgow, Ellen. *A Certain Measure*, 64-76.

Walpole, Hugh. Introduction, *Romance of a Plain Man* (New York, 1926).

GLASGOW, ELLEN, Continued

THE ROMANTIC COMEDIANS
Glasgow, Ellen. *A Certain Measure*, 211-223.

THE SHELTERED LIFE
Canby, Henry Seidel. "Youth and Age," *Saturday Review of Literature* IX (Aug 27, 1932), 63.

Glasgow, Ellen. *A Certain Measure*, 189-210.

McDowell, Frederick P. W. "Theme and Artistry in Ellen Glasgow's *The Sheltered Life*," *Texas Studies in Language and Literature* I (Winter 1960), 502-516.

THEY STOOPED TO FOLLY
Glasgow, Ellen. *A Certain Measure*, 224-245.

VEIN OF IRON
Glasgow, Ellen. *A Certain Measure*, 165-185.

VIRGINIA
Glasgow, Ellen. *A Certain Measure*, 77-96.

THE VOICE OF THE PEOPLE
Glasgow, Ellen. *A Certain Measure*, 48-63.

GENERAL
Baldwin, Alice M. "Ellen Glasgow," *South Atlantic Quarterly* LIV (Jul 1955), 394-404.

Becker, Allen W. "Ellen Glasgow's Social History," *Texas Studies in English* XXXVI (1957), 12-19.

——————. "Ellen Glasgow and the Southern Literary Tradition," *Modern Fiction Studies* V (Winter 1959-1960), 295-303.

Brickell, Herschel. "Miss Glasgow and Mr. Marquand," *Virginia Quarterly Review* XVII (Summer 1941), 405-417.

Cabell, James Branch. "Two Sides of the Shielded," *Some of Us*, 47-58.

Canby, Henry Seidel. "Ellen Glasgow: Ironic Tragedian," *Saturday Review of Literature* XVIII (Sept 10, 1938), 3-4; 14.

——————. "SRL Award to Ellen Glasgow," *Saturday Review of Literature* XXIII (Apr 5, 1941), 10.

Clark, Emily. *Innocence Abroad*, 55-69.

Freeman, Douglas Southall. "Ellen Glasgow: Idealist," *Saturday Review of Literature* XII (Aug 31, 1935), 11-12.

Geismar, Maxwell. "Ellen Glasgow: The Armor of the Legend," *Rebels and Ancestors*, 219-283.

GLASGOW, ELLEN, Continued

Glasgow, Ellen. "One Way to Write Novels," *Saturday Review of Literature* XI (Dec 8, 1934), 335; 344; 350; XXVII (Dec 22, 1945), 12-13; 29-31.
Hardy, John Edward. "Ellen Glasgow," *Southern Renascence*, 236-250.
Hoffman, Frederick J. "Willa Cather and Ellen Glasgow," *The Modern Novel in America*, 52-75.
Holland, Robert. "Miss Glasgow's 'Prufrock,'" *American Quarterly* IX (Winter 1957), 435-440.
Hubbell, Jay B. *The South in American Literature*, 842-845.
Jessup, Josephine Lurie. *The Faith of Our Feminists*.
Kazin, Alfred. "Elegy and Satire: Willa Cather and Ellen Glasgow," *On Native Grounds*, 257-264.
—————. "The Lost Rebel," *The Inmost Leaf*, 136-141.
McDowell, Frederick P. W. "Ellen Glasgow and the Art of the Novel," *Philological Quarterly* XXX (Jul 1951), 328-347.
Monroe, N. Elizabeth. "Contemplation of Manners in Ellen Glasgow," *The Novel and Society*, 139-187.
—————. "Ellen Glasgow: Ironist of Manners," *Fifty Years of the American Novel*, 49-68.
Overton, Grant. "Ellen Glasgow," *The Women Who Make Our Novels*, 157-166.
Patterson, Daniel W. "Ellen Glasgow's Plan for a Social History of Virginia," *Modern Fiction Studies* V (Winter 1959-1960), 353-360.
Quinn, Arthur Hobson. "Ellen Glasgow and the New South," *American Fiction*, 670-682.
Rouse, Blair (ed.). *Letters of Ellen Glasgow*.
Rubin, Louis D., Jr. "Part I. Miss Ellen," *No Place on Earth*, 3-49.
Sherman, Stuart. "Ellen Glasgow: The Fighting Edge of Romance," *Critical Woodcuts*, 73-82.
Steele, Erskine. "Fiction and Social Ethics," *South Atlantic Quarterly* V (Jul 1906), 254-263.
Stone, Grace. "Ellen Glasgow and Her Novels," *Sewanee Review* L (Jul-Sept 1942), 289-301.
Van Doren, Carl. *Contemporary American Novelists*, 132-134.
Wagenknecht, Edward. "Ellen Glasgow: Triumph and Despair," *Cavalcade of the American Novel*, 267-280.

GLASGOW, ELLEN, Continued

———————. "*Great Expectations* and Ellen Glasgow," *Boston University Studies in English*, III (Spring 1957), 57-60.

Whicher, George F. "The Resurgent South," *The Literature of the American People*, 915-918.

BIBLIOGRAPHY

Egly, William H. "Bibliography of Ellen Anderson Gholson Glasgow," *Bulletin of Bibliography* XVII (Sept-Dec 1940), 47-50.

Quesenbery, W. D., Jr. "Ellen Glasgow: A Critical Bibliography," *Bulletin of Bibliography* XXII (May-Aug 1959), 201-206; (Sept-Dec 1959), 230-236.

GOLD, HERBERT

THE OPTIMIST

Hicks, Granville. "Report on Herbert Gold," *Saturday Review* XLII (Apr 25, 1959), 12.

GORDON, CAROLINE

ALECK MAURY, SPORTSMAN

Warren, Robert Penn. "The Fiction of Caroline Gordon," *Southwest Review* XX (Jan 1935), 5-10.

THE MALEFACTORS

Koch, Vivienne. "Companions in the Blood," *Sewanee Review* LXIV (Oct-Dec 1956), 645-651.

GENERAL

Cowan, Louise. "Nature and Grace in Caroline Gordon," *Critique* I (Winter 1956), 11-27.

Hoffman, Frederick J. "Caroline Gordon: The Special Yield," *Critique* I (Winter 1956), 29-35.

Koch, Vivienne. "The Conservatism of Caroline Gordon," *Southern Renascence*, 325-337.

Lytle, Andrew. "Caroline Gordon and the Historic Image," *Sewanee Review* LVII (Oct-Dec 1949), 560-586.

Ross, Danforth. "Caroline Gordon's Golden Ball," *Critique* I (Winter 1956), 67-73.

BIBLIOGRAPHY

Griscom, Joan. "Bibliography of Caroline Gordon," *Critique* I (Winter 1956), 74-78.

GRIFFIN, JOHN HOWARD

THE DEVIL RIDES OUTSIDE
Geismar, Maxwell. *American Moderns,* 251-265.

GUTHRIE, A. B., JR.

THE WAY WEST
Young, Vernon. "An American Dream and Its Parody," *Arizona Quarterly* VI (Summer 1950), 112-123.

GENERAL
Kohler, Dayton. "A. B. Guthrie, Jr., and the West," *College English* XII (Feb 1951), 249-256.

Prescott, Orville. *In My Opinion,* 141-145.

HARTE, BRET

GABRIEL CONROY
Friedrich, Gerhard. "Bret Harte as a Source for James Joyce's 'The Dead,'" *Philological Quarterly* XXXIII (Oct 1954), 442-444.

GENERAL
Clemens, Cyril. "Bret Harte and Henry James as Seen by Marie Belloc Lowndes," *Mark Twain Quarterly* II (Fall 1937), 21-23.

Erskine, John. "Bret Harte," *Leading American Novelists,* 325-369.

Gohdes, Clarence. "Exploitation of the Provinces," *The Literature of the American People,* 642-646.

Howe, M. A. DeWolfe. "Bret Harte and Mark Twain in the Seventies," *Atlantic Monthly* CXXX (1922), 341-348.

Quinn, Arthur Hobson. "Bret Harte and the Fiction of Moral Contrast," *American Fiction,* 232-242.

HAWTHORNE, NATHANIEL

THE BLITHEDALE ROMANCE
Abel, Darrel. "Hawthorne's Skepticism About Social Reform with Especial Reference to *The Blithedale Romance,*" *University of Kansas City Review* XIX (Spring 1953), 181-193.

Bewley, Marius. "James's Debt to Hawthorne (I): *The Blithe-*

HAWTHORNE, NATHANIEL, Continued

    dale Romance and *The Bostonians,*" *Scrutiny* XVI (Sept 1949), 178-195; *The Complex Fate,* 11-30.

Chase, Richard. *The American Novel and Its Tradition,* 82-87.

Crane, Maurice A. "*The Blithedale Romance* as Theatre," *Notes and Queries* 203 (Feb 1958), 84-86.

Crews, Frederick C. "A New Reading of *The Blithedale Romance,*" *American Literature* (May 1957), 147-170.

Davidson, Frank. "Toward a Re-evaluation of *The Blithedale Romance,*" *New England Quarterly* XXV (Sept 1952), 374-383.

Fogle, Richard Harter. *Hawthorne's Fiction,* 140-161.

Howe, Irving. *Politics and the Novel,* 163-175.

Howells, W. D. *Heroines of Fiction,* 175-183.

Lawrence, D. H. *Studies in Classic American Literature,* 111-121.

Lueders, Edward G. "The Melville-Hawthorne Relationship in *Pierre* and *The Blithedale Romance,*" *Western Humanities Review* IV (Autumn 1950), 323-334.

Male, Roy R. *Hawthorne's Tragic Vision,* 139-156.

————————. "Toward *The Waste Land*: The Theme of *The Blithedale Romance,*" *College English* XVI (Feb 1955), 277-283.

Randel, William Peirce. "Hawthorne, Channing, and Margaret Fuller," *American Literature* X (Jan 1939), 472-476.

Rhys, Ernest. Introduction, *Blithedale Romance* (New York, 1912), pp. xi.

Rust, James D. "George Eliot on *The Blithedale Romance,*" *Boston Public Library Quarterly* VII (Oct 1955), 207-215.

Turner, Arlin. "Hawthorne and Reform," *New England Quarterly* XV (Dec 1942), 700-714.

————————. Introduction, *Blithedale Romance* (New York, 1958).

Waggoner, Hyatt H. *Hawthorne,* 174-194.

Yates, Norris. "An Instance of Parallel Imagery in Hawthorne, Melville, and Frost," *Philological Quarterly* XXXVI (Apr 1957), 276-280.

DOCTOR GRIMSHAWE'S SECRET

Davidson, Edward Hutchins. *Hawthorne's Last Phase,* 30-71; 158-162.

HAWTHORNE, NATHANIEL, Continued

----------. Introduction, *Dr. Grimshawe's Secret* (Cambridge, Mass., 1954; New York, 1955).

Kouwenhoven, John A. "Hawthorne's Notebooks and *Doctor Grimshawe's Secret*," *American Literature* V (Jan 1934), 349-358.

Stein, William Bysshe. "A Possible Source for Hawthorne's English Romance," *Modern Language Notes* LXVII (Jan 1952), 52-55.

Wegelin, Christof. "Europe in Hawthorne's Fiction," *ELH* XIV (Sept 1947), 219-245.

A DOLLIVER ROMANCE

Davidson, Edward Hutchins. *Hawthorne's Last Phase*, 122-141.

FANSHAWE

Bode, Carl. "Hawthorne's *Fanshawe*: The Promising of Greatness," *New England Quarterly* XXIII (Jun 1950), 235-242.

Goldstein, Jesse Sidney. "The Literary Source of Hawthorne's *Fanshawe*," *Modern Language Notes* LX (Jan 1945), 1-8.

Orians, G. Harrison. "Scott and Hawthorne's *Fanshawe*," *New England Quarterly* XI (Jun 1938), 388-394.

THE HOUSE OF THE SEVEN GABLES

Abel, Darrel. "Hawthorne's House of Tradition," *South Atlantic Quarterly* LII (Oct 1953), 561-578.

Angoff, Charles. Introduction, *The House of the Seven Gables* (1956).

Beebe, Maurice. "The Fall of the House of Pyncheon," *Nineteenth-Century Fiction* XI (Jun 1956), 1-17.

Brooks, Van Wyck. Introduction, *The House of the Seven Gables* (New York, 1950), pp. xviii.

Castleman, J. H. Introduction, *The House of the Seven Gables* (New York, 1907).

Davidson, H. A. Introduction, *The House of the Seven Gables* (Boston, 1904), pp. xviii.

Dillingham, William B. "Structure and Theme in *The House of the Seven Gables*," *Nineteenth-Century Fiction* XIV (Jun 1959), 59-70.

Fogle, Richard Harter. *Hawthorne's Fiction*, 122-139.

Furst, Clyde. Introduction, *The House of the Seven Gables* (New York, 1905), pp. xxxi.

HAWTHORNE, NATHANIEL, Continued

Hadsell, S. R. Introduction, *The House of the Seven Gables* (New York, 1932).

Havens, Elmer A. "The 'Golden Branch' as Symbol in *The House of the Seven Gables*," *Modern Language Notes* LXXIV (Jan 1959), 20-22.

Male, Roy R. *Hawthorne's Tragic Vision*, 119-138.

Matthiessen, F. O. *American Renaissance*, 322-344.

Merrill, A. Marion. Introduction, *The House of the Seven Gables* (Boston, 1923), pp. xix.

Orel, Harold. "The Double Symbol," *American Literature* XXIII (Mar 1951), 1-6.

Pearce, Roy Harvey. Introduction, *The House of the Seven Gables* (London, 1954).

Waggoner, Hyatt H. *Hawthorne*, 151-173.

Young, Philip. Introduction, *The House of the Seven Gables* (New York, 1957), pp. xxxiii.

THE MARBLE FAUN

Bewley, Marius. "James's Debt to Hawthorne (II): *The Marble Faun* and *The Wings of the Dove*," *Scrutiny* XVI (Winter 1949), 301-317; *The Complex Fate*, 31-54.

Bicknell, John W. "*The Marble Faun* Reconsidered," *University of Kansas City Review* XX (Spring 1954), 193-199.

Brown, Merle E. "The Structure of *The Marble Faun*," *American Literature* XXVIII (Nov 1956), 302-313.

Fogle, Richard Harter. *Hawthorne's Fiction*, 162-183.

——————. "Simplicity and Complexity in *The Marble Faun*," *Tulane Studies in English* II (1950), 103-120.

Howells, W. D. *Heroines of Fiction*, 183-189.

Male, Roy R. *Hawthorne's Tragic Vision*, 157-177.

Marble, Annie Russell. Introduction, *The Marble Faun* (Boston, 1901; 1925).

Matthiessen, F. O. *American Renaissance*, 356-364.

Pearce, Roy Harvey. "Hawthorne and the Twilight of Romance," *Yale Review* XXXVII (Mar 1948), 487-506.

Stephen, Sir Leslie. Introduction, *The Marble Faun* (New York, 1910), pp. xvi.

Waggoner, Hyatt H. *Hawthorne*, 195-222.

Waples, Dorothy. "Suggestions for Interpreting *The Marble*

HAWTHORNE, NATHANIEL, Continued

Faun," *American Literature* XIII (Nov 1941), 224-239.
Wegelin, Christof. "Europe in Hawthorne's Fiction," *ELH* XIV (Sept 1947), 219-245.
Wright, Nathalia. "Hawthorne and the Praslin Murder," *New England Quarterly* XV (Mar 1942), 5-14.

THE SCARLET LETTER

Abel, Darrel. "Hawthorne's Dimmesdale: Fugitive from Wrath," *Nineteenth-Century Fiction* XI (Sept 1956), 81-105.
——————. "Hawthorne's Hester." *College English* XIII (Mar 1952), 303-309.
——————. "Hawthorne's Pearl: Symbol and Character," *ELH* XVIII (Mar 1951), 50-66.
Arvin, Newton. Introduction, *The Scarlet Letter* (New York, 1950), pp. xiii.
Bonham, Sister M. Hilda. "Hawthorne's Symbols *Sotto Voice*," *College English* XX (Jan 1959), 184-186.
Brant, Robert I. "Hawthorne and Marvell," *American Literature* XXX (Nov 1958), 366.
Canfield, Dorothy. Introduction, *The Scarlet Letter* (1941).
Carpenter, Frederic I. "Scarlet A Minus," *College English* V (Jan 1944), 173-180.
Chase, Richard. *The American Novel and Its Tradition*, 67-82.
Cowley, Malcolm. "Five Acts of *The Scarlet Letter*," *College English* XIX (Oct 1957), 11-16; *Twelve Original Essays on Great American Novels*, 23-43.
Davies, Horton. *A Mirror of the Ministry in Modern Novels*, 24-28.
Dony, F. "Romantisme et Puritanisme chez Hawthorne à propos de la *Lettre Pourpre*," *Etudes Anglaises* IV (Jan-Mar 1940), 15-30.
Doubleday, Neal F. "Hawthorne's Hester and Feminism," *PMLA* LIV (1939), 825-828.
Douglas, Harold J. and Robert Daniel. "Faulkner and the Puritanism of the South," *Tennessee Studies in Literature* II (1957), 5-10.
Edgar, Pelham. *The Art of the Novel*, 125-129.
Eisinger, Chester E. "Pearl and the Puritan Heritage," *College English* XII (Mar 1951), 323-329.
Fogle, Richard Harter. *Hawthorne's Fiction*, 104-121.

HAWTHORNE, NATHANIEL, Continued

Gerber, John C. "Form and Content in *The Scarlet Letter*," *New England Quarterly* XVII (Mar 1944), 25-55.

Hanscom, Elizabeth Deering. Introduction, *The Scarlet Letter* (New York, 1927), pp. xxii.

Hart, John E. " 'The Scarlet Letter'—One Hundred Years After," *New England Quarterly* XXIII (Sept 1950), 381-395.

Haugh, Robert F. "The Second Secret in *The Scarlet Letter*," *College English* XVII (Feb 1956), 269-271.

Hoeltje, Hubert H. "The Writing of *The Scarlet Letter*," *New England Quarterly* XXVII (Sept 1954), 326-346.

Howells, W. D. *Heroines of Fiction*, 161-174.

Lawrence, D. H. *Studies in Classic American Literature*, 92-110.

Leavis, Q. D. "Hawthorne as Poet—Part II," *Sewanee Review* LIX (Jul-Sept 1951), 426-458.

Leisy, Ernest E. Introduction, *The Scarlet Letter* (New York, 1929), pp. xxiii.

Levi, Joseph. "Hawthorne's *The Scarlet Letter*: A Psychoanalytic Interpretation," *American Imago* X (Winter 1953), 291-306.

Maclean, Hugh N. "Hawthorne's *Scarlet Letter*: 'The Dark Problem of This Life,' " *American Literature* XXVII (Mar 1955), 12-24.

Male, Roy R. *Hawthorne's Tragic Vision*, 90-118.

Matthiessen, F. O. *American Renaissance*, 275-282.

McNamara, Anne Marie. "The Character of Flame: The Function of Pearl in *The Scarlet Letter*," *American Literature* XXVII (Jan 1956), 537-553.

Michaud, Régis. *The American Novel To-Day*, 25-46.

Orians, G. Harrison. "Hawthorne and the Puritan Punishments," *College English* XIII (May 1952), 424-432.

Pearce, Roy Harvey. "Hawthorne and the Twilight of Romance," *Yale Review* XXXVII (Mar 1948), 487-506.

——————. Introduction, *The Scarlet Letter* (London, 1957).

Phelps, William Lyon. Introduction, *The Scarlet Letter* (New York, 1927), pp. xvi.

Reid, Alfred S. *The Yellow Ruff & The Scarlet Letter*.

Rourke, Constance. *American Humor*, 186-191; (Doubleday Anchor) 50-54.

Ryskamp, Charles. "The New England Sources of *The Scarlet Letter*," *American Literature* XXXI (Nov 1959), 257-272.

HAWTHORNE, NATHANIEL, Continued

Sampson, Edward C. "Motivation in *The Scarlet Letter*," *American Literature* XXVIII (Jan 1957), 511-513.
Schubert, Leland. *Hawthorne, the Artist*, 136-161.
Seay, Claire Soulé. Introduction, *The Scarlet Letter* (New York, 1920), pp. xxiv.
Shipman, Carolyn. "Illustrated Editions of 'The Scarlet Letter,'" *Critic* XLV (Jul 1904), 49-51.
Smith, Harrison. "Hawthorne: The Somber Strain," *Saturday Review of Literature* XXXIII (Nov 18, 1950), 18; 55.
Stein, William Bysshe. *Hawthorne's Faust*, 104-122.
Stone, Edward. "The Antique Gentility of Hester Prynne," *Philological Quarterly* XXXVI (Jan 1957), 90-96.
Thorp, Willard. "Did Melville Review *The Scarlet Letter?*" *American Literature* XIV (Nov 1942), 302-305.
Van Doren, Mark. *Nathaniel Hawthorne*, 143-166.
von Abele, Rudolph. "The 'Scarlet Letter': A Reading," *Accent* XI (Autumn 1951), 211-227.
Waggoner, Hyatt H. *"The Scarlet Letter," Hawthorne*, 118-150; *Interpretations of American Literature*, 3-29.
Walcutt, Charles Child. "'The Scarlet Letter' and Its Modern Critics," *Nineteenth-Century Fiction* VII (Mar 1953), 251-264.
Warren, Austin. Introduction, *The Scarlet Letter* (New York, 1947), pp. xiii.
Werner, W. L. "The First Edition of Hawthorne's *The Scarlet Letter*," *American Literature* V (Jan 1934), 559-564.
Ziff, Larzer. "The Ethical Dimension of 'The Custom House,'" *Modern Language Notes* LXXIII (May 1958), 338-344.

SEPTIMIUS FELTON

Abel, Darrel. "Immortality vs. Mortality in *Septimius Felton*: Some Possible Sources," *American Literature* XXVII (Jan 1956), 566-570.
Davidson, Edward Hutchins. *Hawthorne's Last Phase*, 72-121.

GENERAL

Abel, Darrel. "The Devil in Boston," *Philological Quarterly* XXXII (Oct 1953), 366-381.
Anderson, D. K., Jr. "Hawthorne's Crowds," *Nineteenth-Century Fiction* VII (Jun 1952), 39-50.
Arvin, Newton. *Hawthorne*.

HAWTHORNE, NATHANIEL, Continued

Astrov, Vladimir. "Hawthorne and Dostoevski as Explorers of the Human Conscience," *New England Quarterly* XV (Jun 1942), 296-319.

Beers, Henry A. "Fifty Years of Hawthorne," 33-57.

Bewley, Marius. *The Complex Fate*.

──────────. "Hawthorne's Novels," *The Eccentric Design*, 147-186.

──────────. "James's Debt to Hawthorne (III): The American Problem," *Scrutiny* XVII (Spring 1950), 14-31.

Blair, Walter. "Color, Light, and Shadow in Hawthorne's Fiction," *New England Quarterly* XV (Mar 1942), 74-94.

Brooks, Van Wyck. *The Flowering of New England*, 210-227; 277-285; 380-385.

Brownell, William C. *American Prose Masters*, 63-130.

Brumbaugh, Thomas B. "Concerning Nathaniel Hawthorne and Art as Magic," *American Imago* XI (Winter 1954), 399-405.

Buitenhuis, Peter. "Henry James on Hawthorne," *New England Quarterly* XXXII (Jun 1959), 207-225.

Burdett, Osbert. "Nathaniel Hawthorne," *Critical Essays*, 7-22.

Burton, Richard. "Hawthorne," *Literary Leaders of America*, 99-124.

Canby, Henry Seidel. *Classic Americans*, 226-262.

Cantwell, Robert. *Nathaniel Hawthorne*.

Cargill, Oscar. "Nemesis and Nathaniel Hawthorne," *PMLA* LII (1937), 848-861.

Carpenter, Frederic I. "Puritans Preferred Blondes: The Heroines of Melville and Hawthorne," *New England Quarterly* IX (Jun 1936), 253-272.

Clark, Marden J. "The Wages of Sin in Hawthorne," *Brigham Young University Studies* I (Winter 1959), 21-36.

Clarke, Henel Archibald. *Hawthorne's Country*.

Conway, Moncure D. "My Hawthorne Experience," *Critic* XLV (Jul 1904), 21-25.

Copeland, Charles Townsend. "Hawthorne's Use of his Materials," *Critic* XLV (Jul 1904), 56-60.

Cowie, Alexander. "Nathaniel Hawthorne (1804-1864)," *The Rise of the American Novel*, 327-362.

Cowley, Malcolm. "Hawthorne in the Looking-Glass," *Sewanee Review* LVI (Oct-Dec 1948), 545-563.

HAWTHORNE, NATHANIEL, Continued

Cronin, Morton. "Hawthorne on Romantic Love and the Status of Women," *PMLA* LXIX (Mar 1954), 89-98.

Cunliffe, Marcus. "New England's Day: Nathaniel Hawthorne," *The Literature of the United States*, 96-104.

Davidson, Edward H. "Hawthorne and the Pathetic Fallacy," *Journal of English and Germanic Philology* LIV (Oct 1955), 486-497.

De Casseres, Benjamin. "Hawthorne: Emperor of Shadows," *Critic* XLV (Jul 1904), 37-44.

Doubleday, Neal Frank. "Hawthorne's Criticism of New England Life," *College English* II (Apr 1941), 639-653.

——————. "Hawthorne's Inferno," *College English* I (May 1940), 658-670.

——————. "Hawthorne's Satirical Allegory," *College English* III (Jan 1942), 325-337.

——————. "Hawthorne's Use of Three Gothic Patterns," *College English* VII (Feb 1946), 250-262.

Durr, Robert Allen. "Hawthorne's Ironic Mode," *New England Quarterly* XXX (Dec 1957), 486-495.

Eliot, T. S. "On Henry James: The Hawthorne Aspect," *The Question of Henry James*, 112-119.

Erskine, John. "Nathaniel Hawthorne," *Leading American Novelists*, 179-273.

Fairbanks, Henry G. "Hawthorne amid the Alien Corn," *College English* XVII (Feb 1956), 263-268.

——————. "Hawthorne and the Catholic Church," *Boston University Studies in English* I (Autumn 1955), 148-165.

——————. "Hawthorne and the Machine Age," *American Literature* XXVIII (May 1956), 155-163.

——————. "Hawthorne and the Vanishing Venus," *Texas Studies in English* XXXVI (1957), 52-70.

Faust, Bertha. *Hawthorne's Contemporaneous Reputation*.

Feidelson, Charles, Jr. *Symbolism and American Literature*.

Ferguson, John De Lancey. "Nathaniel Hawthorne," *American Literature in Spain*, 87-108.

Flanagan, John T. "The Durable Hawthorne," *Journal of English and Germanic Philology* LXIX (Jan 1950), 88-96.

Foster, Charles H. "Hawthorne's Literary Theory," *PMLA* LVII (1942), 241-254.

HAWTHORNE, NATHANIEL, Continued

Fussell, Edwin. "Hawthorne, James and 'The Common Doom,' " *American Quarterly* X (Winter 1958), 438-453.

Gribble, Francis. "Hawthorne from an English Point of View," *Critic* XLV (Jul 1904), 60-66.

Guidi, Augusto. "Le Ambiguità Di Hawthorne," *Studi Americani* I (1955), 125-142.

Hall, Lawrence Sargent. *Hawthorne, Critic of Society*.

——————. "Hawthorne: Critic of Society," *Saturday Review of Literature* XXVI (May 22, 1943), 28; 30; 32.

Hawthorne, Julian. "A Group of Hawthorne Letters," *Harper's Magazine* CVIII (Mar 1904), 602-607.

——————. *Hawthorne and His Circle*.

Hayford, Harrison. "Hawthorne, Melville, and the Sea," *New England Quarterly* XIX (Dec 1946), 435-452.

"Herbert Read on Hawthorne," *Notes and Queries* 184 (10 Apr 1943), 211-212.

Howard, Leon. "Hawthorne's Fiction," *Nineteenth-Century Fiction* VII (Mar 1953), 237-250.

Izzo, Carlo. "Un Metafisico Della Narrazione Nathaniel Hawthorne," *Studi Americani* I (1955), 97-124.

Johnson, W. Stacy. "Hawthorne and *The Pilgrim's Progress*," *Journal of English and Germanic Philology* L (1950), 156-166.

Kariel, Henry S. "Man Limited: Nathaniel Hawthorne's Classicism," *South Atlantic Quarterly* LII (Oct 1953), 528-542.

Kesselring, Marion L. "Hawthorne's Reading, 1828-1850," *Bulletin of the New York Public Library* LII (Feb 1949), 55-71; Part II (Mar 1949), 121-138; Part III (Apr 1949), 173-194.

Kling, Carlos. "Hawthorne's View of Sin," *Personalist* XIII (Apr 1932), 119-130.

Knight, Grant C. "Nathaniel Hawthorne," *American Literature and Culture*, 203-214.

Laser, Marvin. " 'Head,' 'Heart,' and 'Will' in Hawthorne's Psychology," *Nineteenth-Century Fiction* X (Sept 1955), 130-140.

Levin, Harry. *The Power of Blackness*.

Lewis, R. W. B. "The Return into Time: Hawthorne," *The American Adam*, 110-126.

Loggins, Vernon. *The Hawthornes*.

HAWTHORNE, NATHANIEL, Continued

Lombardo, Agostino. "Il Primo Romanzo Di Hawthorne," *Studi Americani* I (1955), 73-95.

Lundblad, Jane. *Nathaniel Hawthorne and European Literary Tradition.*

──────────. *Nathaniel Hawthorne and the Tradition of Gothic Romance.*

Lynd, Robert. "Hawthorne," *Books & Authors*, 126-133.

Mabie, Hamilton Wright. "Hawthorne in the New World," *Backgrounds of Literature*, 305-328.

──────────. "Nathaniel Hawthorne," *North American Review* 179 (Jul 1904), 13-23.

Macy, John. "Hawthorne," *The Spirit of American Literature*, 77-96.

Male, Roy R., Jr. "'From the Innermost Germ': The Organic Principle in Hawthorne's Fiction," *ELH* XX (Sept 1953), 218-236.

──────────. "Hawthorne and the Concept of Sympathy," *PMLA* LXVIII (Mar 1953), 138-149.

──────────. *Hawthorne's Tragic Vision.*

Marble, Annie Russell. "Gloom and Cheer in Hawthorne," *Critic* XLV (Jul 1904), 28-34.

Mathews, J. Chesley. "Hawthorne's Knowledge of Dante," *Texas Studies in English* XX (1940), 157-165.

Mathews, James W. "Hawthorne and the Chain of Being," *Modern Language Quarterly* XVIII (Dec 1957), 282-294.

Matthiessen, F. O. *American Renaissance*, 179-274; 282-322; 344-356.

McPherson, Hugo. "Hawthorne's Mythology: A Mirror for Puritans," *University of Toronto Quarterly* XXVIII (Apr 1959), 267-278.

Melchiori, Barbara. "Scenografie Di Hawthorne E Il Dilemma Dell'Artista," *Studi Americani* II (1956), 67-81.

Miller, James E., Jr. "Hawthorne and Melville: The Unpardonable Sin," *PMLA* LXX (Mar 1955), 91-114.

Mills, Barriss. "Hawthorne and Puritanism," *New England Quarterly* XXI (Mar 1948), 78-102.

More, Paul Elmer. "Hawthorne: Looking Before and After," *Shelburne Essays, Second Series*, 173-187.

HAWTHORNE, NATHANIEL, Continued

──────────. "The Solitude of Nathaniel Hawthorne," *Atlantic Monthly* LXXXVIII (1901), 588-599.

Moyer, Patricia. "Time and the Artist in Kafka and Hawthorne," *Modern Fiction Studies* IV (Winter 1958-1959), 295-306.

Mumford, Lewis. *The Golden Day*, 138-142; (Beacon Press) 68-70.

O'Connor, William Van. "Hawthorne and Faulkner: Some Common Ground," *Virginia Quarterly Review* XXXIII (Winter 1957), 105-123.

Parkes, Henry Bramford. "Poe, Hawthorne, Melville: An Essay in Sociological Criticism," *Partisan Review* XVI (Feb 1949), 157-165.

Pattee, Fred Lewis. "Hawthorne," *The First Century of American Literature*, 437-550.

Pearson, Norman Holmes. Introduction, *Complete Novels and Selected Tales* (New York, 1937), pp. xv.

Perry Bliss. "The Centenary of Hawthorne," *Park-Street Papers*, 63-103.

Quinn, Arthur Hobson. "Literature, Politics, and Slavery," *The Literature of the American People*, 433-434.

──────────. "Nathaniel Hawthorne, The Romance of the Moral Life," *American Fiction*, 132-148.

──────────. "The Romance of the Moral Life," *The Literature of the American People*, 308-321.

Rahv, Philip. "The Dark Lady of Salem," *Partisan Review* VIII (Sept-Oct 1941), 362-381.

Read, Herbert. "Hawthorne," *Collected Essays*, 265-279.

Reed, Amy Louise. "Self-Portraiture in the Work of Nathaniel Hawthorne," *Studies in Philology* XXIII (Jan 1926), 40-54.

Ringe, Donald A. "Hawthorne's Psychology of the Head and Heart," *PMLA* LXV (Mar 1950), 120-132.

Schubert, Leland. *Hawthorne, the Artist*.

Schwartz, Joseph. "God and Man in New England," *American Classics Reconsidered*, 121-145.

──────────. "A Note on Hawthorne's Fatalism," *Modern Language Notes* LXX (Jan 1955), 33-36.

Sherman, Stuart P. "Hawthorne: A Puritan Critic of Puritanism," *Americans*, 122-152.

Shroeder, John W. " 'That Inward Sphere': Notes on Hawthorne's

HAWTHORNE, NATHANIEL, Continued

    Heart Imagery and Symbolism," *PMLA* LXV (Mar 1950), 106-119.

Snell, George. "Nathaniel Hawthorne: Bystander," *The Shapers of American Fiction.* 117-129.

Spiller, Robert E. *The Cycle of American Literature,* 78-88; (Mentor) 69-75.

Stanton, Robert. "Dramatic Irony in Hawthorne's Romances," *Modern Language Notes* LXXI (Jun 1956), 420-426.

——————. "Hawthorne, Bunyan, and the American Romance," *PMLA* LXXI (Mar 1956), 155-165.

Stein, William Bysshe. *Hawthorne's Faust.*

Stewart, Randall. "The Golden Age of Hawthorne Criticism," *University of Kansas City Review* XXII (Oct 1955), 44-46.

——————. "Hawthorne and Faulkner," *College English* XVII (Feb 1956), 258-262.

——————. "Hawthorne and the Civil War," *Studies in Philology* XXXIV (Jan 1937), 91-106.

——————. "Hawthorne and *The Faerie Queen,*" *Philological Quarterly* XII (Apr 1933), 196-206.

——————. "Hawthorne in England: The Patriotic Motive in the Note-Books," *New England Quarterly* VIII (Mar 1935), 3-13.

——————. "Melville and Hawthorne," *South Atlantic Quarterly* LI (Jul 1952), 436-446.

——————. *Nathaniel Hawthorne.*

Turner, H. Arlin. "Hawthorne's Literary Borrowings," *PMLA* LI (1936), 543-562.

——————. "Hawthorne as Self-Critic," *South Atlantic Quarterly* XXXVII (Apr 1938), 132-138.

Van Doren, Carl. "Nathaniel Hawthorne," *The American Novel 1789-1939,* 58-83.

Van Doren, Mark. *Nathaniel Hawthorne.*

von Abele, Rudolph. *The Death of the Artist.*

Wagenknecht, Edward. "The Soul's Romance: Hawthorne," *Cavalcade of the American Novel,* 38-57.

Waggoner, Hyatt H. "The Late Romances," *Hawthorne,* 223-242.

——————. "Nathaniel Hawthorne: The Cemetery, the Prison, and the Rose," *University of Kansas City Review* XIV (Spring 1958), 175-190.

HAWTHORNE, NATHANIEL, Continued

Warren, Austin. "Hawthorne, Margaret Fuller, and 'Nemesis,'" *PMLA* LIV (1939), 615-618.
_____. "Hawthorne's Reading," *New England Quarterly* VIII (Dec 1935), 480-497.
_____. "Introduction," *Nathaniel Hawthorne*, xi-lxxiii.
_____. *Rage for Order*, 84-103.
Winters, Yvor. "Maule's Curse: Hawthorne and the Problem of Allegory," *American Review* IX (Sept 1937), 339-361.
_____. "Maule's Curse, or Hawthorne and the Problem of Allegory," *In Defense of Reason*, 157-175; *Maule's Curse*, 3-22.
Woodberry, George Edward. "The Literary Age of Boston," *Harper's Magazine* CVI (Feb 1903), 424-430.
_____. *Nathaniel Hawthorne: How to Know Him.*
Yates, Norris. "Ritual and Reality: Mask and Dance Motifs in Hawthorne's Fiction," *Philological Quarterly* XXXIV (Oct 1955), 56-70.

BIBLIOGRAPHY

Blair, Walter. "Hawthorne," *Eight American Authors*, 100-152.
Browne, Nina Eliza. *A Bibliography of Nathaniel Hawthorne.*
Cathcart, Wallace H. *Bibliography of the Works of Nathaniel Hawthorne.*
Gordan, John D. *Nathaniel Hawthorne: The Years of Fulfillment 1804-1853.*
_____. "Nathaniel Hawthorne, the Years of Fulfillment, 1804-1853," *Bulletin of The New York Public Library* LIX (Mar 1955), 154-165; Part II (Apr 1955), 198-217; Part III (May 1955), 259-269; Part IV (Jun 1955), 316-321.
Warren, Austin. *Nathaniel Hawthorne*, lxxv-lxxxix.

HAYCOX, ERNEST

Fargo, James. "The Western and Ernest Haycox," *Prairie Schooner* XXVI (Summer 1952), 177-184.

HEARN, LAFCADIO

GENERAL
Frost, O. W. *Young Hearn.*

HEARN, LAFCADIO, Continued

Gohdes, Clarence. "Escape from the Commonplace," *The Literature of the American People,* 686-688.
Hicks, Granville. *The Great Tradition,* 148-152.
Quinn, Arthur Hobson. "Lafcadio Hearn and the Later Exotic Romance," *American Fiction,* 509-520.
Salvan, Albert J. "Lafcadio Hearn's Views on the Realism of Zola," *PMLA* LXVII (Dec 1952), 1163-1167.
Snell, George. *The Shapers of American Fiction,* 83-87.

HECHT, BEN

GENERAL
Baldwin, Charles C. "Ben Hecht," *The Men Who Make Our Novels,* 219-226.
Cargill, Oscar. "The Intelligensia," *Intellectual America,* 503-506.
Hansen, Harry. "Ben Hecht: Pagliacci of the Fire Escape," *Midwest Portraits,* 305-357.
Michaud, Régis. *The American Novel To-Day,* 256-283.
Sherman, Stuart. "Ben Hecht and the Supermen," *Critical Woodcuts,* 63-72.

HEMINGWAY, ERNEST

ACROSS THE RIVER AND INTO THE TREES
Baker, Carlos. *Hemingway,* 274-283; 264-268.
Beach, Joseph Warren. "How Do You Like It Now, Gentlemen?" *Sewanee Review* LIX (Apr-Jun 1951), 311-328.
Cousins, Norman. "Hemingway & Steinbeck," *Saturday Review of Literature* XXXIII (Oct 28, 1950), 26-27.
Geismar, Maxwell. "To Have and To Have and To Have," *Saturday Review of Literature* XXXIII (Sept 9, 1950), 18-19.
Redman, Ben Ray. "I. The Champ and the Referees," *Saturday Review of Literature* XXXIII (Oct 28, 1950), 15-16; 38.
Rosenfeld, Isaac. "A Farewell to Hemingway," *Kenyon Review* XIII (Winter 1951), 147-155.
Smith, Harrison. "II. A Titan to Task," *Saturday Review of Literature* XXXIII (Oct 28, 1950), 17; 39.
Stephens, Robert O. "Hemingway's *Across the River and Into the*

HEMINGWAY, ERNEST, Continued

Trees: A Reprise," *Texas Studies in English* XXXVII (1958), 92-101.
Young, Philip. *Ernest Hemingway*, 88-92.
Zaubel, Morton Dauwen. *Craft and Character*, 317-321.

A FAREWELL TO ARMS

Baker, Carlos. *Hemingway*, 94-109.
Canby, Henry Seidel. "Story of the Brave," *Saturday Review of Literature* VI (Oct 12, 1929), 231-232.
"*A Farewell to Arms*," *American Writing Today*, 370-372.
Ford, Ford Madox. Introduction, *A Farewell to Arms* (New York, 1932), pp. xx.
Friedman, Norman. "Criticism and the Novel," *Antioch Review* XVIII (Fall 1958), 352-356.
Hackett, Francis. "Hemingway: 'A Farewell to Arms,'" *Saturday Review of Literature* XXXII (Aug 6, 1949), 32-33.
I., M.S. "Hemingway's *A Farewell to Arms*," *Explicator* II (Jun 1944, Q32; The Editors, "Hemingway's *A Farewell to Arms*," III (Oct 1944), No. 11; Philip Young, "Hemingway's *A Farewell to Arms*," VII (Oct 1948), No. 7.
Moses, W. R. "Water, Water Everywhere: 'Old Man' and 'A Farewell to Arms,'" *Modern Fiction Studies* V (Summer 1959), 172-174.
Richardson, H. Edward. "The 'Hemingwaves' in Faulkner's 'Wild Palms,'" *Modern Fiction Studies* IV (Winter 1958-1959), 357-360.
Russell, H. K. "The Catharsis in *A Farewell to Arms*," *Modern Fiction Studies* I (Aug 1955), 25-30.
Savage, D. S. "Ernest Hemingway," *Hudson Review* I (Autumn 1948), 390-401.
Warren, Robert Penn. Introduction, *A Farewell to Arms* (New York, 1949), vii-xxxvii; [Warren's] *Selected Essays*, 80-118.
West, Ray B., Jr. and Robert Wooster Stallman. "*A Farewell to Arms*," *The Art of Modern Fiction*, 622-634.
Young, Philip. *Ernest Hemingway*, 60-66.

FOR WHOM THE BELL TOLLS

Baker, Carlos. *Hemingway*, 245-259.
Blotner, Joseph L. *The Political Novel*, 15-16; 57-58.
Fadiman, Clifton. *College Prose*, 416-421.

HEMINGWAY, ERNEST, Continued

Fenimore, Edward. "English and Spanish in 'For Whom the Bell Tolls,' " *Ernest Hemingway: The Man and His Work,* 205-220.

Gray, James. *Ernest Hemingway: The Man and His Work,* 226-235.

Kirkwood, M. M. "Value in the Novel Today," *University of Toronto Quarterly* XII (Apr 1943), 290-296.

Moynihan, William T. "The Martyrdom of Robert Jordan," *College English* XXI (Dec 1959), 127-132.

Savage, D. S. "Ernest Hemingway," *Hudson Review* I (Autumn 1948), 393-401.

Schorer, Mark. "The Background of a Style," *Kenyon Review* III (Winter 1941), 101-105.

Young, Philip. *Ernest Hemingway,* 86-88.

THE OLD MAN AND THE SEA

Baker, Carlos. "The Marvel Who Must Die," *Saturday Review* XXXV (Sept 6, 1952), 10-11.

Dupee, F. W. "Hemingway Revealed," *Kenyon Review* XV (Winter 1953), 150-155.

Frohock, W. M. "Mr. Hemingway's Truly Tragic Bones," *Southwest Review* XXXVIII (Winter 1953), 74-77.

Gurko, Leo. "The Old Man and the Sea," *College English* XVII (Oct 1955), 11-15.

Spector, Robert Donald. "Hemingway's *The Old Man and the Sea,*" *Explicator* XI (Mar 1953), No. 38.

Young, Philip. *Ernest Hemingway,* 92-105.

Zaubel, Morton Dauwen. *Craft and Character,* 321-326.

THE SUN ALSO RISES

Baker, Carlos. *Hemingway,* 77-93.

―――――――. "When the Warriors Sleep," *Saturday Review* XXXVI (Jul 4, 1953), 13.

Canby, Henry Seidel. Introduction, *The Sun Also Rises* (New York, 1931), pp. ix.

Cohen, Joseph. "Wouk's Morningstar and Hemingway's Sun," *South Atlantic Quarterly* LVIII (Spring 1959), 213-224.

Farrell, James T. *Ernest Hemingway: The Man and His Work,* 221-225.

Hoffman, Frederick J. *The Twenties,* 80-85.

Levy, Alfred J. "Hemingway's *The Sun Also Rises,*" *Explicator* XVII (Feb 1959), No. 37.

HEMINGWAY, ERNEST, Continued

"Out of Little, Much," *Saturday Review of Literature* III (Dec 11, 1926), 420-421.

Scott, Arthur L. "In Defense of Robert Cohn," *College English* XVIII (Mar 1957), 309-314.

Spilka, Mark. *Twelve Original Essays on Great American Novels,* 238-256.

Young, Philip. *Ernest Hemingway,* 54-60.

TO HAVE AND HAVE NOT

Baker, Carlos. *Hemingway,* 205-222.

DeVoto, Bernard. "Tiger, Tiger!" *Saturday Review of Literature* XVI (Oct 16, 1937), 8.

Young, Philip. *Ernest Hemingway,* 70-73.

TORRENTS OF SPRING

Baker, Carlos. *Hemingway,* 37-42.

Garnett, D. Introduction, *Torrents of Spring* (London, 1933).

GENERAL

Adams, J. Donald. "The Tough Guys," *The Shape of Books to Come,* 103-113.

Aldridge, John W. *After the Lost Generation,* 23-43; 107-116.

──────────. "Hemingway: The Etiquette of the Berserk," *In Search of Heresy,* 149-165.

Atkins, John Alfred. *The Art of Ernest Hemingway.*

Backman, Melvin. "Hemingway: The Matador and the Crucified," *Modern Fiction Studies* I (Aug 1955), 2-11.

Baker, Carlos. *Hemingway.*

──────────. "Hemingway's Wastelanders," *Virginia Quarterly Review* XXVIII (Summer 1952), 373-392.

Bardacke, Theodore. "Hemingway's Women," *Ernest Hemingway: The Man and His Work,* 340-351.

Bartlett, Phyllis. "Other Countries, Other Wenches," *Modern Fiction Studies* III (Winter 1957-1958), 345-347.

Beach, Joseph Warren. "Ernest Hemingway: Empirical Ethics," *American Fiction,* 69-93; 97-119.

──────────. *The Twentieth Century Novel,* 530-538; 540-542.

Beaver, Joseph. "'Technique' in Hemingway," *College English* XIV (Mar 1953), 325-328.

Bishop, John Peale. "Homage to Hemingway," *After the Genteel Tradition,* 186-201; *Collected Essays,* 37-46; *Ernest Hemingway: The Man and His Work,* 292-307.

HEMINGWAY, ERNEST, Continued

Breit, Harvey. *The Writer Observed,* 263-265; 275-279.

Brown, Deming. "Hemingway in Russia," *American Quarterly* V (Summer 1953), 143-156.

Burgum, Edwin Berry. "Ernest Hemingway and the Psychology of the Lost Generation," *The Novel and the World's Dilemma,* 184-204; *Ernest Hemingway: The Man and His Work,* 308-328.

Burnam, Tom. "Primitivism and Masculinity in the Work of Ernest Hemingway," *Modern Fiction Studies* I (Aug 1955), 20-24.

Cargill, Oscar. "The Primitivists," *Intellectual America,* 351-370.

Carpenter, Frederic I. "Hemingway Achieves the Fifth Dimension," *PMLA* LXIX (Dec 1954), 711-718.

Colvert, James B. "Ernest Hemingway's Morality in Action," *American Literature* XXVII (Nov 1955), 372-385.

Cowley, Malcolm. "Ernest Hemingway," *Writers of Today,* 3-18.

——————. "Notes for a Hemingway Omnibus: The Pattern of His Work and Its Relation to His Life," *Saturday Review of Literature* XXVII (Sept 23, 1944), 7-8; 23-25.

——————. "A Portrait of Mister Papa," *Ernest Hemingway: The Man and His Work,* 34-56.

Daiches, David. "Ernest Hemingway," *College English* II (May 1941), 725-736.

Daniel, Robert. "Hemingway and His Heroes," *Queen's Quarterly* LIV (Winter 1947-48), 471-485.

Dewing, Arthur. "The Mistake about Hemingway," *North American Review* 232 (Oct 1931), 364-371.

Eastman, Max. "Bull in the Afternoon," *Art and the Life of Action,* 87-101; *Ernest Hemingway: The Man and His Work,* 66-75.

Fenton, Charles A. *The Apprenticeship of Ernest Hemingway.*

——————. "Ernest Hemingway: the Paris Years," *Atlantic Monthly* CXCIII (May 1954), 39-44.

——————. "Ernest Hemingway: the Young Years," *Atlantic Monthly* CXCIII (Mar 1954), 25-34; (Apr 1954), 49-57.

——————. "Hemingway's Kansas City Apprenticeship," *New World Writing* 2 (1952), 300-315.

Flanagan, John T. "Hemingway's Debt to Sherwood Anderson," *Journal of English and Germanic Philology* LIV (Oct 1955), 507-520.

HEMINGWAY, ERNEST, Continued

Frankenberg, Lloyd. "Themes and Characters in Hemingway's Latest Period," *Southern Review* VII (Spring 1942), 776-788.

Friedrich, Otto. "Ernest Hemingway: Joy Through Strength," *American Scholar* XXVI (Autumn 1957), 470; 518-530.

Frohock, W. M. "Ernest Hemingway: The River and the Hawk," *The Novel of Violence in America*, 167-199.

————. "Ernest Hemingway—Violence and Discipline: I," *Southwest Review* XXXII (Winter 1947), 89-97; Part II (Spring 1947), 184-193; *Ernest Hemingway: The Man and His Work*, 262-291.

Fussell, Edwin. "Hemingway and Mark Twain," *Accent* XIV (Summer 1954), 199-206.

Geismar, Maxwell. "Ernest Hemingway," *American Moderns*, 54-64.

————. "Ernest Hemingway: You Could Always Come Back," *Writers in Crisis*, 39-85; *Ernest Hemingway*, 143-189.

————. "Hemingway and the Nobel Prize," *Saturday Review* XXXVII (Nov 13, 1954), 24; 34.

————. "No Man Alone Now," *Virginia Quarterly Review* XVII (Autumn 1941), 517-534.

Goodheart, Eugene. "The Legacy of Ernest Hemingway," *Prairie Schooner* XXX (Fall 1956), 212-218.

Groth, John. "A Note on Ernest Hemingway," *Ernest Hemingway: The Man and His Work*, 19-24.

Gurko, Leo. "The Achievement of Ernest Hemingway," *College English* XIII (Apr 1952), 368-375.

————. *The Angry Decade*, 187-190; "Hemingway in Spain," *Ernest Hemingway: The Man and His Work*, 258-261.

Halliday, E. M. "Hemingway's Ambiguity: Symbolism and Irony," *American Literature* XXVIII (Mar 1956), 1-22; *Interpretations of American Literature*, 297-319.

————. "Hemingway's Narrative Perspective," *Sewanee Review* LX (Apr-Jun 1952), 202-218.

Hart, Robert C. "Hemingway on Writing," *College English* XVIII (Mar 1957), 314-320.

Hartwick, Harry. "Grace under Pressure," *The Foreground of American Fiction*, 151-159.

Hemphill, George. "Hemingway and James," *Kenyon Review*

HEMINGWAY, ERNEST, Continued

XI, 50-60; *Ernest Hemingway: The Man and His Work,* 329-339.

Henderson, Philip. "Ernest Hemingway," *The Novel Today,* 136-137.

Hersey, John. "The Novel of Contemporary History," *Atlantic Monthly* CLXXXIV (Nov 1949), 80-82.

Hicks, Granville. *The Great Tradition,* 273-277.

Hoffman, Frederick J. "The American Novel Between Wars," *The Modern Novel in America,* 89-103.

——————————. "No Beginning and No End: Hemingway and Death," *Interpretations of American Literature,* 320-331.

——————————. "The Unreasonable Wound," *The Twenties,* 66-76.

Holman, C. Hugh. "Hemingway and Emerson: Notes on the Continuity of an Aesthetic Tradition," *Modern Fiction Studies* I (Aug 1955), 12-16.

Johnson, Edgar. "Farewell the Separate Peace," *Ernest Hemingway: The Man and His Work,* 130-142.

Jones, John A. "Hemingway: The Critics and the Public Legend," *Western Humanities Review* XIII (Autumn 1959), 387-400.

Kashkeen, J. "Ernest Hemingway: A Tragedy of Craftsmanship," *Ernest Hemingway: The Man and His Work,* 76-108.

Kazin, Alfred. "All the Lost Generations," *On Native Grounds,* 327-341; "Hemingway: Synopsis of a Career," *Ernest Hemingway: The Man and His Work,* 190-204.

Kinnamon, Keneth. "Hemingway, the *Corrida,* and Spain," *Texas Studies in Literature and Language* I (Spring 1959), 44-61.

Levin, Harry. "Observations on the Style of Ernest Hemingway," *Kenyon Review* XIII (Autumn 1951), 581-609.

Lewis, Wyndham. "The Dumb Ox: A Study of Ernest Hemingway," *American Review* III (Jun 1934), 289-312; *Men Without Art,* 17-41.

McCaffery, John K. M. *Ernest Hemingway: The Man and His Work,* 9-15.

McCole, John. *Lucifer at Large,* 153-172.

McCormick, John. "Hemingway and History," *Western Review* XVII (Winter 1953), 87-98.

HEMINGWAY, ERNEST, Continued

Mellers, W. H. "Hollywooden Hero," *Scrutiny* VIII (Dec 1939), 335-344.
Moloney, Michael F. "Ernest Hemingway: The Missing Third Dimension," *Fifty Years of the American Novel*, 183-196.
Morris, Lloyd. *Postscript to Yesterday*, 154-156.
Morris, Wright. "The Ability to Function: A Reappraisal of Fitzgerald and Hemingway," *New World Writing* 13 (1958), 43-51.
──────────. "The Function of Style," *The Territory Ahead*, 133-146.
Oldsey, Bernard S. "Hemingway's Old Men," *Modern Fiction Studies* I (Aug 1955), 31-35.
Paul, Elliot. "Hemingway and the Critics," *Saturday Review of Literature* XVII (Nov 6, 1937), 3-4; *Ernest Hemingway: The Man and His Work*, 109-113.
Praz, Mario. "Hemingway in Italy," *Partisan Review* XV (Oct 1948), 1086-1100.
Prescott, Orville. *In My Opinion*, 64-70.
Rosenfeld, Paul. "Hemingway's Perspective," *By Way of Art*, 151-163.
Sartre, Jean-Paul. "American Novelists in French Eyes," *Atlantic Monthly* CLXXVIII (Aug 1946), 114-118.
Savage, D. S. "Ernest Hemingway," *Hudson Review* I (Autumn 1948), 380-401.
Schorer, Mark. "Technique as Discovery," *Hudson Review* I (Spring 1948), 84-86.
Schwartz, Delmore. "Ernest Hemingway's Literary Situation," *Southern Review* III (Spring 1938), 769-782; *Ernest Hemingway: The Man and His Work*, 114-129.
Slochower, Harry. *No Voice Is Wholly Lost*, 36-40.
Snell, George. "Ernest Hemingway and the 'Fifth Dimension,' " *The Shapers of American Fiction*, 156-172.
Spiller, Robert E. *The Cycle of American Literature*, 269-274; (Mentor) 203-207.
Stein, Gertrude. *The Autobiography of Alice B. Toklas*, 261-271; "Hemingway in Paris," *Ernest Hemingway: The Man and His Work*, 25-33.
──────────. "Ernest Hemingway and the Post-War Decade," *Atlantic Monthly* CLII (1953), 197-208.

HEMINGWAY, ERNEST, Continued

Stovall, Floyd. *American Idealism,* 149-152.

Trilling, Lionel. "Hemingway and His Critics," *Partisan Review* VI (Winter 1939), 52-60.

Van Doren, Carl. *The American Novel,* 340-343.

Wagenknecht, Edward. "Ernest Hemingway: Legend and Reality," *Cavalcade of the American Novel,* 368-381.

Walcutt, Charles Child. "Later Trends in Form: Hemingway," *American Literary Naturalism,* 270-280.

Warren, Robert Penn. "Hemingway," *Kenyon Review* IX (Winter 1947), 1-28; *Critiques and Essays on Modern Fiction,* 447-473.

Weeks, Robert P. "Hemingway and the Uses of Isolation," *University of Kansas City Review* XXIV (Dec 1957), 119-125.

West, Ray B., Jr. "Ernest Hemingway: Death in the Evening," *Antioch Review* IV (Dec 1944), 569-580.

――――――. "Ernest Hemingway: The Failure of Sensibility," *Sewanee Review* LIII (Jan-Mar 1945), 120-135; *Forms of Modern Fiction,* 87-101.

――――――. "Three Methods of Modern Fiction," *College English* XII (Jan 1951), 193-203.

Whicher, George F. "Analysts of Decay," *The Literature of the American People,* 882-884.

Wilson, Edmund. "Ernest Hemingway," *Atlantic Monthly* CLXIV (1939), 36-46.

――――――. "Hemingway: Gauge of Morale," *The Wound and the Bow,* 214-242; *Eight Essays,* 92-114; *Ernest Hemingway: The Man and His Work,* 236-257.

――――――. *The Shores of Light,* 115-124; 339-344; 616-629.

――――――. "The Sportsman's Tragedy," *A Literary Chronicle,* 96-101.

Wyrick, Green D. "Hemingway and Bergson: The Élan Vital," *Modern Fiction Studies* I (Aug 1955), 17-19.

Young, Philip. *Ernest Hemingway.*

――――――. *Ernest Hemingway,* University of Minnesota Pamphlets on American Writers, No. 1.

BIBLIOGRAPHY

Beebe, Maurice. "Criticism of Ernest Hemingway: A Selected Checklist with an Index to Studies of Separate Works," *Modern Fiction Studies* I (Aug 1955), 36-45.

HEMINGWAY, ERNEST, Continued

Cohn, Louis H. *A Bibliography of the Works of Ernest Hemingway.*
Critiques and Essays on Modern Fiction, 588-591.
Samuels, Lee. *A Hemingway Check List.*

HENTZ, CAROLINE LEE WHITING
ERNEST LINWOOD

Cowie, Alexander. "The Domestic Sentimentalists and Other Popular Writers (1850-1870): Caroline Lee Whiting Hentz (1800-1856)," *The Rise of the American Novel,* 422-423.

GENERAL

Ellison, Dhoda Coleman. "Mrs. Hentz and the Green-Eyed Monster," *American Literature* XXII (Nov 1950), 345-350.

HERGESHEIMER, JOSEPH
CYTHEREA

Canby, Henry Seidel. *Definitions,* 217-223.

THE LIMESTONE TREE

Kelley, Leon. "America and Mr. Hergesheimer," *Sewanee Review* XL (Apr-Jun 1932), 185-193.

THREE BLACK PENNYS

Hergesheimer, Joseph. Introduction, *Three Black Pennys* (New York, 1930), pp. xv.

GENERAL

Aiken, Conrad. *A Reviewer's A B C,* 143-148.
Baldwin, Charles C. "Joseph Hergesheimer," *The Men Who Make Our Novels,* 227-242.
Beach, Joseph Warren. "Point of View," *The Twentieth Century Novel,* 280-286.
Boynton, Percy H. "Joseph Hergesheimer," *America in Contemporary Fiction,* 53-72.
------------. "Joseph Hergesheimer," *More Contemporary Americans,* 137-156.
Cabell, James Branch. "About One and Another," *Some of Us,* 91-104.
------------. "Diversions of the Anchorite," *Straws and Prayer-Books,* 193-221.
------------. *Joseph Hergesheimer.*
Clark, Emily. *Innocence Abroad,* 87-106.
Hartwick, Harry. "Costumes by Hergesheimer," *The Foreground of American Fiction,* 187-199.

HERGESHEIMER, JOSEPH, Continued

Hatcher, Harlan. "Facing Two Worlds: Joseph Hergesheimer," *Creating the Modern American Novel,* 202-210.
Hicks, Granville. *The Great Tradition,* 219-220.
Kazin, Alfred. "The Exquisites," *On Native Grounds,* 235-238.
Kelley, Leon. "America and Mr. Hergesheimer," *Sewanee Review* XL (Apr-Jun 1932), 171-193.
Knopf, Alfred A. "Reminiscences of Hergesheimer, Van Vechten, and Mencken," *Yale University Library Gazette* XXIV (Apr 1950), 145-164.
Michaud, Régis. "Reinforcements: Willa Cather, Zona Gale, Floyd Dell, Joseph Hergesheimer, Waldo Frank," *The American Novel To-Day,* 238-356.
Sinclair, Upton. "The Ivory Tower," *Money Writes!* 92-99.
Van Doren, Carl. *Contemporary American Novelists,* 122-131.
Van Vechten, Carl. "How I Remember Joseph Hergesheimer," *Yale University Library Gazette* XXII (Jan 1948), 87-92.
Wagenknecht, Edward. "In the Second Decade: Joseph Hergesheimer: 'Brocade and Dream,'" *Cavalcade of the American Novel,* 306-311.
West, Geoffrey. "Joseph Hergesheimer," *Virginia Quarterly Review* VIII (Jan 1932), 95-108.
Whicher, George F. "Loopholes of Retreat," *The Literature of the American People,* 889-890.

HERRICK, ROBERT

TOGETHER
Holland, Robert A. "'Together': A Nietzschean Novel," *Sewanee Review* XVI (Oct 1908), 495-504.

GENERAL
Baldwin, Charles C. "Robert Herrick," *The Men Who Make Our Novels,* 243-250.
Cargill, Oscar. "The Freudians," *Intellectual America,* 582-591.
Duffey, Bernard I. "Realism and the Genteel in Robert Herrick's Chicago Novels," *Western Humanities Review* VI (Summer 1952), 261-271.
——————. "Robert Herrick," *The Chicago Renaissance in American Letters,* 113-123.
Hansen, Harry. "Robert Herrick and Edgar Lee Masters: Interpreters of Our Modern World," *Midwest Portraits,* 227-242.
Herrick, Robert. "A Novelist on His Art," *Dial* LVI (Jan 1, 1914), 5-7.

HERRICK, ROBERT, Continued

Howells, William Dean. "The Novels of Robert Herrick," *North American Review* 189 (Jun 1909), 812-820.

Kazin, Alfred. "Progressivism: The Superman and the Muckrake," *On Native Grounds*, 121-126.

——————. "Three Pioneer Realists," *Saturday Review of Literature* XX (Jul 8, 1939), 3-4; 14-15.

Lüdeke, H. "Robert Herrick: Novelist of American Democracy," *English Studies* XVIII (1936), 49-57.

Lynn, Kenneth S. "The Passion of Robert Herrick," *The Dream of Success*, 208-240.

Nevius, Blake. "The Idealistic Novels of Robert Herrick," *American Literature*, XXI (Mar 1949), 56-70.

Taylor, Walter Fuller. "The Humanism of Robert Herrick," *American Literature* XXVIII (Nov 1956), 287-301.

Van Doren, Carl. *Contemporary American Novelists*, 56-65.

Wagenknecht, Edward. "Voices of the New Century: Robert Herrick, Idealist," *Cavalcade of the American Novel*, 235-244.

Whicher, George F. "The Conscience of Liberalism," *The Literature of the American People*, 830.

HERSEY, JOHN

THE WALL

Geismar, Maxwell. "Experiment in Genocide," *Saturday Review of Literature* XXXIII (Mar 4, 1950), 14-16.

Hersey, John. "The Mechanics of A Novel," *The Yale University Library Gazette*, XXVII (Jul 1952), 1-11.

Prescott, Orville. *In My Opinion*, 238-240.

THE WAR LOVER

Hicks, Granville. "John Hersey's Message," *Saturday Review*, XLII (Oct 3, 1959), 18.

GENERAL

Geismar, Maxwell. "John Hersey: The Revival of Conscience," *American Moderns*, 180-186.

Prescott, Orville. *In My Opinion*, 150-152.

HEYWARD, DUBOSE

MAMBA'S DAUGHTERS

HEYWARD, DUBOSE, Continued

Harrigan, Anthony. "DuBose Heyward: Memorialist and Realist," *Georgia Review* V (Fall 1951), 335-344.
PORGY
Durham, Frank. *DuBose Heyward*, 49-77.
Harrigan, Anthony. "DuBose Heyward: Memorialist and Realist," *Georgia Review* V (Fall 1951), 335-344.
GENERAL
Durham, Frank. *DuBose Heyward*.

HILDRETH, RICHARD

THE SLAVE
Quinn, Arthur Hobson. *The Literature of the American People*, 460.
GENERAL
Cowie, Alexander. "The Mixed Thirties: Richard Hildreth (1807-1865)," *The Rise of the American Novel*, 292-300.

HILLYER, ROBERT

RIVERHEAD
Haraszti, Zoltan. "Robert Hillyer's *Riverhead*," *New England Quarterly* IX (Jun 1936), 273-280.

HOLMES, OLIVER WENDELL

ELSIE VENNER
Oberndorf, Clarence P. *The Psychiatric Novels of Oliver Wendell Holmes*, 20-111.
THE GUARDIAN ANGEL
Oberndorf, Clarence P. *The Psychiatric Novels of Oliver Wendell Holmes*, 112-199.
A MORTAL ANTIPATHY
Oberndorf, Clarence P. *The Psychiatric Novels of Oliver Wendell Holmes*, 200-264.
GENERAL
Boewe, Charles. "Reflex Action in the Novels of Oliver Wendell Holmes," *American Literature* XXVI (Nov 1954), 303-319.
Brooks, Van Wyck. "Dr. Holmes: Forerunner of the Moderns,"

HOLMES, OLIVER WENDELL, Continued

Saturday Review of Literature XIV (Jun 27, 1936), 3-4; 13-15.

Cowie, Alexander. "Experiment and Tradition: Oliver Wendell Holmes (1809-1894)," *The Rise of the American Novel*, 494-504.

Cunliffe, Marcus. "More New Englanders: Holmes," *The Literature of the United States*, 143-145.

Lewis, R. W. B. "The New Adam: Holmes and Whitman," *The American Adam*, 28-53.

Quinn, Arthur Hobson. *The Literature of the American People*, 361-373; 445-447.

————. "The Transition to Realism," *American Fiction*, 164-166.

Roditi, Edouard. "Oliver Wendell Holmes as Novelist," *Arizona Quarterly* I (Winter 1945), 23-33.

Tilton, Eleanor M. "Novelist," *Amiable Autocrat*, 275-292.

Wagenknecht, Edward. *Cavalcade of the American Novel*, 102-104.

HOWE, EDGAR WATSON

THE STORY OF A COUNTRY TOWN

Howells, William Dean. *Prefaces to Contemporaries*, 170-171.

Schorer, C. E. "Mark Twain's Criticism of *The Story of A Country Town*," *American Literature* XXVII (Mar 1955), 109-112.

Stronks, James B., "William Dean Howells, Ed Howe, and *The Story of A Country Town*," *American Literature* XXIX (Jan 1958), 473-483.

GENERAL

Åhnebrink, Lars. "Realism in the Middle West: Edward Eggleston, Edgar Watson Howe, and Joseph Kirkland," *The Beginnings of Naturalism in American Fiction*, 50-59.

Baldwin, Charles C. "E. W. Howe," *The Men Who Make Our Novels*, 260-271.

Gohdes, Clarence. "Exploitation of the Provinces," *The Literature of the American People*, 648.

Schramm, Wilbur L. "Ed Howe versus Time," *Saturday Review of Literature* XVII (Feb 5, 1938), 10-11.

Van Doren, Carl. "Prudence Militant," *Many Minds*, 34-49.

HOWELLS, WILLIAM DEAN

A HAZARD OF NEW FORTUNES
Arms, George. "Howells' New York Novel: Comedy and Belief," *New England Quarterly* XXI (Sept 1948), 313-325.

The Editors. "Howells' *A Hazard of New Fortunes*," *Explicator* I (Nov 1942), No. 14.

AN IMPERATIVE DUTY
Amacher, Anne Ward. "The Genteel Primitivist and the Semi-Tragic Octoroon," *New England Quarterly* XXIX (Jun 1956), 216-227.

INDIAN SUMMER
Gibson, William M. Introduction, *Indian Summer* (New York, 1951; 1958), pp. xxii.

THE LADY OF THE AROOSTOOK
Kar, Annette. "Archetypes of American Innocence: Lydia Blood and Daisy Miller," *American Quarterly* V (Spring 1953), 31-38.

A MODERN INSTANCE
Fryckstedt, Olov W. *In Quest of America.*

Gibson, William M. Introduction, *A Modern Instance* (Boston, 1957).

THE RISE OF SILAS LAPHAM
Arms, George. Introduction, *The Rise of Silas Lapham* (New York, 1949), pp. xviii.

Arms, George and William M. Gibson. "'Silas Lapham,' 'Daisy Miller,' and the Jews," *New England Quarterly* XVI (Mar 1953), 118-122.

Cady, Edwin H. Introduction, *The Rise of Silas Lapham* (Boston, 1957).

Carter, Everett. Introduction, *The Rise of Silas Lapham* (New York, 1958).

Carter, Paul. "A Howells' Letter," *New England Quarterly* XXVIII (Mar 1955), 93-96.

Clark, Harry Hayden. Introduction, *The Rise of Silas Lapham* (New York, 1951), pp. xxii.

Edwards, Herbert. "The Dramatization of *The Rise of Silas Lapham*," *New England Quarterly* XXX (Jun 1957), 235-243.

Fiske, Horace Spencer. *Provincial Types in American Fiction*, 11-42.

Hicks, Granville. *The Great Tradition*, 74-78.

HOWELLS, WILLIAM DEAN, Continued

Mumford, Howard. Introduction, *The Rise of Silas Lapham* (New York, 1948).

Tarkington, Booth. Introduction, *The Rise of Silas Lapham* (Boston, 1937), pp. xv.

THEIR WEDDING JOURNEY

Adrian, Arthur A. "Augustus Hoppin to William Dean Howells," *New England Quarterly* XXIV (Mar 1951), 84-89.

A TRAVELER FROM ALTRURIA

Jones, Howard Mumford. Introduction, *A Traveler from Altruria* (New York, 1957; Gloucester, Mass., 1959).

THE VACATION OF THE KELWYNS

Chase, Richard. *The American Novel and Its Traditions*, 177-184.

A WOMAN'S REASON

Arms, George. "A Novel and Two Letters," *Rutgers University Library Journal* VIII (Dec 1944), 9-13.

GENERAL

Abel, Darrel (ed.). "'Howells or James?'—An Essay by Henry Blake Fuller," *Modern Fiction Studies* III (Summer 1957), 159-164.

Åhnebrink, Lars. "Literary Credos: W. D. Howells and *Criticism and Fiction*, 1891," *The Beginnings of Naturalism in American Fiction*, 129-135.

Arms, George. "'Ever Devotedly Yours' The Whitlock-Howells Correspondence," *Rutgers University Library Journal* X (Dec 1946), 1-19.

——————. "The Literary Background of Howells's Social Criticism," *American Literature* XIV (Nov 1942), 260-276.

Ayers, Robert W. "W. D. Howells and Stephen Crane: Some Unpublished Letters," *American Literature* XXVIII (Jan 1957), 469-477.

Baldwin, Charles C. "William Dean Howells," *The Men Who Make Our Novels*, 272-281.

Becker, George J. "William Dean Howells: The Awakening of Conscience," *College English* XIX (Apr 1958), 283-291.

Brooks, Van Wyck. *The Dream of Arcadia*, 145-154; 197-205.

——————. "End of an Era," *Saturday Review of Literature* XXII (Jun 22, 1940), 3-4; 16.

——————. *Howells: His Life and World*.

HOWELLS, WILLIAM DEAN, Continued

──────────. *New England: Indian Summer.*
Budd, Louis J. "Howells, The *Atlantic Manthly,* and Republicanism," *American Literature* XXIV (May 1952), 139-156.
──────────. "Twain, Howells, and the Boston Nihilists," *New England Quarterly* XXXII (Sept 1959), 351-371.
Cady, Edwin Harrison. "The Gentleman as Socialist: William Dean Howells," *The Gentleman in America,* 184-205.
──────────. "Howells in 1948," *University of Kansas City Review* XV (Winter 1948), 83-91.
──────────. "The Neuroticism of William Dean Howells," *PMLA* LXI (1946), 229-238.
──────────. "A Note on Howells and 'The Smiling Aspects of Life,'" *American Literature* XVII (May 1945), 175-178.
──────────. *The Realist at War.*
──────────. *The Road to Realism.*
Cargill, Oscar. "Henry James's 'Moral Policeman': William Dean Howells," *American Literature* XXIX (Jan 1958), 371-398.
Carter, Everett. *Howells and the Age of Realism.*
──────────. "William Dean Howells' Theory of Critical Realism," *ELH* XVI (Jun 1949), 151-166.
Cooke, Delmar Gross. *William Dean Howells.*
Cowie, Alexander. "William Dean Howells (1837-1920)," *The Rise of the American Novel,* 653-701.
Coyle, Leo P. "Mark Twain and William Dean Howells," *Georgia Review* X (Fall 1956), 302-311.
Cronkhite, G. Ferris. "Howells Turns to the Inner Life," *New England Quarterly* XXX (Dec 1957), 474-485.
Dixon, James M. "The Ideals of William Dean Howells," *Personalist* II (Jan 1921), 35-46.
Dove, John Roland. "Howells' Irrational Heroines," *Texas Studies in English* XXXV (1956), 64-80.
Eble, Kenneth E. "Howells' Kisses," *American Quarterly* IX (Winter 1957), 441-447.
──────────. "The Western Ideals of William Dean Howells," *Western Humanities Review* XI (Autumn 1957), 331-338.
Edwards, Herbert. "Howells and the Controversy over Realism in American Fiction," *American Literature* III (Nov 1931), 237-248.
Ekstrom, William F. "The Equalitarian Principle in the Fiction

HOWELLS, WILLIAM DEAN, Continued

of William Dean Howells," *American Literature* XXIV (Mar 1952), 40-50.

Firkins, O. W. "Last of the Mountaineers," *Saturday Review of Literature* V (Mar 16, 1929), 774-775.

----------. *William Dean Howells.*

----------. "William Dean Howells," *Sewanee Review* XXI (Apr 1921), 171-176.

Foster, Richard. "The Contemporaneity of Howells," *New England Quarterly* XXXII (Mar 1959), 54-78.

Fox, Arnold B. "Howells' Doctrine of Complicity," *Modern Language Quarterly* XIII (Mar 1952), 56-60.

Fryckstedt, Olov W. *In Quest of America.*

Garland, Hamlin. "Sanity in Fiction," *North American Review* 176 (1903), 336-348.

Gibson, William M. "Materials and Form in Howells's First Novels," *American Literature* XIX (May 1947), 158-166.

Gifford, Henry. "W. D. Howells: His Moral Conservatism," *Kenyon Review* XX (Winter 1958), 124-133.

Gohdes, Clarence. "Realism for the Middle Class," *The Literature of the American People*, 665-680.

Gorlier, Claudio. "William Dean Howells E Le Definizioni Del Realismo, " *Studi Americani* II (1956), 83-125.

Grattan, C. Hartley. "Howells: Ten Years After," *American Mercury* XX (May 1930), 42-50.

Gullason, Thomas Arthur. "New Light on the Crane-Howells Relationship," *New England Quarterly* XXX (Sept 1957), 389-392.

Harlow, Virginia. "William Dean Howells & Thomas Sergeant Perry," *Boston Public Library Quarterly* I (Oct 1949), 135-150.

Hartwick, Harry. "Sweetness and Light," *The Foreground of American Fiction*, 315-340.

Harvey, Alexander. *William Dean Howells.*

Hicks, Granville. "The Dean of American Letters," *Saturday Review* XLI (Sept 27, 1958), 16.

----------. *The Great Tradition*, 78-99.

Hoffman, Frederick J. "Henry James, W. D. Howells, and the Art of Fiction," *The Modern Novel in America*, 1-27.

Howells, Mildred, (ed.). *Life in Letters of William Dean Howells.*

HOWELLS, WILLIAM DEAN, Continued

Howells, W. D. "Novel-Writing and Novel-Reading: An Impersonal Explanation" edited by William M. Gibson, *Bulletin of the New York Public Library* LXII (Jan 1958), 15-34.

Kazin, Alfred. "Howells: A Late Portrait," *Antioch Review* I (Jun 1941), 216-233.

Kirk, Clara and Rudolf. "Howells and the Church of the Carpenter," *New England Quarterly* XXXII (Jun 1959), 185-206.

——————. "Howells in Caricature," *The Journal of the Rutgers University Library* XXI (Jun 1958), 69-70.

——————. Introduction, *William Dean Howells*, vii-clxvii.

——————. "Letters to an 'Enchanted Guest': W. D. Howells to Edmund Gosse," *The Journal of the Rutgers University Library* XXII (Jun 1959), 1-25.

——————. "Two Howells Letters," *The Journal of the Rutgers University Library* XXI (Dec 1957), 1-7.

Knight, Grant C. "William Dean Howells," *American Literature and Culture*, 371-378.

Lutwack, Leonard. "William Dean Howells and the 'Editor's Study,'" *American Literature* XXIV (May 1952), 195-207.

Lydenberg, John and Edwin H. Cady. "The Howells Revival: Rounds Two and Three," *New England Quarterly* XXXII (Sept 1959), 394-407.

Macy, John. "Howells," *The Spirit of American Literature*, 278-295.

Martin, Edward S. "W. D. Howells," *Harper's Magazine* CXLI (Jul 1920), 265-266.

Michaud, Régis. "Henry James, Edith Wharton, William Dean Howells and American Society on Parade," *The American Novel To-Day*, 47-70.

——————. "Le Réalisme Assagi: William Dean Howells," *Panorama de la Littérature Américaine Contemporaine*, 111-114.

Morris, Lloyd. "Conscience in the Parlor: William Dean Howells," *American Scholar* XVIII (Autumn 1949), 407-416.

——————. *Postscript to Yesterday*, 101-107.

Mumford, Lewis. *The Golden Day*, 167-170; (Beacon Press edition) 83-85.

——————. "The Disciple Proves Independent: Howells and Lowell," *PMLA* LXXIV (Sept 1959), 484-487.

HOWELLS, WILLIAM DEAN, Continued

Parks, Edd Winfield. "Howells and the Gentle Reader," *South Atlantic Quarterly* L (Apr 1951), 239-247.

Phelps, William Lyon. "An Appreciation," *North American Review* 212 (Jul 1920), 17-20.

───────────. "William Dean Howells," *Essays on Modern Novelists*, 56-81.

───────────. "William Dean Howells," *Yale Review* X (Oct 1920), 99-109.

Quinn, Arthur Hobson. "William Dean Howells and the Establishment of Realism," *American Fiction*, 257-278.

Reeves, John K. "The Way of A Realist: A Study of Howells' Use of the Saratoga Scene," *PMLA* XLV (Dec 1950), 1035-1052.

Sinclair, Robert B. "Howells in the Ohio Valley: An Example for a Generation of Novelists," *Saturday Review of Literature* XXVIII (Jan 6, 1945), 22-23.

Smith, Bernard. *Forces in American Criticism*, 158-175.

───────────. "Howells: The Genteel Radical," *Saturday Review of Literature* XI (Aug 11, 1934), 41-42.

Snell, George. "Howells' Grasshopper," *College English* VII (May 1946), 444-452; *The Shapers of American Fiction*, 198-211.

Sokoloff, B. A. "William Dean Howells and the Ohio Village: A Study in Environment and Art," *American Quarterly* XI (Spring 1959), 58-75.

Spiller, Robert E. *The Cycle of American Literature*, 146-150; (Mentor) 116-119.

Tarkington, Booth. "Mr. Howells," *Harper's Magazine* CXLI (Aug 1920), 246-250.

Taylor, Walter Fuller. "On the Origin of Howells' Interest in Economic Reform," *American Literature* II (Mar 1930), 3-14.

───────────. "William Dean Howells and the Economic Novel," *American Literature* IV (May 1932), 103-113.

───────────. "William Dean Howells: Artist and American," *Sewanee Review* XLVI (Jul-Sept 1938), 288-303.

Tomlinson, May. "Fiction and Mr. Howells," *South Atlantic Quarterly* XX (Oct 1921), 360-367.

Trilling, Lionel. "W. D. Howells and the Roots of Modern

HOWELLS, WILLIAM DEAN, Continued

Taste," *Partisan Review* XVIII (Sept-Oct 1951), 516-536; *The Opposing Self*, 76-103.

Twain, Mark. "William Dean Howells," *Harper's Monthly Magazine* CXIII (Jul 1906), 221-225.

Underwood, John Curtis. "William Dean Howells and Altruria," *Literature and Insurgency*, 87-129.

Van Doren, Carl. "William Dean Howells," *The American Novel 1789-1939*, 120-136.

Wagenknecht, Edward. "The American Mirror: William Dean Howells." *Cavalcade of the American Novel*, 127-144.

Wasserstrom, William. "Willian Dean Howells: The Indelible Stain," *New England Quarterly* XXXII (Dec 1959), 486-495.

Westbrook, Max. "The Critical Implications of Howells' Realism," *Texas Studies in English* XXXVII (1957), 71-79.

Wister, Owen. "William Dean Howells," *Atlantic Monthly* CLX (1937), 704-713.

Woodress, James L., Jr. *Howells & Italy*.

Wyatt, Edith. "A National Contribution," *North American Review* 196 (Sept 1912), 339-352.

BIBLIOGRAPHY

Cady, Edwin H. "Howells Bibliography: A 'Find' and a Clarification," *Studies in Bibliography* XII (1959), 230-234.

Gibson, W. M. and George Arms. *A Bibliography of William Dean Howells*.

Gibson, William M. and George Arms. "A Bibliography of William Dean Howells," *Bulletin of The New York Public Library* L (Sept 1946), 675-698; Part II (Nov 1946), 857-868; Part III (Dec 1946), 909-928; Part IV, LI (Jan 1947), 49-56; Part V (Feb 1947), 91-105; Part VI (Apr 1947), 213-248; Part VII (May 1947), 341-345; Part VIII (Jun 1947), 384-388; Part IX (Jul 1947), 431-457; Part X (Aug 1947), 486-512.

Graham, Philip. "American First Editions at TxU: XI. William Dean Howells (1837-1920)," *Library Chronicle of the University of Texas* VI (Spring 1958), 17-21.

Kirk, Clara and Rudolf. *William Dean Howells*, clxviii-cxcix.

Reeves, John K. (ed.). "The Literary Manuscripts of W. D. Howells: A Descriptive Finding List," *Bulletin of The New York Public Library* XLII (Jun 1958), 267-278; Part II (Jul 1958), 350-363.

HUGHES, RUPERT
GENERAL
Baldwin, Charles C. "Rupert Hughes," *The Men Who Make Our Novels*, 286-296.

HUNEKER, JAMES GIBBONS
GENERAL
Cargill, Oscar. "The Intelligensia," *Intellectual America*, 477-483.
Mencken, H. L. "James Huneker," *A Book of Prefaces*, 151-194.

HURST, FANNIE
LUMMOX
Broun, Heywood. *Fannie Hurst*, 29-32.
Littell, Robert. *Fannie Hurst*, 37-38.
A PRESIDENT IS BORN
James, Winifred. *Fannie Hurst*, 33-36.
GENERAL
Hurston, Zora Neale. "Fannie Hurst," *Saturday Review of Literature* XVI (Oct 9, 1937), 15-16.
Overton, Grant. "Fannie Hurst," *The Women Who Make Our Novels*, 180-186.
————————. "Fannie Hurst: A Critical Appreciation," *Fannie Hurst*, 13-28.

INGRAHAM, JOSEPH HOLT
PIERCE FLEMING
French, Warren G. "A 'Lost' American Novel," *American Literature* XXI (Jan 1950), 477-478.
GENERAL
Cowie, Alexander. "The Mixed Thirties: Joseph Holt Ingraham (1809-1860)," *The Rise of the American Novel*, 288-292.
Hubbell, Jay B. *The South in American Literature*, 623-624.

JACKSON, HELEN HUNT
RAMONA
Dobie, J. Frank. "Helen Hunt Jackson and *Ramona*," *Southwest Review* XLIV (Spring 1959), 93-98.

JACKSON, HELEN HUNT, Continued

Nevins, Allan. "Helen Hunt Jackson, Sentimentalist vs. Realist," *American Scholar* X (Summer 1941), 269-285.

JAMES, HENRY

THE AMBASSADORS

Beach, Joseph Warren. *The Method of Henry James*, 266-270.
Bowden, Edwin T. *The Themes of Henry James*, 97-115.
Brown, E. K. "James and Conrad," *Yale Review* XXXV (Dec 1945), 265-285.
Chase, Richard. *Twelve Original Essays on Great American Novels*, 124-147.
Crews, Frederick C. *The Tragedy of Manners*, 30-56.
Durr, Robert A. "The Night Journey in *The Ambassadors*," *Philological Quarterly* XXXV (Oct 1956), 24-38.
Edel, Leon. "Henry James's Revisions for *The Ambassadors*," *Notes and Queries* 200 (Jan 1955), 37-38.
——————. "A Letter to the Editors," *American Literature* XXIV (Nov 1952), 370-372.
——————. "Time and *The Ambassadors*," *Modern Language Notes* LXXIII (Mar 1958), 177-179.
Edgar, Pelham. *Henry James*, 311-324.
Evans, Patricia. "The Meaning of the Match Image in James's *The Ambassadors*," *Modern Language Notes* LXX (Jan 1955), 36-37.
Foley, Richard Nicholas. *Criticism in American Periodicals of the Works of Henry James*, 92-101.
Forster, E. M. *Aspects of the Novel*, 218-234; *Essays in Modern Literary Criticism*, 433-438.
Gibson, William M. "Metaphor in the Plot of 'The Ambassadors,'" *New England Quarterly* XXIV (Sept 1951), 291-305.
Humphreys, Susan M. "Henry James's Revisions for *The Ambassadors*," *Notes and Queries* 199 (Sept 1954), 397-399.
James, Henry. "Preface to *The Ambassadors*," *The Art of the Novel*, 307-326.
Knox, George. "James's Rhetoric of 'Quotes,'" *College English* XVII (Feb 1956), 293-297.
Lubbock, Percy. *The Craft of Fiction*, 145-149; 156-171.
Matthiessen, F. O. *Henry James*, 18-41.

JAMES, HENRY, Continued

———————. *The Question of Henry James*, 218-235.

Sampson, Martin W. Introduction, *The Ambassadors* (New York, 1930), pp. xv.

Stallman, R. W. " 'The Sacred Rage': The Time-Theme in 'The Ambassadors,' " *Modern Fiction Studies* III (Spring 1957), 41-56.

———————. "Time and the Unnamed Article in *The Ambassadors*," *Modern Language Notes* LXXII (Jan 1957), 27-32.

Stein, William Bysshe. "*The Ambassadors*: The Crucifixion of Sensibility," *College English* XVII (Feb 1956), 289-292.

Swinnerton, Frank. Introduction, *The Ambassadors* (London, 1948; 1957).

Tilford, John E., Jr. "James the Old Intruder," *Modern Fiction Studies* IV (Summer 1958), 157-164.

Ward, J. A. "*The Ambassadors:* Strether's Vision of Evil," *Nineteenth-Century Fiction* XIV (Jun 1959), 45-58.

Williams, Orlo. "*The Ambassadors*," *Criterion* VIII (Sept 1928), 47-64.

Young, Robert E. "An Error in *The Ambassadors*," *American Literature* XXII (Nov 1950), 245-253.

———————. "A Final Note on *The Ambassadors*," *American Literature* XXIII (Jan 1952), 487-490.

THE AMERICAN

Beach, Joseph Warren. Introduction, *The American* (New York, 1949), pp. xix.

———————. *The Method of Henry James*, 199-205.

Bowden, Edwin T. *The Themes of Henry James*, 23-36.

Cargill, Oscar. "The First International Novel," *PMLA* LXXIII (Sept 1958), 418-425.

Clair, John A. "*The American*: A Reinterpretation," *PMLA* LXXIV (Dec 1959), 613-618.

Edgar, Pelham. *Henry James*, 237-245.

Gargano, James W. "Foreshadowing in *The American*," *Modern Language Notes* LXXIV (Nov 1959), 600-601.

Gettmann, Royal A. "Henry James's Revision of *The American*," *American Literature* XVI (Jan 1945), 279-295.

James, Henry. "Preface to *The American*," *The Art of the Novel*, 20-39.

JAMES, HENRY, Continued
Kelley, Cornelia Pulsifer. *The Early Development of Henry James,* 233-244.
Moore, John Robert. "An Imperfection in the Art of Henry James," *Nineteenth-Century Fiction* XIII (Mar 1959), 351-356.
Rourke, Constance. *American Humor,* 245-255; (Doubleday Anchor) 194-202.
──────────. *The Question of Henry James,* 138-159.
Schulz, Max F. "The Bellegardes' Feud with Christopher Newman: A Study of Henry James's Revision of *The American,*" *American Literature* XXVII (Mar 1955), 42-55.
Swan, Michael. Introduction, *The American* (London, 1949).
Traschen, Isadore. "An American in Paris," *American Literature* XXVI (Mar 1954), 67-77.
──────────. "Henry James and the Art of Revision," *Philological Quarterly* XXXV (Oct 1956), 39-47.
──────────. "James's Revisions of the Love Affair in *The American,*" *New England Quarterly* XXIX (Mar 1956), 43-62.
Watkins, Floyd C. "Christopher Newman's Final Instinct," *Nineteenth-Century Fiction* XII (Jun 1957), 85-88.
West, Ray B., Jr. and Robert Wooster Stallman. *The Art of Modern Fiction,* 583-593.

THE ASPERN PAPERS
Baskett, Sam S. "The Sense of the Present in *The Aspern Papers,*" *Papers of the Michigan Academy of Science, Arts, and Letters* XLIV (1959), 381-388.
Bottkol, Joseph M. Introduction, *The Aspern Papers* and *The Europeans* (New York, 1950), pp. xxi.
Edel, Leon. "The Aspern Papers: Great-Aunt Wyckoff and Juliana Bordereau," *Modern Language Notes* LXVII (Jun 1952), 392-395.
James, Henry. "Preface to *The Aspern Papers,*" *The Art of the Novel,* 159-179.
Stein, William Bysshe. "*The Aspern Papers*: A Comedy of Masks," *Nineteenth-Century Fiction* XIV (Sept 1959), 172-178.

THE AWKWARD AGE
Beach, Joseph Warren. *The Method of Henry James,* 243-249.
Bowden, Edwin T. *The Themes of Henry James,* 78-96.

JAMES, HENRY, Continued

Havens, Raymond D. "A Misprint in *The Awkward Age*," *Modern Language Notes* LX (Nov 1945), 497.

THE BOSTONIANS

Anderson, Charles R. "James's Portrait of the Southerner," *American Literature* XXVII (Nov 1955), 309-331.

Beach, Joseph Warren. *The Method of Henry James*, 223-227.

Bewley, Marius. "James's Debt to Hawthorne (I): *The Blithedale Romance* and *The Bostonians*," *Scrutiny* XVI (Sept 1949), 178-195; *The Complex Fate*, 11-30.

Bogan, Louise. *Selected Criticism*, 295-301.

Edgar, Pelham. *Henry James*, 260-269.

Howe, Irving. Introduction, *The Bostonians* (New York, 1956), pp. xxviii.

―――――――. *Politics and the Novel*, 182-200.

Oliver, Clinton. "Henry James as a Social Critic," *Antioch Review* VII (Jun 1947), 243-258.

Rahv, Philip. Introduction, *The Bostonians* (New York, 1945), pp. ix.

Trilling, Lionel. *The Opposing Self*, 104-117.

―――――――. Introduction, *The Bostonians* (London, 1952), pp. xv.

CONFIDENCE

Beach, Joseph Warren. *The Method of Henry James*, 223-227.

Bowden, Edwin T. *The Themes of Henry James*, 37-52.

Kelley, Cornelia Pulsifer. *The Early Development of Henry James*, 275-278.

Levy, Leo B. "Henry James's *Confidence* and the Development of the Idea of the Unconscious," *American Literature* XXVIII (Nov 1956), 347-358.

DAISY MILLER

Arms, George and William M. Gibson. " 'Silas Lapham,' 'Daisy Miller,' and the Jews," *New England Quarterly* XVI (Mar 1953), 118-122.

Buitenhuis, Peter. "From Daisy Miller to Julia Bride: 'A Whole Passage of Intellectual History,' " *American Quarterly* XI (Summer 1959), 136-146.

Burrell, John A. "Henry James: A Rhapsody of Youth," *Dial* LXIII (Sept 27, 1917), 260-262.

JAMES, HENRY, Continued

Cargill, Oscar. Introduction, *Washington Square* and *Daisy Miller* (New York, 1956), pp. xxv.

Dunbar, Viola. "A Note on the Genesis of *Daisy Miller,*" *Philological Quarterly* XXVII (Apr 1948), 184-186; Stone, Edward. "A Further Note on *Daisy Miller* and Cherbuliez," *Philological Quarterly* XXIX (Apr 1950), 213-216.

——————. "The Revision of *Daisy Miller,*" *Modern Language Notes* LXV (May 1950), 311-317.

Howells, W. D. *Heroines of Fiction* II, 164-176.

——————. Introduction, *Daisy Miller* (New York, 1918).

——————. *Prefaces to Contemporaries*, 155-163.

Hoxie, Elizabeth F. "Mrs. Grundy Adopts Daisy Miller," *New England Quarterly* XIX (Dec 1946), 474-484.

James, Henry. "Preface to *Daisy Miller,*" *The Art of the Novel*, 267-287.

Kar, Annette. "Archetypes of American Innocence: Lydia Blood and Daisy Miller," *American Quarterly* V (Spring 1953), 31-38.

Sampson, Martin W. Introduction, *Daisy Miller* (New York, 1927), pp. xv.

THE EUROPEANS

Beach, Joseph Warren. *The Method of Henry James*, 223-227.

Bottkol, Joseph M. Introduction, *The Aspern Papers* and *The Europeans* (New York, 1950), pp. xxi.

Bowden, Edwin T. *The Themes of Henry James*, 37-52.

Leavis, F. R. "The Novel as Dramatic Poem (III): *The Europeans,*" *Scrutiny* XV (Summer 1948), 209-221.

Sackville-West, Edward. Introduction, *The Europeans* (London, 1952).

THE GOLDEN BOWL

Anderson, Quentin. *The American Henry James*, 281-346.

Beach, Joseph Warren. *The Method of Henry James*, 264-266.

Bewley, Marius. "Appearance and Reality in Henry James," *Scrutiny* XVII (Summer 1950), 96-102.

Blackmur, R. P. Introduction, *The Golden Bowl* (New York, 1952), pp. xxi.

Bompard, Paola. "Una Nota Su 'The Golden Bowl,'" *Studi Americani* II (1956), 143-162.

Bowden, Edwin T. *The Themes of Henry James*, 97-115.

JAMES, HENRY, Continued

Brown, E. K. "James and Conrad," *Yale Review* XXXV (Dec 1945), 265-285.
Crews, Frederick C. *The Tragedy of Manners*, 81-114.
Edgar, Pelham. *Henry James*, 324-343.
Fergusson, Francis. "*The Golden Bowl* Revisited," *Sewanee Review* LXIII (Jan-Mar 1955), 13-28.
Foley, Richard Nicholas. *Criticism in American Periodicals of the Works of Henry James*, 101-105.
Girling, H. K. "The Function of Slang in the Dramatic Poetry of 'The Golden Bowl,'" *Nineteenth-Century Fiction* XI (Sept 1956), 130-147.
Gordon, Caroline. "Mr. Verver, Our National Hero," *Sewanee Review* LXIII (Jan-Mar 1955), 29-47.
James, Henry. "Preface to *The Golden Bowl*," *The Art of the Novel*, 327-348.
Kimball, Jean. "Henry James's Last Portrait of a Lady: Charlotte Stant in *The Golden Bowl*," *American Literature* XXVIII (Jan 1957), 449-468.
Matthiessen, F. O. *Henry James*, 81-104.
Spencer, James L. "Symbolism in James's 'The Golden Bowl,'" *Modern Fiction Studies* III (Winter 1957-1958), 333-344.
Spender, Stephen. *The Question of Henry James*, 236-245.
Theobald, John R. "New Reflections on *The Golden Bowl*," *Twentieth Century Literature* III (Apr 1957), 20-26.
Wegelin, Christof. "The 'Internationalism' of 'The Golden Bowl,'" *Nineteenth-Century Fiction* XI (Dec 1956), 161-181.
West, Rebecca. *Henry James*, 105-117.
Wright, Walter. "Maggie Verver: Neither Saint Nor Witch," *Nineteenth-Century Fiction* XII (Jun 1957), 59-71.

THE IVORY TOWER

Matthiessen, F. O. *Henry James*, 105-130.

THE OTHER HOUSE

Bowden, Edwin T. *The Themes of Henry James*, 78-96.
Edel, Leon. Introduction, *The Other House* (New York, 1948), pp. xxi.

THE OUTCRY

Beach, Joseph Warren. *The Method of Henry James*, 249-250.
Bowden, Edwin T. *The Themes of Henry James*, 78-96.

JAMES, HENRY, Continued

Foley, Richard Nicholas. *Criticism in American Periodicals of the Works of Henry James*, 131-134.

THE PORTRAIT OF A LADY

Beach, Joseph Warren. *The Method of Henry James*, 205-211.

Bowden, Edwin T. *The Themes of Henry James*, 53-77.

Bowman, Sylvia E. "Les Heroines d'Henry James dans *The Portrait of A Lady* et d'Yvan Tourgueniev dans a la Veille," *Etudes Anglaises* XI (Apr-Jun 1958), 136-149.

Burrell, John A. "Henry James: A Rhapsody of Youth," *Dial* LXIII (Sept 27, 1917), 260-262.

Cargill, Oscar. " 'The Portrait of a Lady': A Critical Reappraisal," *Modern Fiction Studies* III (Spring 1957), 11-32.

Chase, Richard. *The American Novel and Its Tradition*, 117-137.

Edel, Leon. Introduction, *The Portrait of a Lady* (Boston, 1956), pp. xx.

Edgar, Pelham. *Henry James*, 245-255.

Flinn, H. G. and Howard C. Key. "Henry James and Gestation," *College English* XXI (Dec 1959), 173-175.

Greene, Graham. Introduction, *The Portrait of a Lady* (New York, 1947), pp. xxix.

Hafley, James. "Malice in Wonderland," *Arizona Quarterly* XV (Spring 1959), 512.

James, Henry. "Preface to *The Portrait of a Lady*," *The Art of the Novel*, 40-58.

Kelley, Cornelia Pulsifer. *The Early Development of Henry James*, 284-300.

Krause, Sydney J. "James's Revisions of the Style of *The Portrait of a Lady*," *American Literature* XXX (Mar 1958), 67-88.

Leavis, F. R. *The Great Tradition*, 79-125.

Leavis, Q. D. "A Note on Literary Indebtedness: Dickens, George Eliot, Henry James—," *Hudson Review* VIII (Autumn 1955), 423-428.

Matthiessen, F. O. *Essays in Modern Literary Criticism*, 451-472; *Henry James*, 152-186.

Powers, Lyall H. "*The Portrait of a Lady:* 'The Eternal Mystery of Things,' " *Nineteenth-Century Fiction* XIV (Sept 1959), 143-155.

JAMES, HENRY, Continued

Sackville-West, Edward. *Inclinations,* 58-63.

Sandeen, Ernest. "*The Wings of the Dove* and *The Portrait of a Lady*: A Study of Henry James's Later Phase," *PMLA* LXIX (Dec 1954), 1060-1075.

Snow, Lotus. "The Disconcerting Poetry of Mary Temple: A Comparison of the Imagery of *The Portrait of A Lady* and *The Wings of the Dove*," *New England Quarterly* XXXI (Sept 1958), 312-339.

Stallman, R. W. "Who Was Gilbert Osmond?," *Modern Fiction Studies* IV (Summer 1958), 127-135.

Van Ghent, Dorothy. *Interpretations of American Literature,* 244-261.

THE PRINCESS CASAMASSIMA

Beach, Joseph Warren. *The Method of Henry James,* 212-215.

Bogan, Louise. *Selected Criticism,* 112-121.

Bowden, Edwin T. *The Themes of Henry James,* 53-77.

Edgar, Pelham. *Henry James,* 269-283.

Firebaugh, Joseph J. "A Schopenhauerian Novel: James's *The Princess Casamassima*," *Nineteenth-Century Fiction* XIII (Dec 1958), 177-197.

H., J. "Henry James and Dumas, fils," *Notes and Queries* 185 (28 Aug 1943), 132-133.

Howe, Irving. *Politics and the Novel,* 139-156.

James, Henry. "Preface to *The Princess Casamassima,*" *The Art of the Novel,* 59-78.

Kretsch, Robert W. "Political Passion in Balzac and Henry James," *Nineteenth-Century Fiction* XIV (Dec 1959), 265-270.

Oliver, Clinton. "Henry James as a Social Critic," *Antioch Review* VII (Jun 1947), 243-258.

Spanos, Bebe. "The Real Princess Christina," *Philological Quarterly* XXXVIII (Oct 1959), 488-496.

Trilling, Lionel. Introduction, *The Princess Casamassima* (New York, 1948; 1954).

————. *The Liberal Imagination,* 58-92.

Wilkins, M. S. "A Note on the Princess Casamassima," *Nineteenth-Century Fiction* XII (Jun 1957), 88.

Woodcock, George. "Henry James and the Conspirators," *Sewanee Review* LX (Apr-Jun 1952), 219-229.

JAMES, HENRY, Continued

THE REVERBERATOR
Bowden, Edwin T. *The Themes of Henry James*, 37-52.
James, Henry. "Preface to *The Reverberator*," *The Art of the Novel*, 180-197.

RODERICK HUDSON
Beach, Joseph Warren. *The Method of Henry James*, 191-199.
Bowden, Edwin T. *The Themes of Henry James*, 23-36.
Cooney, Séamus. "Grammar vs. Style in a Sentence From *Roderick Hudson*," *Notes and Queries* 204 (Jan 1959), 32-33.
Dunbar, Viola R. "The Problem in *Roderick Hudson*," *Modern Language Notes* LXVII (Feb 1952), 109-113.
———. "A Source for *Roderick Hudson*," *Modern Language Notes* LXIII (May 1948), 303-310.
Edel, Leon. "Henry James and Vernon Lee," *PMLA* LXIX (Jun 1954), 677-678.
Edgar, Pelham. *Henry James*, 232-237.
H., J. "Henry James and Dumas, fils," *Notes and Queries* 185 (28 Aug 1943), 132-133.
Harvitt, Hélène. "How Henry James Revised *Roderick Hudson*: A Study in Style," *PMLA* XXXIX (1924), 203-227.
Havens, Raymond D. "The Revision of *Roderick Hudson*," *PMLA* XL (1925), 433-434.
James, Henry. "Preface to *Roderick Hudson*," *The Art of the Novel*, 3-19.
Kelley, Cornelia Pulsifer. *The Early Development of Henry James*, 182-194.
"Rossetti and Henry James," *Notes and Queries* 184 (5 Jun 1943), 327-328.

THE SACRED FOUNT
Beach, Joseph Warren. *The Method of Henry James*, 250-254.
Blackmur, R. P. "The Sacred Fount," *Kenyon Review* IV (Autumn 1942), 328-352.
Bowden, Edwin T. *The Themes of Henry James*, 78-96.
Edel, Leon. Introduction, *Sacred Fount* (New York, 1953), pp. xxxii.
Foley, Richard Nicholas. *Criticism in American Periodicals of the Works of Henry James*, 80-82.

JAMES, HENRY, Continued

Hoffmann, Charles G. "The Art of Reflection in James's *The Sacred Fount*," *Modern Language Notes* LXIX (Nov 1954), 507-508.

Raeth, Claire J. "Henry James's Rejection of *The Sacred Fount*," *ELH*, XVI (Dec 1949), 308-324.

Sackville-West, Edward. *Inclinations*, 63-71.

THE SENSE OF THE PAST

Stone, Edward. "Henry James's Last Novel," *Boston Public Library Quarterly* II (Oct 1950), 348-353.

THE SPOILS OF POYNTON

Beach, Joseph Warren. *The Method of Henry James*, 233-236.

Bowden, Edwin T. *The Themes of Henry James*, 53-77.

Broderick, John C. "Nature, Art, and Imagination in *The Spoils of Poynton*," *Nineteenth-Century Fiction* XIII (Mar 1959), 295-312.

James, Henry. "Preface to *The Spoils of Poynton*," *The Art of the Novel*, 119-139.

Volpe, Edmond L. "The Spoils of Art," *Modern Language Notes* LXXIV (Nov 1959), 601-608.

THE TRAGIC MUSE

Beach, Joseph Warren. *The Method of Henry James*, 216-220.

Bowden, Edwin T. *The Themes of Henry James*, 53-77.

Cargill, Oscar. "Gabriel Nash—Somewhat Less than Angel?" *Nineteenth-Century Fiction* XIV (Dec 1959), 231-239.

——————. "Mr. James's Aesthetic Mr. Nash," *Nineteenth-Century Fiction* XII (Dec 1957), 171-187.

Edgar, Pelham. *Henry James*, 284-298.

James, Henry. "Preface to *The Tragic Muse*," *The Art of the Novel*, 79-97.

Powers, Lyall H. "James's *The Tragic Muse*—Ave Atque Vale," *PMLA* LXXIII (Jun 1958), 270-274.

——————. "Mr. James's Aesthetic Mr. Nash—Again," *Nineteenth-Century Fiction* XIII (Mar 1959), 341-349.

WASHINGTON SQUARE

Beach, Joseph Warren. *The Method of Henry James*, 228-232.

Bowden, Edwin T. *The Themes of Henry James*, 37-52.

Cargill, Oscar. Introduction, *Washington Square* and *Daisy Miller* (New York, 1956), pp. xxv.

JAMES, HENRY, Continued

Dobree, Valentine. Introduction, *Washington Square* (London, 1949).

Fadiman, Clifton. Introduction, *Washington Square* (New York, 1950), pp. xii.

Kelley, Cornelia Pulsifer. *The Early Development of Henry James*, 278-283.

WATCH AND WARD

Stone, Edward. "Henry James's First Novel," *Boston Public Library Quarterly* II (Apr 1950), 167-171.

WHAT MAISIE KNEW

Beach, Joseph Warren. *The Method of Henry James*, 238-242.

Bewley, Marius. "Appearance and Reality in Henry James," *Scrutiny* XVII (Summer 1950), 102-114.

——————. "Maisie, Miles and Flora, the Jamesian Innocents: A Rejoinder," *Scrutiny* XVII (Autumn 1950), 255-263.

Bowden, Edwin T. *The Themes of Henry James*, 78-96.

Brebner, Adele. "How to Know Maisie," *College English* XVII (Feb 1956), 283-285.

James, Henry. "Preface to *What Maisie Knew*," *The Art of the Novel*, 140-158.

Leavis, F. R. "James's *What Maisie Knew*: A Disagreement," *Scrutiny* XVII (Summer 1950), 115-127; *The Complex Fate*, 114-131.

Wilson, Harris W. "What *Did* Maisie Know?" *College English* XVII (Feb 1956), 279-282.

Worden, Ward S. "A Cut Version of *What Maisie Knew*," *American Literature* XXIV (Jan 1953), 493-504.

——————. "Henry James's *What Maisie Knew*: A Comparison with the Plans in the Notebooks," *PMLA* LXVIII (Jun 1953), 371-383.

THE WINGS OF THE DOVE

Allott, Miriam. "A Ruskin Echo in *The Wings of the Dove*," *Notes and Queries* 201 (Feb 1956), 87.

Anderson, Quentin. "Manifest Providence: II," *The American Henry James*, 233-280.

Beach, Joseph Warren. *The Method of Henry James*, 262-263.

Bewley, Marius. "James's Debt to Hawthorne (II): *The Marble Faun* and *The Wings of the Dove*," *Scrutiny* XVI (Winter 1949), 301-317; *The Complex Fate*, 31-54.

JAMES, HENRY, Continued

Bowden, Edwin T. *The Themes of Henry James*, 78-96.
Brown, E. K. "James and Conrad," *Yale Review* XXXV (Dec 1945), 265-285.
Crews, Frederick C. *The Tragedy of Manners*, 57-80.
Crow, Charles R. "The Style of Henry James: *The Wings of the Dove*," *English Institute Essays* (1958), 172-189.
Edgar, Pelham. *Henry James*, 299-310.
Foley, Richard Nicholas. *Criticism in American Periodicals of the Works of Henry James*, 82-87.
James, Henry. "Preface to *The Wings of the Dove*," *The Art of the Novel*, 288-306.
Kimball, Jean. "The Abyss and the Wings of the Dove: The Image as a Revelation," *Nineteenth-Century Fiction* X (Mar 1956), 281-300.
Lewis, R. W. B. "The Vision of Grace: James's 'The Wings of the Dove,'" *Modern Fiction Studies* III (Spring 1957), 33-40.
Lubbock, Percy. *The Craft of Fiction*, 172-187.
Matthiessen, F. O. *Henry James*, 42-80.
Muecke, D. C. "The Dove's Flight," *Nineteenth-Century Fiction* IX (Jun 1954), 76-78.
Read, Sir Herbert. Introduction, *The Wings of the Dove* (London, 1948).
Sandeen, Ernest. "*The Wings of the Dove* and *The Portrait of A Lady*: A Study of Henry James's Later Phase," *PMLA* LXIX (Dec 1954), 1060-1075.
Snow, Lotus. "The Disconcerting Poetry of Mary Temple: A Comparison of Imagery of *The Portrait of A Lady* and *The Wings of the Dove*," *New England Quarterly* XXXI (Sept 1958), 312-339.
Wegelin, Christof. "Henry James's *The Wings of the Dove* as an International Novel," *Jahrbuch für Amerikastudien* III (1958), 151-161.

GENERAL

Abel, Darrel (ed.). "'Howells or James?'—An Essay by Henry Blake Fuller," *Modern Fiction Studies* III (Summer 1957), 159-164.
Åhnebrink, Lars. "Literary Credos: Henry James and 'The Art of Fiction.' 1884," *The Beginnings of Naturalism in American Fiction*, 128-129.

JAMES, HENRY, Continued

Anderson, Quentin. *The American Henry James.*

——————. "Henry James and the New Jerusalem," *Kenyon Review* XVIII (Autumn 1946), 515-566.

——————. "Henry James: His Symbolism and His Critics," *Scrutiny* XV (Dec 1947), 12-19.

——————. "The Two Henry Jameses," *Scrutiny* XIV (Sept 1947), 242-251.

Andreas, Osborn. *Henry James and the Expanding Horizon.*

Auden, W. H. "At the Grave of Henry James," *The Question of Henry James,* 246-250.

Barrett, Laurence. "Young Henry James, Critic," *American Literature* XX (Jan 1949), 385-400.

Barzun, Jacques. "Henry James, Melodramatist," *The Question of Henry James,* 254-266; *The Energies of Art,* 227-244.

——————. "James the Melodramatist," *Kenyon Review* V (Autumn 1943), 508-521.

Beach, Joseph Warren. "The Figure in the Carpet," *The Question of Henry James,* 92-104.

——————. *The Method of Henry James.*

——————. *The Twentieth Century Novel,* 177-228.

——————. "The Witness of the Notebooks," *Forms of Modern Fiction,* 46-60.

Beebe, Maurice. "The Turned Back of Henry James," *South Atlantic Quarterly* LIII (Oct 1954), 521-539.

Beer, Thomas. "Henry James and Stephen Crane," *The Question of Henry James,* 105-107.

Beerbohm, Max. "The Mote in the Middle Distance," *The Question of Henry James,* 40-43.

Bell, Millicent. "Edith Wharton and Henry James: The Literary Relation," *PMLA* LXXIV (Dec 1959), 619-637.

Bethurum, Dorothy. "Morality and Henry James," *Sewanee Review* XXXI (Jul 1923), 324-330.

Bewley, Marius. "Appearance and Reality in Henry James," *Scrutiny* XVII (Summer 1950), 90-114.

——————. *The Complex Fate.*

——————. *The Eccentric Design,* 220-258.

——————. "Henry James and 'Life,'" *Hudson Review* XI (Summer 1958), 167-185.

JAMES, HENRY, Continued

──────────. "James's Debt to Hawthorne (III): The American Problem," *Scrutiny* XVII (Spring 1950), 14-31.

Blackmur, Richard P. "In the Country of the Blue," *Kenyon Review* V (Autumn 1943), 595-617; *The Question of Henry James*, 191-211; *Critiques and Essays on Modern Fiction*, 303-318.

──────────. *The Lion and the Honeycomb*, 240-288.

──────────. Introduction. *The Art of the Novel*, vii-xxxix.

──────────. "The Loose and Baggy Monsters of Henry James," *Accent* XI (Spring 1951), 129-146.

Bode, Carl. "Henry James and Owen Wister," *American Literature* XXVI (May 1954), 250-252.

Booth, Bradford A. "Henry James and the Economic Motif," *Nineteenth-Century Fiction* VIII (Sept 1953), 141-150.

Bosanquet, Theodora. "The Record of Henry James," *Yale Review* X (Oct 1920), 143-156.

Bradford, Gamaliel. "Portrait of Henry James," *North American Review* 213 (Feb 1921), 211-224.

Brooks, Van Wyck. *The Dream of Arcadia*, 155-175.

──────────. "Henry James: An International Episode," *Dial* LXXV (Sept 1923), 225-238.

──────────. "Henry James of Boston," *Saturday Review of Literature* XXII (Jul 15, 1940), 3-4; 16-17.

──────────. "Henry James: The American Scene," *Dial* LXXV (Jul 1923), 29-42.

──────────. "Henry James: The First Phase," *Dial* LXXIX (May 1923), 433-450.

──────────. *New England: Indian Summer*.

──────────. *The Pilgrimage of Henry James*.

──────────. "Two Phases of Henry James," *The Question of Henry James*, 120-127.

Brown, E. K. "Two Formulas for Fiction: Henry James and H. G. Wells," *College English* VIII (Oct 1946), 7-17.

Brownell, William C. *American Prose Masters*, 339-398.

Buitenhuis, Peter. "Henry James on Hawthorne," *New England Quarterly* XXXII (Jun 1959), 207-225.

Bynner, Witter. "On Henry James's Centennial: Lasting Impressions of a Great American Writer," *Saturday Review of Literature* XXVI (May 22, 1943), 23; 26; 28.

JAMES, HENRY, Continued

Canby, Henry Seidel. "He Knew His Women," *Saturday Review of Literature* XXXIV (Nov 10, 1951), 9-10; 34-36.

——————. "Henry James & the Observant Profession," *Saturday Review of Literature* XXXIII (Dec 2, 1950), 11-12; 70-71.

——————. "The Return of Henry James," *Saturday Review of Literature* XXXI (Jan 24, 1948), 9-10; 34-35.

——————. *Turn West, Turn East.*

Cargill, Oscar. "Henry James's 'Moral Policeman': William Dean Howells," *American Literature* XXIX (Jan 1958), 371-398.

Cary, Elisabeth Luther. *The Novels of Henry James.*

Catalani, G. "Henry James and American Criticism," *Notes and Queries* 176 (18 Mar 1939), 194-195.

Chase, Richard. "James on the Novel vs. the Romance," *The American Novel and Its Tradition,* 21-28.

Chislett, William, Jr. "Henry James: His Range and Accomplishment," *Moderns and Near-Moderns,* 11-66.

Clemens, Cyril. "Bret Harte and Henry James as Seen by Marie Belloc Lowndes," *Mark Twain Quarterly* II (Fall 1937), 21-23.

Colby, Frank Moore. "In Darkest James," *The Question of Henry James,* 20-27.

Conrad, Joseph. "Henry James: An Appreciation," *North American Review* 180 (Jan 1905), 102-108; reprinted 203 (Apr 1916), 585-591; *Notes on Life and Letters,* 11-19.

——————. "The Historian of Fine Consciences," *The Question of Henry James,* 44-46.

Cornelius, Roberta D. "The Clearness of Henry James," *Sewanee Review* XXVII (Jan 1919), 1-8.

Cowie, Alexander. "Henry James (1843-1916)," *The Rise of the American Novel,* 702-742.

Crews, Frederick C. "Society and the Hero," *The Tragedy of Manners,* 13-29.

Croly, Herbert. "Henry James and His Countrymen," *The Question of Henry James,* 28-39.

Daiches, David. "Sensibility and Technique," *Kenyon Review* V (Autumn 1943), 569-579.

Dauner, Louise. "Henry James and the Garden of Death," *University of Kansas City Review* XIX (Winter 1952), 137-143.

Dupee, F. W. *Henry James.*

JAMES, HENRY, Continued

————. "Henry James in the Great Grey Babylon," *Partisan Review* XVIII (Mar-Apr 1951), 183-190.
Edel, Leon. "The Architecture of Henry James's 'New York Edition,'" *New England Quarterly* XXIV (Jun 1951), 169-178.
————. *Henry James.*
————. "Hugh Walpole and Henry James: The Fantasy of the 'Killer and the Slain,'" *American Imago* VIII (Dec 1951), 351-369.
————. "The Literary Convictions of Henry James," *Modern Fiction Studies* III (Spring 1957), 3-10.
————. *The Prefaces of Henry James.*
————. *The Psychological Novel.*
———— and Gordon N. Ray. *Henry James and H. G. Wells.*
———— and Lyall H. Powers. "Henry James and the *Bazar* Letters," *Bulletin of The New York Public Library* LXII (Feb 1958), 75-103.
Edgar, Pelham. *Henry James.*
————. "Henry James, the Essential Novelist," *Queen's Quarterly* XXXIX (May 1932), 181-192.
Edwards, Herbert. "Henry James and Ibsen," *American Literature* XXIV (May 1952), 208-223.
Eliot, T. S. "On Henry James," *The Question of Henry James*, 108-119.
Fadiman, Clifton. "Three Notes on Henry James," *Party of One*, 154-175.
Falk, Robert P. "Henry James and the 'Age of Innocence,'" *Nineteenth-Century Fiction* VII (Dec 1952), 171-188.
Ferguson, Alfred R. "The Triple Quest of Henry James: Fame, Art, and Fortune," *American Literature* XXVII (Jan 1956), 475-498.
Firebaugh, Joseph J. "Coburn: Henry James's Photographer," *American Quarterly* VII (Fall 1955), 215-233.
————. "The Pragmatism of Henry James," *Virginia Quarterly Review* XXVII (Summer 1951), 419-435.
Foley, Richard Nicholas. *Criticism in American Periodicals of the Works of Henry James.*
Ford, Ford Madox. "Henry James: The Master," *Portraits from Life*, 1-20.

JAMES, HENRY, Continued

Fox, Hugh, Jr. "Henry James and the Antimonian James Household: A Study of Selfhood and Selflessness," *Arizona Quarterly* XV (Spring 1959), 49-55.
Friend, Albert C. "A Forgotten Story by Henry James," *South Atlantic Quarterly* LIII (Jan 1954), 100-108.
Fussell, Edwin. "Hawthorne, James and 'The Common Doom,'" *American Quarterly* X (Winter 1958), 438-453.
Gale, Robert L. "Art Imagery in Henry James's Fiction," *American Literature* XXIX (Mar 1957), 47-63.
——————————. "Freudian Imagery in James's Fiction," *American Imago* XI (Summer 1954), 181-190.
——————————. "Henry James and Italy," *Studi Americani* III (1957), 189-203; *Nineteenth-Century Fiction* XIV (Sept 1959), 157-170.
——————————. "Henry James's Dream Children," *Arizona Quarterly* XV (Spring 1959), 56-63.
——————————. "Religion Imagery in Henry James's Fiction," *Modern Fiction Studies* III (Spring 1957), 64-72.
Gass, William H. "The High Brutality of Good Intentions," *Accent* XVIII (Winter 1958), 62-71.
Gastón, Nilita Vientós. *Introducción a Henry James.*
Gibson, Pricilla. "The Uses of James's Imagery: Drama Through Metaphor," *PMLA* LXIX (Dec 1954), 1076-1084.
Gide, André. "Henry James," *The Question of Henry James,* 251-253.
Gohdes, Clarence. "Escape from the Commonplace," *The Literature of the American People,* 688-700.
Goldsmith, Arnold L. "Henry James's Reconciliation of Free Will and Fatalism," *Nineteenth-Century Fiction* XIII (Sept 1958), 109-126.
Gordon, Caroline. "Henry James and His Critics," *How to Read a Novel,* 111-119.
Gurko, Leo. *The Angry Decade,* 129-132.
Hale, Edward Everett. "Henry James," *Dial* LX (Mar 16, 1916), 259-263.
Hamblen, Abigail Ann. "Henry James and the Press: A Study of Protest," *Western Humanities Review* XI (Spring 1957), 169-175.

JAMES, HENRY, Continued

Harlow, Virginia. "Thomas Sergeant Perry and Henry James," *Boston Public Library Quarterly* I (Jul 1949), 43-60.
Hartwick, Harry. "Caviar to the General," *The Foreground of American Fiction,* 341-368.
Hemphill, George. "Hemingway and James," *Kenyon Review* XI (1949), 50-60; *Ernest Hemingway: Man and Hero,* 329-339.
Herrick, Robert. "A Visit to Henry James," *Yale Review,* XII (Jul 1923), 724-741.
Hicks, Granville. *The Great Tradition,* 105-124.
Higginson, Thomas Wentworth. "Henry James, Jr.," *The Question of Henry James,* 1-5.
Hoffman, Charles G. *The Short Novels of Henry James.*
Hoffman, Frederick J. "Henry James, W. D. Howells, and the Art of Fiction," *The Modern Novel in America,* 1-27.
Hoskins, Katherine. "Henry James and the Future of the Novel," *Sewanee Review* LIV (Jan-Mar 1946), 87-101.
Howe, Irving. "Henry James and the Political Vocation," *Western Review* XVIII (Spring 1954), 199-208.
Howells, William Dean. "Mr. Henry James's Later Work," *North American Review* 176 (Jan 1903), 125-137; reprinted in 203 (Apr 1916), 572-584; *The Question of Henry James,* 6-19.
Hueffer, Ford Madox. *Henry James.*
Izzo, Carlo. "Henry James Scrittore Sintattico," *Studi Americani* II (1956), 127-142.
Josephson, Matthew. *Portrait of the Artist as American,* 70-138; 265-288.
Kazin, Alfred. "William and Henry James: 'Our Passion Is Our Task,'" *The Inmost Leaf,* 9-20.
Kelley, Cornelia Pulsifer. *The Early Development of Henry James.*
Kenton, Edna. "Henry James in the World," *The Question of Henry James.* 131-137.
Knight, Grant C. "Henry James," *American Literature and Culture,* 379-388.
Knights, L. C. "Henry James and the Trapped Spectator," *Southern Review* IV (Winter 1939), 600-615.
Krook, Dorothea. "Principles and Method in the Later Works of Henry James," *Interpretations of American Literature,* 262-279.
Leavis, F. R. *The Great Tradition,* 126-172.

JAMES, HENRY, Continued

——————. "Henry James," *Scrutiny* V (Mar 1937), 398-417.
——————. "Henry James and the Function of Criticism," *Scrutiny* XV (Spring 1948), 98-104.
LeClair, Robert C. *Young Henry James.*
Levy, Leo. B. "Henry James and the Jews," *Commentary* XXVI (Sept 1958), 243-249.
Lewis, Wyndham. "Henry James: The Arch-Enemy of 'Low Company,'" *Men Without Art,* 138-157.
——————. *Versions of Melodrama.*
Leyburn, Ellen Douglass. "Virginia Woolf's Judgment of Henry James," *Modern Fiction Studies* V (Summer 1959), 166-169.
Lind, Ilse Dusoir. "The Inadequate Vulgarity of Henry James," *PMLA* LXVI (Dec 1951), 886-910.
Lubbock, Percy. "The Mind of an Artist," *The Question of Henry James,* 54-69.
MacCarthy, Desmond. "The World of Henry James," *Saturday Review of Literature* VIII (Aug 29, 1931), 81-83.
Macy, John. "Henry James," *The Spirit of American Literature,* 324-339.
Matthiessen, F. O. *American Renaissance,* 292-305; 351-368.
——————. *Henry James,* 1-18; 131-151.
——————. "Henry James' Portrait of the Artist," *Partisan Review* XI (Winter 1944), 71-87.
——————. Introduction, *American Novels and Stories* (New York, 1947), pp. xxvi.
——————. "James and the Plastic Arts," *Kenyon Review* V (Autumn 1943), 533-550.
——————. *The James Family.*
McCarthy, Harold T. "Henry James and 'The Personal Equation,'" *College English* XVII (Feb 1956), 272-278.
——————. *Henry James: The Creative Process.*
McCormick, John O. "The Rough and Lurid Vision: Henry James, Graham Greene and the International Theme," *Jahrbuch für Amerikastudien* II (1957), 158-167.
McElderry, B. R., Jr. "Hamlin Garland and Henry James," *American Literature* XXIII (Jan 1952), 433-446.
Melchiori, Barbara. "The Taste of Henry James," *Studi Americani* III (1957), 171-187.

JAMES, HENRY, Continued

Melchiori, Giorgio. "Un Personaggio Di Henry James," *Studi Americani* II (1956), 179-194.

Michaud, Régis. "Henry James, Edith Wharton, William Dean Howells and American Society on Parade," *The American Novel To-Day*, 47-70.

----------. "Un Splendide Exile: Henry James," *Panorama de la Littérature Américaine Contemporaine*, 115-120.

Morley, Robert. "Meetings with Some Men of Letters," *Queen's Quarterly* XXXIX (Feb 1932), 67-71.

Morris, Lloyd. *Postscript to Yesterday*, 89-96.

Morris, Wright. *The Territory Ahead*, 93-112; 187-214.

Murray, Donald M. "Henry James and the English Reviewers, 1882-1890," *American Literature* XXIV (Mar 1952), 1-20.

----------. "James and Whistler at the Grosvenor Gallery," *American Quarterly* IV (Spring 1952), 49-65.

Neff, John C. "Henry James the Reporter," *New Mexico Quarterly* VIII (Feb 1938), 9-14.

O'Connor, Frank. "Transition: Henry James," *The Mirror in the Roadway*.

Pacey, W. C. D. "Henry James and His French Contemporaries," *American Literature* XIII (Nov 1941), 240-256.

Parrington, Vernon Louis. "Henry James and the Nostalgia of Culture," *The Question of Henry James*, 128-130.

Phelps, William Lyon. "Henry James," *Yale Review* V (Jul 1916), 783-797.

Porter, Katherine Anne. *The Days Before*, 3-22; *Kenyon Review* V (Autumn 1943), 481-494.

Pound, Ezra. "Henry James," *Literary Essays*, 295-338.

Quinn, Arthur Hobson. "Henry James and the Fiction of International Relations," *American Fiction*, 279-304.

Rahv, Philip. "Attitudes Toward Henry James," *The Question of Henry James*, 273-280.

----------. "The Heiress of All the Ages," *Partisan Review* X (May-Jun 1943), 227-247.

Raleigh, John Henry. "Henry James: The Poetics of Empiricism," *PMLA* LXVI (Mar 1951), 107-123.

Read, Herbert. "Henry James," *Collected Essays*, 354-366.

"Religion and Henry James," *Notes and Queries* 184 (8 May 1943), 271-272.

JAMES, HENRY, Continued

Richardson, Lyon N. "Henry James—Introduction," *Henry James,* ix-xc.
Roberts, Morris. "Henry James's Final Period," *Yale Review* XXXVII (Sept 1947), 60-67.
Roditi, Edouard. "Oscar Wilde and Henry James," *University of Kansas City Review* XV (Autumn 1948), 52-56.
Rogers, Robert. "The Beast in Henry James," *American Imago* XIII (Winter 1956), 427-453.
Rosenbaum, S. P. "Letters to the Pell-Clarkes from Their 'Old Cousin and Friend' Henry James," *American Literature* XXXI (Mar 1959), 46-58.
Rosenzweig, Saul. "The Ghost of Henry James," *Partisan Review* XI (Fall 1944), 436-455.
Rourke, Constance. "The American," *American Humor,* 235-265; (Doubleday Anchor) 186-208.
Rouse, H. Blair. "Charles Dickens and Henry James: Two Approaches to the Art of Fiction," *Nineteenth-Century Fiction* V (Sept 1950), 151-157.
Rypins, Harold L. "Henry James in Harley Street," *American Literature* XXIV (Jan 1953), 481-492.
Sackville-West, Edward. "James: An American in Europe," *Saturday Review of Literature* XXXIV (Jan 20, 1951), 24-25.
──────. "The Personality of Henry James," *Inclinations,* 42-58.
Scott, Arthur L. "A Protest against the James Vogue," *College English* XIII (Jan 1952), 194-201.
Seznac, Jean. "Lettres de Tourguéneff à Henry James," *Comparative Literature* I (Summer 1959), 193-209.
Sherman, Stuart P. "The Aesthetic Idealism of Henry James," *On Contemporary Literature,* 226-255; *The Question of Henry James,* 70-91.
Short, R. W. "Henry James's World of Images," *PMLA* LXVIII (Sept 1958), 943-960.
──────. "The Sentence Structure of Henry James," *American Literature* XVIII (May 1946), 71-88.
──────. "Some Critical Terms of Henry James," *PMLA* (Sept 1950), 667-680.
Smith, Bernard. *Forces in American Criticism,* 202-220.

JAMES, HENRY, Continued

Smith, S. Stephenson. "The Psychological Novel," *The Craft of the Critic*, 185-190.

Snell, George. "Henry James: Life Refracted by Temperament," *The Shapers of American Fiction*, 129-140.

Snow, Lotus. "The Pattern of Innocence through Experience in the Characters of Henry James," *University of Toronto Quarterly* XXII (Apr 1953), 230-236.

Spiller, Robert E. "Seer of the Gem-like Flame," *Saturday Review* XXXVI (May 9, 1953), 13-14.

Stafford, William T. "Henry James the American: Some Views of His Contemporaries," *Twentieth Century Literature* I (Jul 1955), 69-76.

————. "James Examines Shakespeare: Notes on the Nature of Genius," *PMLA* LXXIII (Mar 1958), 123-128.

Stevens, George. "The Return of Henry James: Exploring the Relationship Between James and His Audience," *Saturday Review of Literature* XXVIII (Mar 3, 1945), 7-8; 30; 32-33.

Stevenson, Elizabeth. *The Crooked Corridor*.

Stewart, Randall. "The Moral Aspect of Henry James's 'International Situation,'" *University of Kansas City Review* X (Winter 1943), 109-112.

Stovall, Floyd. *American Idealism*, 121-123.

Swan, Michael. *Henry James* [1950].

————. *Henry James* [1952].

Tintner, Adeline R. "The Spoils of Henry James," *PMLA* LXI (1946), 239-251.

Troy, William. "The Altar of Henry James," *The Question of Henry James*, 267-272.

Underwood, John Curtis. "Henry James: Expatriate," *Literature and Insurgency*, 41-86.

Van Doren, Carl. "Henry James," *The American Novel 1789-1939*, 163-189.

Vivas, Eliseo. "Henry and William (Two Notes)," *Kenyon Review* V (Autumn 1943), 580-594.

Volpe, Edmond L. "The Childhood of James's American Innocents," *Modern Language Notes* LXXI (May 1956), 345-347.

————. "James's Theory of Sex in Fiction," *Nineteenth-Century Fiction* XIII (Jun 1958), 36-45.

JAMES, HENRY, Continued

──────────. "The Prefaces of George Sand and Henry James," *Modern Language Notes* LXX (Feb 1955), 107-108.
Wagenknecht, Edward. "The American as Artist: Henry James," *Cavalcade of the American Novel*, 145-165.
──────────. "Our Contemporary Henry James," *College English* X (Dec 1948), 123-132.
Ward, J. A. "Social Criticism in James's London Fiction," *Arizona Quarterly* XV (Spring 1959), 36-48.
Warren, Austin. "Henry James: Symbolic Imagery in the Later Novels," *Rage for Order*, 142-161.
──────────. "Myth and Dialectic in the Later Novels," *Kenyon Review* V (Autumn 1943), 551-568.
Weber, Carl J. "Henry James and His Tiger-Cat," *PMLA* LXVIII (Sept 1953), 672-687.
──────────. "Henry James and Thomas Hardy," *Mark Twain Quarterly* V (Spring 1943), 3-4.
Wegelin, Christof. *The Image of Europe in Henry James.*
Wellek, René. "Henry James's Literary Theory and Criticism," *American Literature* XXX (Nov 1958), 293-321.
West, Rebecca. *Henry James.*
Williams, Blanche Colton. "The Depth of Henry James," *Mark Twain Quarterly* V (Spring 1943), 5-6.
Wilson, Edmund. "The Ambiguity of Henry James," *The Triple Thinkers*, 122-164; *The Question of Henry James*, 160-190.
──────────. "The Last Phase of Henry James," *Partisan Review* IV (Feb 1938), 3-8.
──────────. "The Pilgrimage of Henry James," *The Shores of Light*, 217-228.
Winters, Yvor. "Henry James and the Relation of Morals to Manners," *American Review* IX (Oct 1937), 482-503.
──────────. "Maule's Well or Henry James and the Relation of Morals to Manners," *In Defense of Reason*, 300-343; *Maule's Curse*, 169-216.
Wright, Nathalia. "Henry James and the Greenough Data," *American Quarterly* X (Fall 1958), 338-343.
Wyatt, Edith. "Henry James: An Impression," *North American Review* 203 (Apr 1916), 592-599; *Great Companions*, 83-99.
Zabel, Morton Dauwen. "Henry James: The Act of Life," *Craft and Character*, 114-143.

JAMES, HENRY, Continued

――――. "The Poetics of Henry James," *The Question of Henry James*, 212-217.

BIBLIOGRAPHY

Beebe, Maurice and William T. Stafford. "Criticism of Henry James: A Selected Checklist with an Index to Studies of Separate Works," *Modern Fiction Studies* III (Spring 1957), 73-96.

Critiques and Essays on Modern Fiction, 592-599.

Dunbar, Viola R. "Addenda to 'Biographical and Critical Studies of Henry James, 1941-1948,' *American Literature* XX, 424-435 (January, 1949)," *American Literature* XXII (Mar 1950), 56-61.

Hamilton, Eunice C. "Biographical and Critical Studies of Henry James, 1941-1948," *American Literature* XX (Jan 1949), 424-435.

Hoffman, Charles G. *The Short Novels of Henry James*, 134-139.

Kelley, Cornelia Pulsifer. *The Early Development of Henry James*, 301-304.

LeClair, Robert C. *Young Henry James*, 455-462.

Nowell-Smith, Simon. *The Legend of the Master*, 172-176.

Richardson, Lyon N. *Henry James*, xci-cxi; *The Question of Henry James*, 281-297.

Spiller, Robert E. "Henry James," *Eight American Authors*, 364-418.

JEWETT, SARAH ORNE

THE TORY LOVER

Bishop, Ferman. "Henry James Criticizes *The Tory Lover*," *American Literature* XXVII (May 1955), 262-264.

GENERAL

Bishop, Ferman. *The Sense of the Past in Sarah Orne Jewett*.

Cather, Willa. "Miss Jewett," *Not Under Forty*, 76-95.

Chapman, Edward M. "The New England of Sarah Orne Jewett," *Yale Review* III (Oct 1913), 157-172.

Cunliffe, Marcus. "Minor Key," *The Literature of the United States*, 177-179.

Matthiessen, Francis Otto. *Sarah Orne Jewett*.

Wagenknecht, Edward. "Novelists of the 'Eighties: [Miss Jewett]," *Cavalcade of the American Novel*, 171-173.

JEWETT, SARAH ORNE, Continued
BIBLIOGRAPHY
Weber, Clara and Carl J. *A Bibliography of the Published Writings of Sarah Orne Jewett.*

JOHNSTON, MARY
GENERAL
Hubbell, Jay B. "Cavalier and Indentured Servant in Virginia Fiction," *South Atlantic Quarterly* XXVI (Jan 1927), 22-39.
Wagenknecht, Edward. "Some Southern Novelists of the 'Nineties and After: Allotropes and Mary Johnston," *Cavalcade of the American Novel,* 197-203.

JONES, JAMES
FROM HERE TO ETERNITY
Adams, Richard P. "A Second Look at *From Here to Eternity,*" *College English* XVII (Jan 1956), 205-210.
Breit, Harvey. *The Writer Observed,* 178-181.
Burress, Lee A., Jr. "James Jones on Folklore and Ballad." *College English* XXI (Dec 1959), 161-165.
Fiedler, Leslie. "James Jones' Dead-End Young Werther: The Bum as American Culture Hero," *Commentary* XII (Sept 1951), 252-255; *An End to Innocence,* 183-190.
Geismar, Maxwell. *American Moderns,* 225-238.
Griffith, Ben W., Jr. "Rear Rank Robin Hood: James Jones's Folk Hero," *Georgia Review* X (Spring 1956), 41-46.
Leslie, Warren. "Never Had It So Bad," *Southwest Review* XXXVI (Summer 1951), xxiii, 241-244.
Prescott, Orville. *In My Opinion,* 159-161.
THE PISTOL
Hicks, Granville. "The Shorter and Better Jones," *Saturday Review* XLII (Jan 10, 1959), 12.
SOME CAME RUNNING
Childs, Barney. "*Some Came Running,*" *Arizona Quarterly* XIV (Spring 1958), 86-88.
GENERAL
Fuller, Edmund. "The Female Zombies," *Man in Modern Fiction,* 94-118.

JUDD, SYLVESTER

GENERAL
Brockway, Philip Judd. "Sylvester Judd: Novelist of Transcendentalism," *New England Quarterly* XIII (Dec 1940), 654-677.

KANTOR, MacKINLAY

ANDERSONVILLE
Hesseltine, William B. "Andersonville Revisited," *Georgia Review* X (Spring 1956), 92-100.

KENNEDY, JOHN PENDLETON

HORSE-SHOE ROBINSON
Ellison, Rhoda Coleman. "An Interview with Horse-Shoe Robinson," *American Literature* XXXI (Nov 1959), 329-332.

Gwathney, Edward M. *John Pendleton Kennedy*, 106-120.

Leisy, Ernest E. Introduction, *Horse-Shoe Robinson* (New York, 1937), pp. xxxii.

Moore, John Robert. "Kennedy's Horse-Shoe Robinson: Fact or Fiction?" *American Literature* IV (May 1932), 160-166.

ROB OF THE BOWL
Gwathney, Edward M. *John Pendleton Kennedy*, 120-126.

GENERAL
Cowie, Alexander. "Contemporaries and Immediate Followers of Cooper, II: John Pendleton Kennedy (1795-1870)," *The Rise of the American Novel*, 258-270.

Gwathney, Edward M. *John Pendleton Kennedy*.

Hubbell, Jay B. *The South in American Literature*, 481-495.

Quinn, Arthur Hobson. "The Romance of History and the Frontier," *The Literature of the American People*, 239.

Uhler, John Earle. "Kennedy's Novels and His Posthumous Works," *American Literature* III (Jan 1932), 471-479.

KEROUAC, JACK

MAGGIE CASSIDY
Ciardi, John. "In Loving Memory of Myself," *Saturday Review* XLII (Jul 25, 1959), 22-23.

KEROUAC, JACK, Continued
DR. SAX
Conrad, Barnaby. "Barefoot Boy with Dreams of Zen," *Saturday Review* XLII (May 2, 1959), 23-24.
ON THE ROAD
Fuller, Edmund. *Man in Modern Fiction,* 148-163.
Podhoretz, Norman. "The Know-Nothing Bohemians," *Partisan Review* XXV (Spring 1958), 305-318.
THE SUBTERRANEANS
Podhoretz, Norman. "The Know-Nothing Bohemians," *Partisan Review* XXV (Spring 1958), 305-318.
GENERAL
Kerouac, Jack. "Belief & Technique for Modern Prose," *Evergreen Review* II (Spring 1959), 57.
Kerouac, Jack. "Essentials of Spontaneous Prose," *Evergreen Review* II, No. 6 (Summer 1958), 72-73.

KIRKLAND, JOSEPH
THE CAPTAIN OF COMPANY K
Holaday, Clayton A. "Kirkland's *Captain of Company K*: A Twice-Told Tale," *American Literature* XXV (Mar 1953), 62-68.
ZURY: THE MEANEST MAN IN SPRING COUNTY
Flanagan, John T. Introduction, *Zury: The Meanest Man in Spring County* (Urbana, Ill., 1956).
LaBudde, Kenneth J. "A Note on the Text of Joseph Kirkland's *Zury,*" *American Literature* XX (Jan 1949), 452-455.
Lease, Benjamin. "Realism and Joseph Kirkland's *Zury,*" *American Literature* XXIII (Jan 1952), 464-466.
GENERAL
Åhnebrink, Lars. "Realism in the Middle West: Edward Eggleston, Edgar Watson Howe, and Joseph Kirkland," *The Beginnings of Naturalism in American Fiction,* 50-59.
Flanagan, John T. "Joseph Kirkland, Pioneer Realist," *American Literature* XI (Nov 1939), 273-284.
Henson, Clyde E. "Joseph Kirkland's Influence on Hamlin Garland," *American Literature* XXIII (Jan 1952), 458-463.

KYNE, PETER B.

GENERAL
Bode, Carl. "Cappy Ricks and the Monk in the Garden," *PMLA* LXIV (Mar 1949), 59-69.

LA FARGE, OLIVER

GENERAL
Allen, Charles. "The Fiction of Oliver La Farge," *Arizona Quarterly* I (Winter 1945), 74-81.

LANGLEY, ADRIA LOCKE

A LION IN THE STREETS
Rubin, Louis D., Jr. "All the King's Meanings," *Georgia Review* VIII (Winter 1954), 422-434.

LANIER, SIDNEY

TIGER-LILIES
Starke, Aubrey Harrison. *Sidney Lanier*, 90-107.
Wright, Nathalia. "The East Tennessee Background of Sidney Lanier's *Tiger-Lilies*," *American Literature* XIX (May 1947), 127-138.
GENERAL
Hubbell, Jay B. *The South in American Literature*, 758-777.

LEA, TOM

THE BRAVE BULLS
Bromfield, Louis. "Triumphs in the Arena," *Saturday Review of Literature* XXXII (Apr 23, 1949), 10-12.

LEWIS, JANET

GENERAL
Swallow, Alan. "The Mavericks," *Critique* II (Winter 1959), 77-79.

LEWIS, SINCLAIR

ANN VICKERS
DeVoto, Bernard. "Sinclair Lewis," *Saturday Review of Literature* IX (Jan 28, 1933), 397-398.

ARROWSMITH
Richardson, Lyon N. *"Arrowsmith:* Genesis, Development, Versions," *American Literature* XXVII (May 1955), 225-244.

Smith, Harrison (ed.). *From Main Street to Stockholm*, 121-189.

BABBITT
Bruccoli, Matthew J. "Textual Variants in Sinclair Lewis's *Babbitt,*" *Studies in Bibliography* XI (1958), 263-268.

Hoffman, Frederick J. *The Twenties*, 364-370.

Smith, Harrison (ed.). *From Main Street to Stockholm*, 71-117.

CASS TIMBERLANE
Colum, Mary M. "Sinclair Lewis's New Thesis Novel," *Saturday Review of Literature* XXVIII (Oct 6, 1945), 8-9.

DODSWORTH
Canby, Henry Seidel. "Sex War," *Saturday Review of Literature* V (Mar 30, 1929), 821-822.

"Dodsworth," *American Writing Today*, 368-370.

Fadiman, Clifton. *Party of One*, 132-135.

Smith, Harrison (ed.). *From Main Street to Stockholm*, 249-302.

ELMER GANTRY
Canby, Henry Seidel. "Vicious Ignorance," *Saturday Review of Literature* III (Mar 12, 1927), 637; 640.

Davies, Horton. *A Mirror of the Ministry in Modern Novels*, 28-35.

Smith, Harrison (ed.). *From Main Street to Stockholm*, 193-245.

West, Rebecca. *The Strange Necessity*, 295-308.

GIDEON PLANISH
Jones, Howard Mumford. "Sinclair Lewis and the Do-Gooders," *Saturday Review of Literature* XXVI (Apr 24, 1943), 6.

THE GOD-SEEKER
Davies, Horton. *A Mirror of the Ministry in Modern Novels*, 35-40.

IT CAN'T HAPPEN HERE
Blotner, Joseph L. *The Political Novel*, 14-15.

LEWIS, SINCLAIR, Continued

KINGSBLOOD ROYAL
Fadiman, Clifton. " 'The American Problem,' " *Saturday Review of Literature* XXX (May 24, 1947), 9-10.

MAIN STREET
Cousins, Norman. " 'Main Street' Comes into the Home," *Saturday Review* XXXVIII (Dec 17, 1955), 22.

Gannett, Lewis. "Looking Backwards—Sinclair Lewis: 'Main Street,' " *Saturday Review of Literature* XXXII (Aug 6, 1949), 31-32.

Smith, Harrison, (ed.). *From Main Street to Stockholm*, 3-67.

THE MAN WHO KNEW COOLIDGE
Canby, Henry Seidel. "Schmaltz, Babbit & Co.," *Saturday Review of Literature* IV (Mar 24, 1928), 697-698.

Richardson, Lyon N. "Revision in Sinclair Lewis's *The Man Who Knew Coolidge*," *American Literature* XXV (Nov 1953), 326-333.

OUR MR. WRENN
Smith, Harrison. Introduction, *Our Mr. Wrenn* (New York, 1951), pp. x.

WORK OF ART
Canby, Henry Seidel. "Sinclair Lewis's Art of Work," *Saturday Review of Literature* X (Feb 10, 1934), 465; 473.

GENERAL
Adams, J. Donald. "Main Street and the Dust Bowl," *The Shape of Books to Come*, 131-143.

Ames, Russell. "Sinclair Lewis Again," *College English* X (Nov 1948), 77-80.

Anderson, Carl. *The Swedish Acceptance of American Literature*, 45-63; 84-102.

Austin, Allen. "An Interview with Sinclair Lewis," *University of Kansas City Review* XXIV (Mar 1958), 199-210.

Baldwin, Charles C. "Sinclair Lewis," *The Men Who Make Our Novels*, 321-334.

Beach, Joseph Warren. *The Twentieth Century Novel*, 263-266.

Beck, Warren. "How Good Is Sinclair Lewis?" *College English* IX (Jan 1948), 173-180.

Becker, George J. "Sinclair Lewis: Apostle to the Philistines," *American Scholar* XX (Autumn 1952), 423-432.

LEWIS, SINCLAIR, Continued

Benét, William Rose. "The Earlier Lewis," *Saturday Review of Literature* X (Jan 20, 1934), 421-422.

Boynton, Percy H. "Sinclair Lewis," *America in Contemporary Fiction*, 164-184.

_____. "Sinclair Lewis," *More Contemporary Americans*, 179-198.

Breasted, Charles. "The 'Sauk-Centricities' of Sinclair Lewis," *Saturday Review* XXXVII (Aug 14, 1954), 7-8; 33-36.

Brown, Deming. "Sinclair Lewis: The Russian View," *American Literature* XXV (Mar 1953), 1-12.

Cabell, James Branch. "Goblins in Winnemac," *Some of Us*, 61-73.

_____. "A Note as to Sinclair Lewis," *American Mercury* XX (Aug 1930), 394-397.

Canby, Henry Seidel. "Sinclair Lewis," *Saturday Review of Literature* VII (Nov 22, 1930), 357.

Cantwell, Robert. "Sinclair Lewis," *After the Genteel Tradition*, 112-126.

Carpenter, Frederic I. "Sinclair Lewis and the Fortress of Reality," *College English* XVI (Apr 1955), 416-423.

Edgar, Pelham. "The Way of Irony and Satire," *The Art of the Novel*, 293-300.

Feinberg, Leonard. *Sinclair Lewis as a Satirist*.

Flanagan, John T. "A Long Way to Gopher Prairie: Sinclair Lewis's Apprenticeship," *Southwest Review* XXXII (Autumn 1947), 403-413.

Geismar, Maxwell. "Diarist of the Middle-Class," *Saturday Review of Literature* XXX (Nov 1, 1947), 9-10; 42-45.

_____. "Sinclair Lewis," *American Moderns*, 107-118.

_____. "Sinclair Lewis: The Cosmic Bourjoyce," *The Last of the Provincials*, 69-150.

Grebstein, Sheldon. "Sinclair Lewis and the Nobel Prize," *Western Humanities Review* XIII (Spring 1959), 163-171.

_____. "Sinclair Lewis's Unwritten Novel," *Philological Quarterly* XXXVII (Oct 1958), 400-409.

_____. "The Education of A Rebel: Sinclair Lewis at Yale," *New England Quarterly* XXVIII (Sept 1955), 372-382.

Gurko, Leo and Miriam Gurko. "The Two Main Streets of Sinclair Lewis," *College English* IV (Feb 1943), 288-292.

LEWIS, SINCLAIR, Continued

Harrison, Oliver. *Sinclair Lewis*.
Hartwick, Harry. "The Village Virus," *The Foreground of American Fiction*, 250-281.
Hatcher, Harlan. "Sinclair Lewis," *Creating the Modern American Novel*, 109-126.
Hicks, Granville. *The Great Tradition*, 230-236.
Hollis, C. Carroll. "Sinclair Lewis: Reviver of Character," *Fifty Years of the American Novel*, 89-106.
Horton, Thomas D. "Sinclair Lewis: The Symbol of an Era," *North American Review* 248 (Winter 1939-40), 374-393.
Karlfeldt, Erik Axel. "Sinclair Lewis and the Nobel Prize," *Saturday Review of Literature* VII (Jan 10, 1931), 524-525.
────── and Sinclair Lewis. *Why Sinclair Lewis Got the Nobel Prize*.
Kazin, Alfred. "The New Realism: Sherwood Anderson and Sinclair Lewis," *On Native Grounds*, 217-226.
Lewis, Grace Hegger. "I Wrote A Biography," *Virginia Quarterly Review* XXIV (Winter 1958), 18-25.
──────. *With Love from Gracie*.
Lippmann, Walter. *Men of Destiny*, 71-92.
Loiseau, J. "La Crusade de Sinclair Lewis," *Etudes Anglaises* II (Apr-Jun 1938), 120-133.
Macafee, Helen. "Some Novelists in Mid-Stream," *Yale Review* XV (Jan 1926), 338-340.
Michaud, Régis. "Sinclair Lewis," *Panorama de la Littérature Américaine Contemporaine*, 174-177.
──────. "Sinclair Lewis and the Average Man," *The American Novel To-Day*, 128-153.
Miller, Perry. "The Incorruptible Sinclair Lewis," *Atlantic Monthly* CLXXXVII (Apr 1951), 30-34.
Morris, Lloyd. *Postscript to Yesterday*, 134-142.
──────. "Sinclair Lewis—His Critics and the Public," *North American Review* 245 (Summer 1938), 381-390.
Parrington, Vernon Louis. *Sinclair Lewis*.
Prescott, Orville. *In My Opinion*, 50-58.
Quinn, Arthur Hobson. "Critics and Satirists—The Radicals," *American Fiction*, 661-669.
Schorer, Mark. "Sinclair Lewis and the Method of Half-Truths," *English Institute Essays* (1955), 117-144.

LEWIS, SINCLAIR, Continued

――――――. "Two Houses, Two Ways: The Florentine Villas of Lewis and Lawrence, Respectively," *New Directions* 4 (1953), 136-154.

Sherman, Stuart P. "The Significance of Sinclair Lewis," *Points of View*, 189-226.

Smith, Harrison. "Sinclair Lewis: Remembrance of the Past," *Saturday Review of Literature* XXXIV (Jan 27, 1951), 7-8; 36-38.

Stovall, Floyd. *American Idealism*, 143-147.

Van Doren, Carl. *Contemporary American Novelists*, 161-164.

――――――. *Sinclair Lewis*.

――――――. "Sinclair Lewis," *The American Novel 1789-1939*, 303-314.

von Hibler, Leo. "Sinclair Lewis und die Amerkanische Wirtschaft," *Anglia* LIX (1935), 448-460.

Wagenknecht, Edward. "Sinclair Lewis and the Babbitt Warren," *Cavalcade of the American Novel*, 354-367.

Walker, Franklin. "Jack London's Use of Sinclair Lewis Plots, Together with a Printing of Three of the Plots," *Huntington Library Quarterly* XVII (Nov 1953), 59-74.

Warren, Dale. "Notes on a Genius," *Harper's Magazine* CCVIII (Jan 1954), 61-69.

Waterman, Margaret. "Sinclair Lewis as Teacher," *College English* XIII (Nov 1951), 87-90.

Whicher, George F. "Respectability Defined," *The Literature of the American People*, 854-855.

Whipple, T. K. "Sinclair Lewis," *Spokesmen*, 208-229.

Woodward, W. E. "Sinclair Lewis Gets the Job," *Saturday Review of Literature* XXX (Nov 1, 1947), 10-11.

BIBLIOGRAPHY

Van Doren, Carl. *Sinclair Lewis*, 175-184.

LEWISOHN, LUDWIG

THE CASE OF MR. CRUMP

Bates, Ernest Sutherland. "Lewisohn into Crump," *American Mercury* XXXI (Apr 1934), 441-450.

LEWISOHN, LUDWIG, Continued

GENERAL

Bates, Ernest Sutherland. "Lewisohn into Crump," *American Mercury* XXXI (Apr 1934), 441-450.

Cargill, Oscar. "The Freudians," *Intellectual America*, 727-735.

LIPPARD, GEORGE

GENERAL

Cowie, Alexander. "The Mixed Thirties: George Lippard (1882-1854)," *The Rise of the American Novel*, 319-326.

LOCKE, DAVID

GENERAL

Jones, Joseph. "Petroleum V. Nasby Tries the Novel: David Ross Locke's Excursions into Political and Social Fiction," *Texas Studies in English* XXX (1951), 202-218.

LOCKRIDGE, ROSS, JR.

RAINTREE COUNTY

Blotner, Joseph L. "Raintree County Revisited," *Western Humanities Review* X (Winter 1955-1956), 57-64.

Tindall, William York. "Many-leveled Fiction: Virginia Woolf to Ross Lockridge," *College English* X (Nov 1948), 65-71.

GENERAL

Kutner, Nanette. "Ross Lockridge, Jr.—Escape from Main Street," *Saturday Review of Literature* XXXI (Jun 12, 1948), 6-7; 31.

LONDON, JACK

THE CALL OF THE WILD

Mitchell, Theodore C. Introduction, *The Call of the Wild* (New York, 1917; 1947).

Mott, Frank Luther. Introduction, *The Call of the Wild* (New York, 1926, pp. xxxv.

THE IRON HEEL

LONDON, JACK, Continued

Baskett, Sam S. "A Source for *The Iron Heel*," *American Literature* XXVII (May 1955), 268-270.
Blotner, Joseph L. *The Political Novel*, 37-38.
Lerner, Max. Introduction, *The Iron Heel* (New York, 1957).
JOHN BARLEYCORN
Baskett, Sam S. "Jack London on the Oakland Waterfront," *American Literature* XXVII (Nov 1955), 363-371.
Noel, Joseph. *Footloose in Arcadia*, 275-281.
MARTIN EDEN
Baskett, Sam S. Introduction, *Martin Eden* (New York, 1956), pp. xxvi.
THE ROAD
Mullin, Glen. Introduction, *The Road* (New York, 1926).
THE SEA WOLF
Noel, Joseph. *Footloose in Arcadia*, 232-241.
GENERAL
Anderson, Carl. "Swedish Criticism Before 1920: The Reception of Jack London and Upton Sinclair," *The Swedish Acceptance of American Literature*, 33-44.
Austin, Mary. "George Sterling at Carmel," *American Mercury* XI (May 1927), 68-70.
Bamford, Georgia L. *The Mystery of Jack London*.
Baskett, Sam S. "Jack London's Heart of Darkness," *American Quarterly* X (Spring 1958), 66-77.
Bosworth, Hobart. "My Jack London," *Mark Twain Quarterly* V (Summer 1942), 2-5.
Brooks, Van Wyck. "Frank Norris and Jack London," *The Confident Years*, 217-238.
Friedland, L. S. "Jack London as Titan," *Dial* LXII (Jan 25, 1917), 49-51.
Geismar, Maxwell. "Jack London: The Short Cut," *Rebels and Ancestors*, 139-216.
Hartwick, Harry. "Men with the Bark On," *The Foreground of American Fiction*, 67-84.
Hicks, Granville. *The Great Tradition*, 186-196.
Kazin, Alfred. "Progressivism: The Superman and the Muckrake," *On Native Grounds*, 111-116.
London, Charmian. *The Book of Jack London*.
London, Joan. *Jack London and His Times*.

LONDON, JACK, Continued

Lynn, Kenneth S. "Jack London: The Brain Merchant," *The Dream of Success,* 75-118.

Mencken, H. L. *Prejudices,* 236-239.

Mills, Gordon. "Jack London's Quest for Salvation," *American Quarterly* VII (Spring 1955), 3-14.

———. "The Symbolic Wilderness: James Fenimore Cooper and Jack London," *Nineteenth-Century Fiction* XIII (Mar 1959), 329-340.

Morris, Lloyd. *Postscript to Yesterday,* 115-121.

Mumford, Lewis. *The Golden Day,* 246-250; (Beacon Press edition) 125-127.

Noel, Joseph. *Footloose in Arcadia.*

Pattee, Fred Lewis. "The Prophet of the Last Frontier," *Sidelights on American Literature,* 98-160.

Quinn, Arthur Hobson. "The Journalists," *American Fiction,* 541-545.

Stone, Irving. *Sailor on Horseback.*

Stovall, Floyd. *American Idealism,* 129-134.

Wagenknecht, Edward. "Towards Naturalism: Jack London and the Cult of Primitive Sensation," *Cavalcade of the American Novel,* 222-229.

Walcutt, Charles Child. "Jack London: Blond Beasts and Supermen," *American Literary Naturalism,* 87-113.

Walker, Franklin. "Jack London's Use of Sinclair Lewis Plots, Together with a Printing of Three of the Plots," *Huntington Library Quarterly* XVII (Nov 1953), 59-74.

Whicher, George F. "Respectability Defied," *The Literature of the American People,* 846-847.

Whipple, T. K. "Jack London—Wonder Boy," *Saturday Review of Literature* XVIII (Sept 24, 1938), 3-4; 16-17.

BIBLIOGRAPHY

Chomet, Otto. "Jack London: Works, Reviews, and Criticism Published in German," *Bulletin of Bibliography* XIX (Jan-Apr, 1949), 211-215; (May-Aug 1949), 239-240.

Foner, Philip S. (ed.). *Jack London, American Rebel,* 531-533.

LONGFELLOW, HENRY W.
GENERAL
Cowie, Alexander. "The Mixed Thirties: Henry W. Longfellow 1807-1882," *The Rise of the American Novel*, 309-318.

LOOMIS, EDWARD
GENERAL
Swallow, Alan. "The Mavericks," *Critique* II (Winter 1959), 90-92.

LYTLE, ANDREW
THE VELVET HORN
Ghiselin, Brewster. "Trial of Light," *Sewanee Review* LXV (Oct-Dec 1957), 657-665.
Macauley, Robie. "Big Novel," *Kenyon Review* XIX (Autumn 1957), 644-646.

MACAULEY, ROBIE
THE DISGUISES OF LOVE
Hoffman, Frederick J. "The Secret Feud," *Saturday Review* XXXV (Nov 22, 1952), 17-18.
Hyman, Stanley Edgar. "Some Notes on the Albertine Strategy," *Hudson Review* VI (Autumn 1953), 417-422; "Communications," *Hudson Review* VI (Winter 1954), 634-636.
Rosenfeld, Isaac. "*Liebestod*," *Kenyon Review* XV (Winter 1953), 147-150.

MAILER, NORMAN
BARBARY SHORE
Blotner, Joseph L. *The Political Novel*, 17.
THE DEER PARK
Alpert, Hollis. "Hollywood Saturnalia," *Saturday Review* XXXVIII (Oct 15, 1955), 15.
Fuller, Edmund. *Man in Modern Fiction*, 101-105.
THE NAKED AND THE DEAD
Aldridge, John W. *After the Lost Generation*, 133-156.
Geismar, Maxwell. "Nightmare on Anopopei," *Saturday Review of Literature* XXXI (May 8, 1948), 10-11.
Healey, Robert C. *Fifty Years of the American Novel*, 257-264.

MAILER, NORMAN, Continued

GENERAL

Breit, Harvey. *The Writer Observed,* 199-201.

Geismar, Maxwell. "Norman Mailer: The Bohemian of the National Letters," *American Moderns,* 171-179.

Mailer, Norman. "Hip, Hell, and the Navigator," *Western Review* XXIII (Winter 1959), 101-109.

Prescott, Orville. *In My Opinion,* 155-159.

MANFRED, FREDERICK F.

GENERAL

Milton, John R. "Frederick Feikema Manfred," *Western Review* XXII (Spring 1958), 181-199.

──────. "Voice from Siouxland: Frederick Feikema Manfred." *College English* XIX (Dec 1957), 104-111.

Swallow, Alan. "The Mavericks," *Critique* II (Winter 1959), 88-92.

"West of the Mississippi: An Interview with Frederick Manfred," *Critique* II (Winter 1959), 35-56.

MARCH, WILLIAM

THE BAD SEED

Fuller, Edmund. *Man in Modern Fiction,* 25-29.

GENERAL

Cooke, Alistair. Introduction, *A William March Omnibus* (New York and Toronto, 1956).

Crowder, Richard. "The Novels of William March," *University of Kansas City Review* XV (Winter 1948), 111-129.

Tallant, Robert. "Poor Pilgrim, Poor Stranger," *Saturday Review* XXXVII (Jul 17, 1954), 9; 33-34.

MARQUAND, JOHN PHILLIPS

B. F.'s DAUGHTER

Woodburn, John. "Mr. Marquand's Sound Wine," *Saturday Review of Literature* XXIX (Nov 2, 1946), 13.

H. M. PULHAM, ESQUIRE

Jones, Howard Mumford. "Think Fast, Mr. Marquand," *Saturday Review of Literature* XXIII (Feb 22, 1941), 5.

MARQUAND, JOHN PHILLIPS, Continued

MELVILLE GOODWIN, USA

Geismar, Maxwell. "The Struggle with Authority," *Saturday Review of Literature* XXXIV (Sept 29, 1951), 11.

SINCERELY, WILLIS WAYDE

Barrett, William. "Soul for Sale," *Saturday Review* XXXVIII (Feb 26, 1955), 12.

SO LITTLE TIME

Redman, Ben Ray. "J. P. Marquand's Literary Wizardry," *Saturday Review of Literature* XXVI (Aug 21, 1943), 4-5.

GENERAL

Beach, Joseph Warren. "John P. Marquand: The Moonlight of Culture," *American Fiction*, 253-270.

Bisbee, Thayer Donovan. "J. P. Marquand's Tales of Two Cities," *Saturday Review of Literature* XIV (Jul 5, 1941), 11; 14.

Brady, Charles A. "John Phillips Marquand: Martini-Age Victorian," *Fifty Years of the American Novel*, 107-134.

Breit, Harvey. *The Writer Observed*, 47-51.

Brickell, Herschel. "Miss Glasgow and Mr. Marquand," *Virginia Quarterly Review* XVII (Summer 1941), 405-417.

Fiske, Constance M. "John P. Marquand: 'Something of an Apley Himself,' " *Saturday Review of Literature* XIX (Dec 10, 1938), 10-11.

Flick, Nathan. "Marquand's Vanishing American Aristocracy: Good Manners and the Good Life," *Commentary* X (May 1950), 435-441.

Geismar, Maxwell. "J. P. Marquand," *American Moderns*, 156-167.

Gurko, Leo. *The Angry Decade*, 208-212.

——————. "The High-Level Formula of J. P. Marquand," *American Scholar* XX (Autumn 1952), 443-453.

Hamburger, Philip, *J. P. Marquand Esquire.*

Hatcher, Harlan. "John Phillips Marquand," *College English* I (Nov 1939), 107-118.

Hicks, Granville. "Marquand of Newburyport," *Harper's Magazine* CC (Apr 1950), 101-108.

Marquand, John P. "Apley, Wickford Point, and Pulham: My Early Struggles," *Atlantic Monthly* CXCVIII (1956), 71-74.

Oppenheimer, Franz M. "Lament for Unbought Grace," *Antioch Review* XVIII (Mar 1958), 41-61.

MARQUAND, JOHN PHILLIPS, Continued

Prescott, Orville. *In My Opinion,* 174-179.

Roberts, Kenneth. "The Memories of John P. Marquand," *Saturday Review* XXXIX (Sept 15, 1956), 14-15.

Wagenknecht, Edward. *Cavalcade of the American Novel,* 438-443.

BIBLIOGRAPHY

White, William. "John P. Marquand: A Preliminary Checklist," *Bulletin of Bibliography* XIX (Sept-Dec 1949), 268-271; XX (Jan-Apr 1950), 8-12.

——————. "John P. Marquand Since 1950," *Bulletin of Bibliography* XXI (May-Aug 1956), 230-234.

MASTERS, EDGAR LEE

CHILDREN OF THE MARKET PLACE

Blotner, Joseph L. *The Political Novel,* 34.

GENERAL

Flanagan, John T. "The Novels of Edgar Lee Masters," *South Atlantic Quarterly* XLIX (Jan 1950), 82-95.

Whicher, George F. "Analysts of Decay," *The Literature of the American People,* 869-870.

MATHEWS, CORNELIUS

BEHEMOTH: A LEGEND OF THE MOUND-BUILDERS

Dahl, Curtis. "Moby Dick's Cousin Behemoth," *American Literature* XXXI (Mar 1959), 21-29.

GENERAL

Miller, Perry. *The Raven and the Whale.*

McCARTHY, MARY

A CHARMED LIFE

Kelly, James. "New Faces and New Leeds," *Saturday Review* XXXVIII (Nov 5, 1955), 17.

Macauley, Robie. "A McCarthy Inquiry," *Kenyon Review* XVIII (Winter 1956), 155-157.

THE COMPANY SHE KEEPS

Southard, W. P. "Lady Flat on Her Back," *Kenyon Review* V (Winter 1943), 140-142.

McCULLERS, CARSON

THE BALLAD OF THE SAD CAFE
Evans, Oliver. "The Theme of Spiritual Isolation in Carson McCullers," *New World Writing* I (1952), 304-310.

THE HEART IS A LONELY HUNTER
Durham, Frank. "God and No God in *The Heart Is a Lonely Hunter,*" *South Atlantic Quarterly* LVI (Autumn 1957), 494-499.

Evans, Oliver. "The Theme of Spiritual Isolation in Carson McCullers," *New World Writing* I (1952), 298-300.

THE MEMBER OF THE WEDDING
Dangerfield, George. "An Adolescent's Four Days," *Saturday Review of Literature* XXIX (Mar 30, 1946), 15.

Evans, Oliver. "The Theme of Spiritual Isolation in Carson McCullers," *New World Writing* I (1952), 301-304.

Young, Marguerite. "Metaphysical Fiction," *Kenyon Review* IX (Winter 1947), 151-155.

REFLECTIONS IN A GOLDEN EYE
Evans, Oliver. "The Theme of Spiritual Isolation in Carson McCullers," *New World Writing* I (1952), 300-301.

GENERAL
Evans, Oliver. "The Theme of Spiritual Isolation in Carson McCullers," *New World Writing* I (1952), 297-310.

Hart, Jane. "Carson McCullers, Pilgrim of Loneliness," *Georgia Review* XI (Spring 1957), 53-58.

Hassan, Ihab H. "Carson McCullers: The Alchemy of Love and Aesthetics of Pain," *Modern Fiction Studies* V (Winter 1959-1960), 311-326.

Kohler, Dayton. "Carson McCullers: Variations on a Theme," *College English* XIII (Oct 1951), 1-8.

BIBLIOGRAPHY
Stewart, Stanley. "Carson McCullers, 1940-1956: A Selected Checklist," *Bulletin of Bibliography* XXII (Jan-Apr 1959), 182-185.

MELVILLE, HERMAN

THE CONFIDENCE MAN
Cawelti, John G. "Some Notes on the Structure of *The Confidence-Man,*" *American Literature* XXIX (Nov 1957), 278-288.

MELVILLE, HERMAN, Continued

Chase, Richard. "Melville's *Confidence Man*," *Kenyon Review* XI (Winter 1949), 122-140.

Fuller, Roy. Introduction, *The Confidence-Man* (London, 1948), pp. xiii.

Hayford, Harrison. "Poe in *The Confidence-Man*," *Nineteenth-Century Fiction* XIV (Dec 1959), 207-218.

Hoffman, Dan G. "Melville's 'Story of China Aster,'" *American Literature* XXII (May 1950), 137-149.

Horsford, Howard C. "Evidence of Melville's Plans for a Sequel to *The Confidence-Man*," *American Literature* XXIV (Mar 1952), 85-89.

Mason, Ronald. *The Spirit Above the Dust: A Study of Herman Melville*, 198-207.

Miller, James E., Jr. "The Confidence-Man: His Guises," *PMLA* LXXIV (March 1959), 102-111.

Mumford, Lewis. *Herman Melville*, 247-255.

Oliver, Egbert S. "Melville's Goneril and Fanny Kemble," *New England Quarterly* XVIII (Dec 1945), 489-506.

——————. "Melville's Picture of Emerson and Thoreau in *The Confidence Man*," *College English* VIII (Nov 1946), 61-72.

Pearce, Roy Harvey. "Melville's Indian Hater: A Note on the Meaning of *The Confidence Man*," *PMLA* LXVII (Dec 1952), 942-948.

Rosenberry, Edward H. *Melville and the Comic Spirit*, 146-178.

Sedgwick, William Ellery. *Herman Melville: The Tragedy of Mind*, 186-193.

Shroeder, John W. "Sources and Symbols for Melville's *Confidence-Man*," *PMLA* LXVI (Jun 1951), 363-380.

Stone, Geoffrey. *Melville*, 228-234.

Thompson, Lawrance. *Melville's Quarrel with God*, 297-328.

Wright, Nathalia. "The Confidence Men of Melville and Cooper: an American Indictment," *American Quarterly* IV (Fall 1952), 266-268.

ISRAEL POTTER

Chase, Richard. *Melville: A Critical Study*, 176-184.

McCutcheon, Roger P. "The Technique of Melville's *Israel Potter*," *South Atlantic Quarterly* XXVII (Apr 1928), 161-174.

Page, C. A. Introduction, *Israel Potter* (New York, 1925), pp. xviii.

MELVILLE, HERMAN, Continued

Weaver, Raymond M. Introduction, *Israel Potter* (New York, 1924), pp. xvii.

Yates, Norris. "An Instance of Parallel Imagery in Hawthorne, Melville, and Frost," *Philological Quarterly* XXXVI (Apr 1957), 276-280.

MARDI

Arvin, Newton. "Melville's *Mardi*," *American Quarterly* II (Spring 1950), 71-81.

Birss, J. H. "A Note on Melville's *Mardi*," *Notes and Queries* CLXII (4 Jun 1932), 404.

Braswell, William. *Melville's Religious Thought*, 86-106.

Collins, Carvel. "Melville's *Mardi*," *Explicator* XII (May 1954), No. 42.

Davis, Merrell R. "The Flower Symbolism in *Mardi*," *Modern Language Quarterly* II (Dec 1941), 625-638.

——————. *Melville's Mardi: A Chartless Voyage*.

Day, A. Grove. "Hawaiian Echoes in Melville's *Mardi*," *Modern Language Quarterly* XVIII (Mar 1957), 3-8.

Freeman, John. *Herman Melville*, 95-108.

Graham, Philip. "The Riddle of Melville's *Mardi*: A Re-Interpretation," *Texas Studies in English* XXXVI (1957), 93-99.

Hillway, Tyrus. "Taji's Abdication in Herman Melville's *Mardi*," *American Literature* XVI (Nov 1944), 204-207.

——————. "Taji's Quest for Certainty," *American Literature* XVIII (Mar 1946), 27-34.

Jaffé, David. "Some Sources of Melville's *Mardi*," *American Literature* IX (Mar 1937), 56-69.

Larrabee, Stephen A. "Melville against the World," *South Atlantic Quarterly* XXXIV (Oct 1935), 410-418.

Mason, Ronald. *The Spirit Above the Dust: A Study of Herman Melville*, 38-65.

Miller, James E., Jr. "The Many Masks of *Mardi*," *Journal of English and Germanic Philology* LVIII (Jul 1959), 400-413.

Mills, Gordon. "The Significance of 'Arcturus' in *Mardi*," *American Literature* XIV (May 1942). 158-161.

Mumford, Lewis. *Herman Melville*, 93-107.

Rosenberry, Edward H. *Melville and the Comic Spirit*, 57-89.

Sealts, Merton M., Jr. "Melville's 'Friend Atahalph,'" *Notes and Queries* 194 (22 Jan 1949), 37-38.

MELVILLE, HERMAN, Continued

Sedgwick, William Ellery. *Herman Melville: The Tragedy of Mind,* 37-61.

Stern, Milton R. *The Fine Hammered Steel of Herman Melville,* 66-149.

Stone, Geoffrey. *Melville,* 86-108.

Thompson, Lawrance. *Melville's Quarrel with God,* 59-69.

Wright, Nathalia. "The Head and the Heart in Melville's *Mardi,*" *PMLA* LXVI (Jun 1951), 351-362.

——————. "A Note on Melville's Use of Spenser: Hautia and the Bower of Bliss," *American Literature* XXIV (Mar 1952), 83-85.

MOBY DICK

Ament, William S. "Bowdler and the Whale: Some Notes on the First English and American Editions of Moby-Dick," *American Literature* IV (Mar 1932), 39-46.

——————. Introduction, *Moby Dick* (New York, 1928), pp. xxxvii.

Anderson, Charles Roberts. *Melville in the South Seas,* 11-65.

Arms, George. "*Moby Dick* and *The Village Blacksmith,*" *Notes and Queries* 192 (3 May 1947), 187-188.

Arvin, Newton. *Herman Melville,* 143-193.

——————. Introduction, *Moby Dick* (New York, 1948), pp. xxxiii.

Auden, W. H. *The Enchafèd Flood,* 61-84; 115-144.

Battenfeld, David H. "The Source for the Hymn in *Moby-Dick,*" *American Literature* XXVII (Nov 1955), 393-396.

Beach, Joseph Warren. "Hart Crane and Moby Dick," *Western Review* XX (Spring 1956), 183-196.

Belgion, Montgomery. "Heterodoxy in *Moby-Dick,*" *Sewanee Review* LV (Jan-Mar 1947), 108-125.

Bell, Millicent. "Melville and Hawthorne at the Grave of St. John (A Debt to Pierre Bayle)," *Modern Language Notes* LXVII (Feb 1952), 116-118.

——————. "Pierre Bayle and *Moby Dick,*" *PMLA* LXVI (Sept 1951), 626-648.

Bezanson, Walter E. *Moby-Dick Centennial Essays,* 30-58.

Braswell, William. *Melville's Religious Thought,* 57-73.

Burnam, Tom. "Tennyson's 'Ringing Grooves' and Captain Ahab's Grooved Soul," *Modern Language Notes* LXVII (Jun 1952), 423-424.

MELVILLE, HERMAN, Continued

Calhoon, Herbert. "Herman Melville and W. H. Hudson," *American Notes & Queries* VIII (Dec 1949), 131-132.
Chase, Richard. *Herman Melville: A Critical Study*, 43-102.
——————. *The American Novel and Its Tradition*, 80-82; 89-113.
Collins, Carvel. "Melville's *Moby Dick*," *Explicator* IV (Feb 1946), No. 27; G. Giovannini, "Melville's *Moby Dick*," V (Oct 1946), No. 7.
Colum, Padraic. *A Half-Day's Ride*, 175-179.
Cook, Charles H., Jr. "Ahab's 'Intolerable Allegory,'" *Boston University Studies in English* I (Spring-Summer 1955), 45-52.
Cook, Reginald L. "Big Medicine in 'Moby Dick,'" *Accent* VIII (Winter 1948), 102-109.
Dahl, Curtis. *"Moby Dick* and Reviews of *The Cruise of The Cachelot*," *Modern Language Notes* LXVII (Nov 1952), 471-472.
——————. "Moby Dick's Cousin Behemoth," *American Literature* XXXI (Mar 1959), 21-29.
Dale, T. R. "Melville and Aristotle: The Conclusion of *Moby-Dick* as a Classical Tragedy," *Boston University Studies in English* III (Spring 1957), 45-50.
Don, Ralph. Introduction, *Moby Dick* (New York, 1929), pp. xli.
Edgar, Pelham. *The Art of the Novel*, 130-135.
Erskine, John. *The Delight of Great Books*, 223-240.
Fadiman, Clifton. "Herman Melville," *Atlantic Monthly* CLXXII (Oct 1943), 88-91.
——————. Introduction, *Moby Dick* (New York, 1950; 1956).
——————. *Party of One*, 136-144.
Fagin, N. Bryllion. "Herman Melville and the Interior Monologue," *American Literature* VI (Jan 1935), 433-434.
Forsythe, Robert S. "An Oversight by Herman Melville," *Notes and Queries* 172 (24 Apr 1937), 296.
——————. "Emerson and *Moby Dick*," *Notes and Queries* 177 (23 Dec 1939), 457-458.
——————. "Herman Melville's 'The Town-Ho's Story,'" *Notes and Queries* 168 (4 May 1935), 314.
Frédérix, Pierre. *Herman Melville*, 185-203.
Freeman, John. *Herman Melville*, 114-131.

MELVILLE, HERMAN, Continued

Friedrich, Gerhard. *In Pursuit of Moby Dick: Melville's Image of Man.*

Geiger, Don. "Demonism in 'Moby Dick': A Study of Twelve Chapters," *Perspective* VI (Spring 1953), 111-124.

——————. "Melville's Black God: Contrary Evidence in 'The Town-Ho's Story,'" *American Literature* XXV (Jan 1954), 464-471.

Gleim, William S. *The Meaning of Moby Dick.*

——————. "A Theory of *Moby Dick*," *New England Quarterly* II (Jul 1929), 402-419.

Granger, Bruce Ingham. "The Gams in Moby Dick," *Western Humanities Review* VIII (Winter 1953-1954), 41-47.

Grdseloff, Dorothee. "A Note on the Origin of Fedallah in *Moby-Dick*," *American Literature* XXVII (Nov 1955), 396-403.

Hall, James B. "Moby Dick: Parable of A Dying System," *Western Review* XIV (Spring 1950), 223-226; Eugene R. Spangler, "Harvest in a Barren Field: A Countercomment," (Summer 1950), 305-307.

Hanley, James. Introduction, *Moby Dick* (London, 1952), pp. xxxix.

Harding, Walter. "A Note on the Title 'Moby-Dick,'" *American Literature,* XXII (Jan 1951), 500-501.

Hawley, Hattie L. Introduction, *Moby Dick* (New York, 1924), pp. xiv.

Heflin, Wilson L. *Moby-Dick Centennial Essays,* 165-179.

——————. "The Source of Ahab's Lordship over the Level Loadstone," *American Literature* XX (Nov 1948), 323-327.

Hetherington, Hugh W. *Moby-Dick Centennial Essays,* 89-122.

Hicks, Granville. *Twelve Original Essays on Great American Novels,* 44-68.

Hillway, Tyrus. *Melville and the Whale.*

——————. *Moby-Dick Centennial Essays,* 22-29.

Holman, C. Hugh. "The Reconciliation of Ishmael: *Moby-Dick* and the Book of Job," *South Atlantic Quarterly* LVII (Autumn 1958), 477-490.

Howard, Leon. "A Predecessor of *Moby-Dick*," *Modern Language Notes* XLIX (May 1934), 310-311.

Hutchinson, William H. "A Definitive Edition of *Moby-Dick*," *American Literature* XXV (Jan 1954), 472-478.

MELVILLE, HERMAN, Continued

Jaffé, David. "Some Origins of *Moby-Dick*: New Finds in an Old Source," *American Literature* XXIX (Nov 1957), 263-277.

Jones, Joseph. "Ahab's 'Blood-Quench': Theater or Metallurgy?" *American Literature* XVIII (Mar 1946), 35-37.

————. "Humor in *Moby Dick*," *Texas Studies in English* XXV (1945-1946), 51-71.

Kazin, Alfred. Introduction, *Moby Dick* (Boston, 1956).

Kendall, Lyle H., Jr. "On 'the Whiteness of The Whale,' " *Notes and Queries* 200 (Jun 1955), 266.

————. "Ishmael and Ahab," *Atlantic* CXCVIII (Nov 1956), 81-85.

Lash, Kenneth. "Captain Ahab and King Lear," *New Mexico Quarterly* XIX (Winter 1949), 438-445.

Lawrence, D. H. *Studies in Classic American Literature*, 156-174.

Leisy, Ernest E. *Moby-Dick Centennial Essays*, 76-88.

Leiter, Louis. "Queequeg's Coffin," *Nineteenth-Century Fiction* XIII (Dec 1958), 249-254.

Lowry, Thomas C. F. "Melville's *Moby-Dick*, XXXI," *Explicator* XVI (Jan 1958), No. 22.

Mabbott, T. O. "Melville's *Moby Dick*," *Explicator* VIII (Nov 1949), No. 15.

————. "A Source for the Conclusion of *Moby Dick*," *Notes and Queries* 181 (26 Jul 1941), 47-48.

Mason, Ronald. *The Spirit Above the Dust*, 111-157.

Matthiessen, F. O. *American Renaissance*, 282-291; 409-466.

Maugham, W. Somerset. *Ten Novels and Their Authors*, 178-203.

————. "Moby Dick," *Atlantic Monthly* CLXXXI (Jun 1948), 98-104.

McCloskey, John C. "*Moby Dick* and the Reviewers," *Philological Quarterly* XXV (Jan 1946), 20-31.

McDermott, John Francis. "The *Spirit of the Times* Reviews *Moby Dick*," *New England Quarterly* XXX (Sept 1957), 392-395.

McFee, William. Introduction, *Moby Dick* (Philadelphia, 1931; 1934).

Meynell, Viola. Introduction, *Moby Dick* (New York, 1920), pp. xiii.

Miller, Paul W. "Sun and Fire in Melville's *Moby Dick*," *Nineteenth-Century Fiction* XIII (Sept 1958), 139-144.

MELVILLE, HERMAN, Continued

Mills, Gordon H. "The Castaway in *Moby-Dick*," *Texas Studies in English* XXIX (1950), 231-248.

Mumford, Lewis. *The Golden Day*, 144-152; (Beacon Press edition) 72-76.

——————. "Moby Dick," *Herman Melville*, 158-195.

——————. "The Writing of *Moby Dick*," *American Mercury* XV (Dec 1928), 482-490.

Murray, Henry A. "In Nomine Diaboli," *New England Quarterly* XXIV (Dec 1951), 435-452; *Princeton University Library Chronicle* XIII (Winter 1952), 47-62; *Moby-Dick Centennial Essays*, 3-21.

Myers, Henry Alonzo. "Captain Ahab's Discovery: The Tragic Meaning of *Moby Dick*," *New England Quarterly* XV (Mar 1942), 15-34.

Newman, Robert G. "An Early Berkshire Appraisal of *Moby-Dick*," *American Quarterly* IX (Fall 1957), 365-366.

O'Daniel, Therman B. "An Interpretation of the Relation of the Chapter Entitled 'The Symphony,'" *CLA Journal* II (Sept 1958), 55-57.

Olson, Charles. *Call Me Ishmael*.

Parke, John. "Seven Moby-Dicks," *New England Quarterly* XXVIII (Sept 1955), 319-338; *Interpretations of American Literature*, 84-101.

Paul, Sherman. "Hawthorne's Ahab," *Notes and Queries* 196 (9 Jun 1951), 255-257.

——————. Introduction, *Moby Dick* (London, 1954), pp. xxx.

——————. "Melville's 'The Town-Ho's Story,'" *American Literature* XXI (May 1949), 212-221.

——————. "Morgan Neville, Melville and the Folk-Hero," *Notes and Queries* 194 (25 Jun 1949), 278.

Percival, M. O. *A Reading of Moby-Dick*.

Phelps, Leland R. "*Moby Dick* in Germany," *Comparative Literature* X (Fall 1958), 349-355.

Potter, David. "Reviews of *Moby-Dick*," *Rutgers University Library Journal* III (Jun 1940), 62-65.

Rice, Howard C., Jr., *et al*. "*Moby-Dick* by Herman Melville: A Century of an American Classic 1851-1951: Catalogue of an Exhibition Princeton University Library October 15-December

MELVILLE, HERMAN, Continued

15, 1951," *Princeton University Library Chronicle* XIII (Winter 1952), 63-118.

Rockwell, Frederick S. "DeQuincey and the Ending of 'Moby-Dick,'" *Nineteenth-Century Fiction* IX (Dec 1954), 161-168.

Rosenbach, A. S. W. Introduction, *Moby Dick* (New York, 1928).

Rosenberry, Edward H. *Melville and the Comic Spirit*, 93-138.

——————. "Queequeg's Coffin-Canoe: Made in Typee," *American Literature* XXX (Jan 1959), 529-530.

Rourke, Constance. *American Humor*, 191-200; (Doubleday Anchor) 154-160.

Russell, C. H. St. L. Introduction, *Moby Dick* (New York, 1931).

Satterfield, John. "Perth: An Organic Digression in *Moby-Dick*," *Modern Language Notes* LXXIV (Feb 1959), 106-107.

Scott, Sumner W. D. "Some Implications of the Typhoon Scenes in *Moby Dick*," *American Literature* XII (Mar 1940), 91-98.

Sealts, Merton M., Jr. "Melville and the Shakers," *Studies in Bibliography* II (1949-50), 105-114.

Sedgwick, William Ellery. *Herman Melville: The Tragedy of Mind*, 82-136.

Sherbo, Arthur. "Melville's 'Portugese Catholic Priest,'" *American Literature* XXVI (Jan 1955), 563-564.

Short, R. W. "Melville as Symbolist," *University of Kansas City Review* XV (Autumn 1948), 38-46; *Interpretations of American Literature*, 102-113.

Slochower, Harry. "*Moby Dick*: The Myth of Democratic Expectancy," *American Quarterly* II (Fall 1950), 259-269.

Smith, Henry Nash. *Moby-Dick Centennial Essays*, 59-75.

Spiller, Robert E. "Melville: Our First Tragic Poet," *Saturday Review of Literature* XXXIII (Nov 25, 1950), 24-25.

Stern, Milton R. "The Whale and the Minnow: *Moby Dick* and the Movies," *College English* XVII (May 1956), 470-473.

Stewart, George R. "The Two Moby-Dicks," *American Literature*, XXV (Jan 1954), 417-448.

Stone, Edward. "Melville's Pip and Coleridge's Servant Girl," *American Literature* XXV (Nov 1953), 358-360.

Stone, Geoffrey. *Melville*, 160-186.

Stovall, Floyd. *American Idealism*, 69-72.

MELVILLE, HERMAN, Continued

Sullivan, J. N. Introduction, *Moby Dick* (London, 1953; New York, 1959).

Thompson, Lawrance. *Melville's Quarrel with God*, 127-243.

Tomlinson, H. M. "Two Americans and a Whale," *Harper's* CLII (Apr 1926), 618-621.

Van Doren, Carl. *American Criticism*, 308-325.

Vincent, Howard P. *The Trying-Out of Moby-Dick*.

Vogel, Dan. "The Dramatic Chapters in *Moby-Dick*," *Nineteenth-Century Fiction* XIII (Dec 1958), 239-247.

Walcutt, Charles Child. "The Fire Symbolism in *Moby Dick*," *Modern Language Notes* LIX (May 1944), 304-310.

Ward, J. A. "The Function of the Cetological Chapters in *Moby-Dick*," *American Literature* XXVIII (May 1956), 164-183.

Watters, R. E. "The Meanings of the White Whale," *University of Toronto Quarterly* XX (Jan 1951), 155-168.

Weaver, Raymond M. Introduction, *Moby Dick* (New York, 1924; 1925; 1926).

Weeks, Donald. "Two Uses of *Moby Dick*," *American Quarterly* II (Summer 1950), 155-164.

Wells, W. H. "*Moby Dick* and Rabelais," *Modern Language Notes* XXXVIII (Feb 1923), 123.

Welsh, Alexander. "A Melville Debt to Carlyle," *Modern Language Notes* LXXIII (Nov 1958), 489-491.

Wheeler, Otis. "Humor in *Moby-Dick*: Two Problems," *American Literature* XXIX (May 1957), 203-206.

White, William. "*Moby Dick*: A New Source?" *Notes and Queries* 180 (7 Jun 1941), 403.

Winters, Yvor. *In Defense of Reason*, 200-221; *Maule's Curse*, 53-76.

Wright, Nathalia. "*Mosses from an Old Manse* and *Moby-Dick*: The Shock of Discovery," *Modern Language Notes* LXVII (Jun 1952), 387-392.

Young, James Dean. "The Nine Gams of the *Pequod*," *American Literature* XXV (Jan 1954), 449-463.

OMOO

Anderson, Charles Roberts. "Contemporary American Opinions of *Typee* and *Omoo*," *American Literature* IX (Mar 1937), 1-25.

MELVILLE, HERMAN, Continued

──────. "Melville's English Debut," *American Literature* XI (Mar 1939), 23-38.

──────. *Melville in the South Seas,* 199-345.

Birss, John Howard. "Whitman and Herman Melville," *Notes and Queries* 164 (22 Apr 1933), 280.

Forsythe, Robert S. "Herman Melville in the Marquesas," *Philological Quarterly* XV (Jan 1936), 1-15.

──────. "Herman Melville in Tahiti," *Philological Quarterly* XVI (Oct 1937), 344-357.

──────. "More Upon Herman Melville in Tahiti," *Philological Quarterly* XVII (Jan 1938), 1-17.

Frédérix, Pierre. *Herman Melville,* 132-147.

Kaplan, Sidney. "Herman Melville and the Whaling Enderbys," *American Literature* XXIV (May 1952), 224-230.

Lawrence, D. H. *Studies in Classic American Literature,* 142-156.

Mason, Ronald. *The Spirit Above the Dust,* 31-37.

Rhys, Ernest. Introduction, *Omoo* (New York, 1908).

Russell, W. Clark. Introduction, *Omoo* (New York, 1904), pp. xii.

PIERRE

Braswell, William. "The Early Love Scenes in Melville's *Pierre,*" *American Literature* XXII (Nov 1950), 283-289.

──────. "Melville's Opinion of *Pierre,*" *American Literature* XXIII (May 1951), 246-250.

──────. *Melville's Religious Thought,* 75-106.

──────. "The Satirical Temper of Melville's *Pierre,*" *American Literature* VII (Jan 1936), 424-438.

Chase, Richard. *Herman Melville,* 103-141.

Frédérix, Pierre. *Herman Melville,* 204-213.

Freeman, John. *Herman Melville,* 108-113.

Giovannini, G. "Melville's *Pierre* and Dante's *Inferno,*" *PMLA* LXIV (Mar 1949), 70-78; J. Chesley Mathews, "Melville and Dante," *PMLA* LXIV (Dec 1949), 1238; G. Giovannini, "Melville and Dante," *PMLA* LXV (Mar 1950), 329.

Hillway, Tyrus. "Pierre, the Fool of Virtue," *American Literature* XXI (May 1949), 201-211.

Kissane, James. "Imagery, Myth, and Melville's *Pierre,*" *American Literature* XXVI (Jan 1955), 564-572.

MELVILLE, HERMAN, Continued

Lueders, Edward G. "The Melville-Hawthorne Relationship in *Pierre* and *The Blithedale Romance*," *Western Humanities Review* IV (Autumn 1950), 323-344.

Mason, Ronald. *The Spirit Above the Dust*, 158-178.

McCorquodale, Marjorie Kimball. "Melville's Pierre as Hawthorne," *Texas Studies in English* XXXIII (1954), 97-102.

Moore, John Brooks. Introduction, *Pierre* (New York, 1929), pp. xxvii.

Moorman, Charles. "Melville's *Pierre* and the Fortunate Fall," *American Literature* XXV (Mar 1953), 13-30.

——————. "Melville's Pierre in the City," *American Literature* XXVII (Jan 1956), 571-577.

Mumford, Lewis. *Herman Melville*, 203-222.

Sedgwick, William Ellery. *Herman Melville: The Tragedy of Mind*, 137-172.

Stern, Milton R. *The Fine Hammered Steel of Herman Melville*, 150-205.

Stone, Geoffrey. *Melville*, 187-210.

Thompson, Lawrance. *Melville's Quarrel with God*, 247-294.

Watson, E. L. Grant. "Melville's *Pierre*," *New England Quarterly* III (Apr 1930), 195-234.

Yaggy, Elinor. "Shakespeare and Melville's *Pierre*," *Boston Public Library Quarterly* VI (Jan 1954), 43-51.

Zolla, Elémire. "Il linguaggio di Pierre," *Studi Americani* III (1957), 63-97.

REDBURN

Freeman, John. *Herman Melville*, 84-88.

Gilman, William H. *Melville's Early Life and Redburn.*

——————. "Melville's Liverpool Trip," *Modern Language Notes* LXI (Dec 1946), 543-547.

Gross, John J. "The Rehearsal of Ishmael: Melville's 'Redburn,'" *Virginia Quarterly Review* XXVII (Summer 1951), 581-600.

Huntress, Keith. "A Note on Melville's *Redburn*," *New England Quarterly* XVIII (Jun 1945), 259-260.

Mason, Ronald. "*Redburn*: the Assault upon Innocence," *The Spirit Above the Dust*, 67-79.

Miller, James E., Jr. "*Redburn* and *White Jacket*: Initiation and Baptism," *Nineteenth-Century Fiction* XIII (Mar 1959), 273-293.

MELVILLE, HERMAN, Continued

Plomer, William. Introduction, *Redburn* (London, 1937).
Sedgwick, William Ellery. *Herman Melville: The Tragedy of Mind*, 62-81.
Thompson, Lawrance. *Melville's Quarrel with God*, 73-89.
Thorp, Willard. "Redburn's Prosy Old Guidebook," *PMLA* LIII (1938), 1146-1156.

TYPEE

Adkins, Nelson F. "A Note on Melville's *Typee*," *New England Quarterly* V (Apr 1932), 248-351.
Anderson, Charles Roberts. "Contemporary American Opinions of *Typee* and *Omoo*," *American Literature* IX (Mar 1937), 1-25.
_____. "Melville's English Debut," *American Literature* XI (Mar 1939), 23-38.
_____. *Melville in the South Seas*, 69-195.
Babcock, C. Merton. Introduction, *Typee* (New York, 1959).
Birss, John H. "*The Story of Toby*, a Sequel to *Typee*," *Harvard Library Bulletin* I (Winter 1947), 118-119.
_____. "Whitman and Herman Melville," *Notes and Queries* 164 (22 Apr 1933), 280.
DeVoto, Bernard. "Editions of *Typee*," *Saturday Review of Literature* V (Nov 24, 1928), 406.
Firebaugh, Joseph J. "Humorist as Rebel: The Melville of *Typee*," *Nineteenth-Century Fiction* IX (Sept 1954), 108-120.
Forsythe, Robert S. "Herman Melville in the Marquesas," *Philological Quarterly* XV (Jan 1936). 1-15.
Frédérix, Pierre. *Herman Melville*, 132-147.
Freeman, John. *Herman Melville*, 74-80.
Gibbings, Robert. Introduction, *Typee* (London, 1951).
Gohdes, Clarence. "Gossip about Melville in the South Seas," *New England Quarterly* X (Sept 1937), 526-531.
_____. "Melville's Friend 'Toby,'" *Modern Language Notes* LIX (Jan 1944), 52-55.
Lawrence, D. H. *Studies in Classic American Literature*, 142-156.
Leonad, Sterling Andrus. Introduction, *Typee* (New York, 1920), pp. viii.
Mason, Ronald. *The Spirit Above the Dust*, 21-30.
Petrullo, Helen B. "The Neurotic Hero of *Typee*," *American Imago* XII (1955), 317-323.

MELVILLE, HERMAN, Continued

Russell, W. Clark. Introduction, *Typee* (New York, 1904) pp. xx.
Sedgwick, William Ellery. *Herman Melville: The Tragedy of Mind*, 19-35.
Stanton, Robert. "*Typee* and Milton: Paradise Well Lost," *Modern Language Notes* LXXIV (May 1959), 407-411.
Stedman, Arthur. Introduction, *Typee* (Boston, 1900), pp. xxxv.
Stern, Milton R. *The Fine Hammered Steel of Herman Melville*, 29-65.
──────. Introduction, *Typee* and *Billy Budd* (New York, 1958), pp. xxx.
Thomas, Russell. "Yarn for Melville's *Typee*," *Philological Quarterly* XV (Jan 1936), 16-29.
Thompson, Lawrance. *Melville's Quarrel with God*, 45-55.
Thorp, Willard. "'Grace Greenwood' Parodies *Typee*," *American Literature* IX (Jan 1938), 455-457.
Trent, W. P. Introduction, *Typee* (Boston, 1902), pp. ix.
Weaver, Raymond. Introduction, *Typee* (1935), pp. xxviii.
Yates, Norris. "A Traveller's Comments on Melville's *Typee*," *Modern Language Notes* LXIX (Dec 1954), 581-583.

WHITE-JACKET

Anderson, Charles Roberts. *Melville in the South Seas*, 349-434.
──────. "A Reply to Herman Melville's *White Jacket* by Rear-Admiral Thomas O. Selfridge, Sr.," *American Literature* VII (May 1935), 123-144.
Freeman, John. *Herman Melville*, 88-94.
Hayford, Harrison. "The Sailor Poet of *White Jacket*," *Boston Public Library Quarterly* III (Jul 1951), 221-228.
Huntress, Keith. "Melville's Use of a Source for *White-Jacket*," *American Literature* XVII (Mar 1945), 66-74.
Mason, Ronald. *The Spirit Above the Dust*, 80-95.
Miller, James E., Jr. "*Redburn* and *White Jacket*: Initiation and Baptism," *Nineteenth-Century Fiction* XIII (Mar 1959), 273-293.
Mordell, Albert. "Melville and 'White Jacket,'" *Saturday Review of Literature* VII (Jul 4, 1931), 946.
Nichol, John W. "Melville's '"Soiled" Fish of the Sea,'" *American Literature* XXI (Nov 1949), 338-339.

MELVILLE, HERMAN, Continued

Philbrick, Thomas L. "Another Source for *White-Jacket*," *American Literature* XXIX (Jan 1958), 431-439.

Plomer, William. Introduction, *White Jacket* (London, 1952).

Procter, Page S., Jr. "A Source for the Flogging Incident in *White-Jacket*," *American Literature* XXII (May 1950), 176-182.

Sedgwick, William Ellery. *Herman Melville: The Tragedy of Mind*, 62-81.

Stone, Geoffrey. *Melville*, 125-135.

Thompson, Lawrance. *Melville's Quarrel with God*, 93-124.

Van Doren, Carl. Introduction, *White Jacket* (New York, 1924; 1929), pp. xx.

Vincent, Howard P. " '*White-Jacket*': An Essay in Interpretation," *New England Quarterly* XXII (Sept 1949), 304-315.

Walker, Warren S. "A Note on Nathaniel Ames," *American Literature* XXVI (May 1954), 239-241.

GENERAL

Aaron, Daniel. "An English Enemy of Melville," *New England Quarterly* VIII (Dec 1935), 561-567.

----------. "Melville and the Missionaries," *New England Quarterly* VIII (Sept 1935), 404-408.

Arvin, Newton. *Herman Melville*.

----------. "Melville and the Gothic Novel," *New England Quarterly* XXII (Mar 1949), 33-48.

Baird, James. *Ishmael*.

Bergler, Edmund. "A Note on Herman Melville," *American Imago* XI (Winter 1954), 385-397.

Bewley, Marius. "Melville," *The Eccentric Design*, 187-219.

----------. "A Truce of God for Melville," *Sewanee Review* LXI (Autumn 1953), 682-700.

Bezanson, Walter E. "Melville's Reading of Arnold's Poetry," *PMLA* LXIX (Jun 1954), 365-391.

Blackmur, R. P. "The Craft of Herman Melville," *Virginia Quarterly Review* XIV (Spring 1938), 266-282.

----------. "The Craft of Herman Melville: A Putative Statement," *The Lion and the Honeycomb*, 124-144; *The Expense of Greatness*, 139-166.

Bond, William H. "Melville and *Two Years Before the Mast*," *Harvard Library Bulletin* VII (Autumn 1953), 362-365.

MELVILLE, HERMAN, Continued

Botta, Guido. "L'ultimo romanzo di Melville," *Studi Americani* III (1957), 109-131.
Boynton, Percy H. "Herman Melville," *More Contemporary Americans,* 29-50.
Braswell, William. *Melville's Religious Thought.*
—————————. "Melville's Use of Seneca," *American Literature* XIII (Mar 1940), 98-104.
—————————. "A Note on 'The Anatomy of Melville's Fame,'" *American Literature* V (Jan 1934), 360-364.
Brooks, Van Wyck. "Notes on Herman Melville," *Emerson and Others,* 171-205.
—————————. *The Times of Melville and Whitman.*
Canby, Henry Seidel. *Classic Americans,* 226-262.
Carpenter, Frederic I. "Melville: the World in a Man-of-War," *University of Kansas City Review* XIX (Summer 1953), 257-264.
—————————. "Puritans Preferred Blondes: The Heroines of Melville and Hawthorne," *New England Quarterly* IX (Jun 1936), 253-272.
Charvat, William. "Melville and the Common Reader," *Studies in Bibliography* XII (1959), 41-57.
Chase, Richard. "An Approach to Melville," *Partisan Review* XIV (May-Jun 1947), 285-294.
—————————. *Herman Melville.*
Chittick, V. L. O. "The Way Back to Melville—Sea-Chart of a Literary Revival," *Southwest Review* XL (Summer 1955), 238-248.
Cowie, Alexander. "Herman Melville (1819-1891)," *The Rise of the American Novel,* 363-411.
Cunliffe, Marcus. "Melville and Whitman," *The Literature of the United States,* 107-119.
Damon, S. Foster. "Why Ishmael Went to Sea," *American Literature* II (Nov 1930), 281-283.
Feidelson, Charles, Jr. *Symbolism and American Literature.*
Fiess, Edward. "Melville as A Reader and Student of Byron," *American Literature* XXIV (May 1952), 186-194.
Fiske, John C. "Herman Melville in Soviet Criticism," *Comparative Literature* V (Winter 1953), 30-39.

MELVILLE, HERMAN, Continued

Floan, Howard R. "Melville," *The South in Northern Eyes*, 131-147.

Forsythe, Robert S. "Herman Melville in Honolulu," *New England Quarterly* VIII (Mar 1935), 99-105.

Foster, Elizabeth S. "Another Note on Melville and Geology," *American Literature* XXII (Jan 1951), 479-487.

----------. "Melville and Geology," *American Literature* XVII (Mar 1945), 50-65.

Frédérix, Pierre. *Herman Melville*.

Freeman, F. Barron. "The Enigma of Melville's 'Daniel Orme,'" *American Literature* XVI (Nov 1944), 208-211.

Freeman, John. *Herman Melville*.

Hart, James D. "Melville and Dana," *American Literature* IX (Mar 1937), 49-55.

Hayford, Harrison. "Hawthorne, Melville, and the Sea," *New England Quarterly* XIX (Dec 1946), 435-452.

----------. "Melville's *Usable* or *Visible Truth*," *Modern Language Notes* LXXIV (Dec 1959), 702-705.

----------. "The Significance of Melville's 'Agatha' Letters," *ELH* XIII (Dec 1946), 299-310.

----------. "Two New Letters of Herman Melville," *ELH* XI (Mar 1944), 76-83.

Hetherington, Hugh W. "A Tribute to the Late Hiram Melville," *Modern Language Quarterly* XVI (Dec 1955), 325-331.

Hewett-Thayer, Harvey W. "The Voice of New England; and Melville," *American Literature As Viewed in Germany 1818-1861*, 38-56.

Hillway, Tyrus. "Melville and the Spirit of Science," *South Atlantic Quarterly* XLVIII (Jan 1949), 77-88.

----------. "Melville as Amateur Zoologist," *Modern Language Quarterly* XII (Jun 1951), 159-164.

----------. "Melville as Critic of Science," *Modern Language Notes* LXV (Jun 1950), 411-414.

----------. "Melville's Art: One Aspect," *Modern Language Notes* LXII (Nov 1947), 477-480.

----------. "Melville's Geological Knowledge," *American Literature* XXI (May 1949), 232-237.

Homans, George C. "The Dark Angel: The Tragedy of Herman Melville," *New England Quarterly* V (Oct 1932), 699-730.

MELVILLE, HERMAN, Continued

Howard, Leon. *Herman Melville.*
——————. "Melville's Struggle with the Angel," *Modern Language Quarterly* I (Jun 1940), 195-206.
Hyman, Stanley Edgar. "Melville the Scrivener," *New Mexico Quarterly* XXIII (Winter 1953), 381-415.
James, C. L. R. *Mariners, Renegades and Castaways.*
Jerman, Bernard R. " 'With Real Admiration': More Correspondence between Melville and Bentley," *American Literature* XXV (Nov 1953), 307-313.
Josephson, Matthew. *Portrait of the Artist as American,* 26-36.
Kazin, Alfred. "On Melville as Scripture," *Partisan Review* XVII (Jan 1950), 67-75; *The Inmost Leaf,* 197-207.
Klingerman, Charles. "The Psychology of Herman Melville," *Psychoanalytic Review* XL (Apr 1953), 125-143.
Knight, Grant C. "Herman Melville," *American Literature and Culture,* 214-221.
Lacy, Patricia. "The Agatha Theme in Melville's Stories," *Texas Studies in English* XXXV (1956), 96-105.
Levin, Harry. *The Power of Blackness.*
Lewis, R. W. B. "Melville on Homer," *American Literature* XXII (May 1950), 166-176.
——————. "Melville: The Apotheosis of Adam," *The American Adam,* 127-155.
Leyda, Jay. "Another Friendly Critic for Melville," *New England Quarterly* XXVII (Jun 1954), 243-249.
——————. "Ishmael Melville: Remarks on Board of Ship Amazon," *Boston Public Library Quarterly* I (Oct 1949), 119-134.
Lombardo, Agostino. "Introduzione a Melville," *Studi Americani* III (1957), 29-61.
Lucas, F. L. "Herman Melville," *Authors Dead & Living,* 105-114.
Lucid, Robert F. "The Influence of *Two Years Before the Mast* on Herman Melville," *American Literature* XXXI (Nov 1959), 243-256.
Lutwack, Leonard. "Herman Melville and *Atlantic Monthly* Critics," *Huntington Library Quarterly* XIII (Aug 1950), 414-416.
MacDonald, Allan. "A Sailor among the Transcendentalists, *New England Quarterly* VIII (Sept 1935), 307; 319.

MELVILLE, HERMAN, Continued

Macshane, Frank. "Conrad on Melville," *American Literature* XXIX (Jan 1958), 463-464.

Mather, Frank Jewett, Jr. "Herman Melville," *Saturday Review of Literature* V (Apr 27, 1929), 945-946.

Matthiessen, F. O. *American Renaissance*, 119-132; 179-191; 371-408; 467-514.

Metcalf, Eleanor Melville. *Herman Melville: Cycle and Epicycle.*

Miller, James E., Jr. "The Achievement of Melville," *University of Kansas City Review* XXVI (Autumn 1959), 59-67.

—————. "The Complex Figure in Melville's Carpet," *Arizona Quarterly* XV (Autumn 1959), 197-210.

—————. "Hawthorne and Melville: The Unpardonable Sin," *PMLA* LXX (Mar 1955), 91-114.

—————. "Melville's Quest in Life and Art," *South Atlantic Quarterly* LVIII (Autumn 1959), 587-602.

Miller, Perry. "Melville and Transcendentalism," *Virginia Quarterly Review* XXIX (Autumn 1953), 556-575; *Moby-Dick Centennial Essays*, 123-152.

—————. *The Raven and the Whale.*

Morris, Wright. "The High Seas," *The Territory Ahead*, 67-77.

Mumford, Lewis. *Herman Melville.*

—————. "The Young Olympian," *Saturday Review of Literature* V (Dec 15, 1928), 514-515.

Murry, John Middleton. "The End of Herman Melville," *John Clare and Other Studies*, 208-212.

Nichol, John W. "Melville and the Midwest," *PMLA* LXVI (Sept 1951), 613-625.

O'Connor, William Van. "Melville on the Nature of Hope," *University of Kansas City Review* XXII (Dec 1955), 123-130.

Parkes, Henry Bramford. "Poe, Hawthorne, Melville: An Essay in Sociological Criticism," *Partisan Review* XVI (Feb 1949), 157-165.

Pattee, Fred Lewis. "Herman Melville," *American Mercury* X (Jan 1927), 33-43.

Pommer, Henry F. "Herman Melville and the Wake of *The Essex*," *American Literature* XX (Nov 1948), 290-304.

—————. *Milton and Melville.*

Powys, John Cowper. "Melville and Poe," *Enjoyment of Literature*, 379-390.

MELVILLE, HERMAN, Continued

Quinn, Arthur Hobson. "Herman Melville and the Exotic Romance," *American Fiction*, 149-158.

——————. "The Romance of History and the Frontier," *The Literature of the American People*, 243-247.

Riegel, O. W. "The Anatomy of Melville's Fame," *American Literature* III (May 1931), 195-203.

Ritchie, Mary C. "Herman Melville," *Queen's Quarterly* XXXVII (Winter 1930), 36-61.

Rizzardi, Alfredo. "La Poesia Di Herman Melville," *Studi Americani* I (1955), 159-203.

Rosenberry, Edward H. *Melville and the Comic Spirit*.

Rosenheim, Frederick. "Flight from Home: Some Episodes in the Life of Herman Melville," *American Imago* I (1939-40), 1-30.

Sealts, Merton M., Jr. "Melville's Reading: A Checklist of Books Owned and Borrowed," *Harvard Library Bulletin* II (Spring 1948), 141-163; (Autumn 1948), 378-392; III (Winter 1949), 119-130; (Spring 1949), 268-277; (Autumn 1949), 407-421; IV (Winter 1950), 98-109; VI (Spring 1952), 239-247.

Snell, George. "Herman Melville: The Seeker," *The Shapers of American Fiction*, 60-78.

Spiller, Robert E. *The Cycle of American Literature*, 89-99; (Mentor) 76-83.

Stein, William Bysshe. "Melville Roasts Thoreau's Cock," *Modern Language Notes* LXXIV (Mar 1959), 218-219.

Stern, Milton R. *The Fine Hammered Steel of Herman Melville*.

——————. "Some Techniques of Melville's Perception," *PMLA* LXXIII (Jun 1958), 251-259.

Stewart, Randall. "Melville and Hawthorne," *South Atlantic Quarterly* LI (Jul 1952), 436-446; *Moby-Dick Centennial Essays*, 153-164.

Stone, Geoffrey. "Loyalty to the Heart," *American Classics Reconsidered*, 210-228.

——————. *Melville*.

Sundermann, K. H. *Herman Melvilles Gedankengut: Ein kritische Untersuchung seiner weltanschaulichen Grundiden*.

Thorp, Willard. "Introduction," *Herman Melville*, xi-cxxix.

Van Doren, Carl. "Herman Melville," *The American Novel 1789-1939*, 84-102.

MELVILLE, HERMAN, Continued

Wagenknecht, Edward. "The Ambiguities of Herman Melville," *Cavalcade of the American Novel*, 58-81.

──────. "Our Contemporary, Herman Melville," *College English* XI (Mar 1950), 301-308.

Watters, R. E. "Melville's 'Isolatoes,'" *PMLA* LX (1945), 1138-1148.

──────. "Melville's Metaphysics of Evil," *University of Toronto Quarterly* IX (Jan 1940), 170-182.

──────. "Melville's 'Sociality,'" *American Literature* XVII (Mar 1945), 33-49.

Weaks, Mabel. "Long Ago and 'Faraway,'" *Bulletin of The New York Public Library* LII (Jul 1948), 362-369.

Weaver, Raymond M. *Herman Melville, Mariner and Mystic*.

Weber, Walter. "Some Characteristic Symbols in Herman Melville's Works," *English Studies* XXX (1949), 217-224.

West, Ray B., Jr. "Primitivism in Melville," *Prairie Schooner* XXX (Winter 1956), 369-385.

Williams, Mentor L. "Some Notices and Reviews of Melville's Novels in American Religious Periodicals, 1846-1849," *American Literature* XXII (May 1950), 119-127.

Williams, Stanley T. "Spanish Influences in American Fiction: Melville and Others," *New Mexico Quarterly* XXII (Spring 1952), 5-14.

Winters, Yvor. "Herman Melville and The Problems of Moral Navigation," *In Defense of Reason*, 200-233; *Maule's Curse*, 53-89.

Wright, Nathalia. "Biblical Allusion in Melville's Prose," *American Literature* XII (May 1940), 185-199.

──────. *Melville's Use of the Bible*.

BIBLIOGRAPHY

Cahoon, Herbert. "Herman Melville: A Check List of Books and Manuscripts in the Collections of The New York Public Library," *Bulletin of The New York Public Library* LV (Jun 1951), 263-275; Part II (Jul 1951), 325-338.

Minnigerode, Meade. *Some Personal Letters of Herman Melville and a Bibliography*.

Sadlier, Michael. "Herman Melville," *Excursions in Victorian Bibliography*, 217-234.

Sealts, Merton M. *Melville's Reading*.

MELVILLE, HERMAN, Continued

Stern, Milton R. "A Checklist of Melville Studies," *The Fine Hammered Steel of Herman Melville*, 252-291.
Thorp, Willard. *Herman Melville*, cxxiii-clxi.
Williams, Stanley T. "Melville," *Eight American Authors*, 207-270.

MICHENER, JAMES

GENERAL
Havighurst, Walter. "Michener of the South Pacific," *College English* XIV (Oct 1952), 1-6.

MILLER, HENRY

TROPIC OF CANCER
Fraenkel, Michael. *The Genesis of the 'Tropic of Cancer'; The Happy Rock*, 38-56.
Nin, Anais. *Preface to Henry Miller's Tropic of Cancer.*
Orwell, George. *Inside the Whale*, 131-188.
——————. *A Collection of Essays*, 215-256.
Wilson, Edmund. *A Literary Chronicle*, 211-216.

GENERAL
Bald, Wambly. "La Vie de Boheme," *The Happy Rock*, 25-27.
Chiaromonte, Nocola. "The Return of Henry Miller," *Of-By-and About Henry Miller*, 6-10.
Durrell, Lawrence. "The Happy Rock," *The Happy Rock*, 1-6.
Fauchery, Pierre. "Une Epopee Du Sexe: Le feuilleton bebdomadaire," *Of-By-and About Henry Miller*, 40-43.
Finch, Roy. "Three Americans," *The Happy Rock*, 116-118.
Fowlie, Wallace. "Shadow of Doom: an Essay on Henry Miller," *Accent* V (Autumn 1944), 49-53; *Of-By-And About Henry Miller*, 18-24; *The Happy Rock*, 102-107.
Gilbert, Rudolph. "Between Two Worlds," *The Happy Rock*, 126-132.
Gilbert, Thomas R. "Rocamadour," *The Happy Rock*, 62-63.
Glicksberg, Charles I. "Henry Miller: Individualism in Extremis," *Southwest Review* XXXIII (Summer 1948), 289-295.
Haverstick, John and William Barrett. "Henry Miller: Man in Quest of Life," *Saturday Review* XL (Aug 3, 1957), 8-10.
Kazin, Alfred. "The Rhetoric and the Agony," *On Native Grounds*, 465-470.

MILLER, HENRY, Continued

Kronhausen, Eberhard and Phyllis. *Pornography and the Law,* 125-130.
Laughlin, James. "Three Americans," *The Happy Rock,* 114-116.
Lee, Alwyn. "Henry Miller—The Pathology of Isolation," *New World Writing* 2 (1952), 340-347.
Leite, George. "The Autochthon," *The Happy Rock,* 140-146.
Maine, Harold. "Henry Miller: Bigotry's Whipping Boy," *Arizona Quarterly* VII (Autumn 1951), 197-208.
Manning, Hugo. "British Notes," *The Happy Rock,* 119-121.
Merrild, Knud. "All the Animals in the Zoo," *The Happy Rock,* 77-88.
Miller, Henry. "Defence of the Freedom to Read," *Evergreen Review* III (Summer 1959), 12-20.
——————. "The Situation in American Writing," *Partisan Review* VI (Summer 1939), 50-51.
Moore, Nicholas. *Henry Miller.*
——————. "Henry Miller in England," *The Happy Rock,* 147-151.
Moore, Reginald. "Miller's Impact upon an English Writer," *The Happy Rock,* 136-139.
Muller, Herbert J. "The World of Henry Miller," *Kenyon Review* II (Summer 1940), 312-318.
Neiman, Gilbert. "No Rubbish, No Albatrosses," *The Happy Rock,* 89-96.
Osborn, Richard G. "No. 2 Rue Auguste Bartholdi," *The Happy Rock,* 28-37.
Perlès, Alfred. "Henry Miller in Villa Seurat," *The Happy Rock,* 57-61.
——————. *My Friend Henry Miller.*
Read, Herbert. "View and Reviews: Henry Miller," *Of-By-and About Henry Miller,* 14-17.
Rexroth, Kenneth. "The Reality of Henry Miller," *Bird in the Bush,* 154-167.
Rosenfeld, Paul. "Hellenism," *The Happy Rock,* 64-72.
——————. "The Traditions and Henry Miller," *Of-By-and About Henry Miller,* 10-14.
Schnellock, Emil. "Just a Brooklyn Boy," *The Happy Rock,* 7-24.
Tyler, Parker. "Three Americans," *The Happy Rock,* 113-114.
Weiss, Paul. "Art and Henry Miller," *The Happy Rock,* 133-135.

MILLER, HENRY, Continued

West, Herbert Faulkner. "Camerado," *The Happy Rock*, 109-112.

MITCHELL, MARGARET

GONE WITH THE WIND

Drake, Robert Y., Jr. "Tara Twenty Years After," *Georgia Review* XII (Summer 1958), 142-150.

Nolan, Edward F. "The Death of Bryan Lyndon: An Analogue in 'Gone With the Wind,'" *Nineteenth-Century Fiction* VIII (Dec 1953), 225-228.

MITCHELL, SILAS WEIR

ROLAND BLAKE

Richardson, Lyon N. "S. Weir Mitchell at Work," *American Literature* XI (Mar 1939), 58-65.

GENERAL

Burr, Anna Robeson. *Weir Mitchell*.

Earnest, Ernest. "Weir Mitchell As Novelist," *American Scholar* XVII (Summer 1948), 314-322.

——————. *S. Weir Mitchell*.

Gohdes, Clarence. "A Challenge of Social Problems and of Science," *The Literature of the American People*, 776-778.

Quinn, Arthur Hobson. "Weir Mitchell, Pioneer and Patrician," *American Fiction*, 305-322.

Wagenknecht, Edward. "Novelists of the 'Eighties: S. Weir Mitchell: Medicine and Romance," *Cavalcade of the American Novel*, 177-179..

MORLEY, CHRISTOPHER

GENERAL

Baldwin, Charles C. "Christopher Morley," *The Men Who Make Our Novels*, 384-393.

Breit, Harvey. *The Writer Observed*, 67-71.

Canby, Henry Seidel. "Christopher Morley," *American Estimates*, 61-70.

Hatcher, Harlan. "Fantasy as a Way of Escape," *Creating the Modern American Novel*, 211-218.

Hughes, Babette. *Christopher Morley*.

MORRIS, WRIGHT

THE HUGE SEASON
Webster, Harvey Curtis. "Journey Between Two Eras," *Saturday Review* XXXVII (Oct 2, 1954), 29.
GENERAL
Booth, Wayne C. "The Two Worlds in the Fiction of Wright Morris," *Sewanee Review* XLV (Jul-Sept 1957), 375-399.
Carpenter, Frederic L. "Wright Morris and the Territory Ahead," *College English* XXI (Dec 1959), 147-156.

MURFREE, MARY NOAILLES

THE PROPHET OF THE GREAT SMOKY MOUNTAINS
Fiske, Horace Spencer. *Provincial Types in American Fiction,* 133-143.
GENERAL
Brooks, Van Wyck. "The South: Miss Murfree and Cable," *The Times of Melville and Whitman,* 378-394.
Cowie, Alexander. "Local-Color, Frontier, and Regional Ficiton: Charles Egbert Craddock (1850-1922) (Mary Noailles Murfree)," *The Rise of the American Novel,* 592-598.
Parks, Edd Winfield. *Charles Egbert Craddock.*
Toulmin, Harry Aubrey. "Charles Egbert Craddock," *Social Historians,* 59-97.

NATHAN, ROBERT

WINTER IN APRIL
Fay, Eliot G. "Borrowings from Anatole France by Willa Cather and Robert Nathan," *Modern Language Notes* LVI (May 1941), 377.
GENERAL
Breit, Harvey. *The Writer Observed,* 119-121.
Dorian, Edith McEwen. "While a Little Dog Dances: Robert Nathan: Novelist of Simplicity," *Sewanee Review* XLI (Apr-Jun 1933), 129-140.
Hatcher, Harlan. "Fantasy as a Way of Escape," *Creating the Modern American Novel,* 211-218.
Redman, Ben Ray. "Expert in Depressions," *Saturday Review of Literature* XI (Oct 13, 1934), 206.

NATHAN, ROBERT, Continued

Wagenknecht, Edward. "Novelists of the 'Twenties: Romance and Fantasy: Robert Nathan," *Cavalcade of the American Novel*, 399-405.

NEAL, ROBERT

GENERAL

Cowie, Alexander. "Contemporaries and Immediate Followers of Cooper, I: John Neal (1793-1895)," *The Rise of the American Novel*, 165-177.

Lease, Benjamin. "Yankee Poetics: John Neal's Theory of Poetry and Fiction," *American Literature* XXIV (Jan 1953), 505-519.

Martin, Harold C. "The Colloquial Tradition in the Novel: John Neal," *New England Quarterly* XXXII (Dec 1959), 455-475.

Quinn, Arthur Hobson. "National and Universal Themes," *The Literature of the American People*, 220-222.

Yorke, Dane. "Yankee Neal," *American Mercury* XIX (Mar 1930), 361-368.

NORRIS, FRANK

BLIX

Norris, Kathleen. Introduction, *Blix* (New York, 1925), pp. viii.

A MAN'S WOMAN

Sherwood, John C. "Norris and the *Jeannette*," *Philological Quarterly* XXXVII (Apr 1958), 245-252.

McTEAGUE

Chase, Richard. *The American Novel and Its Tradition*, 188-192.

Collins, Carvel. Introduction, *McTeague* (New York, 1950), pp. xix.

Kaplan, Charles. "Fact into Fiction in *McTeague*," *Harvard Library Bulletin* VIII (1954), 381-385.

Norris, Charles G. Introduction, *McTeague* (San Francisco, 1941).

Pancoast, Henry S. Introduction, *McTeague* (New York, 1918).

THE OCTOPUS

Chase, Richard. "*The Octopus*," *The American Novel and Its Tradition*, 193-198.

NORRIS, FRANK, Continued

Lundy, Robert D. Introduction, *Octopus* (New York, 1957).
Lynn, Kenneth S. Introduction, *Octopus* (Boston, 1958).
Meyer, George Wilbur. "A New Interpretation of *The Octopus*," *College English* IV (Mar 1943), 351-359.
Pizer, Donald. "Another Look at 'The Octopus,'" *Nineteenth-Century Fiction* X (Dec 1955), 217-224.
Reninger, H. Willard. "Norris Explains *The Octopus*: A Correlation of His Theory and Practice," *American Literature* XII (May 1940), 218-227.
Walcutt, Charles Child. "Frank Norris on Realism and Naturalism," *American Literature* XIII (Mar 1941), 61-63.

THE PIT

Kaplan, Charles. "Norris's Use of Sources in *The Pit*," *American Literature* XXV (Mar 1953), 75-84.

VANDOVER AND THE BRUTE

Walcutt, Charles Child. *Forms of Modern Fiction*, 254-268.

GENERAL

Åhnebrink, Lars. *The Beginnings of Naturalism in American Fiction*, 104-124; 155-165; 277-314; 332-342; 381-409.
──────────. *The Influence of Emile Zola on Frank Norris*.
Bixler, Paul H. "Frank Norris's Literary Reputation," *American Literature* VI (May 1934), 107-121.
Brooks, Van Wyck. "Frank Norris and Jack London," *The Confident Years*, 217-238.
Cargill, Oscar. "The Naturalists," *Intellectual America*, 89-107.
Chase, Richard. "Norris and Naturalism," *The American Novel and Its Tradition*, 185-187; 198-204.
Cooperman, Stanley. "Frank Norris and the Werewolf of Guilt," *Modern Language Quarterly* XX (Sept 1959), 252-258.
Dobie, Charles Caldwell. "Frank Norris or Up from Culture," *American Mercury* XIII (Apr 1928), 412-424.
Geismar, Maxwell. "Frank Norris: And the Brute," *Rebels and Ancestors*, 3-66.
Gohdes, Clarence. "The Facts of Life *Versus* Pleasant Reading," *The Literature of the American People*, 749-754.
Hartwick, Harry. "Norris and the Brute," *The Foreground of American Fiction*, 45-66.
Hicks, Granville. *The Great Tradition*, 168-175.

NORRIS, FRANK, Continued

Hoffman, Charles G. "Norris and the Responsibility of the Novelist," *South Atlantic Quarterly* LIV (Oct 1955), 508-515.

Howells, William Dean. "Frank Norris," *North American Review* 175 (Sept 1902), 769-778.

Kazin, Alfred. "Progressivism: The Superman and the Muckrake," *On Native Grounds*, 97-102.

——————————. "Three Pioneer Realists," *Saturday Review of Literature* XX (Jul 8, 1939), 3-4; 14-15.

Knight, Grant C. "Frank Norris," *American Literature and Culture*, 389-395.

Kwiat, Joseph J. "The Newspaper Experience: Crane, Norris, and Dreiser," *Nineteenth-Century Fiction* VIII (Sept 1953), 99-117.

Lynn, Kenneth S. "Frank Norris: Mama's Boy," *The Dream of Success*, 158-207.

Marchand, Ernest. *Frank Norris*.

Martin, Willard E., Jr. "Frank Norris's Reading at Harvard College," *American Literature*, VII (May 1935), 203-204.

Norris, Frank. "The Responsibilities of the Novelist," *Critic* XLI (Dec 1902), 537-540.

Peixotto, Ernest. "Romanticist Under the Skin," *Saturday Review of Literature* IX (May 27, 1933), 613-615.

Piper, Henry Dan. "Frank Norris and Scott Fitzgerald," *Huntington Library Quarterly* XIX (Aug 1956), 393-400.

Pizer, Donald. "Romantic Indiviualism in Garland, Norris, and Crane," *American Quarterly* X (Winter 1958), 463-475.

Quinn, Arthur Hobson. "Critics and Satirists—The Liberals," *American Fiction*, 624-630.

Snell, George. "Naturalism Nascent: Crane and Norris," *The Shapers of American Fiction*, 226-233.

Taylor, Walter F. "Frank Norris," *The Economic Novel in America*, 282-306.

Todd, Edgeley W. "The Frontier Epic: Frank Norris and John G. Neihardt," *Western Humanities Review* XIII (Winter 1959), 40-45.

Underwood, John Curtis. "Frank Norris," *Literature and Insurgency*, 130-178.

Wagenknecht, Edward. "Towards Naturalism: The Achievement of Frank Norris," *Cavalcade of the American Novel*, 216-222.

NORRIS, FRANK, Continued

Walcutt, Charles Child. *American Literary Naturalism,* 114-156.
──────────. "Frank Norris on Realism and Naturalism," *American Literature* XIII (Mar 1941), 61-63.
──────────. "Frank Norris and the Search for Form," *University of Kansas City Review* XIV (Winter 1947), 126-136.
Walker, Franklin Dickerson. *Frank Norris.*
BIBLIOGRAPHY
Lohf, Kenneth A. and Eugene P. Sheehy. *Frank Norris,* 66-86.
White, William. "Frank Norris: Bibliographical Addenda," *Bulletin of Bibliography* XXII (Sept-Dec 1959), 227-228.

NORRIS, KATHLEEN

GENERAL
Overton, Grant. "Kathleen Norris," *The Women Who Make Our Novels,* 227-242.

O'CONNOR, FLANNERY

WISE BLOOD
Gordon, Caroline. "Flannery O'Connor's *Wise Blood,*" *Critique* II (Fall 1958), 3-10.
Hart, Jane. "Strange Earth, the Stories of Flannery O'Connor," *Georgia Review* XII (Summer 1958), 215-222.
GENERAL
Quinn, Sister M. Bernetta. "View from a Rock: The Fiction of Flannery O'Connor & J. F. Powers," *Critique* II (Fall 1958), 19-27.
Rubin, Louis D., Jr. "Flannery O'Connor: A Note on Literary Fashions," *Critique* II (Fall 1958), 11-18.
BIBLIOGRAPHY
Wedge, George F. "Flannery O'Connor," *Critique* II (Fall 1958), 59-63.

O'HARA, JOHN

TEN NORTH FREDERICK
Kelly, James. "Under the Million Dollars," *Saturday Review* XXXVIII (Nov 26, 1955), 13-14.

O'HARA, JOHN, Continued

GENERAL

Breit, Harvey. *The Writer Observed*, 81-83.

Fadiman, Clifton. "A Period Sample: Three Reviews of John O'Hara," *Party of One*, 446-454.

Gibbs, Wolcott. "Watch Out for Mr. O'Hara," *Saturday Review of Literature* XVII (Feb 19, 1938), 10-12.

Gurko, Leo. *The Angry Decade*, 113-116.

Kazin, Alfred. "The Revival of Naturalism," *On Native Grounds*, 387-393.

Portz, John. "John O'Hara Up to Now," *College English* XVI (May 1955), 493-499; 516.

Prescott, Orville. *In My Opinion*, 70-74.

Waterman, Rollene. "Appt. with O'Hara," *Saturday Review* XLI (Nov 29, 1958), 15.

Wilson, Edmund. "The Boys in the Back Room: John O'Hara," *Classics and Commercials*, 22-26; *A Literary Chronicle*, 219-222.

PAGE, THOMAS NELSON

GENERAL

Hubbell, Jay B. *The South in American Literature*, 795-804.

Mims, Edwin. "Thomas Nelson Page," *Atlantic Monthly* C (Jul 1907), 109-115.

——————. "Thomas Nelson Page," *South Atlantic Quarterly* VI (1907), 263-271.

Page, Rosewell. *Thomas Nelson Page*.

Quinn, Arthur H. *American Fiction*, 357-362.

Toulmin, Harry Aubrey. *Social Historians*, 1-32.

PARKMAN, FRANCIS

VASSALL MORTON

Schramm, Wilbur L. "Parkman's Novel," *American Literature* IX (May 1937), 218-227.

PAULDING, JAMES K.

THE DUTCHMAN'S FIRESIDE

Dondore, Dorothy. "The Debt of Two Dyed-in-the-Wool Americans to Mrs. Grant's Memoirs: Cooper's *Satanstoe* and Pauld-

PAULDING, JAMES K., Continued

ing's *The Dutchman's Fireside*," *American Literature* XII (Mar 1940), 52-58.

THE PURITAN AND HIS DAUGHTER
Davidson, Frank. "Paulding's Treatment of The Angel of Hadley," *American Literature* VII (Nov 1935), 330-332.

SHEPPARD LEE
Quinn, Arthur Hobson. *The Literature of the American People*, 461-462.

GENERAL
Aderman, Ralph M. "James Kirke Paulding on Literature and the West," *American Literature* XXVII (Mar 1955), 97-101.

Cowie, Alexander. "Contemporaries and Immediate Followers of Cooper, I: James Kirke Paulding (1778-1860)," *The Rise of the American Novel*, 185-200.

Herold, Amos L. *James Kirke Paulding*.

Quinn, Arthur Hobson. "National and Universal Themes," *The Literature of the American People*, 219-220.

Watkins, Floyd C. "James Kirke Paulding and the South," *American Quarterly* V (Fall 1953), 219-230.

PETERKIN, JULIA

GENERAL
Clark, Emily. *Innocence Abroad*, 213-231.

Overton, Grant. "Julia Peterkin," *The Women Who Make Our Novels*, 257-261.

PETRY, ANN

THE STREET
Hughes, Carl Milton. "Portrayals of Bitterness," *The Negro Novelist*, 86-96.

PHILLIPS, DAVID GRAHAM

THE PLUM TREE
Blotner, Joseph L. *The Political Novel*, 36-37.

GENERAL
Baldwin, Charles C. "David Graham Phillips," *The Men Who Make Our Novels*, 423-426.

PHILLIPS, DAVID GRAHAM, Continued

Cargill, Oscar. "The Freudians," *Intellectual America*, 592-596.
Filler, Louis. "Murder in Gramercy Park," *Antioch Review* VI (Dec 1946), 495-508.
——————. "The Reputation of David Graham Phillips," *Antioch Review* XI (Dec 1951), 475-488.
Kazin, Alfred. "Progressivism: The Superman and the Muckrake," *On Native Grounds*, 107-109.
——————. "Three Pioneer Realists," *Saturday Review of Literature* XX (Jul 8, 1939), 3-4; 14-15.
Lynn, Kenneth S. "David Graham Phillips: The Dream Panderer," *The Dream of Success*, 121-157.
Underwood, John Curtis. "David Graham Phillips and Results," *Literature and Insurgency*, 179-253.
Whicher, George F. "The Conscience of Liberalism," *The Literature of the American People*, 829.

BIBLIOGRAPHY

Feldman, Abraham. "David Graham Phillips—His Works and His Critics," *Bulletin of Bibliography* XIX (May-Aug 1948), 144-146; (Sept-Dec 1948), 177-179.

POE, EDGAR ALLAN

THE NARRATIVE OF ARTHUR GORDON PYM

Bailey, J. O. "Sources of Poe's *Arthur Gordon Pym*, 'Hans Pfaal,' and other Pieces," *PMLA* LVII (Jun 1942), 513-535.
Bonaparte, Marie. *The Life and Works of Edgar Allan Poe*, 290-352.
Cowie, Alexander. "The Mixed Thirties," *The Rise of the American Novel*, 300-306.
Davidson, Edward H. *Poe: A Critical Study*, 156-180.
Huntress, Keith. "Another Source for Poe's *Narrative of Arthur Gordon Pym*," *American Literature* XVI (Mar 1944), 19-25.
McKeithan, D. M. "Two Sources of Poe's Narrative of Arthur Gordon Pym," *University of Texas Studies in English* XIII (1933), 116-137.
Quinn, Patrick F. *The French Face of Edgar Poe*, 169-215.
——————. "Poe's Imaginary Voyage," *Hudson Review* IV (Winter 1952), 562-585.

PROKOSCH, FREDERIC

GENERAL
Carpenter, Richard C. "The Novels of Frederic Prokosch," *College English* XVIII (Feb 1957), 261-267.

RAND, AYN

THE FOUNTAINHEAD
Aaron, Daniel. "Remarks on A Bestseller," *Partisan Review* XIV Jul-Aug 1947), 442-445.

RAWLINGS, MARJORIE KINNAN

THE SOJOURNER
Bromfield, Louis. "Case of the Wandering Wits," *Saturday Review* XXXVI (Jan 3, 1953), 9-10.
THE YEARLING
Rawlings, Marjorie Kinnan. Introduction, *The Yearling* (New York, 1952), pp. xiii.

RICHTER, CONRAD

GENERAL
Carpenter, Frederic I. "Conrad Richter's Pioneers: Reality and Myth," *College English* XII (Nov 1950), 77-83.
Flanagan, John T. "Conrad Ritcher: Romancer of the Southwest," *Southwest Review* XLIII (Summer 1958), 189-196.
Kohler, Dayton. "Conrad Richter: Early Americana," *College English* VIII (Feb 1947), 221-227.
Prescott, Orville. *In My Opinion*, 137-140.
Whicher, George F. "Loopholes of Retreat," *The Literature of the American People*, 891-892.

RINEHART, MARY ROBERTS

GENERAL
Breit, Harvey. *The Writer Observed*, 227-229.
Overton, Grant. "Mary Roberts Rinehart," *The Women Who Make Our Novels*, 273-285.
—————. "The Vitality of Mary Roberts Rinehart," *When Winter Comes to Main Street*, 102-117.

ROBERTS, ELIZABETH MADOX

A BURIED TREASURE
Campbell, Harry Modean and Ruel E. Foster. *Elizabeth Madox Roberts*, 168-181.

BLACK IS MY TRUELOVE'S HAIR
Campbell, Harry Modean and Ruel E. Foster. *Elizabeth Madox Roberts*, 181-197.

THE GREAT MEADOW
Campbell, Harry Modean and Ruel E. Foster. *Elizabeth Madox Roberts*, 135-152.

HE SENT FORTH A RAVEN
Campbell, Harry Modean and Ruel E. Foster. *Elizabeth Madox Roberts*, 217-229.

JINGLING IN THE WIND
Campbell, Harry Modean and Ruel E. Foster. *Elizabeth Madox Roberts*, 199-216.

MY HEART AND MY FLESH
Campbell, Harry Modean and Ruel E. Foster. *Elizabeth Madox Roberts*, 153-167.

THE TIME OF MAN
Campbell, Harry Modean and Ruel E. Foster. *Elizabeth Madox Roberts*, 122-135.

GENERAL
Adams, J. Donald. "Elizabeth Madox Roberts," *Virginia Quarterly Review* XII (Jan 1936), 80-90.

Buchan, Alexander M. "Elizabeth Madox Roberts," *Southwest Review* XXV (Jul 1940), 463-481.

Campbell, Harry Modean. "The Poetic Prose of Elizabeth Madox Roberts," *Southwest Review* XXXIX (Autumn 1954), 337-346.

Janney, F. Lamar. "Elizabeth Madox Roberts," *Sewanee Review* XLV (Oct-Dec 1937), 388-410.

Van Doren, Mark. "Elizabeth Madox Roberts: Her Mind and Style," *The Private Reader*, 97-109.

Wagenknecht, Edward. "Novelists of the 'Twenties: The Inner Vision: Elizabeth Madox Roberts," *Cavalcade of the American Novel*, 389-396.

ROBERTS, KENNETH

LYDIA BAILEY
Nevins, Allan. "The Past as Pageant," *Saturday Review of Literature* XXX (Jan 4, 1947), 14-15.
GENERAL
Kenneth Roberts: An American Novelist.
Williams, Ben Ames. "Kenneth Roberts," *Saturday Review of Literature* XVIII (Jun 25, 1938), 8-10.

RÖLVAAG, OLE

GIANTS IN THE EARTH
Baker, Joseph E. "Western Man Against Nature: *Giants in the Earth*," *College English* IV (Oct 1942), 19-26.
GENERAL
Boynton, Percy H. "Ole Edvart Rölvaag," *America in Contemporary Fiction*, 225-240.
Nelson, Pearl. "Rölvaag," *Prairie Schooner* III (Spring 1929), 156-159.
Whicher, George F. "In the American Grain," *The Literature of the American People*, 912-913.

RUTHERFORD, MARK
(See WHITE, WILLIAM HALE)

SALINGER, J. D.

CATCHER IN THE RYE
Aldridge, John W. "The Society of Three Novels," *In Search of Heresy*, 126-148.
Branch, Edgar. "Mark Twain and J. D. Salinger: A Study in Literary Continuity," *American Quarterly* IX (Summer 1957), 144-158.
Gwynn, Frederick L. and Joseph Blotner (eds.). *Faulkner in the University*, 244-245; 247.
——————. *The Fiction of J. D. Salinger*, 28-31.
Heiserman, Arthur and James E. Miller, Jr. "J. D. Salinger: Some Crazy Cliff," *Western Humanities Review* X (Spring 1956), 129-137.

SALINGER, J. D., Continued

Kaplan, Charles. "Holden and Huck: The Odysseys of Youth," *College English* XVIII (Nov 1956), 76-80.

Kegel, Charles H. "Incommunicability in Salinger's *The Catcher in the Rye*," *Western Humanities Review* XI (Spring 1957), 188-190.

Smith, Harrison. "Manhattan Ulysses, Junior," *Saturday Review of Literature* XXXIV (Jul 14, 1951), 12-13.

GENERAL

Geismar, Maxwell. "J. D. Salinger: The Wise Child and the New Yorker School of Fiction," *American Moderns*, 195-209.

Hassan, Ihab H. "Rare Quixotic Gesture: The Fiction of J. D. Salinger," *Western Review* XXI (Summer 1957), 261-280.

Hicks, Granville. "J. D. Salinger: Search for Wisdom," *Saturday Review* XLII (Jul 25, 1959), 13; 30.

Levine, Paul. "J. D. Salinger: The Development of the Misfit Hero," *Twentieth Century Literature* IV (Oct 1958), 92-99.

Wakefield, Dan. "Salinger and the Search for Love," *New World Writing* 14 (1958), 65-85.

BIBLIOGRAPHY

Gwynn, Frederick L. and Joseph L. Blotner. *The Fiction of J. D. Salinger*, 57-59.

SALTUS, EDGAR

GENERAL

Gohdes, Clarence. "The Facts of Life *Versus* Pleasant Reading," *The Literature of the American People*, 741-742.

McKitrick, Eric. "Edgar Saltus of the Obsolete," *American Quarterly* III (Spring 1951), 22-35.

SANTAYANA, GEORGE

THE LAST PURITAN

Aiken, Conrad. *A Reviewer's A B C*, 352-354.

Binsse, Harry Lorin. "A New Novelist," *American Review* VI (Mar 1936), 612-617.

Buchler, Justur. "George Santayana's *The Last Puritan*," *New England Quarterly* (Jun 1936), 273-280; Daniel Aaron, "A Postscript to *The Last Puritan*," *The New England Quarterly* IX (Dec 1936), 683-686.

SANTAYANA, GEORGE, Continued

Canby, Henry Seidel. "The Education of a Puritan," *Saturday Review of Literature* XIII (Feb 1, 1936), 3-4; 12.
Howgate, George W. *George Santayana*, 262-272.
Smith, Dane Farnsworth. "George Santayana and the Last Puritan," *New Mexico Quarterly* VII (Feb 1937), 39-45.
GENERAL
Cargill, Oscar. "The Naturalists," *Intellectual America*, 134-142.
Howgate, George W. *George Santayana*.
Santayana, George. "Brief History of Myself," *Saturday Review of Literature* XIII (Feb 1, 1936), 13.

SAROYAN, WILLIAM

THE ADVENTURES OF WESLEY JACKSON
Smith, Harrison. "Saroyan's War," *Saturday Review of Literature* XXIX (Jun 1, 1946), 7-8.
THE HUMAN COMEDY
Burgum, Edwin Berry. "The Lonesome Young Man on the Flying Trapeze," *The Novel and the World's Dilemma*, 269-271.
GENERAL
Fisher, William J. "What Ever Happened to Saroyan?" *College English* XVI (Mar 1955), 336-340.
Remenyi, Joseph. "William Saroyan: A Portrait," *College English* VI (Nov 1944), 92-99.
Wilson, Edmund. "The Boys in the Back Room," *A Literary Chronicle*, 222-227.

SCHAEFER, JACK

GENERAL
Mikkelsen, Robert. "The Western Writer: Jack Schaefer's Use of the Western Frontier," *Western Humanities Review* VIII (Spring 1954), 151-155.

SCHULBERG, BUDD

THE DISENCHANTED
Alpert, Hollis. "Golden Boy of Letters Badly Tarnished," *Saturday Review of Literature* XXXIII (Oct 28, 1950), 11.

SCHULBERG, BUDD, Continued

Robinson, Jean Joseph. "Harry James and Schulberg's *The Disenchanted*," *Modern Language Notes* LXVII (Nov 1952), 472-473.

GENERAL

Breit, Harvey. *The Writer Observed*, 139-141.

Schulberg, Budd. "Collision with the Party Line," *Saturday Review* XXXV (Aug 30, 1952), 6-8; 31-37.

SCOTT, EVELYN

GENERAL

Cargill, Oscar. "The Freudians," *Intellectual America*, 723-724.

Hatcher, Harlan. "Eroticism and the Psychological Novel: Evelyn Scott," *Creating the Modern American Novel*, 179-183.

SEDGWICK, ANN DOUGLAS

GENERAL

Beach, Joseph Warren. *The Twentieth Century Novel*, 287-291.

Quinn, Arthur Hobson. *American Fiction*, 582-595.

Whicher, George F. "Lingering Urbanity," *The Literature of the American People*, 819.

SEDGWICK, CATHERINE MARIA

GENERAL

Cowie, Alexander. "Contemporaries and Immediate Followers of Cooper, I: Catherine Maria Sedgwick (1789-1867)," *The Rise of the American Novel*, 200-212.

Quinn, Arthur Hobson. "The Development of Idealistic Romance," *American Fiction*, 103-105.

SHAW, IRWIN

THE YOUNG LIONS

Aldridge, John W. *After the Lost Generation*, 133-156.

Rogow, Lee. "The Folks to Fight With," *Saturday Review of Literature* XXXI (Oct 2, 1948), 12-13.

SHAW, IRWIN, Continued

GENERAL

Evans, Bergen. "Irwin Shaw," *College English* XIII (Nov 1951), 71-77.

Fiedler, Leslie A. "Irwin Shaw: Adultery, the Last Politics," *Commentary* XXII (Jul 1956), 71-74.

Shaw, Irwin. "If You Write About the War," *Saturday Review of Literature* XXVIII (Feb 17, 1945), 5-6.

SHELDON, CHARLES M.

IN HIS STEPS

Mott, Frank Luther. "*In His Steps*: The Myth of Thirty Millions," *Golden Multitudes*, 193-198.

SIMMS, WILLIAM GILMORE

MARTIN FABER

Stone, Edward. "*Caleb Williams* and *Martin Faber*: A Contrast," *Modern Language Notes* LXII (Nov 1947), 480-483.

THE PARTISAN

Vandiver, Edward P., Jr. "Simms's Porgy and Cooper," *Modern Language Notes* LXX (Apr 1955), 272-274.

YEMASSEE

Cowie, Alexander. Introduction, *Yemassee* (New York, 1937), pp. xliv.

Spencer, M. Lyle. Introduction, *Yemassee*.

GENERAL

Brooks, Van Wyck. "Charleston and the Southwest: Simms," *The World of Washington Irving*, 291-314.

Cowie, Alexander. "Contemporaries and Immediate Followers of Cooper, II: William Gilmore Simms (1806-1870)," *The Rise of the American Novel*, 228-246.

Holman, C. Hugh. "The Influence of Scott and Cooper on Simms," *American Literature* XXIII (May 1951), 203-218.

──────. "Simms and the British Dramatists," *PMLA* LXV (Jun 1950), 346-359.

──────. "The Status of Simms," *American Quarterly* X (Summer 1958), 181-185.

SIMMS, WILLIAM GILMORE, Continued

Hoole, William Stanley. "A Note on Simms's Visits to the Southwest," *American Literature* VI (Nov 1934), 334-336.

Hubbell, Jay B. *The South in American Literature*, 572-602.

Jarrell, Hampton M. "Falstaff and Simms's Porgy," *American Literature* III (May 1931), 204-212.

------. "Simms's Visits to the Southwest," *American Literature* V, (Mar 1933), 29-35.

Keiser, Albert. "Simms' Romantic Naturalism," *The Indian in American Literature*, 154-174.

Parks, Edd Winfield. "Simms: A Candid Self-Portrait," *Georgia Review* XII (Spring 1958), 94-103.

Quinn, Arthur Hobson. "The Development of Idealistic Romance," *American Fiction*, 114-123.

------. "The Romance of History and the Frontier," *The Literature of the American People*, 239-242.

Turner, Arlin. "William Gilmore Simms in His Letters," *South Atlantic Quarterly* LIII (Jul 1954), 404-415.

Wagenknecht, Edward. "William Gilmore Simms," *Cavalcade of the American Novel*, 32-37.

Whaley, Grace Wine. "A Note on Simms's Novels," *American Literature* II (May 1930), 173-174.

SINCLAIR, UPTON

DRAGON HARVEST

Jones, Howard Mumford. "The Continuing Story of Lanny Budd," *Saturday Review of Literature* XXVIII (Jun 16, 1945), 9-10.

THE JUNGLE

Fischer, John. Introduction, *The Jungle* (New York, 1951), pp. xviii.

KING COAL

Brandes, Dr. Georg. Introduction, *King Coal* (New York, 1917; London, 1930).

OIL!

Blotner, Joseph L. *The Political Novel*, 38.

PRESIDENTIAL AGENT

Blotner, Joseph L. *The Political Novel*, 40.

SINCLAIR, UPTON, Continued

THE RETURN OF LANNY BUDD

Lee, Charles. "More About Superbudd," *Saturday Review* XXXVI (Apr 18, 1953), 23; 41.

GENERAL

Anderson, Carl. "Swedish Criticism Before 1920: The Reception of Jack London and Upton Sinclair," *The Swedish Acceptance of American Literature*, 33-44.

Baldwin, Charles C. "Upton Sinclair," *The Men Who Make Our Novels*, 450-459.

Becker, George J. "Upton Sinclair: Quixote in a Flivver," *College English* XXI (Dec 1959), 133-140.

Brooks, Van Wyck. "The Novels of Upton Sinclair," *Emerson and Others*, 209-217.

Cantwell, Robert. "Upton Sinclair," *After the Genteel Tradition*, 37-51.

Dell, Floyd. *Upton Sinclair.*

Gurko, Leo. *The Angry Decade*, 99-103.

Harris, Frank. "Upton Sinclair," *Contemporary Portraits* (third series), 15-30.

Hartwick, Harry. "Plain Talk," *The Foreground of American Fiction*, 231-249.

Hatcher, Harlan. *Creating the Modern American Novel*, 127-132.

Hicks, Granville. *The Great Tradition*, 196-203.

——————. "The Survival of Upton Sinclair," *College English* IV (Jan 1943), 213-220.

Kazin, Alfred. "Progressivism: The Superman and the Muckrake," *On Native Grounds*, 116-121.

Lippmann, Walter. "Upton Sinclair," *Saturday Review of Literature* IV (Mar 3, 1928), 641-643.

Quinn, Arthur Hobson. "Critics and Satirists—The Radicals," *American Fiction*, 652-656.

Quint, Howard H. "Upton Sinclair's Quest for Artistic Independence—1909," *American Literature* XXIX (May 1957), 194-202.

Sinclair, Upton. "Farewell to Lanny Budd," *Saturday Review of Literature* XXXII (Aug 13, 1949), 18-19; 38.

Van Doren, Carl. *Contemporary American Novelists*, 65-74.

Whicher, George F. "The Conscience of Liberalism," *The Literature of the American People*, 829-830.

SINCLAIR, UPTON, Continued

BIBLIOGRAPHY

Bantz, Elizabeth. "Upton Sinclair: Book Reviews and Criticisms Published in German and French Periodicals and Newspapers," *Bulletin of Bibliography* XVIII (Jan-Apr 1946), 204-206.

SMITH, BETTY

A TREE GROWS IN BROOKLYN

Prescott, Orville. *In My Opinion*, 47-49.

SMITH, F. HOPKINSON

COLONEL CARTER OF CARTERSVILLE

Fiske, Horace Spencer. *Provincial Types in American Fiction*, 97-105.

GENERAL

Hornberger, Theodore. "The Effect of Painting on the Fiction of F. Hopkinson Smith (1838-1915)," *Texas Studies in English* XXIII (1943), 162-192.

SMITH, LILLIAN

STRANGE FRUIT

DeVoto, Bernard. "The Decision in *The Strange Fruit* Case: The Obscenity Statute in Massachusetts," *New England Quarterly* XIX (Jun 1946), 147-183.

Moore, Harry Estill. "*Strange Fruit*," *Southwest Review* XXX (Autumn 1944), 98-99.

Smith, Lillian. "Personal History of 'Strange Fruit': A Statement of Purposes and Intentions," *Saturday Review of Literature* XXVIII (Feb 17, 1945), 9-10.

SOUTHWORTH, EMMA DOROTHY ELIZA NEVILLE

GENERAL

Cowie, Alexander. "The Domestic Sentimentalists and Other Popular Writers (1850-1870): Emma Dorothy Eliza Neville Southworth (1819-1899)," *The Rise of the American Novel*, 418-419.

SOUTHWORTH, E. D. E. N.. Continued

Mott, Frank Luther. "Mrs. E.D.E.N. Southworth," *Golden Multitudes,* 136-142.

SPILLANE, MICKEY
GENERAL
Rolo, Charles J. "Simenon and Spillane: The Metaphysics of Murder for the Millions," *New World Writing* I (1952), 234-245.

SPRINGS, ELLIOTT WHITE
GENERAL
Olney, Clarke. "The Literary Career of Elliott White Springs," *Georgia Review* XI (Winter 1957), 400-411.

STAFFORD, JEAN
GENERAL
Breit, Harvey. *The Writer Observed,* 223-225.
Hassan, Ihab H. "Jean Stafford: The Expense of Style and The Scope of Sensibility," *Western Review* XIX (Spring 1955), 185-203.

STEIN, GERTRUDE
GENERAL
Brinnin, John Malcolm. *The Third Rose: Gertrude Stein and Her World.*
Burgum, Edwin Berry. "The Genius of Miss Gertrude Stein," *The Novel and the World's Dilemma,* 157-183.
Cargill, Oscar. "The Decadents," *Intellectual America,* 293-300, "The Primitivists," 311-322.
Eagleson, Harvey. "Gertrude Stein: Method in Madness," *Sewanee Review* XLIV (Apr-Jun 1936), 164-177.
Fadiman, Clifton. "Gertrude Stein," *Party of One,* 85-97.
Fay, Bernard. "A Rose Is a Rose," *Saturday Review of Literature* X (Sept 2, 1933), 77-79.
Gallup, Donald. "Carl Van Vechten's Gertrude Stein," *Yale University Library Gazette* XXVII (Oct 1952), 77-86.

STEIN, GERTRUDE, Continued

———————. "The Gertrude Stein Collection," *The Yale University Library Gazette* XXII (Oct 1947), 21-32.
Gass, W. H. "Gertrude Stein: Her Escape from Protective Language," *Accent* XVIII (Autumn 1958), 233-244.
Haines, George, IV. "Gertrude Stein and Composition," *Sewanee Review* LVII (Jul-Sept 1949), 411-424.
Herbst, Josephine. "Miss Porter and Miss Stein," *Partisan Review* XV (May 1948), 568-572.
Hoffman, Frederick J. "Gertrude Stein: The Method and the Subject," *The Modern Novel in America*, 76-88.
Miller, Rosalind S. *Gertrude Stein*.
Porter, Katherine Anne. *The Days Before*, 36-60.
Reid, B. L. *Art by Subtraction*.
Rogers, W. G. *When This You See, Remember Me*.
Rosenfeld, Paul. "The Place of Gertrude Stein," *By Way of Art*, 111-131.
Russell, Francis. "Gertrude Stein," *Three Studies in Twentieth Century Obscurity*, 66-122.
Sherman, Stuart P. "A Note on Gertrude Stein," *Points of View*, 263-268.
Smith, Harrison. "A Rose for Remembrance," *Saturday Review of Literature* XXIX (Aug 10, 1946), 11.
Sprigge, Elizabeth. *Gertrude Stein*.
———————. "Gertrude Stein's American Years," *Reporter* XIII (Aug 11, 1955), 46-52.
Stein, Gertrude. "The Situation in American Writing," *Partisan Review* VI (Summer 1939), 40-41.
Stewart, Allegra. "The Quality of Gertrude Stein's Creativity," *American Literature* XXVIII (Jan 1957), 488-506.
Sutherland, Donald. *Gertrude Stein*.
Van Doren, Carl. *The American Novel, 1784-1939*, 338-341.
Van Vechten, Carl. "A Stein Song," *Selected Writings of Gertrude Stein* (New York, 1946), ix-xv.
Whicher, George F. "Impressionists and Experimenters," *The Literature of the American People*, 864-866.
Wilson, Edmund. *The Shores of Light*, 575-586.
BIBLIOGRAPHY
Miller, Rosalind S. *Gertrude Stein*, 157-160.
Reid, B. L. *Art by Subtraction*, 211-216.

STEINBECK, JOHN

CANNERY ROW
Lisca, Peter. *The Wide World of John Steinbeck,* 197-217.
Rothman, Nathan L. "A Small Miracle," *Saturday Review of Literature* XXVII (Dec 30, 1944), 5.

CUP OF GOLD
Lisca, Peter. *The Wide World of John Steinbeck,* 21-38.
Moore, Harry Thornton. *The Novels of John Steinbeck,* 11-18.

EAST OF EDEN
Fuller, Edmund. *Man in Modern Fiction,* 25-29.
Hobson, L. Z. "Trade Winds," *Saturday Review* XXXV (Aug 30, 1952), 4.
Krutch, Joseph Wood. *Steinbeck and His Critics,* 302-305.
Leonard, Frank G. "Cozzens without Sex; Steinbeck without Sin," *Antioch Review* XVIII (Summer 1958), 209-218.
Lisca, Peter. *The Wide World of John Steinbeck,* 261-275.
Webster, Harvey Curtis. "Out of the New-born Sun," *Saturday Review* XXXV (Sept 20, 1952), 11-12.

THE GRAPES OF WRATH
Bluestone, George. *Novels into Film,* 147-169.
Bowron, Bernard. " 'The Grapes of Wrath': A 'Wagons West' Romance," *Colorado Quarterly* III (Summer 1954), 84-91; French, Warren G. "Another Look at 'The Grapes of Wrath,' " *Colorado Quarterly* III (Winter 1955), 337-343; Steinbeck, John. "A Letter on Criticism," *Colorado Quarterly* IV (Autumn 1955), 218-219.
Canby, Henry Seidel. "The Right Question," *Saturday Review of Literature* XXI (Mar 23, 1940), 8.
Carpenter, Frederic I. "The Philosophical Joads," *College English* II (Jan 1941), 315-325; *Steinbeck and His Critics,* 241-249.
Eisinger, Chester E. "Jeffersonian Agrarianism in *The Grapes of Wrath,*" *University of Kansas City Review* XIV (Winter 1957), 149-154.
Fairley, Barker. "John Steinbeck and the Coming Literature," *Sewanee Review* L (Apr-Jun 1942), 145-161.
"Grapes of Wrath," *American Writing Today,* 398-399.
Isherwood, Christopher. "The Tragedy of Eldorado," *Kenyon Review* I (Autumn 1939), 450-453.
Jackson, Joseph Henry. Introduction, *Grapes of Wrath* (New York, 1940) pp. xxii.

STEINBECK, JOHN, Continued

Kronenberger, Louis. *College Prose.* 424-427.
Lisca, Peter. "*The Grapes of Wrath* as Fiction," *PMLA* LXXII (Mar 1957), 296-309.
——————. *The Wide World of John Steinbeck,* 144-177.
Long, Louise. "*The Grapes of Wrath,*" *Southwest Review* XXIV (Jul 1939), 495-498.
Longstreet, Stephen. *College Prose,* 428-430.
McElderry, B. R., Jr. "*The Grapes of Wrath*: In the Light of Modern Critical Theory," *College English* V (Mar 1944), 308-313.
Miron, George Thomas. *The Truth About John Steinbeck and the Migrants.*
Moore, Harry Thornton. *The Novels of John Steinbeck,* 53-72.
Pollock, Theodore. "On the Ending of 'The Grapes of Wrath,'" *Modern Fiction Studies* IV (Summer 1958), 177-178.
Poore, Charles. Introduction, *The Grapes of Wrath* (New York, 1951).
Shockley, Martin Staples. "The Reception of *The Grapes of Wrath* in Oklahoma," *American Literature* XV (Jan 1944), 351-361; *Steinbeck and His Critics,* 231-240.
——————. "Christian Symbolism in *The Grapes of Wrath,*" *College English* XVIII (Nov 1956), 87-90; Carlson, Eric W. "Rebuttal: Symbolism in *The Grapes of Wrath,*" *College English* XIX (Jan 1958), 172-175; De Schweinitz, George. "Steinbeck and Christianity," *College English* XIX (May 1958), 369.
——————. *Steinbeck and His Critics,* 266-271.
Slochower, Harry. *No Voice Is Wholly Lost,* 299-306.
Stevens, George. "Steinbeck's Uncovered Wagon," *Saturday Review of Literature* XIX (Apr 15, 1939), 3-4.
Stovall, Floyd. *American Idealism,* 161-166.
Tedlock, E. W., Jr. and C. V. Wicker. *Steinbeck and His Critics,* xxxii-xxxv.
Van Doren, Carl. Introduction, *The Grapes of Wrath* (Cleveland, 1947), pp. vii.

IN DUBIOUS BATTLE

Blotner, Joseph L. "John Steinbeck: The Party Organizer," *The Political Novel,* 14.
Lisca, Peter. *The Wide World of John Steinbeck,* 108-129.

STEINBECK, JOHN, Continued

Moore, Harry Thornton. *The Novels of John Steinbeck,* 40-47.

OF MICE AND MEN

Jackson, Joseph Henry. Introduction, *Of Mice and Men* (New York, 1958), pp. xx.

Lisca, Peter. *The Wide World of John Steinbeck,* 130-143.

——————. "Motif and Pattern in 'Of Mice and Men,'" *Modern Fiction Studies* II (Winter 1956-1957), 228-234.

Moore, Harry Thornton. *The Novels of John Steinbeck,* 47-53.

Van Doren, Mark. "Wrong Number," *The Private Reader,* 255-257.

THE PASTURES OF HEAVEN

Lisca, Peter. *The Wide World of John Steinbeck,* 56-71.

Moore, Harry Thornton. *The Novels of John Steinbeck,* 18-23.

THE PEARL

Lisca, Peter. *Steinbeck and His Critics,* 291-301.

——————. *The Wide World of John Steinbeck,* 218-230.

SWEET THURSDAY

Lisca, Peter. *The Wide World of John Steinbeck,* 276-284.

Webster, Harvey Curtis. "'Cannery Row,' Continued," *Saturday Review* XXXVII (Jun 5, 1954), 11.

TO A GOD UNKNOWN

Lisca, Peter. *The Wide World of John Steinbeck,* 39-55.

Moore, Harry Thornton. *The Novels of John Steinbeck,* 23-33.

TORTILLA FLAT

Lisca, Peter. *The Wide World of John Steinbeck,* 72-91.

Moore, Harry Thornton. *The Novels of John Steinbeck,* 35-40.

Schumann, Hildegard. "*Tortilla Flat,* John Steinbecks erster schrifstellerischer Erfolg," *Zeitschrift für Anglistik und Amerikanistik* IV (Heft 3 1956), 331-342.

THE WAYWARD BUS

Brown, J. M. "Upright Bus," *Saturday Review of Literature* XXX (Apr 19, 1947), 24-27.

Lisca, Peter. *Steinbeck and His Critics,* 281-290.

——————. *The Wide World of John Steinbeck,* 231-247.

GENERAL

Adams, J. Donald. "Main Street and the Dust Bowl," *The Shape of Books to Come,* 131-143.

Beach, Joseph Warren. "John Steinbeck: Art and Propaganda," *American Fiction,* 327-347.

STEINBECK, JOHN, Continued

──────────. "John Steinbeck: Journeyman Artist," *American Fiction*, 309-324; *Steinbeck and His Critics*, 80-91.

Bidwell, Martin. "John Steinbeck: An Impression," *Prairie Schooner* XII (Spring 1938), 10-15.

Boynton, Percy H. "John Steinbeck," *America in Contemporary Fiction*, 241-257.

Bracher, Frederick. "Steinbeck and the Biological View of Man," *Steinbeck and His Critics*, 183-196.

Burgum, Edwin Berry. "The Fickle Sensibility of John Steinbeck," *The Novel and the World's Dilemma*, 272-291; *Steinbeck and His Critics*, 104-118.

Carpenter, Frederic I. "John Steinbeck: American Dreamer," *Southwest Review* XXVI (Summer 1941), 454-467; *Steinbeck and His Critics*, 68-79.

Champney, Freeman. "John Steinbeck, Californian," *Antioch Review* VIII (Sept 1947), 345-362; *Steinbeck and His Critics*, 135-151.

Cody, W. F. "Steinbeck Will Get You if You Don't Watch Out," *Saturday Review of Literature* XXVIII (Jul 7, 1945), 18-19.

Cousins, Norman. "Bankrupt Realism," *Saturday Review of Literature* XXX (Mar 8, 1947), 22-23.

──────────. "Who Are the Real People?" *Saturday Review of Literature* XXVIII (Mar 17, 1945), 14.

Fairley, Barker. "John Steinbeck and the Coming Literature," *Sewanee Review* L (Apr-Jun 1942), 145-161.

Frohock, W. M. "John Steinbeck's Men of Wrath," *Southwest Review* XXXI (Spring 1946), 144-152.

──────────. "John Steinbeck: The Utility of Wrath," *The Novel of Violence in America*, 147-164.

Gannett, Lewis. Introduction, *The Portable Steinbeck* (New York, 1958), vii-xviii.

──────────. "John Steinbeck: Novelist at Work," *Atlantic Monthly*, CLXXVI (Dec 1945), 55-60.

Geismar, Maxwell. "John Steinbeck," *American Moderns*, 151-156.

──────────. "John Steinbeck: Of Wrath or Joy," *Writers in Crisis*, 239-270.

Gibbs, Lincoln R. "John Steinbeck, Moralist," *Antioch Review* II (Jun 1942), 172-184; *Steinbeck and His Critics*, 92-103.

STEINBECK, JOHN, Continued

Gurko, Leo. "The Joads in California," *The Angry Decade,* 201-221.

Gurko, Leo and Miriam. "The Steinbeck Temperament," *Rocky Mountain Review* IX (Fall 1954), 17-22.

Hyman, Stanley E. "*Some Notes on John Steinbeck*," *Antioch Review* II (Jun 1942), 185-200; *Steinbeck and His Critics,* 152-166.

Jackson, Joseph Henry. Introduction, *Short Novels* (New York, 1953).

——————. "John Steinbeck: A Portrait," *Saturday Review of Literature* XVI (Sept 25, 1937), 11-12; 18.

Jones, Claude E. "Proletarian Writing and John Steinbeck," *Sewanee Review* XLVIII (Oct-Dec 1940), 445-456.

Kazin, Alfred. "The Revival of Naturalism," *On Native Grounds,* 393-399.

Kennedy, John S. "John Steinbeck: Life Affirmed and Dissolved," *Fifty Years of the American Novel,* 217-236; *Steinbeck and His Critics,* 119-134.

Lewis, R. W. B. "The Steinbeck Perspective," *The Picaresque Saint,* 179-193.

Lisca, Peter. "John Steinbeck: A Literary Biography," *Steinbeck and His Critics,* 3-22.

——————. *The Wide World of John Steinbeck,* 3-20; 288-295.

Magny, Claude-Edmonde. "Steinbeck, or The Limits of the Impersonal Novel," *Steinbeck and His Critics,* 216-227.

Mayo, Thomas F. "The Great Pendulum," *Southwest Review* XXXVI (Summer 1951), 190-201.

Moore, Harry Thornton. *The Novels of John Steinbeck,* 73-96.

Morris, Lloyd. *Postscript to Yesterday,* 167-171.

Nevius, Blake. "Steinbeck: One Aspect," *Steinbeck and His Critics,* 197-206.

Prescott, Orville. *In My Opinion,* 58-64.

Rascoe, Burton. "John Steinbeck," *Steinbeck and His Critics,* 57-67.

Richards, Edmund C. "The Challenge of John Steinbeck," *North American Review* 243 (Summer 1937), 406-413.

Ross, Woodburn O. "John Steinbeck: Earth and Stars," *Steinbeck and His Critics,* 167-182.

STEINBECK, JOHN, Continued

——————. "John Steinbeck: Naturalism's Priest," *College English* X (May 1949), 432-438; *Steinbeck and His Critics*, 206-215.

Sartre, Jean-Paul. "American Novelists in French Eyes," *Atlantic Monthly* CLXXVIII (Aug 1946), 114-118.

Schramm, Wilbur L. "Careers at Crossroads," *Virginia Quarterly Review* XV (Oct 1939), 628-632.

Seixas, Antonia. *Steinbeck and His Critics*, 275-280.

Snell, George. "John Steinbeck: Realistic Whimsy," *The Shapers of American Fiction*, 187-197.

Steinbeck, John. "My Short Novels," *Steinbeck and His Critics*, 38-40.

Tedlock, E. W., Jr. and C. V. Wicker. Introduction, *Steinbeck and His Critics*, xi-xxii; xxxv-xli.

Wagenknecht, Edward. *Cavalcade of the American Novel*, 443-448.

Walcutt, Charles Child. "Later Trends in Form: Steinbeck," *American Literary Naturalism*, 258-269.

Whicher, George F. "Proletarian Leanings," *The Literature of the American People*, 958-961.

Whipple, Thomas K. "Steinbeck: Through a Glass, Though Brightly," *Study Out the Land*, 105-111.

Wilson, Edmund. "The Boys in the Back Room: John Steinbeck," *Classics and Commercials*, 35-45; *A Literary Chronicle*, 230-239.

STILL, JAMES

GENERAL

Kohler, Dayton. "Jesse Stuart and James Still: Mountain Regionalists," *College English* III (Mar 1942), 523-533.

STOCKTON, FRANK

GENERAL

Chislett, William, Jr. "The Stories and Novels of Frank Stockton," *Moderns and Near-Moderns*, 67-97.

Griffin, Martin I. J. *Frank R. Stockton*.

Quinn, Arthur Hobson. "The Fiction of Fantasy," *American Fiction*, 220-231.

STOWE, HARRIET BEECHER

DRED: A TALE OF THE GREAT DISMAL SWAMP
Foster, Charles H. *The Rungless Ladder,* 71-78.

THE MINISTER'S WOOING
Foster, Charles H. *The Rungless Ladder,* 86-128.

──────────. "The Genesis of Harriet Beecher Stowe's 'The Minister's Wooing,'" *New England Quarterly* XXI (Dec 1948), 493-517.

MY WIFE AND I
Wyman, Margaret. "Harriet Beecher Stowe's Topical Novel on Woman Suffrage," *New England Quarterly* XXV (Sept 1952), 383-391.

OLDTOWN FOLKS
Foster, Charles H. *The Rungless Ladder,* 165-202.

Suckow, Ruth. "An Almost Lost American Classic," *College English* XIV (Mar 1953), 315-325.

THE PEARL OF ORR'S ISLAND
Foster, Charles H. *The Rungless Ladder,* 145-160.

UNCLE TOM'S CABIN
Blotner, Joseph L. *The Political Novel,* 10-11.

Burns, Wayne and Emerson Grant Sutcliffe. "Uncle Tom and Charles Reade," *American Literature* XVII (Jan 1946), 334-347.

Downs, Robert B. *Books That Changed the World,* 76-85.

Duvall, S. P. C. "W. G. Simms's Review of Mrs. Stowe," *American Literature* XXX (Mar 1958), 107-117.

Foster, Charles H. *The Rungless Ladder,* 12-63.

Furnas, J. C. *Goodbye to Uncle Tom.*

Gaines, Francis Pendleton. Introduction, *Uncle Tom's Cabin* (New York, 1926), pp. xiv.

Maycock, Willoughby. "Prefaces to *Uncle Tom's Cabin*," *Notes and Queries* 11 S.XII (Jul 17, 1915), 58.

Mott, Frank Luther. *Golden Multitudes,* 114-122.

Nicholas, Herbert G. "*Uncle Tom's Cabin,* 1852-1952," *Georgia Review* VIII (Summer 1954), 140-148.

Page, John T.; S.; W. B.; and Willoughby Maycock. "The Original 'Uncle Tom,'" *Notes and Queries* 11 S. VI (1912), 367; 436; 493.

STOWE, HARRIET BEECHER, Continued

Roppolo, Joseph P. "Harriet Beecher Stowe and New Orleans: A Study in Hate," *New England Quarterly* XXX (Sept 1957), 346-362.

Scudder, Harold H. "Mrs. Trollope and Slavery in America," *Notes and Queries* 187 (29 Jul 1944), 46-48.

Stone, Harry. "Charles Dickens and Harriet Beecher Stowe," *Nineteenth-Century Fiction* XII (Dec 1957), 188-202.

Stowe, Lyman Beecher. "Uncle Tom's Cabin," *Saturday Review of Literature* II (Dec 12, 1925), 422.

Weaver, Raymond. Introduction, *Uncle Tom's Cabin* (New York, 1938; 1948).

GENERAL

Andrews, Kenneth R. *Nook Farm.*

Bradford, Gamaliel. "Portraits of American Woman: Harriet Beecher Stowe," *Atlantic Monthly* CXXII (1918), 84-94; *Portraits of American Women*, 101-130.

Cowie, Alexander. "Experiment and Tradition: Harriet Beecher Stowe (1811-1896)," *The Rise of the American Novel*, 447-463.

Cunliffe, Marcus. "Minor Key," *The Literature of the United States*, 176-177.

Eaton, G. D. "Harriet Beecher Stowe," *American Mercury* X (Apr 1927), 445-459.

Erskine, John. "Harriet Beecher Stowe," *Leading American Novelists*, 275-323.

Foster, Charles H. *The Rungless Ladder.*

Gilbertson, Catherine. *Harriet Beecher Stowe.*

Hubbell, Jay B. *The South in American Literature*, 385-393.

Quinn, Arthur Hobson. "Literature, Politics, and Slavery," *The Literature of the American People*, 460-461.

——————. "The Transition to Realism," *American Fiction*, 159-163.

Seiler, Grace. "Harriet Beecher Stowe," *College English* XI (Dec 1949), 127-137.

Wagenknecht, Edward. *Cavalcade of the American Novel*, 91-102.

Westbrook, Percy D. *Acres of Flint*, 21-26.

Wilson, Forrest. *Crusader in Crinoline.*

STREET, JAMES

GENERAL

Davies, Horton. *A Mirror of the Ministry in Modern Novels,* 40-47.

STRIBLING, T. S.

GENERAL

Dickens, Byrom. "T. S. Stribling and the South," *Sewanee Review* XLII (Jul-Sept 1934), 341-349.

Warren, Robert Penn. "T. S. Stribling: a Paragraph in the History of Critical Realism," *American Review* II (Feb 1934), 463-486.

STUART, JESSE

GENERAL

Kohler, Dayton. "Jesse Stuart and James Still: Mountain Regionalists," *College English* III (Mar 1942), 523-533.

Stuart, Jesse. "What Happens to a Writer in His Home Town," *Saturday Review of Literature* XXVIII (Apr 21, 1945), 5-7.

STYRON, WILLIAM

LIE DOWN IN DARKNESS

Aldridge, John W. *In Search of Heresy,* 126-148.

Geismar, Maxwell. "Domestic Tragedy in Virginia," *Saturday Review of Literature* XXXVI (Sept 15, 1951), 12-13.

GENERAL

Geismar, Maxwell. "William Styron: The End of Innocence," *American Moderns,* 239-250.

Matthiesen, Peter and George Plimpton. "William Styron," *Writers at Work,* 267-282.

SUCKOW, RUTH

THE FOLKS

Baker, Joseph E. "Regionalism in the Middle West," *American Review* V (Mar 1935), 603-614.

GENERAL

Hatcher, Harlan. "Newer Arrivals," *Creating the Modern American Novel,* 99-106.

TARKINGTON, BOOTH

ALICE ADAMS
Woodress, James. *Booth Tarkington*, 245-250.
THE HERITAGE OF HATCHER IDE
Marquand, J, P. "Tarkington and Social Significance," *Saturday Review of Literature* XXIII (Mar 1, 1941), 7.
THE MAGNIFICENT AMBERSONS
Woodress, James. *Booth Tarkington*, 194-198.
THE MIDLANDER
Sherman, Stuart P. *Points of View*, 229-233.
PENROD
Woodress, James. *Booth Tarkington*, 174-180.
THE PLUTOCRAT
Woodress, James. *Booth Tarkington*, 265-269.
THE TURMOIL
Woodress, James. "Booth Tarkington's Attack on American Materialism," *Georgia Review* VIII (Winter 1954), 440-446.
GENERAL
Baldwin, Charles C. "Booth Tarkington," *The Men Who Make Our Novels*, 474-486.
Boynton, Percy H. "Booth Tarkington," *Some Contemporary Americans*, 108-125.
Quinn, Arthur Hobson. *American Fiction*, 596-622.
Van Doren, Carl. *Contemporary American Novelists*, 84-95.
Wagenknecht, Edward. "Voices of the New Century: Booth Tarkington, Success," *Cavalcade of the American Novel*, 244-251.
Whicher, George F. "Spokesmen of the Plain People," *The Literature of the American People*, 838-839.
Woodress, James. *Booth Tarkington*.
Wyatt, Edith. "Booth Tarkington: The Seven Ages of Man," *North American Review* 216 (Oct 1922), 499-512.
BIBLIOGRAPHY
Curries, Barton. *Booth Tarkington*.
Russo, Dorothy Ritter and Thelma L. Sullivan. *A Bibliography of Booth Tarkington*.

TAYLOR, BAYARD

GENERAL
Beatty, Richmond Croom. *Bayard Taylor*, 229-242.
Cary, Richard. *The Genteel Circle.*
Cowie, Alexander. "Experiment and Tradition: Bayard Taylor (1825-1878)," *The Rise of the American Novel*, 475-486.
Taylor, Marie Hansen. *On Two Continents.*

TATE, ALLEN

THE FATHERS
Baker, Howard. "The Shattered Door," *Kenyon Review* I (Winter 1939), 90-93.
Mizener, Arthur. "*The Fathers* and Realistic Fiction," *Accent* 7 (Winter 1947), 101-109.

THIELEN, BENEDICT

THE LOST MEN
Carlson, Eric W. "Thielen's *The Lost Men*," *Arizona Quarterly* XI (Autumn 1955), 238-250.

THOMPSON, DANIEL PIERCE

THE GREEN MOUNTAIN BOYS
Flitcroft, John E. *The Novelist of Vermont*, 79-113.
LOCKE AMSDEN
Flitcroft, John E. *The Novelist of Vermont*, 91-127.
GENERAL
Cowie, Alexander. "Contemporaries and Immediate Followers of Cooper, II: Daniel Pierce Thompson (1795-1868)," *The Rise of the American Novel*, 270-275.
Flitcroft, John E. *The Novelist of Vermont.*

TOURGÉE, ALBION WINEGAR

A FOOL'S ERRAND
Blotner, Joseph L. *The Political Novel*, 34-35.
Dibble, Roy F. *Albion W. Tourgée*, 59-83.
GENERAL
Becker, George J. "Albion W. Tourgée: Pioneer in Social Criticism," *American Literature* XIX (Mar 1947), 59-72.

TOURGÉE, ALBION WINEGAR, Continued

Cowie, Alexander. "Civil War and Reconstruction: Albion W. Tourgée (1838-1905)," *The Rise of the American Novel*, 521-535.

Dibble, Roy F. *Albion W. Tourgée*.

Gohdes, Clarence. "A Challenge of Social Problems of Science," *The Literature of the American People*, 765-766.

TRILLING, LIONEL

THE MIDDLE OF THE JOURNEY

Beresnack, Lillian. "The Journey of Lionel Trilling," *Perspective* I (Spring 1948), 177-183.

Zaubel, Morton Dauwen. *Craft and Character*, 312-317.

TWAIN, MARK

A CONNECTICUT YANKEE IN KING ARTHUR'S COURT

Canby, Henry Seidel. "Hero of the Great Know-How," *Saturday Review of Literature* XXXIV (Oct 20, 1951), 7-8; 40-41.

Edwards, Peter G. "The Political Economy of Mark Twain's 'Connecticut Yankee,'" *Mark Twain Quarterly* VIII (Winter 1950), 2.

Foner, Philip. *Mark Twain*, 103-115.

Hoben, John B. "Mark Twain's *A Connecticut Yankee:* A Genetic Study," *American Literature* XVIII (Nov 1946), 197-218.

Howells, W. D. *My Mark Twain*, 145-149.

Lorch, Fred W. "Hawaiian Feudalism and Mark Twain's *A Connecticut Yankee in King Arthur's Court*," *American Literature* XXX (Mar 1958), 50-66.

Roades, Sister Mary Teresa. "Don Quixote and a Connecticut Yankee in King Arthur's Court," *Mark Twain Quarterly* II (Summer-Fall 1938), 8-9.

Trainor, Juliette A. "Symbolism in *A Connecticut Yankee in King Arthur's Court*," *Modern Language Notes* LXVI (Jun 1951), 382-385.

Van Doren, Carl. Introduction, *A Connecticut Yankee in King Arthur's Court* (New York, 1948), pp. vii.

THE GILDED AGE

Foner, Philip. *Mark Twain*, 69-86.

TWAIN, MARK, Continued

Kitzhaber, Albert R. "Mark Twain's Use of the Pomeroy Case in *The Gilded Age*," *Modern Language Quarterly* XV (Mar 1954), 42-56.

Leisy, Ernest E. "Mark Twain's Part in *The Gilded Age*," *American Literature* VIII (Jan 1937), 445-447.

Paine, Albert Bigelow. *A Short Life of Mark Twain*, 154-156.

Turner, Arlin. "James Lampton, Mark Twain's Model for Colonel Sellers," *Modern Language Notes* LXX (Dec 1955), 592-594.

Walker, Franklin. "An Influence from San Francisco on Mark Twain's *The Gilded Age*," *American Literature* VIII (Mar 1936), 63-66.

Weatherly, Edward H. "Beau Tibbs and Colonel Sellers," *Modern Language Notes* LIX (May 1944), 310-313.

HUCKLEBERRY FINN, THE ADVENTURES OF

A., P. B. "Clemens'. . .*Huckleberry Finn*," *Explicator* IV (Nov 1945), Q7; Ferguson, DeLancey. "Clemens . . . *Huckleberry Finn*," IV (Apr 1946), No. 42.

Adams, Richard P. "The Unity and Coherence of *Huckleberry Finn*," *Tulane Studies in English* VI (1956), 87-103; *Mark Twain's Huckleberry Finn*, 82-94.

Allen, Walter. Introduction, *The Adventures of Huckleberry Finn* (London, 1949).

Altenbernd, Lynn. "Huck Finn, Emancipator," *Criticism* I (Fall 1959), 298-307.

Baldanza, Frank. "The Structure of *Huckleberry Finn*," *American Literature* XXVII (Nov 1955), 347-355; *Mark Twain's Huckleberry Finn*, 75-81.

Blair, Walter. "When Was *Huckleberry Finn* Written?" *American Literature* XXX (Mar 1958), 1-25.

---------------. "Why Huck and Jim Went Downstream," *College English* XVIII (Nov 1956), 106-107.

Blassingame, Wyatt. "The Use of the Lie in 'Huckleberry Finn' as a Technical Device," *Mark Twain Quarterly* IX (Winter 1952), 11-12.

Branch, Edgar. "Mark Twain and J. D. Salinger: A Study in Literary Continuity," *American Quarterly* IX (Summer 1957), 144-158.

TWAIN, MARK, Continued

———. "The Two Provinces: Thematic Form in 'Huckleberry Finn,'" *College English* XI (Jan 1950), 188-195.
Brownell, Frances V. "The Role of Jim in *Huckleberry Finn*," *Boston University Studies in English* I (Spring-Summer 1955), 74-83.
Cardwell, Guy A. *Twins of Genius*, 68-77.
Chase, Richard. *The American Novel and Its Tradition*, 139-149.
Cowie, Alexander. "Mark Twain Controls Himself," *American Literature* X (Jan 1939), 488-491.
Cox, James M. "Remarks on the Sad Initiation of Huckleberry Finn," *Sewanee Review* LXII (Jul-Sept 1954), 389-405; *Interpretations of American Literature*, 229-243; *Mark Twain's Huckleberry Finn*, 65-74.
Da Ponte, Durant. "*Life* Reviews *Huckleberry Finn*," *American Literature* XXXI (Mar 1959), 78-81.
De Voto, Bernard. Introduction, *The Adventures of Huckleberry Finn* (1942), pp. lxxvi.
———. "Mark Twain at Work," *Mark Twain's Huckleberry Finn*, 28-43.
———. *Mark Twain at Work*, 45-104.
———. "Tom, Huck, and America," *Saturday Review of Literature* IX (Aug 13, 1932), 37-39.
Eliot, T. S. Introduction, *The Adventures of Huckleberry Finn* (London, 1950), pp. xvi.
Elliott, George P. *Twelve Original Essays on Great American Novels*, 69-95.
Fadiman, Clifton. *Party of One*, 129-131.
Fiedler, Leslie. "Come Back to the Raft Ag'in, Huck Honey!" *Partisan Review*, XV (Jun 1948), 664-671; *An End to Innocence*, 142-151.
Fiske, Horace Spencer. *Provincial Types in American Fiction*, 152-166.
Foner, Philip S. *Mark Twain*, 204-219.
Frantz, Ray W., Jr. "The Role of Folklore in *Huckleberry Finn*," *American Literature* XXVIII (Nov 1956), 314-327.
Gerber, Helmut E. "Twain's *Huckleberry Finn*," *Explicator* XII (Mar 1954), No. 28.
Gullason, Thomas Arthur. "The 'Fatal' Ending of *Huckleberry Finn*," *American Literature* XXIX (Mar 1957), 86-91.

TWAIN, MARK, Continued

Harrison, James G. "A Note on the Duke in 'Huck Finn': The Journeyman Printer as a Picaro," *Mark Twain Quarterly* VIII (Winter 1947), 1-2.

Hunting, Robert. "Mark Twain's Arkansaw Yahooes," *Modern Language Notes* LXXIII (Apr 1958), 254-268.

Jones, Joseph. "The 'Duke's' Tooth-Powder Racket: A Note on *Huckleberry Finn*," *Modern Language Notes* LXI (Nov 1946), 468-469.

Kaplan, Charles. "Holden and Huck: The Odysseys of Youth," *College English* XVIII (Nov 1956), 76-80.

Klaus, Rosemarie. "Mark Twain und die Negerfrage—*Huckleberry Finn*," *Zeitschrift für Anglistik und Amerikanistik* V Heft 2 (1957), 166-181.

Lane, Lauriat, Jr. "Why *Huckleberry Finn* Is a Great World Novel," *College English* XVII (Oct 1955), 1-5; *Mark Twain's Huckleberry Finn*, 95-100.

Leary, Lewis. "Tom and Huck: Innocence on Trial," *Virginia Quarterly Review* XXX (Summer 1954), 417-430.

Lorch, Fred W. "A Note on Tom Blankenship (Huckleberry Finn)," *American Literature* XII (Nov 1940), 351-353.

Lynn, Kenneth S. "Huck and Jim," *Yale Review* XLVII (Mar 1958), 421-431.

Marx, Leo. "Mr. Eliot, Mr. Trilling and *Huckleberry Finn*," *American Scholar* XXII (Autumn 1953), 423-440; *Mark Twain's Huckleberry Finn*, 53-64; *Interpretations of American Literature*, 212-228.

————. "The Pilot and the Passenger: Landscape Conventions and the Style of *Huckleberry Finn*," *American Literature* XXVIII (May 1956), 129-146.

Matthews, Brander. Introduction, *The Adventures of Huckleberry Finn* (New York, 1918), pp. xix.

Matthews, Brander and Dixon Wecter. Introduction, *The Adventures of Huckleberry Finn* (New York, 1948), pp. xxv.

Morley, Christopher. Introduction, *The Adventures of Tom Sawyer* and *The Adventures of Huckleberry Finn* (New York, 1954).

Morris, Courtland P. "The Model for Huck Finn," *Mark Twain Quarterly* II (Summer-Fall 1938), 22-23.

TWAIN, MARK, Continued

O'Connor, William Van. "Why *Huckleberry Finn* Is Not The Great American Novel," *College English* XVII (Oct 1955), 6-10; *Mark Twain's Huckleberry Finn,* 101-106.

Ornstein, Robert. "The Ending of *Huckleberry Finn,*" *Modern Language Notes* LXXIV (Dec 1959), 698-702.

Paine, Albert Bigelow. *A Short Life of Mark Twain,* 168-171; 196-199.

Rubenstein, Gilbert M. "The Moral Structure of *Huckleberry Finn,*" *College English* XVIII (Nov 1956), 72-76.

Schwartz, Edward. "Huckleberry Finn: The Inward Thoughts of a Generation," *Mark Twain Quarterly* IX (Winter 1952), 11-16.

Scott, Arthur L. "The *Century Magazine* Edits *Huckleberry Finn,* 1884-1885," *American Literature* XXVII (Nov 1955), 356-362.

Slater, Joseph. "Music at Col. Grangerford's: A Footnote to *Huckleberry Finn,*" *American Literature* XXI (Mar 1949), 108-111.

Stallman, R. W. "Letters to the Editor: Huck Finn Again," *College English* XVIII (May 1957), 425-426.

Swinton, Marjory. Introduction, *The Adventures of Tom Sawyer* and *The Adventures of Huckleberry Finn* (New York, 1959).

Tarkington, Booth. Introduction, *The Adventures of Huckleberry Finn* (1933).

Trilling, Lionel. Introduction, *The Adventures of Huckleberry Finn* (New York, 1948), pp. xxii.

——————. "The Greatness of *Huckleberry Finn,*" *Mark Twain's Huckleberry Finn,* 44-52.

——————. *The Liberal Imagination,* 104-117.

Vogelback, Arthur Lawrence. "The Publication and Reception of *Huckleberry Finn* in America," *American Literature* XI (Nov 1939), 260-272.

Williams, Stanley T. Introduction, *The Adventures of Huckleberry Finn* (New York, 1953).

Young, Philip. *Ernest Hemingway,* 181-212.

JOAN OF ARC

Holloway, T. E. "Mark Twain's Turning Point," *Mark Twain Quarterly* VIII (Summer-Fall 1948), 1-3.

TWAIN, MARK, Continued

Howells, W. D. *My Mark Twain,* 150-156.

Paine, Albert Bigelow. *A Short Life of Mark Twain,* 232-236; 240-242.

THE MYSTERIOUS STRANGER

Fussell, E. S. "The Structural Problem of *The Mysterious Stranger,*" *Studies in Philology* LXIX (Jan 1952), 95-104.

Laverty, Carroll D. "The Genesis of The Mysterious Stranger," *Mark Twain Quarterly* VII (Spring-Summer), 15-19.

THE PRINCE AND THE PAUPER

Baetzhold, Howard G. "Mark Twain's *The Prince and the Pauper,*" *Notes and Queries* 199 (Sept 1954), 401-403.

Becker, May Lamberton. Introduction, *The Prince and the Pauper* (Cleveland, 1948), pp. xiv.

Quinn, Arthur Hobson. Introduction, *The Prince and the Pauper* (New York, 1920), pp. xxx.

Vogelback, Arthur Lawrence. "*The Prince and the Pauper:* A Study in Critical Standards," *American Literature* XIV (Mar 1942), 48-54.

PUDD'NHEAD WILSON

Chase, Richard. *The American Novel and Its Tradition,* 149-156.

Cox, James M. "Pudd'nhead Wilson: The End of Mark Twain's American Dream," *South Atlantic Quarterly* LVIII (Summer 1959), 351-363.

Foner, Philip. *Mark Twain,* 210-213.

Ford, Thomas W. "The Miscegenation Theme in Pudd'nhead Wilson," *Mark Twain Quarterly* X (Summer 1955), 13-14.

Leavis, F. R. Introduction, *Pudd'nhead Wilson* (New York, 1955).

──────────. "Mark Twain's Neglected Classic: The Moral Astringency of 'Pudd'nhead Wilson,'" *Commentary* XXI (Feb 1956), 128-136.

Wigger, Anne P. "The Source of Fingerprint Material in Mark Twain's *Pudd'nhead Wilson* and *Those Extraordinary Twins,*" *American Literature,* XXVIII (Jan 1957), 517-520.

THOSE EXTRAORDINARY TWINS

Wigger, Anne P. "The Source of Fingerprint Material in Mark Twain's *Pudd'nhead Wilson* and *Those Extraordinary Twins,*" *American Literature,* XXVIII (Jan 1957), 517-520.

Wiggins, Robert A. "The Original of Mark Twain's *Those Extraordinary Twins,*" *American Literature* XXIII (Nov 1951), 355-357.

TWAIN, MARK, Continued

TOM SAWYER, THE ADVENTURES OF

Becker, May Lamberton. Introduction, *The Adventures of Tom Sawyer* (Cleveland, 1946; 1950).

Boynton, Percy. Introduction, *The Adventures of Tom Sawyer* (New York, 1920).

De Voto, Bernard. Introduction, *The Adventures of Tom Sawyer* (1939), pp. xxx.

──────. *Mark Twain at Work*, 3-24.

Hillway, Tyrus. "Tom Sawyer's Fence," *College English* XIX (Jan 1958), 165-166; McElderry, B. R., Jr. "Tom Sawyer's Fence—Original Illustrations," *College English* XIX (May 1958), 370.

Howells, W. D. *My Mark Twain*, 125-128.

Hutton, Graham. Introduction, *The Adventures of Tom Sawyer* (London, 1947).

Leary, Lewis. "Tom and Huck: Innocence on Trial," *Virginia Quarterly Review* XXX (Summer 1954), 417-430.

Morley, Christopher. Introduction, *The Adventures of Tom Sawyer* (Philadelphia, 1942), pp. xiv.

──────. Introduction, *The Adventures of Tom Sawyer* and *The Adventures of Huckleberry Finn* (New York, 1954).

Petersen, Svend. "Splendid Days and Fearsome Nights," *Mark Twain Quarterly* VIII (Winter-Spring 1949), 3-8.

Rubin, Louis D., Jr. "Tom Sawyer and the Use of Novels," *American Quarterly* IX (Summer 1957), 209-216.

Salomon, Louis B. Introduction, *The Adventures of Tom Sawyer* (New York, 1958).

Santayana, George. "Tom Sawyer and Don Quixote," *Mark Twain Quarterly* IX (Winter 1952), 1-3.

Swinton, Marjory. Introduction, *The Adventures of Tom Sawyer* and *The Adventures of Huckleberry Finn* (New York, 1959).

Ward, Bertha Evans. Introduction, *The Adventures of Tom Sawyer* (New York, 1931), pp. xxiv.

TOM SAWYER ABROAD

Byrd, R. E. Introduction, *Tom Sawyer Abroad* (New York, 1928), pp. xi.

McKeithan, D. M. "Mark Twain's *Tom Sawyer Abroad* and Jules Verne's *Five Weeks in A Balloon*," *Texas Studies in English* XXVIII (1949), 257-270.

TWAIN, MARK, Continued
GENERAL
Allen, Jerry. *The Adventures of Mark Twain.*
Altick, Richard D. "Mark Twain's Despair: An Explanation in Terms of His Humanity," *South Atlantic Quarterly* XXXIV (Oct 1935), 359-367.
Andrews, Kenneth R. *Nook Farm.*
Baetzhold, Howard G. "Mark Twain: England's Advocate," *American Literature* XXVIII (Nov 1956), 328-346.
Bell, Robert E. "How Mark Twain Comments on Society through Use of Folklore," *Mark Twain Quarterly* X (Summer 1955), 1-8.
Bellamy, Gladys Carmen. *Mark Twain as a Literary Artist.*
Blair, Walter. "Mark Twain and Native American Humor," *Mark Twain's Huckleberry Finn*, 19-27.
Blearsides, Oliver. "Mark Twain's Characters Come from Real People," *Mark Twain Quarterly* IV (Summer-Fall 1941), 16-19.
Bowen, Edwin W. "Mark Twain," *South Atlantic Quarterly* XV (Jul 1916), 250-268.
Bradford, Gamaliel. "Mark Twain," *Atlantic Monthly* CXXV (1920), 462-472.
Branch, Edgar Marquess. *The Literary Apprenticeship of Mark Twain.*
Brashear, Minnie M. *Mark Twain, Son of Missouri.*
Brooks, Van Wyck. *The Ordeal of Mark Twain.*
——————. "The Ordeal of Mark Twain," *Mark Twain's Huckleberry Finn*, 1-18.
——————. "Mark Twain's Humor," *Dial* LXVIII (Mar 1920), 275-291.
——————. "Mark Twain's Satire," *Dial* LXVIII (Apr 1920), 424-443.
——————. *The Times of Melville and Whitman*, 283-300; 448-464.
Budd, Louis J. "The Idea of Progress: II. At the Close of the Gilded Age," *Georgia Review* XI (Fall 1957), 278-284.
——————. "Twain, Howells, and the Boston Nihilists," *New England Quarterly* XXXII (Sept 1959), 351-371.
Canby, Henry Seidel. "Mark Twain: Anti-Victorian," *Saturday Review of Literature* XII (Oct 12, 1935), 3-4; 14.

TWAIN, MARK, Continued

———. "Mark Twain Himself," *Saturday Review of Literature* IX (Oct 29, 1932), 201-202.

———. "Mark Twain—Radical," *Saturday Review of Literature* I (Nov 1, 1924), 241.

———. *Turn West, Turn East.*

Carter, Paul J., Jr. "The Influence of the Nevada Frontier on Mark Twain," *Western Humanities Review* XIII (Winter 1959), 61-70.

Childs, Marquis W. "The Home of Mark Twain," *American Mercury* IX (Sept 1926), 101-105.

Clark, George Peirce. "Mark Twain in Bret Harte: Selections from Two Unpublished Letters," *Journal of English and Germanic Philology* LVII (Apr 1958), 208-210.

Clemens, Clara. *My Father Mark Twain.*

Clemens, Cyril. "Mark Twain and St. Louis," *Mark Twain Quarterly* IV (Summer 1940), 15-16.

Compton, Charles H. "Who Reads Mark Twain?" *American Mercury* XXXI (Apr 1934), 465-471.

Consiglio, Carla. "La Prosa Di Mark Twain E I Suoi Influssi," *Studi Americani* IV (1958), 175-208.

Cowie, Alexander. "Mark Twain (1835-1910)," *The Rise of the American Novel*, 599-652.

Coyle, Leo P. "Mark Twain and William Dean Howells," *Georgia Review* X (Fall 1956), 302-311.

Cummings, Sherwood. "Mark Twain's Social Darwinism," *Huntington Library Quarterly* XX (Feb 1957), 163-175.

———. "Science and Mark Twain's Theory of Fiction," *Philological Quarterly* XXXVII (Jan 1958), 26-33.

Cunliffe, Marcus. "American Humor and the Rise of the West: Mark Twain," *The Literature of the United States*, 151-169.

Currie, H. MacL. "Aristophanes and Mark Twain," *Notes and Queries* 203 (Apr 1958), 165-168.

DeVoto, Bernard. "Introduction," *The Portable Mark Twain* (New York, 1946), 1-34.

———. "Mark Twain: a Caricature," *Saturday Review of Literature* XVII (Mar 19, 1938), 5.

———. *Mark Twain's America.*

———. "The Mark Twain Papers," *Saturday Review of Literature* XIX (Dec 10, 1938), 3-4; 14-15.

TWAIN, MARK, Continued

Douglas, Robert. "The Pessimism of Mark Twain," *Mark Twain Quarterly* IX (Winter 1951), 1-4.

Eastman, Max. "Mark Twain's Elmira," *Harpers Magazine* 176 (May 1938), 620-632.

Emberson, Frances Guthrie. *Mark Twain's Vocabulary.*

Erskine, John. "Huckleberry Finn," *The Delight of Great Books*, 263-274.

Feinstein, George W. "Mark Twain on the Immanence of Authors in Their Writing," *Mark Twain Quarterly* VIII (Winter 1947), 13-14.

——————. "Mark Twain's Idea of Story Structure," *American Literature* XVIII (May 1946), 160-163.

——————. "Mark Twain's Regionalism in Fiction," *Mark Twain Quarterly* VII (Winter-Spring 1945-1946), 7.

Foner, Philip S. *Mark Twain.*

Francis, Raymond L. "Mark Twain and H. L. Mencken," *Prairie Schooner* (Spring 1950), 31-39.

Fussell, Edwin. "Hemingway and Mark Twain," *Accent* XIV (Summer 1954), 199-206.

Gay, Robert M. "The Two Mark Twains," *Atlantic Monthly* CLXVI (1940), 724-726.

Gerber, John C. "The Relation between Point of View and Style in the Works of Mark Twain," *English Institute Essays* (1958), 142-171.

Gohdes, Clarence. "Mirth for the Millions," *The Literature of the American People*, 708-720.

Goold, Edgar H., Jr. "Mark Twain on the Writing of Fiction," *American Literature* XXVI (May 1954), 141-153.

Guest, Boyd. "Twain's Concept of Woman's Sphere," *Mark Twain Quarterly* VII (Winter-Spring 1945-1946), 1-4.

Harris, Frank. "Memories of Mark Twain," *Contemporary Portraits*, fourth series, 162-173.

Henderson, Archibald. "The International Fame of Mark Twain," *North American Review* 192 (Dec 1910), 805-815.

——————. *Mark Twain.*

——————. "Mark Twain," *Harper's Monthly Magazine* CXVIII (May 1909), 948-955.

Herrick, George H. "Mark Twain, Reader and Critic of Travel Literature," *Mark Twain Quarterly* X (Summer 1955), 9-12.

TWAIN, MARK, Continued

Herrick, Robert. "Mark Twain and the American Tradition," *Mark Twain Quarterly* II (Winter 1937-38), 8-11.

Hewlett, Maurice. "Mark on Sir Walter," *Sewanee Review* XXI (Apr 1921), 130-133.

Hicks, Granville. *The Great Tradition*, 38-49.

Hollenbach, John W. "Mark Twain, Story-Teller, at Work," *College English* VII (Mar 1946), 303-312.

Hornstein, Simon. *Mark Twain.*

Howe, M. A. DeWolfe. "Bret Harte and Mark Twain in the 'Seventies," *Atlantic Monthly* CXXX (1922), 341-348.

Howells, William Dean. "Editor's Easy Chair," *Harper's Magazine* CXXVI (Jan 1913), 310-312; CXXXVI (Mar 1918), 602-605.

———————. "Mark Twain: An Inquiry," *North American Review* 172 (Feb 1901), 306-321; reprinted 191 (Jun 1910), 836-850.

———————. *My Mark Twain.*

———————. "My Memories of Mark Twain," *Harper's Monthly Magazine* CXXI (Jul 1910), 165-178; (Aug 1910), 340-348; (Sept 1910), 512-529.

Hubbell, Jay B. *The South in American Literature*, 822-836.

Johnson, Burgess. "A Ghost for Mark Twain," *Atlantic Monthly* CLXXXIX (May 1952), 65-66.

Lawton, Mary. *A Lifetime with Mark Twain.*

Leacock, Stephen. "Mark Twain and Canada," *Queen's Quarterly* XLII (Spring 1935), 68-81.

———————. "Two Humorists: Charles Dickens and Mark Twain," *Yale Review* XXIV (Sept 1934), 118-129.

Lederer, Max. "Mark Twain in Vienna," *Mark Twain Quarterly* VII (Summer-Fall 1945), 1-12.

Long, E. Hudson. *Mark Twain Handbook.*

Lundy, Robert D. "Mark Twain and Italy," *Studi Americani* IV (1958), 135-149.

Lynn, Kenneth S. *Mark Twain and Southwestern Humor.*

Macy, John. "Mark Twain," *The Spirit of American Literature*, 248-277.

Marcosson, Isaac F. "Mark Twain as Collaborator," *Mark Twain Quarterly* II (Winter 1937-38), 7

Masters, Edgar Lee. *Mark Twain.*

TWAIN, MARK, Continued

Matthews, Brander. "Mark Twain," *Inquiries and Opinions*, 139-166.

——————. "Mark Twain and the Art of Writing," *Harper's Magazine* CXLI (Oct 1920), 635-643.

McKeithan, D. M. "More About Mark Twain's War with English Critics of America," *Modern Language Notes* LXIII (Apr 1948), 221-228.

Meyer, Harold. "Mark Twain on the Comstock," *Southwest Review* XII (Apr 1927), 197-207.

Mirizzi, Piero. "Il Mondo Di Mark Twain," *Studi Americani* IV (1958), 151-174.

Moore, Olin Harris. "Mark Twain and Don Quixote," *PMLA* XXXVII (1922), 324-346.

Morris, Lloyd. *Postscript to Yesterday*, 98-101.

Morris, Wright. "The Available Past," *The Territory Ahead*, 79-90.

Mumford, Lewis. *The Golden Day*, 170-179; (Beacon Press edition) 85-90.

——————. "Prophet, Pedant and Pioneer," *Saturday Review of Literature* IX (May 6, 1933), 573-575.

Paine, Albert Bigelow. "Mark Twain: Some Chapters from an Extraordinary Life," *Harper's Monthly Magazine* CXXIII (Nov 1911), 813-828; CXXIV (Dec 1911), 42-53; (Jan 1912), 215-228; (Feb 1912), 419-433; (Mar 1912), 583-597; (Apr 1912), 737-751; (May 1912), 934-947; CXXV (Jun 1912), 104-119; (Jul 1912), 249-263; (Aug 1912), 405-417; (Sept 1912), 593-605; (Oct 1912), 767-780; (Nov 1912), 923-935.

——————. *A Short Life of Mark Twain*.

—————— (ed.). 'Some Mark Twain Letters," *Harper's Magazine* CXXXIV (May 1917), 781-794; CXXXV (Jul 1917), 177-186; (Aug 1917), 378-388; (Sept 1917), 569-577; (Oct 1917), 638-647; (Nov 1917), 812-819.

—————— (ed.). "Unpublished Chapters from the Autobiography of Mark Twain," *Harper's Magazine* CXLIV (Feb 1922), 273-280; (Mar 1922), 455-460; CXLV (Aug 1922), 310-315.

Parry, Albert. "Mark Twain in Russia," *Books Abroad* XV (Apr 1941), 168-175.

Parsons, Coleman O. "The Devil and Samuel Clemens," *Virginia Quarterly Review* XXIII (Autumn 1947), 582-606.

TWAIN, MARK, Continued

Pattee, Fred Lewis. "On the Rating of Mark Twain," *American Mercury* XIV (Jun 1928), 183-191.

———. "Mark Twain: Introduction," *Mark Twain*, xi-lii.

Phelps, William Lyon. "Mark Twain," *North American Review* 185 (Jul 5, 1907), 540-548; *Yale Review* XXV (Dec 1935), 291-310.

Peckham, H. Houston. "The Literary Status of Mark Twain, 1877-1890," *South Atlantic Quarterly* XIX (Oct 1920), 332-340.

Putnam, Samuel. "The Americanism of Mark Twain," *Mark Twain Quarterly* II (Summer-Fall 1938), 13.

Quinn, Arthur Hobson. "Mark Twain and the Romance of Youth," *American Fiction*, 243-256.

Roades, Sister Mary Teresa. "Was Mark Twain Influenced by the Prolog to 'Don Quixote'?" *Mark Twain Quarterly* IX (Winter 1952), 4-6.

Robertson, Stuart. "Mark Twain in German," *Mark Twain Quarterly* II (Fall 1937), 10-12.

Rourke, Constance. *American Humor*, 209-221; (Doubleday Anchor) 167-175.

Rowe, Ida. "Mark Twain's Interest in Nature," *Mark Twain Quarterly* I (Summer 1937), 7.

Sedgwick, Henry Dwight. *The New American Type*, 281-313.

Sherman, Stuart. "Mark Twain's Last Phase," *The Main Stream*, 80-88.

———. "The Democracy of Mark Twain," *On Contemporary Literature*, 18-49.

Slade, William G. "Mark Twain's Educational Views," *Mark Twain Quarterly* IV (Summer-Fall 1941), 5-10.

Smith, Henry Nash. "Mark Twain's Images of Hannibal: From St. Petersburg to Eseldorf," *Texas Studies in English* XXXVII (1958), 3-23.

Snell, George. "Mark Twain: Realism and the Frontier," *The Shapers of American Fiction*, 211-222.

Spiller, Robert E. *The Cycle of American Literature*, 150-162; (Mentor) 119-127.

Stovall, Floyd. *American Idealism*, 112-116.

Taylor, Walter Fuller. "Mark Twain and the Machine Age," *South Atlantic Quarterly* XXXVII (Oct 1938), 384-396.

TWAIN, MARK, Continued

Twain, Mark. "Mark Twain Speaks Out," *Harper's Magazine* CCXVII (Dec 1958), 36-41.
Underwood, John Curtis. "Democracy and Mark Twain," *Literature and Insurgency,* 1-40.
Van Doren, Carl. "Mark Twain," *The American Novel 1789-1939,* 137-162.
Van Doren, Mark. "A Century of Mark Twain," *The Private Reader,* 110-118.
Wagenknecht, Edward. "The Lincoln of Our Literature," *Cavalcade of the American Novel,* 109-126.
──────────. "Twain: A Literary Lincoln," *Saturday Review of Literature* XXXIV (Jan 20, 1951), 25-26.
Waggoner, Hyatt Howe. "Science in the Thought of Mark Twain," *American Literature* VIII (Jan 1937), 357-370.
Webster, Samuel Charles (ed.). *Mark Twain.*
Webster, Samuel Charles. "Mark Twain, Business Man," *Atlantic Monthly* CLXXIII (Jun 1944), 37-46; CLXXIV (Jul 1944), 72-80; (Aug 1944), 71-77; (Sep 1944), 90-96; (Oct 1944), 74-80; (Nov 1944), 100-106.
Wecter, Dixon. "Mark Twain's River," *Atlantic Monthly* CLXXXII (Oct 1948), 45-47.
──────────. *Sam Clemens of Hannibal.*
West, Ray B., Jr. "Mark Twain's Idyl of Frontier America," *University of Kansas City Review* XV (Winter 1948), 92-104.
Wiggins, Robert A. "Mark Twain and the Drama," *American Literature* XXV (Nov 1953), 279-286.
Wister, Owen. "In Homage to Mark Twain," *Harpers Magazine* 171 (Oct 1935), 547-556.
Wood, Grant. "My Debt to Mark Twain," *Mark Twain Quarterly* II (Fall 1937), 6.
Wyatt, Edith. "An Inspired Critic," *North American Review* 205 (Apr 1917), 603-615.
Yates, Paulene M. "Mark Twain on Writing and Speaking," *Prairie Schooner* XIX (Summer 1945), 169-178.

BIBLIOGRAPHY

Adams, Lucille. *Huckleberry Finn,* 30-39.
Bellamy, Gladys Carmen. *Mark Twain as a Literary Artist,* 378-382.
Brashear, Minnie M. *Mark Twain, Son of Missouri,* 264-284.

TWAIN, MARK, Continued

Brashear, Minnie M. and Robert M. Rodney (eds.). *The Art, Humor, and Humanity of Mark Twain*, 411-517.
Clark, Harry Hayden. "Mark Twain," *Eight American Authors*, 319-363.
Emberson, Frances Guthrie. *Mark Twain's Vocabulary*, 50-53.
Foner, Philip S. *Mark Twain*, 326-330.
Henderson, Archibald. *Mark Twain*, 220-230.
Johnson, Merle. *A Bibliography of the Works of Mark Twain*.
Long, E. Hudson. *Mark Twain Handbook*, 428-434.
Pattee, Fred Lewis. *Mark Twain*, liii-lxi.
Troxell, Gilbert McCoy. "Samuel Langhorne Clemens, 1835-1910," *Yale University Library Gazette* XVIII (Jul 1943), 1-5.
Wecter, Dixon. *Sam Clemens of Hannibal*, 318-321.

ULLMAN, JAMES RAMSEY

THE WHITE TOWER
Redman, Ben Ray. "High Adventure in Interdependence," *Saturday Review of Literature* XXVIII (Sept 22, 1945), 11-12.

URIS, LEON

BATTLE CRY
Miller, Merle. "The Backdrop Is Victory," *Saturday Review* XXXVI (Apr 25, 1953), 16-17.

VAN VECHTEN, CARL

GENERAL
Baldwin, Charles C. "Carl Van Vechten," *The Men Who Make Our Novels*, 523-529.
Cargill, Oscar. "The Intelligensia," *Intellectual America*, 507-511.
Clark, Emily. *Innocence Abroad*, 129-145.
Jonas, Klaus W. *Carl Van Vechten*.
Kazin, Alfred. "The Exquisites," *On Native Grounds*, 244-246.
Knopf, Alfred A. "Reminiscences of Hergesheimer, Van Vechten, and Mencken," *Yale University Library Gazette* XXIV (Apr 1950), 145-164.

VAN VECHTEN, CARL, Continued

Lueders, Edward. "Literature: Exquisite and Rowdy," *Carl Van Vechten and the Twenties*, 53-98.

BIBLIOGRAPHY

Cunningham, Scott. *A Bibliography of the Writings of Carl Van Vechten.*

VIDAL, GORE

GENERAL

Aldridge, John W. "Gore Vidal: The Search for a King," *After the Lost Generation*, 170-183.

WARD, ELIZABETH STUART PHELPS

GENERAL

Quinn, Arthur Hobson. *American Fiction*, 192-203.

WARE, WILLIAM

GENERAL

Quinn, Arthur Hobson. "The Romance of History and the Frontier," *The Literature of the American People*, 242-243.

WARNER, CHARLES DUDLEY

GENERAL

Andrews, Kenneth R. *Nook Farm.*

WARNER, SUSAN

GENERAL

Cowie, Alexander. "The Domestic Sentimentalists and Other Popular Writers (1850-1870): Susan Warner ('Elizabeth Wetherell') (1819-1885)," *The Rise of the American Novel*, 416-418.

Warner, Anna B. *Susan Warner.*

WARREN, ROBERT PENN

ALL THE KING'S MEN

Baker, Joseph E. "Irony in Fiction: 'All the King's Men,'" *College English* IX (Dec 1947), 122-130.

Cottrell, Beekman W. *All the King's Men: A Symposium*, 39-49.

Girault, Norton R. "The Narrator's Mind as Symbol: An Analysis of *All the King's Men*," *Accent* VII (Summer 1947), 220-234; *Critiques and Essays on Modern Fiction*, 200-216.

Gross, Seymour L. "Conrad and *All the King's Men*," *Twentieth Century Literature* III (Apr 1957), 27-32.

Hart, John A. *All the King's Men: A Symposium*, 63-74.

Rubin, Louis D., Jr. "All the King's Meanings," *Georgia Review* VIII (Winter 1954), 422-434.

Ruoff, James. "Humpty Dumpty and *All the King's Men*: A Note on Robert Penn Warren's Teleology," *Twentieth Century Literature* III (Oct 1957), 128-134.

Satterwhite, Joseph N. "Robert Penn Warren and Emily Dickinson," *Modern Language Notes* LXXI (May 1956), 347-349.

Schutte, William M. *All the King's Men: A Symposium*, 75-90.

Sillars, Malcolm O. "Warren's *All the King's Men*: A Study in Populism," *American Quarterly* IX (Fall 1957), 345-353.

Slack, Robert C. *All the King's Men: A Symposium*, 29-38.

Sochatoff, A. Fred. *All the King's Men: A Symposium*, 3-15.

Steinberg, Erwin R. *All the King's Men: A Symposium*, 17-28.

Stewart, James T. "Two Uses of Maupassant by R. P. Warren," *Modern Language Notes* LXX (Apr 1955), 279-280.

Wood, James P. "Mr. Warren's 'Modern Realism,'" *Saturday Review of Literature* XXIX (Aug 17, 1946), 11.

Woodruff, Neal, Jr. *All the King's Men*, 51-62.

AT HEAVEN'S GATE

Hendry, Irene. "The Regional Novel: The Example of Robert Penn Warren," *Sewanee Review* LIII (Jan-Mar 1945), 84-102.

Lytle, Andrew. "At Heaven's Gate," *Sewanee Review* LI (Oct-Dec 1943), 599-602.

BAND OF ANGELS

Baker, Carlos. "Souls Lost in a Blind Lobby," *Saturday Review* XXXVIII (Aug 13, 1955), 9-10.

Flint, F. Cudworth. "Mr. Warren and the Reviewers," *Sewanee Review* LXIV (Oct-Dec 1956), 632-645.

WARREN, ROBERT PENN, Continued

THE CAVE
Hicks, Granville. "Melodrama with Meaning," *Saturday Review* XLII (Aug 22, 1959), 13.

NIGHT RIDER
Hendry, Irene. "The Regional Novel: The Example of Robert Penn Warren," *Sewanee Review* LIII (Jan-Mar 1945), 84-102.

Long, Louise. "Night Rider," *Southwest Review* XXIV (Jul 1939), 498-500.

Muller, Herbert J. "Violence upon the Roads," *Kenyon Review* I (Summer 1939), 323-324.

WORLD ENOUGH AND TIME
Campbell, Harry Modean. *Southern Renascence*, 225-235.

Frank, Joseph. "Romanticism and Reality in Robert Penn Warren," *Hudson Review* III (Summer 1951), 248-258.

Guthrie, A. B., Jr. "Virtue Plundered in Kentucky," *Saturday Review of Literature* XXXIII (Jun 24, 1950), 11-12.

Heilman, Robert B. "Tangled Web," *Sewanee Review* LIX (Jan-Mar 1951), 107-119.

McDowell, Frederick P. "The Romantic Tragedy of Self in *World Enough and Time*," *Critique* I (Summer 1957), 34-48.

GENERAL
Anderson, Charles R. "Violence and Order in the Novels of Robert Penn Warren," *Southern Renascence*, 207-224.

Beatty, Richmond C. "The Poetry and Novels of Robert Penn Warren," *Vanderbilt Studies in the Humanities* I (1951), 142-160.

Bentley, Eric. "The Meaning of Robert Penn Warren's Novels," *Kenyon Review* X (Summer 1948), 407-424; *Forms of Modern Fiction*, 269-286.

Bradbury, John M. "Robert Penn Warren's Novels: The Symbolic and Textual Patterns," *Accent* XIII (Spring 1953), 77-89.

Breit, Harvey. *The Writer Observed*, 131-133.

Cargill, Oscar. "Anatomist of Monsters," *College English* IX (1947), 1-8.

Douglas, Wallace W. "Drug Store Gothic: The Style of Robert Penn Warren," *College English* XV (Feb 1954), 265-272.

Ellison, Ralph and Eugene Walter. "Robert Penn Warren," *Writers at Work*, 183-207.

WARREN, ROBERT PENN, Continued

Frank, William. "Warren's Achievement," *College English* XIX (May 1958), 365-366.

Frohock, W. M. "Mr. Warren's Albatross," *Southwest Review* XXXVI (Winter 1951), 48-59.

Gross, Seymour L. "The Achievement of Robert Penn Warren," *College English* XIX (May 1959), 361-365.

Hynes, Sam. "Robert Penn Warren: The Symbolic Journey," *University of Kansas City Review* XVII (Summer 1951), 279-285.

Joost, Nicholas. " 'Was All for Naught?': Robert Penn Warren and New Directions in the Novel," *Fifty Years of the American Novel*, 273-284.

Kelvin, Norman. "The Failure of Robert Penn Warren," *College English* XVIII (Apr 1957), 355-364.

King, Roma A., Jr. "Time and Structure in the Early Novels of Robert Penn Warren," *South Atlantic Quarterly* LVI (Autumn 1957), 486-493.

Prescott, Orville. *In My Opinion*, 24-27.

Stewart, John L. "The Achievement of Robert Penn Warren," *South Atlantic Quarterly* XLVII (Oct 1948), 562-579.

Wagenknecht, Edward. *Cavalcade of the American Novel*, 456-457.

Watkins, Floyd C. "Thomas Wolfe and the Nashville Agrarians," *Georgia Review* VII (Winter 1953), 410-423.

White, Robert. "Robert Penn Warren and the Myth of the Garden," *Faulkner Studies* III (Winter 1954), 59-67.

BIBLIOGRAPHY

Stallman, Robert Wooster. "Robert Penn Warren: A Checklist of His Critical Writings," *University of Kansas City Review* XIV (Autumn 1947), 78-83.

WATERS, FRANK

GENERAL

Swallow, Alan. "The Mavericks," *Critique* II (Winter 1959), 86-88.

WELLER, GEORGE
THE CRACK IN THE COLUMN
Blotner, Joseph L. *The Political Novel*, 16-17; 58.

WELTY, EUDORA
DELTA WEDDING
Dangerfield, George. "A Family Rarely in Repose," *Saturday Review of Literature* XXIX (Apr 20, 1946), 12.

Hardy, John Edward. "*Delta Wedding* as Region and Symbol," *Sewanee Review* LX (Jul-Sept 1952), 396-417.

Ransom, John Crowe. "Delta Fiction," *Kenyon Review* XVIII (Summer 1946), 503-507.

THE PONDER HEART
Drake, Robert Y., Jr. "The Reasons of the Heart," *Georgia Review* XI (Winter 1957), 420-426.

GENERAL
Baldanza, Frank. "Plato in Dixie," *Georgia Review* XII (Summer 1958), 150-167.

Daniel, Robert. "The World of Eudora Welty," *Southern Renascence*, 306-315.

Hicks, Granville. "Eudora Welty," *College English* XIV (Nov 1952), 69-76.

Read, Martha. "Eudora Welty," *Prairie Schooner* XVIII (Spring 1944), 74-76.

WESCOTT, GLENWAY
THE GRANDMOTHERS
Langdon, Mabel. "Glenway Wescott," *Prairie Schooner* IV (Spring 1930), 117-123.

GENERAL
Schorer, C. E. "The Maturing of Glenway Wescott," *College English* XVIII (Mar 1957), 320-326.

BIBLIOGRAPHY
Kahn, Sy M. "Glenway Wescott: A Bibliography," *Bulletin of Bibliography* XXII (Sept-Dec 1958), 156-160.

WEST, JESSAMYN
THE WITCH DIGGERS
Bergler, Edmund. "Writers of Half-Talent," *American Imago* XIV (Summer 1957), 155-164.

WEST, NATHANAEL

THE DAY OF THE LOCUST
Aaron, Daniel. "Waiting for Apocalypse," *Hudson Review* III (Winter 1951), 634-636.

Collins, Carvel. "Nathanael West's *The Day of the Locust* and *Sanctuary*," *Faulkner Studies* II (Summer 1953), 23-24.

Gehman, Richard B. Introduction, *Day of the Locust* (New York, 1950), pp. xxiii.

THE DREAM LIFE OF BALSO SNELL
Light, James. "Nathanael West, 'Balso Snell,' and the Mundane Millstone," *Modern Fiction Studies* IV (Winter 1958-1959), 319-328.

MISS LONELYHEARTS
Coates, Robert M. Introduction, *Miss Lonelyhearts* (New York, 1933).

Light, James F. "*Miss Lonelyhearts:* The Imagery of Nightmare," *American Quarterly* (Winter 1956), 316-327.

GENERAL
Carlisle, Henry. "The Comic Tradition," *American Scholar* XXVIII (Winter 1958-59), 96-108.

Gehman, Richard B. "Nathanael West: A Novelist Apart," *Atlantic Monthly* CLXXXVI (Sept 1950), 69-72.

Light, James F. "Genius on Campus: Nathanael West at Brown," *Contact* 3 (1959), 97-111.

_____. "Violence, Dreams, and Dostoevsky: The Art of Nathanael West," *College English* XIX (Feb 1958), 208-213.

Ross, Alan. Introduction, *Complete Works* (New York, 1957), pp. xxii.

Schneider, Cyril M. "The Individuality of Nathanael West," *Western Review* XX (Autumn 1955), 7-28.

Schwartz, Edward Greenfield. "The Novels of Nathanael West," *Accent* XVII (Autumn 1957), 251-262.

Wilson, Edmund. "The Boys in the Back Room," *A Literary Chronicle*, 246-249.

_____. *Classics and Commercials*, 51-55.

BIBLIOGRAPHY
White, William. "Nathanael West: A Bibliography," *Studies in Bibliography* XI (1958), 207-224.

WHARTON, EDITH

THE AGE OF INNOCENCE
Canby, Henry Seidel. *Definitions,* 212-216.
Hopkins, Viola. "The Ordering Style of *The Age of Innocence,*" *American Literature* XXX (Nov 1958), 345-357.
Mosely, Edwin M. "*The Age of Innocence:* Edith Wharton's Weak Faust," *College English* XXI (Dec 1959), 156-160.
Wyndham, Francis. Introduction, *Age of Innocence* (London, 1953).

CUSTOM OF THE COUNTRY
Nevius, Blake. Introduction, *Custom of the Country* (New York, 1956).
Wyndham, Francis. Introduction, *Custom of the Country* (London, 1953).

ETHAN FROME
De Voto, Bernard. Introduction, *Ethan Frome* (New York, 1938), pp. xviii.
Fadiman, Clifton. Introduction, *Ethan Frome* (New York, 1939), pp. xi.
Nevius, Blake. " 'Ethan Frome' and the Themes of Edith Wharton's Fiction," *New England Quarterly* XXIV (Jun 1951), 197-207.
Thomas, J. D. "Marginalia on *Ethan Frome,*" *American Literature* XXVII (Nov 1955), 405-409.
Trilling, Lionel. "The Morality of Inertia," *Great Moral Dilemmas in Literature, Past and Present,* 37-46.

THE HOUSE OF MIRTH
Rideout, Walter B. "Edith Wharton's *The House of Mirth,*" *Twelve Original Essays on Great American Novels,* 148-176.
Steele, Erskine. "Fiction and Social Ethics," *South Atlantic Quarterly* V (Jul 1906), 254-263.
Wyndham, Francis. Introduction, *The House of Mirth* (London, 1953).

GENERAL
Auchincloss, Louis. "Edith Wharton and Her New Yorks," *Partisan Review* XVIII (Jul-Aug 1951), 411-419.
Beach, Joseph Warren. *The Twentieth Century Novel,* 291-303; 311-314.
Bell, Millicent. "Edith Wharton and Henry James: The Literary Relation," *PMLA* LXXIV (Dec 1959), 619-637.

WHARTON, EDITH, Continued

―――――. "Lady into Author: Edith Wharton and the House of Scribner," *American Quarterly* IX (Fall 1957), 295-315.
Bogan, Louise. "The Decoration of Novels," *Selected Criticism*, 83-85.
Boynton, Percy H. "Edith Wharton," *Some Contemporary Americans*, 89-107.
Brooks, Van Wyck. "The Collectors: Edith Wharton," *The Dream of Arcadia*, 237-245.
―――――. "Edith Wharton," *The Confident Years*, 283-300.
Brown, E. K. "Edith Wharton," *Etudes Anglaises* II (Jan-Mar 1938), 16-26.
Canby, Henry Seidel. "Edith Wharton," *Saturday Review of Literature* XVI (Aug 21, 1937), 6-7.
Dooley, R. B. "A Footnote to Edith Wharton," *American Literature* XXVI (Mar 1954), 78-85.
Edgar, Pelham. "Edith Wharton," *The Art of the Novel*, 196-205.
Fremantle, Anne. "Edith Wharton: Values and Vulgarity," *Fifty Years of the American Novel*, 15-32.
Gelfant, Blanche Housman. *The American City Novel*, 107-119.
Hartwick, Harry. "Vanity Fair," *The Foreground of American Fiction*, **369-388.**
Harvey, John. "Contrasting Worlds: A Study in the Novels of Edith Wharton," *Etudes Anglaises* VII (Apr 1954), 190-198.
Hicks, Granville. *The Great Tradition*, 216-219.
Hoffman, Frederick J. "Points of Moral Reference: a Comparative Study of Edith Wharton and F. Scott Fitzgerald," *English Institute Essays* (1949), 147-176.
James, Henry. *Notes on Novelists*, 280-283.
Jessup, Josephine Lurie. *The Faith of Our Feminists.*
Kazin, Alfred. "Two Educations: Edith Wharton and Theodore Dreiser," *On Native Grounds*, 73-82.
Knight, Grant C. "Edith Wharton," *American Literature and Culture*, 413-421.
LaGuardia, Eric. "Edith Wharton on Critics and Criticism," *Modern Language Notes* LXXIII (Dec 1958), 587-589.
Leach, Nancy R. "Edith Wharton's Unpublished Novel," *American Literature* XXV (Nov 1953), 334-353.

WHARTON, EDITH, Continued

──────────. "New England in the Stories of Edith Wharton," *New England Quarterly* XXX (Mar 1957), 90-98.

Leavis, Q. D. "Henry James's Heiress: The Importance of Edith Wharton," *Scrutiny* VII (Dec 1938), 261-276.

Lovett, Robert Morss. *Edith Wharton.*

Lubbock, Percy. *Portrait of Edith Wharton.*

Lyde, Marilyn Jones. *Edith Wharton.*

Lynskey, Winifred. "The 'Heroes' of Edith Wharton," *University of Toronto Quarterly* XXIII (Jul 1954), 354-361.

Michaud, Régis. "Henry James, Edith Wharton, William Dean Howells and American Society on Parade," *The American Novel To-Day,* 47-70.

──────────. "Mrs. Wharton et le Roman de Moeurs," *Panorama de la Littérature Américaine Contemporaine,* 148-151.

Monroe, N. Elizabeth. "Moral Situation in Edith Wharton," *The Novel in Society,* 111-138.

Nevius, Blake. *Edith Wharton: A Study of Her Fiction.*

Overton, Grant. "Edith Wharton," *The Women Who Make Our Novels,* 324-342.

Quinn, Arthur Hobson. *American Fiction,* 550-581.

Russell, Frances Theresa. "Melodramatic Mrs. Wharton," *Sewanee Review* XL (Oct-Dec 1932), 425-437.

Sedgwick, Henry Dwight. *The New American Type,* 53-96.

Sherman, Stuart. "Edith Wharton: Costuming the Passions," *The Main Stream,* 204-212.

Snell, George. "The James Influence," *The Shapers of American Fiction,* 140-150.

Trueblood, Charles K. "Edith Wharton," *Dial* LXVIII (Jan 1920), 80-91.

Underwood, John Curtis. "Culture and Edith Wharton," *Literature and Insurgency,* 346-390.

Van Doren, Carl. *Contemporary American Novelists,* 95-104.

──────────. "Edith Wharton," *The American Novel 1789-1939,* 273-280.

Wagenknecht, Edward. "Edith Wharton: Social Background and Ethical Dilemma," *Cavalcade of the American Novel,* 252-266.

Wharton, Edith. "Permanent Values in Fiction," *Saturday Review of Literature* X (Apr 17, 1934), 603-604.

WHARTON, EDITH, Continued

Whicher, George F. "Lingering Urbanity," *The Literature of the American People,* 816-819.
Wilson, Edmund. "Edith Wharton: A Memoir by An English Friend," *Classics and Commercials,* 412-418.
──────────. "Justice to Edith Wharton," *The Wound and the Bow,* 195-213.

BIBLIOGRAPHY

Nevius, Blake. *Edith Wharton,* 364-365.

WHITE, STEWART EDWARD

GENERAL

Underwood, John Curtis. "Stewart Edward White and All Outdoors," *Literature and Insurgency,* 254-298.
Whicher, George F. "Loopholes of Retreat," *The Literature of the American People,* 892.

WHITE, WILLIAM ALLEN

GENERAL

Van Doren, Carl. *Contemporary American Novelists,* 134-136.

WHITE, WILLIAM HALE

THE AUTOBIOGRAPHY OF MARK RUTHERFORD

Davies, Horton. *A Mirror of the Ministry in Modern Novels,* 52-63.

CATHERINE FURZE

Stock, Irvin. *William Hale White,* 175-195.

CLARA HOPGOOD

Stock, Irvin. *William Hale White,* 196-220.

GENERAL

Maclean, Catherine MacDonald. *Mark Rutherford.*
Stock, Irvin. *William Hale White.*
Stone, Wilfred. *Religion and Art of William Hale White,* 143-198.
Taylor, A. E. "The Novels of Mark Rutherford," *Essays and Studies by Members of the English Association,* 51-74.

BIBLIOGRAPHY

Stone, Wilfred. *Religion and Art of William Hale White,* 222-232.

WHITLOCK, BRAND
GENERAL
Arms, George. " 'Ever Devotedly Yours' The Whitlock-Howells Correspondence," *Rutgers University Library Journal* X (Dec 1946), 1-19.
Howells, William Dean. "A Political Novelist and More," *North American Review* 192 (Jul 1910), 93-100.

WHITMAN, WALT
FRANKLIN EVANS
Cowie, Alexander. *The Rise of the American Novel*, 306-309.

WILDER, THORNTON
THE BRIDGE OF SAN LUIS REY
Fischer, Walther. "Thornton Wilder's *The Bridge of San Luis Rey* und Prosper Mérimées *Le Carosse Du Saint-Sacrement*," *Anglia* LX (1936), 234-240.
THE IDES OF MARCH
American Writing Today, 402-403. Reprinted from *The Times Literary Supplement*, July 31, 1948.
Davis, Elmer. "Caesar's Last Months," *Saturday Review of Literature* XXXI (Feb 21, 1948), 11-12.
THE WOMAN OF ANDROS
Wilson, Edmund. *A Literary Chronicle*, 138-141.
GENERAL
Brown, E. K. "A Christian Humanist: Thornton Wilder," *University of Toronto Quarterly* IV (No. 3), 356-370.
Cargill, Oscar. "The Intelligensia," *Intellectual America*, 532-536.
Cowley, Malcolm. "The Man Who Abolished Time: Thornton Wilder and the Spirit of Anti-History," *Saturday Review* XXXIX (Oct 6, 1956), 13-14; 50-52.
Drew, Fraser. "Another Look at Thornton Wilder," *Trace* XXXIII (Aug-Sept 1959), 23-26.
Fuller, Edmund. "Thornton Wilder: The Notation of the Heart," *American Scholar* XXVIII (Spring 1959), 210-217.
Gardner, Martin. "Thornton Wilder and the Problem of Providence," *University of Kansas City Review* VIII (Dec 1940), 83-91.

WILDER, THORNTON, Continued

Goldstone, Richard H. "Thornton Wilder," *Writers at Work*, 99-118.
Hartwick, Harry. *The Foreground of American Fiction*, 407-409.
Henderson, Philip. "Thornton Wilder," *The Novel Today*, 137-141.
Hicks, Granville. *The Great Tradition*, 272-273.
Morgan, H. Wayne. "The Early Thornton Wilder," *Southwest Review* XLIII (Summer 1958), 245-253.
Parmenter, Ross. "Novelist into Playwright," *Saturday Review of Literature* XVIII (Jun 11, 1938), 10-11.
Wagenknecht, Edward. "Novelists of the Twenties: Romance and Fantasy: Thornton Wilder," *Cavalcade of the American Novel*, 405-408.
Wilson, Edmund. *The Shores of Light*, 384-391; 442-450; "The Economic Interpretation of Wilder," 500-503; 587-592.
——————. "Thornton Wilder," *A Literary Chronicle*, 102-108.

WILKINS, MARY E.
(See FREEMAN, MARY E. WILKINS)

WILLIAMS, TENNESSEE

THE ROMAN SPRING OF MRS. STONE
Alpert, Hollis. "Sex Fringed with Horror," *Saturday Review of Literature* XXXIII (Sept 30, 1950), 18-19.
Prescott, Orville. *In My Opinion*, 118-119.

WILLIAMS, WILLIAM CARLOS

GENERAL
Koch, Vivienne. "The Novels and Short Stories," *William Carlos Williams*, 187-246.

WILLIS, NATHANIEL PARKER

GENERAL
Brooks, Van Wyck. *The World of Washington Irving*, 426-442.
Quinn, Arthur Hobson. "National and Universal Themes," *The Literature of the American People*, 222-225.

WILSON, EDMUND
MEMOIRS OF HECATE COUNTY
Kronhausen, Eberhard and Phyllis. *Pornography and the Law,* 245-249.

WISTER, OWEN
THE VIRGINIAN
Bode, Carl. "Henry James and Owen Wister," *American Literature* XXVI (May 1954), 250-252.

Fiske, Horace Spencer. *Provincial Types in American Fiction,* 215-240.

Wister, Fanny Kemble. "Owen Wister's West," *Atlantic Monthly* CXCV (May 1955), 29-35; (Jun 1955), 52-57.

GENERAL
Baldwin, Charles C. "Owen Wister," *The Men Who Make Our Novels,* 590-600.

Boatright, Mody C. "The American Myth Rides the Range: Owen Wister's Man on Horseback," *Southwest Review* XXXVI (Summer 1951), 157-163.

Boynton, H. W. "Some American Novelists and the Lame Art," *Dial* LIX (Dec 9, 1915), 548-549.

Lewis, Marvin. "Owen Wister: Caste Imprints in Western Letters," *Arizona Quarterly* X (Summer 1954), 147-156.

WOLFE, THOMAS
LOOK HOMEWARD, ANGEL
Albrecht, W. P. "The Titles of *Look Homeward, Angel:* A Story of the Buried Life," *Modern Language Quarterly* XI (Mar 1950), 50-57.

Budd, Louis J. "The Grotesques of Anderson and Wolfe," *Modern Fiction Studies* V (Winter 1959-1960), 304-310.

Evans, Robert O. "Wolfe's Use of *Iliad* I.49," *Modern Language Notes* LXX (Dec 1955), 594-595.

Johnson, Pamela Hansford. *Thomas Wolfe,* 34-45.

"Look Homeward, Angel," *American Writing Today,* 374-376. Reprinted from *TLS* of Jul 24, 1930.

McElderry, B. R., Jr. "The Durable Humor of *Look Homeward, Angel,*" *Arizona Quarterly* XI (Summer 1955), 123-128.

Perkins, Maxwell E. Introduction, *Look Homeward, Angel* (New York, 1952), pp. xvi.

Watkins, Floyd C. *Thomas Wolfe's Characters,* 4-37.

WOLFE, THOMAS, Continued

Wolfe, Thomas. "The Story of a Novel," *Saturday Review of Literature* XIII (Dec 14, 1935), 3-4, 12, 14, 16; (Dec 21, 1935), 3-4, 15; (Dec 28, 1935), 3-4, 14-16.

OF TIME AND THE RIVER

Canby, Henry Seidel. "The River of Youth," *Saturday Review of Literature* XI (Mar 9, 1935), 529-530.

Halperin, Irving. "Wolfe's *Of Time and the River*," *Explicator* XVIII (Nov 1949), No. 9.

Johnson, Pamela Hansford. *Thomas Wolfe*, 45-54.

Warren, Robert Penn. "A Note on the Hamlet of Thomas Wolfe," *American Review* V (May 1935), 191-208; *Selected Essays*, 170-183.

Watkins, Floyd C. *Thomas Wolfe's Characters*, 49-65.

THE WEB AND THE ROCK

Braswell, William. Introduction, *The Web and the Rock* (New York, 1958).

Johnson, Pamela Hansford. *Thomas Wolfe*, 55-69.

Stevens, George. "Always Looking Homeward," *Saturday Review of Literature* XX (Jun 24, 1939), 5-6.

Watkins, Floyd C. *Thomas Wolfe's Characters*, 84-110.

YOU CAN'T GO HOME AGAIN

Beach, Joseph Warren. "Thomas Wolfe: Discovery of Brotherhood," *American Fiction*, 197-215.

Benét, Stephen Vincent. "Thomas Wolfe's Torrent of Recollection," *Saturday Review of Literature* XXII (Sept 21, 1940), 5.

Johnson, Pamela Hansford. *Thomas Wolfe*, 69-77.

Watkins, Floyd C. *Thomas Wolfe's Characters*, 111-132.

GENERAL

Adams, Agatha Boyd. *Thomas Wolfe*.

Albrecht, W. P. "Time as Unity in Thomas Wolfe," *New Mexico Quarterly* XIX (Autumn 1949), 320-329.

Armstrong, Anne W. "As I Saw Thomas Wolfe," *Arizona Quarterly* II (Spring 1946), 5-15.

Aswell, Edward C. "Thomas Wolfe Did Not Kill Maxwell Perkins," *Saturday Review of Literature* XXXIV (Oct 6, 1951), 16-17, 44-46.

─────── and John Skally Terry. "En Route to a Legend: Two Interpretations of Thomas Wolfe," *Saturday Review of Literature* XXXI (Nov 27, 1948), 7-9, 34-36.

WOLFE, THOMAS, Continued

Basso, Hamilton. "Thomas Wolfe," *After the Genteel Tradition,* 202-212.

Beach, Joseph Warren. "Thomas Wolfe: The Search for a Father," *American Fiction,* 173-193.

Bishop, John Peale. "The Sorrows of Thomas Wolfe," *Kenyon Review* I (Winter 1939), 7-17; *Critiques and Essays on Modern Fiction,* 362-369.

Blythe, LeGette. "The Thomas Wolfe I Knew," *Saturday Review of Literature* XXVIII (Aug 25, 1945), 18-19.

Boynton, Percy H. "Thomas Wolfe," *America in Contemporary Fiction,* 204-224.

Bridgers, Ann Preston. "Thomas Wolfe: Legends of a Man's Hunger in His Youth," *Saturday Review of Literature* XI (Apr 6, 1935), 599, 609.

Brown, E. K. "Thomas Wolfe: Realist and Symbolist," *University of Toronto Quarterly* X (Jan 1941), 153-166.

Burgum, Edwin Berry. "Thomas Wolfe's Discovery of America," *Virginia Quarterly Review* XXII (Summer 1946), 421-437; *The Novel and the World's Dilemma,* 302-321.

Church, Margaret. "Thomas Wolfe: Dark Time," *PMLA* LXIV (Sept 1949), 629-638.

Collins, Thomas Lyle. "Thomas Wolfe," *Sewanee Review* L (Oct-Dec 1942), 487-504.

Daniels, Jonathan. "Thomas Wolfe," *Saturday Review of Literature* XVIII (Sept 24, 1938), 8.

Delakas, Daniel L. "Thomas Wolfe and Anatole France: A Study of Some Unpublished Experiments," *Comparative Literature* IX (Winter 1957), 33-50.

──────. *Thomas Wolfe, La France et les Romanciers Français.*

DeVoto, Bernard. "Genius Is Not Enough," *Saturday Review of Literature* XIII (Apr 25, 1936), 3-4; 14-15.

Falk, Robert P. "Thomas Wolfe and the Critics," *College English* V (Jan 1944), 186-192.

Foster, Ruel E. "Fabulous Tom Wolfe," *University of Kansas City Review* XXIII (Jun 1957), 260-264.

Frohock, W. M. "Thomas Wolfe: Of Time and Neurosis," *Southwest Review* XXXIII (Autumn 1948), 349-360; *The Novel of Violence in America,* 47-66.

WOLFE, THOMAS, Continued

Geismar, Maxwell. "Thomas Wolfe," *American Moderns,* 119-144.

———. "Thomas Wolfe: The Hillman and the Furies," *Yale Review* XXXV (Jun 1946), 649-665.

———. "Thomas Wolfe: The Unfound Door," *Writers in Crisis,* 187-235.

Gelfant, Blanche Housman. *The American City Novel,* 119-132.

Gurko, Leo. "The Laying of the Wind-Grieved Ghosts," *The Angry Decade,* 148-170.

Halperin, Irving. "Faith as Dilemma in Thomas Wolfe," *Prairie Schooner* XXVII (Summer 1953), 213-217.

Heiderstadt, Dorothy. "Studying Under Thomas Wolfe," *Mark Twain Quarterly* VIII (Winter 1950), 7-8.

Johnson, Pamela Hansford. *Hungry Gulliver.*

———. *Thomas Wolfe.*

Kazin, Alfred. "The Rhetoric and the Agony." *On Native Grounds,* 471-484.

Kennedy, Robert S. "Thomas Wolfe at Harvard, 1920-1923," *Harvard Library Bulletin* IV (Spring 1950), 172-190; (Autumn 1950), 304-319.

Kohler, Dayton. "Thomas Wolfe: Prodigal and Lost," *College English* I (Oct 1939), 1-10.

Kussy, Bella. "The Vitalist Trend and Thomas Wolfe," *Sewanee Review* L (Jul-Sept 1942), 306-324.

McCole, John. *Lucifer at Large,* 231-253.

McElderry, B. R., Jr. "The Autobiographical Problem in Thomas Wolfe's Earlier Novels," *Arizona Quarterly* IV (Winter 1948), 315-324.

———. "Wolfe and Emerson on 'Flow,'" *Modern Fiction Studies* II (May 1956), 77-78.

Meade, Robert D. "You Can't Escape Autobiography," *Atlantic Monthly* CLXXXVI (Nov 1950), 80-83.

Morris, Wright. "The Function of Appetite," *The Territory Ahead,* 147-155.

Muller, Herbert J. *Thomas Wolfe.*

Norwood, Hayden. "Julia Wolfe: Web of Memory," *Virginia Quarterly Review* XX (Spring 1944), 236-250.

———. *The Marble Man's Wife.*

Nowell, Elizabeth (ed.). *The Letters of Thomas Wolfe.*

WOLFE, THOMAS, Continued

Pollock, Thomas Clark and Oscar Cargill. *Thomas Wolfe at Washington Square.*

Powell, Desmond. "Of Thomas Wolfe," *Arizona Quarterly* (Spring 1945), 28-36.

Pugh, C. Elton. "Of Thomas Wolfe," *Mark Twain Quarterly* VII (Summer-Fall 1945), 13-14.

Rothman, Nathan L. "Thomas Wolfe and James Joyce," *A Southern Vanguard,* 52-77.

Rubin, Louis D., Jr. *Thomas Wolfe.*

———. "Thomas Wolfe in Time and Place," *Southern Renascence,* 290-305.

Shorer, Mark. "Technique as Discovery," *Hudson Review* I (Spring 1948), 80-81.

Simpson, Claude. "Thomas Wolfe: A Chapter in His Biography," *Southwest Review* XXV (Apr 1940), 308-321.

Slochower, Harry. *No Voice Is Wholly Lost,* 99-102.

Sloyan, Gerard S. "Thomas Wolfe: A Legend of a Man's Youth in His Hunger," *Fifty Years of the American Novel,* 197-215.

Snell, George. "The Education of Thomas Wolfe," *The Shapers of American Fiction,* 173-187.

Spiller, Robert E. *The Cycle of American Literature,* 263-269; (Mentor), 199-203.

Stearns, Monroe M. "The Metaphysics of Thomas Wolfe," *College English* VI (Jan 1945), 193-199.

Stovall, Floyd. *American Idealism,* 154-159.

Taylor, Walter Fuller. "Thomas Wolfe and the Middle-Class Tradition," *South Atlantic Quarterly* LII (Oct 1953), 543-554.

Terry, John Skally (ed.). *Thomas Wolfe's Letters to His Mother.*

Thompson, Betty. "Thomas Wolfe: Two Decades of Criticism," *South Atlantic Quarterly* XLIX (Jul 1950), 378-392.

Van Doren, Carl. *The American Novel,* 343-348.

Volkening, Henry T. "Tom Wolfe: Penance No More," *Virginia Quarterly Review* XV (Spring 1939), 196-215.

Wagenknecht, Edward. "Novelists of the 'Thirties: Gargantua as Novelist: Thomas Wolfe," *Cavalcade of the American Novel,* 409-415.

Walser, Richard Gaither. *The Enigma of Thomas Wolfe.*

Watkins, Floyd C. "Rhetoric in Southern Writing: Wolfe," *Georgia Review* XII (Spring 1958), 79-82.

WOLFE, THOMAS, Continued

──────────. "Thomas Wolfe and the Nashville Agrarians," *Georgia Review* VII (Winter 1953), 410-423.

──────────. "Thomas Wolfe and the Southern Mountaineer," *South Atlantic Quarterly* L (Jan 1951), 58-71.

──────────. *Thomas Wolfe's Characters.*

──────────. "Thomas Wolfe's High Sinfulness of Poetry," *Modern Fiction Studies* II (Winter 1956-1957), 197-206.

Whicher, George F. "The Resurgent South," *The Literature of the American People,* 924-925.

Williams, Cecil B. "Thomas Wolfe Fifteen Years After," *South Atlantic Quarterly* LIV (Oct 1955), 523-537.

Wolfe, Julia Elizabeth. "Look Homeward, Angel," *Saturday Review of Literature* XXIX (Jan 5, 1946), 13-14; 31-32.

Wolfe, Thomas. "Something of My Life," *Saturday Review of Literature* XXXI (Feb 7, 1948), 6-8.

──────────. "Writing Is My Life," *Atlantic Monthly* CLXXIX (Feb 1947), 55-61.

BIBLIOGRAPHY

Holman, C. Hugh. "Thomas Wolfe: A Bibliographical Study," *Texas Studies in Literature and Language* I (Autumn 1959), 427-445.

Kauffman, Bernice. "Bibliography of Periodical Articles on Thomas Wolfe," *Bulletin of Bibliography* XVII (Aug-May 1942), 162-165.

Pollock, Thomas Clark and Oscar Cargill. *Thomas Wolfe at Washington Square,* 154-163.

Preston, George R., Jr. *Thomas Wolfe.*

WOLFERT, IRA

GENERAL

Aldridge, John W. "Ira Wolfert: The Failure of A Form," *In Search of Heresy,* 177-185.

WOOLSON, CONSTANCE FENIMORE

GENERAL

Brooks, Van Wyck. "The South: Constance Fenimore Woolson," *The Times of Melville and Whitman,* 323-350.

WOOLSON, CONSTANCE FENIMORE, Continued

Cowie, Alexander. "Local-Color, Frontier, and Regional Fiction: Constance Fenimore Woolson (1840-1890)," *The Rise of the American Novel*, 568-578.

Hubbell, Jay B. *The South in American Literature*, 733-737.

Kern, John Dwight. *Constance Fenimore Woolson*.

Pattee, Fred Lewis. "Constance Fenimore Woolson and the South," *South Atlantic Quarterly* XXXVI (Apr 1939), 130-141.

Richardson, Lyon N. "Constance Fenimore Woolson, 'Novelist Laureate' of America," *South Atlantic Quarterly* XXXIX (Jan 1940), 18-36.

Wagenknecht, Edward. "Novelists of the 'Eighties: Miss Woolson," *Cavalcade of the American Novel*, 173-177.

WOUK, HERMAN

THE CAINE MUTINY

Bierstedt, Robert. *Great Moral Dilemmas in Literature, Past and Present*, 1-14.

Browne, James R. "Distortion in *The Caine Mutiny*," *College English* XVII (Jan 1956), 216-218.

Frankel, Theodore. "Second Thoughts on *The Caine Mutiny*," *Western Humanities Review* IX (Autumn 1955), 333-339.

Fuller, Edmund. *Man in Modern Fiction*, 134-145.

Prescott, Orville. *In My Opinion*, 163-164.

Swados, Harvey. "Popular Taste and 'The Caine Mutiny,'" *Partisan Review* XX (Mar-Apr 1953), 248-256.

THE CITY BOY

Gehman, Richard B. "Bronx Penrod," *Saturday Review of Literature* XXXI (Aug 21, 1948), 10.

MARJORIE MORNINGSTAR

Cohen, Joseph. "Wouk's Morningstar and Hemingway's Sun," *South Atlantic Quarterly* LVIII (Spring 1959), 213-224.

Fitch, Robert E. "The Bourgeois and the Bohemian," *Antioch Review* XVI (Jun 1956), 131-145.

Geismar, Maxwell. *American Moderns*, 38-45.

Levin, Meyer. "Central Park West Revisited," *Saturday Review* XXXVIII (Sept 3, 1955), 9-10.

GENERAL

Carpenter, Frederic I. "Herman Wouk," *College English* XVII (Jan 1956), 211-215.

WOUK, HERMAN, Continued

McElderry, B. R., Jr. "The Conservative as Novelist: Herman Wouk," *Arizona Quarterly* XV (Summer 1959), 128-136.

WRIGHT, HAROLD BELL

GENERAL

Baldwin, Charles C. "Harold Bell Wright," *The Men Who Make Our Novels*, 601-612.

Boynton, H. W. "A Word on 'The Genteel Critic,'" *Dial* LIX (Oct 14, 1915), 303-306.

----------. "Some American Novelists and the Lame Art," *Dial* LIX (Dec 9, 1915), 548-549.

Mott, Frank Luther. "Harold Bell Wright," *Golden Multitudes*, 225-233.

WRIGHT, RICHARD

NATIVE SON

Burgum, Edwin Berry. *The Novel and the World's Dilemma*, 223-259.

Canby, Henry Seidel. "The Right Question," *Saturday Review of Literature* XXI (Mar 23, 1940), 8.

Creekmore, Hubert. "Social Factors in *Native Son*," *University of Kansas City Review* VIII (Winter 1941), 136-143.

Ellison, Ralph. "Richard Wright's Blues," *Antioch Review* V (Jun 1945), 198-211.

Hughes, Carl Milton. *The Negro Novelist*, 41-68.

Slochower, Harry. *No Voice Is Wholly Lost*, 87-92.

Wright, Richard. "How 'Bigger' Was Born," *Saturday Review of Literature* XXII (Jun 1, 1940), 3-4; 17-20.

GENERAL

Bone, Robert A. *The Negro Novel in America*, 140-152.

Cohn, David L. "The Negro Novel: Richard Wright," *Atlantic Monthly* CLXV (May 1940), 659-661.

Embree, Edwin R. "Native Son," *13 Against the Odds*, 25-46.

Ford, Nick Aaron. "The Ordeal of Richard Wright," *College English* XV (Nov 1953), 87-94.

Hicks, Granville. "The Power of Richard Wright," *Saturday Review* XLI (Oct 18, 1958), 13; 65.

Prescott, Orville. *In My Opinion*, 42-43.

WRIGHT, RICHARD, Continued

Scott, Nathan A. "Search for Beliefs: Fiction of Richard Wright," *University of Kansas City Review* XXIII (1956), 19-24.

Whicher, George F. "The Resurgent South," *The Literature of the American People*, 920.

BIBLIOGRAPHY

Sprague, M. D. "Richard Wright: A Bibliography," *Bulletin of Bibliography* XXI (Sept-Dec 1953), 39.

WYLIE, ELINOR

GENERAL

Benét, William Rose. *The Prose and Poetry of Elinor Wylie.*

Cabell, James Branch. "Sanctuary in Porcelain," *Some of Us*, 15-26.

Cargill, Oscar. "The Intelligensia," *Intellectual America*, 511-514.

Clark, Emily. *Innocence Abroad*, 167-183.

Hatcher, Harlan. "Fantasy as a Way of Escape," *Creating the Modern American Novel*, 211-218.

Hoyt, Nancy. *Elinor Wylie.*

Kazin, Alfred. "The Exquisites," *On Native Grounds*, 242-244.

Kohler, Dayton. "Elinor Wylie: Heroic Mask," *South Atlantic Quarterly* XXXVI (Apr 1939), 218-228.

Overton, Grant. "Elinor Wylie," *The Women Who Make Our Novels*, 350-352.

Van Doren, Carl. "Elinor Wylie: A Portrait from Memory," *Harpers Magazine* 173 (Sept 1936), 358-367.

Wagenknecht, Edward. "Novelists of the 'Twenties: Romance and Fantasy: Elinor Wylie," *Cavalcade of the American Novel*, 396-399.

Wainstein, Lia. "Il cerchio magico di Elinor Wylie," *Studi Americani* III (1957), 265-291.

Wilson, Edmund. "The Death of Elinor Wylie," *A Literary Chronicle*, 109-113.

YOUNG, STARK

SO RED THE ROSE

Davidson, Donald. *Southern Renascence*, 262-277.

Erskine, Albert Russel, Jr. "The Sempiternal Rose," *Southwest Review* XX (Apr 1935), 21-27.

GENERAL STUDIES

EIGHTEENTH CENTURY

Cowie, Alexander. "John Trumbull Glances at Fiction," *American Literature* XII (Mar 1940), 69-73.

Loshe, Lillie Deming. *The Early American Novel.*

McDowell, Tremaine. "The Big Three in Yankee Fiction," *Sewanee Review* XXXVI (Apr-Jun 1928), 157-163.

──────────. "Sensibility in the Eighteenth-Century American Novel," *Studies in Philology* XXIV (Jul 1927), 383-402.

Orians, G. Harrison. "Censure of Fiction in American Romances and Magazines," *PMLA* LII (1937), 195-214.

Wyatt, Edith Franklin. "The First American Novel," *Atlantic Monthly* CXLIV (1929), 466-475.

NINETEENTH CENTURY

Adams, R. P. "Romanticism and the American Renaissance," *American Literature* XXIII (Jan 1951), 419-432.

Åhnebrink, Lars. "Aspects of European Realistic and Naturalistic Literature in America Prior to 1900," *The Beginnings of Naturalism in American Fiction,* 34-49.

Beer, Thomas. "The Mauve Decade," *Hanna, Crane, and the Mauve Decade,* 3-207.

Berkelman, Robert. "Mrs. Grundy and Richard Watson Gilder," *American Quarterly* IV (Spring 1952), 66-72.

Brooks, Van Wyck. "Writers of the Eighties," *Saturday Review of Literature* XXII (Jun 8, 1940), 3-4; 18-19.

Brown, Herbert R. "The Great American Novel," *American Literature* VII (Mar 1935), 1-14.

Carter, Everett. "The Haymarket Affair in Literature," *American Quarterly* II (Fall 1950), 270-278.

Cassady, Edward E. "Muckraking in the Gilded Age," *American Literature* XIII (May 1941), 134-141.

Collins, Carvel Emerson. "Nineteenth Century Fiction of the Southern Appalachians," *Bulletin of Bibliography* XVII (Sept-Dec 1942), 186-190; (Jan-Apr 1943), 215-218.

Cowie, Alexander. "The Vogue of the Domestic Novel 1850-1870," *South Atlantic Quarterly* XLI (Oct 1942), 416-424.

Curti, Merle. "Dime Novels and the American Tradition," *Yale Review* XXVI (Jun 1937), 761-778.
DeVoto, Bernard. "Fiction Fights the Civil War," *Saturday Review of Literature* XVII (Dec 18, 1937), 3-4; 15-16.
Ernest, Joseph M., Jr. "Whittier and the 'Feminine Fifties,'" *American Literature* XXVIII (May 1956), 184-196.
Falk, Robert P. "The Rise of Realism 1871-1891," *Transitions in American Literary History*, 381-442.
Fidler, William Perry. "Recipe for an Old-Fashioned Best-Seller," *Georgia Review* VIII (Spring 1954), 5-16.
Fiske, Horace Spencer. *Provincial Types in American Fiction*.
Flanagan, John T. "A Half-Century of Middlewestern Fiction," *Critique* II (Winter 1959), 16-34.
Frailberg, Louis. "The *Westminster Review* and American Literature, 1824-1885," *American Literature* XXIV (Nov 1952), 310-329.
Gohdes, Clarence. *American Literature in Nineteenth-Century England*.
——————. "Exploitation of the Provinces," *The Literature of the American People*, 651-660.
Hart, James D. "Platitudes of Piety: Religion and the Popular Modern Novel," *American Quarterly*, VI (Winter 1954), 311-322.
Hewett-Thayer, Harvey W. *American Literature as Viewed in Germany 1818-1861*.
Howells, William Dean. "The New Historical Romance," *North American Review* 171 (Dec 1900), 935-948.
Hubbell, Jay B. "Cavalier and Indentured Servant in Virginia Fiction," *South Atlantic Quarterly* XXVI (Jan 1927), 22-39.
Hudson, Ruth. "A Literary 'Area of Freedom' Between Irving and Twain," *Western Humanities Review* XIII (Winter 1959), 46-60.
Kazin, Alfred. "American Fin-de-Siècle," *Saturday Review of Literature* XXI (Feb 3, 1940), 3-4; 11-12; *On Native Grounds*, 51-72.
Keeler, Clinton. "Children of Innocence: The Agrarian Crusade in Fiction," *Western Humanities Review* VI (Autumn 1952), 363-376.
Knight, Grant C. *The Critical Period in American Literature*.
Landrum, Grace Warren. "Sir Walter Scott and His Literary

Rivals in the Old South," *American Literature* II (Nov 1930), 256-276.

Lash, John S. "The American Negro and American Literature: A Check-List of Significant Commentaries," *Bulletin of Bibliography* XIX (Sept-Dec 1946), 12-15; (Jan-Apr 1947), 33-36.

Lively, Robert A. *Fiction Fights the Civil War: An Unfinished Chapter in the Literary History of the American People.*

Martin, Harold C. "The Development of Style in Nineteenth-Century American Fiction," *English Institute Essays* (1958), 114-141.

Matthiessen, F. O. *American Renaissance.*

McDowell, Tremaine. "The Negro in the Southern Novel Prior to 1850," *Journal of English and Germanic Philology* XXV (Oct 1926), 455-473.

Miller, Perry. *The Raven and the Whale.*

Muller, Herbert J. "The New Psychology in Old Fiction," *Saturday Review of Literature* XVI (Aug 21, 1937), 3-4; 11.

Oakes, Frances Etheridge. "The Swoon, the Kayo and the Blackout," *Georgia Review* IX (Winter 1955), 433-442.

Orians, G. Harrison. "The Romance Ferment after Waverly," *American Literature* III (Jan 1932), 408-431.

Papashvily, Helen Waite. *All the Happy Endings.*

Parks, Edd Winfield. "Agrarianism as a Theme in Southern Literature: The Ante-Bellum Period," *Georgia Review* XI (Summer 1957), 147-149.

——————. "Early American Novels," *Southwest Review* XXII (Jan 1937), 204-208.

——————. "The Three Streams of Southern Humor," *Georgia Review* VII (Winter 1954), 147-159.

Rose, Lisle Abbott. "A Bibliographical Survey of Economic and Political Writings, 1865-1900," *American Literature* XV (Jan 1944), 381-410.

——————. "Shortcomings of 'Muckraking in the Gilded Age,'" *American Literature* XIV (May 1942), 161-164.

Satterwhite, Joseph N. "The Tremulous Formula: Form and Technique in *Godey's* Fiction," *American Quarterly* VIII (Summer 1958), 99-113.

Schwab, Arnold T. "James Huneker's Criticism of American Literature," *American Literature* XXIX (Mar 1957), 64-78.

Shurter, Robert I. "The Utopian Novel in America: 1888-1900," *South Atlantic Quarterly* XXXIV (Apr 1935), 137-144.

Smith, Henry Nash. "The Dime Novel Heroine," *Southwest Review* XXXIV (Spring 1949), 182-188; *Virgin Land*, 112-122.

——————. "The Western Hero in the Dime Novel," *Southwest Review* XXXIII (Summer 1948), 276-284; *Virgin Land*, 90-111.

Smith, Rebecca W. "Catalogue of the chief novels and short stories by American authors dealing with the Civil War and its effects, 1861-1899," *Bulletin of Bibliography* XVI (Sept-Dec 1939), 193-194; XVII (Jan-Apr 1940), 10-12: (May-Aug 1940), 33-35; (Sept-Dec 1940), 53-55; XVIII (Jan-Apr 1941), 72-75.

Spencer, Benjamin T. "A National Literature: Post-Civil War Decade," *Modern Language Quarterly* IV (Mar 1943), 71-86.

——————. "The New Realism and a National Literature," *PMLA* LVI (1941), 1116-1132.

Spiller, Robert E. "Critical Standards in the American Romantic Movement," *College English* VIII (Apr 1947), 344-352.

Starke, Aubrey. " 'No Names' and 'Round Robins,' " *American Literature* VI (Jan 1935), 400-412.

Stovall, Floyd. "The Decline of Romantic Idealism 1855-1871," *Transitions in American Literary History*, 317-378.

Tandy, Jeannette Reid. "Pro-Slavery Propaganda in American Fiction of the Fifties," *South Atlantic Quarterly* XXI (Jan 1922), 41-50; XXI (Apr 1922), 170-178.

Taylor, Walter Fuller. "In Behalf of the Gilded Age," *College English* VI (Oct 1944), 13-17.

Wasserstrom, William. *Heiress of all Ages*.

Woodberry, George Edward. "Knickerbocker Era of American Letters," *Harper's Magazine* CV (Oct 1902), 677-683.

TWENTIETH CENTURY

Adams, J. Donald. *The Shape of Books to Come*.

Adams, Samuel Hopkins. "Apollyon vs. Pollyanna," *The Novel of Tomorrow*, 3-7.

Albrecht, W. P. "War and Fraternity: A Study of Some Recent American War Novels," *New Mexico Quarterly* XXI (Winter 1951), 461-474.

Aldridge, John W. *After the Lost Generation*.

——————. "America's Young Novelists," *Saturday Review of Literature* XXXII (Feb 12, 1949), 6-8; 36-37; 42.

——————. *In Search of Heresy.*
Allen, Frederick Lewis. "Best-Sellers: 1900-1935," *Saturday Review of Literature* XIII (Dec 7, 1935), 3-4; 20; 24; 26.
Anderson, Sherwood. *The Modern Writer.*
Austin, Mary. "The American Form of the Novel," *The Novel of Tomorrow*, 11-22.
Banning, Margaret Culkin. "Changing Moral Standards in Fiction," *Saturday Review of Literature* XX (Jul 1, 1939), 4-5; 14.
Barrett, William. "American Fiction and American Values," *Partisan Review* XVIII (Nov-Dec 1951), 681-690.
Beach, Joseph Warren. *American Fiction.*
——————. "American Letters Between Wars," *College English* III (Oct 1941), 1-12.
——————. "Eight Novelists Between Wars," *Saturday Review of Literature* XXIII (Mar 29, 1941), 3-4; 17-19.
——————. "New Intentions in the Novel," *North American Review* 218 (Aug 1923), 233-245.
——————. *The Twentieth Century Novel.*
Becker, Stephen, Simon Michael Bessie, Ralph Ellison, Albert Erskine, Jean Stafford, William Styron, and Hiram Haydn: "What's Wrong With the American Novel?" *American Scholar* XXIV (Autumn 1955), 464-503.
Bellow, Saul. "Distractions of a Fiction Writer," *New World Writing* 12 (1957), 229-243.
Bernard, Harry. *Le Roman Régionaliste aux Etats-Unis (1913-1940).*
Bishop, John Peale. "The Myth and Modern Literature," *Saturday Review of Literature* XX (Jul 22, 1939), 3-4; 14.
Bodenheim, Maxwell. "American Novels," *Saturday Review of Literature* III (Mar 26, 1927), 673-674.
——————. "Tendencies in Modern Prose and Poetry," *North American Review* 213 (Apr 1921), 553-555.
Bourjaily, Vance. "No More Apologies: A Critical Note," *discovery* 2 (1953), 186-190.
Bowron, Bernard R., Jr. "Realism in America," *Comparative Literature* III (Summer 1951), 268-285.
Brace, Marjorie. "Thematic Problems of the American Novelist," *Accent* VI (Autumn 1945), 44-53.
Brooks, Cleanth. "What Deep South Literature Needs," *Saturday Review of Literature* XXV (Sept 19, 1942), 8-9; 29-30.

Brooks, Van Wyck. "Fashions in Defeatism," *Saturday Review of Literature* XXIII (Mar 22, 1941), 3-4; 14.
Burt, Struthers. "What's Left for the Novel?" *North American Review* 232 (Aug 1931), 118-125.
Cabell, James Branch. "A Note on Alcoves," *The Novel of Tomorrow*, 25-35.
――――――. "Vitality en Vogue: A Plea of an Average Novel Reader," *Sewanee Review* XXIII (Jan 1915), 66-74.
Caldwell, Erskine. "A Writer Looks at Writing," *Saturday Review* XLI (Aug 9, 1958), 10; 35.
Calmer, Alan. "Portrait of the Artist as a Proletarian," *Saturday Review of Literature* XVI (Jul 31, 1937), 3-4; 14.
Calverton, V. F. "Land of Literary Plenty," *Saturday Review of Literature* XXII (May 11, 1940), 3-4; 16-17.
Canby, Henry Seidel. "Footnotes to 1949," *Saturday Review of Literature* XXXII (Aug 6, 1949), 17-19; 175-176.
――――――. "Humor and the Twenties," *Saturday Review of Literature* VIII (Nov 28, 1931), 325; 328.
――――――. "The Imitationists," *Saturday Review of Literature* II (Dec 5, 1925), 357.
――――――. "The Threatening Thirties," *Saturday Review of Literature* XVI (May 22, 1937), 3-4; 14.
Cargill, Oscar. "Anatomist of Monsters," *College English* IX (Oct 1947), 1-8.
Cash, W. J. "Literature and the South," *Saturday Review of Literature* XXIII (Dec 28, 1940), 3-4; 18-19.
Cestre, Charles. "American Literature through French Eyes," *Yale Review* X (Oct 1920), 85-98.
Champney, Freeman. "Literature Takes to the Woods," *Antioch Review* IV (Jun 1944), 244-256.
――――――. "Protofascism in American Literature," *Antioch Review* IV (Sept 1944), 338-348.
Clark, Harry Hayden. "Pandora's Box in American Fiction," *Humanism and America*, 170-204.
Clay, George R. "The Jewish Hero in American Fiction," *Reporter* (Sept 19, 1957), 43-46.
Coates, Robert M. "The State of the Novel," *Yale Review* XXXVI (Jun 1947), 604-610.
Colum, Mary M. "Literature and the Social Left," *Saturday Review of Literature* XIII (Nov 2, 1935), 3-4; 18.

Cousins, Norman. "Letter to a Novelist, 1960," *Saturday Review of Literature* XXV (Jan 17, 1942), 3-4; 16-18.

Cowie, Alexander. "My Case Against Contemporary Fiction," *Saturday Review of Literature* XXVIII (Sept 29, 1945), 15; 44-46.

Cowley, Malcolm. *Exile's Return.*

——————. "The Generation That Wasn't Lost," *College English* V (Feb 1944), 233-239.

——————. *The Literary Situation.*

——————. "Twenty-five Years After," *Saturday Review of Literature* XXXIV (Jun 2, 1951), 6-7; 33-34.

Crandall, Norma. "The Decline of Liberalism and of the Modern Novel," *Trace* No. 33 (Aug-Sept 1959), 1-5.

Crane, Maurice. "Impaled on a Horn: The Jazz Trumpeter as Tragic Hero," *Critique* I (Summer 1957), 64-72.

Cross, Wilbur. "The New Fiction," *Yale Review* XI (Apr 1922), 449-466.

Current-Garcia, E. "Writers in the 'Sticks,'" *Prairie Schooner* XII (Winter 1938), 294-309.

Davis, Joe Lee. "An American Novelist Between Wars," *College English* V (May 1944), 428-434.

Dell, Floyd. "The Difference Between Life and Fiction," *The Novel of Tomorrow,* 39-48.

Derleth, August. "Contemporary Science-Fiction," *College English* XIII (Jan 1952), 187-194.

DeVoto, Bernard. "American Novels: 1939," *Atlantic Monthly* CLXV (Jan 1940), 66-74.

——————. "Fiction and the Everlasting *If*: Notes on the Contemporary Historical Novel," *Harpers Magazine* 177 (Jun 1938), 42-49.

Edel, Leon. *The Psychological Novel.*

Fadiman, Clifton. "The American Novel of the Truce," *Saturday Review of Literature* XXVII (Aug 5, 1944), 19-21.

Farber, Marjorie. "Subjectivity in Modern Fiction," *Kenyon Review* VII (Autumn 1945), 645-652.

Farrell, James T. *The Coming of Age of a Great Book,* 18.

——————. "The Decline of the Serious Writer," *Antioch Review* XVII (Jun 1957), 147-160.

——————. "Some Observations on Naturalism, So Called, in American Fiction," *Antioch Review* X (Jun 1950), 247-264.

Fenton, Charles A. "Ambulance Drivers in France and Italy: 1914-1918," *American Quarterly* III (Winter 1951), 326-343.

———. "The Writers Who Came Out of the War," *Saturday Review* XL (Aug 3, 1957), 5-7; 24.

Fiedler, Leslie A. "Adolescence and Maturity in the American Novel," *An End to Innocence,* 191-210.

Field, Louise M. "American Novelists vs. the Nation," *North American Review* 235 (Jun 1933), 552-560.

———. "Emancipating the Novel," *North American Review* 240 (Sept 1935), 318-324.

———. "Heroines Back at the Hearth," *North American Review* 236 (Aug 1933), 176-183.

———. "The Modern Novelists," *North American Review* 235 (Jan 1933), 63-69.

Filler, Louis. "Political Literature: A Post-Mortem," *Southwest Review* XXXIX (Summer 1954), 185-193.

Flesch, Rudolf. "What the War Did to Prose," *Saturday Review of Literature* XXXII (Aug 13, 1949), 6-7; 36-37.

Frank, Waldo. "The Major Issue," *The Novel of Tomorrow,* 51-62.

Frederick, John T. "Costain and Company: The Historical Novel Today," *College English* XV (Apr 1954), 373-379.

———. "Fiction of the Second World War," *College English* XVII (Jan 1956), 197-204.

Frey, John R. "Postwar German Reactions to American Literature," *Journal of English and Germanic Philology* LIV (Apr 1955), 173-194.

Frohock, W. M. *The Novel of Violence in America.*

Fuller, Edmund. *Man in Modern Fiction.*

———. "The New Compassion in the American Novel," *American Scholar* XXVI (Spring 1957), 155-163.

Gaines, Francis P. "The Racial Bar Sinister in American Romance," *South Atlantic Quarterly* XXV (Oct 1926), 396-402.

Gale, Zona. "The Novel and the Spirit," *Yale Review* XII (Oct 1922), 41-55.

———. "The Novel of Tomorrow," *The Novel of Tomorrow,* 65-72.

———. "Period Realism," *Yale Review* XXIII (Sept 1933), 111-124.

Garvin, Harry R. "Camus and the American Novel," *Compara-*

tive Literature VIII (Summer 1956), 194-204; Philip Thody, A Note on Camus and the American Novel," *Comparative Literature* IX (Summer 1957), 243-249.

Geismar, Maxwell. *American Moderns.*

──────────. *The Last of the Provincials.*

──────────. "The Postwar Generation in Arts & Letters," *Saturday Review* XXXVI (Mar 14, 1953), 11-12; 60.

──────────. "Years of Gain," *Rebels and Ancestors*, 383-415.

Gerould, Katherine Fullerton. "Stream of Consciousness," *Saturday Review of Literature* IV (Oct 22, 1927), 231-233.

Glasgow, Ellen. "Heroes and Monsters," *Saturday Review of Literature* XII (May 4, 1935), 3-4.

Gold, Herbert. "Fiction of the Fifties," *Hudson Review* XII (Summer 1959), 192-201.

──────────. "The Mystery of Personality in the Novel," *Partisan Review* XXIV (Summer 1957), 453-462.

──────────. "The New Upper-Middle Soap Opera (A Tribute to Herman Wouk, Sloan Wilson, Cameron Hawley, and Makers of Fine Face-Cream Everywhere)," *Hudson Review* IX (Winter 1956-57), 585-591.

Guerard, Albert J. "The Ivory Tower and the Dust Bowl," *New World Writing* 3 (1953), 344-356.

Gurko, Leo. *The Angry Decade.*

Hackett, Alice. "New Novelists of 1944," *Saturday Review of Literature* XXVIII (Feb 17, 1945), 12-14; 41.

──────────. "New Novelists of 1945," *Saturday Review of Literature* XXIX (Feb 16, 1946), 8-10.

──────────. "New Novelists of 1946," *Saturday Review of Literature* XXX (Feb 15, 1947), 11-13.

Hatcher, Harlan. *Creating the Modern American Novel.*

Healey, Robert C. "Novelists of the War: A Bunch of Dispossessed," *Fifty Years of the American Novel*, 257-271.

Henderson, Philip. *The Novel Today.*

Hergesheimer, Joseph. "The Feminine Nuisance in American Literature," *Yale Review* X (Jul 1921), 716-725.

──────────. "The Profession of Novelist," *The Novel of Tomorrow*, 75-87.

Herrick, Robert. "The Background of the American Novel," *Yale Review* III (Jan 1914), 213-233.

_____. "The New Novel," *The Novel of Tomorrow*, 91-102.
Herzberg, Max J. "Literary 1947 in Retrospect," *College English* IX (Mar 1948), 293-299.
Hicks, Granville. "The Fighting Decade," *Saturday Review of Literature* XXII (Jul 6, 1940), 3-5; 16-17.
_____. "Literature in This Global War," *College English* IV (May 1943), 453-459.
_____. "1959: Books in Review," *Saturday Review* XLII (Dec 26, 1959), 10.
_____. "Our Novelists' Shifting Reputations," *College English* XII (Jan 1951), 187-193.
_____. "The Shape of Postwar Literature," *College English* V (May 1944), 407-412.
Hoffman, Frederick J. "Grace, Violence, and Self: Death and Modern Literature," *Virginia Quarterly Review* XXXIV (Summer 1958), 439-454.
_____. *The Modern Novel in America*.
_____. *The Twenties*.
Holman, Harriet R. "Chivalry's Last Stand: Some Comment on American Fiction, 1900-1920," *Georgia Review* X (Summer 1956), 161-167.
Howe, Irving. "The Novel in Mid-Century," *The Reporter* III (Dec 26, 1950), 35-38.
Hughes, Carl Milton. *The Negro Novelist*.
Hyman, Stanley Edgar. "Some Trends in the Novel," *College English* XX (Oct 1958), 1-9.
Jack, Peter Monro. "The James Branch Cabell Period," *After the Genteel Tradition*, 141-154.
Jackson, Blyden. "A Golden Mean for the Negro Novel," *CLA Journal* III (Dec 1959), 81-87.
Jarrett, Thomas D. "Recent Fiction by Negroes," *College English* XVI (Nov 1954), 85-91; Byrd, James W. "Letters to the Editor: Negro Fiction," *College English* XVI (Apr 1955), 451.
Johnson, James William. "The Adolescent Hero: A Trend in Modern Fiction," *Twentieth Century Literature* V (Apr 1959), 3-11.
Josephson, Matthew. "The Younger Generation: Its Young Novelists," *Virginia Quarterly Review* IX (Apr 1933), 243-261.

Kain, Richard M. "The American Novel—1936 Models," *American Scholar* VII (Winter 1938), 121-124.

Knight, Grant C. *The Strenuous Age in American Literature.*

Kohler, Dayton. "Time in the Modern Novel," *College English* X (Oct 1948), 15-24.

Lenormand, H.-R. "American Literature in France," *Saturday Review of Literature* XI (Oct 27, 1934), 244-245.

Lewisohn, Ludwig. "The Crisis of the Novel," *Yale Review* XXII (Mar 1933), 533-544.

"The Limits of the Possible: Accepting the Reality of the Human Situation," *London Times Literary Supplement,* Nov 6, 1959, xvi.

The Living Novel: A Symposium.

Lydenberg, John. "Mobilizing our Novelists," *American Quarterly* IV (Spring 1952), 35-48.

Macauley, Robie. "Fiction of the 'Forties," *Western Review* XVI (Autumn 1951), 59-69.

Maclean, Hugh. "Conservatism in Modern American Fiction," *College English* XV (Mar 1954), 315-325.

MacLeish, Archibald. "The New Age and the New Writers," *Yale Review* XII (Jan 1923), 314-321.

Magyar, Francis. "American Literature in Hungary," *Books Abroad* VI (Apr 1932), 150-151.

Marble, Annie Russell. *A Study of the Modern Novel.*

Marley, Harold P. "The Negro in Recent American Literature," *South Atlantic Quarterly* XXVII (Jan 1928), 29-41.

Mendelson, M. *Soviet Interpretation of Contemporary American Literature.*

Michaelson, L. W. "Science Fiction, Censorship, and Pie-in-the-Sky," *Western Humanities Review* XIII (Autumn 1959), 409-413.

Mitchell, Stephen O. "Alien Vision: The Techniques of Science Fiction," *Modern Fiction Studies* IV (Winter 1958-1959), 346-356.

Mizener, Arthur. "The Novel of Manners in America," *Kenyon Review* XII (Winter 1950), 1-19.

Monkhouse, Allan. "Society and the Novel," *Atlantic Monthly* CLVI (1935), 369-371.

Moore, Virginia. "The Youngest Generation," *Saturday Review of Literature* VI (Jan 25, 1930), 672-673.

Morris, Lloyd. *Postscript to Yesterday.*
Muir, Edwin. "Time and the Modern Novel," *Atlantic Monthly* CLXV (Apr 1940), 535-537.
Muller, Herbert. "Impressionism in Fiction: Prism vs. Mirror," *American Scholar* VII (Summer 1938), 355-367.
O'Connor, William Van. "The Grotesque in Modern American Fiction," *College English* XX (Apr 1959), 342-346.
Odum, Gertrude Gilmer. "Georgia Fiction: 1926-1950," *Georgia Review* V (Summer 1951), 244-257.
O'Higgins, Harvey. "A Note on the Novel," *The Novel of Tomorrow*, 105-109.
Parkes, H. B. "The American Cultural Scene (IV): The Novel," *Scrutiny* IX (Jun 1940), 2-8.
Peckham, H. Houston. "Do We Need More Literature?" *South Atlantic Quarterly* XXI (Jul 1922), 270-274.
----------. "Lopsided Realism," *South Atlantic Quarterly* XV (Jul 1916), 276-281.
Phelps, Ruth Shepard. "A Use for Contemporary Fiction," *North American Review* 204 (Nov 1916), 745-750.
Pick, Robert. "Old-World Views on New-World Writing," *Saturday Review of Literature* XXXII (Aug 20, 1949), 7-9; 35-38.
Podhoretz, Norman. "The New Nihilism and the Novel," *Partisan Review* XXV (Fall 1958), 576-590.
Prescott, Orville. *In My Opinion.*
Priestley, J. B. "Contemporary American Fiction As An English Critic Sees It," *Harpers Magazine* 152 (Jan 1926), 230-234.
Rahv, Philip. "Proletarian Literature: A Political Autopsy," *Southern Review* IV (Winter 1939), 616-628.
Rawlings, Marjorie Kinnan. "Regional Literature of the South," *College English* I (Feb 1940), 381-389.
Redding, J. Saunders. "American Negro Literature," *American Scholar* XVIII (Spring 1949), 137-148.
Redman, Ben Ray. "Decline & Fall of the Whodunit," *Saturday Review of Literature* XXXV (May 31, 1952), 8-9; 31-32.
Ribalow, Harold U. "From *Hungry Hearts* to *Marjorie Morningstar*: The Progress of an American Minority Told in Fiction," *Saturday Review* XL (Sept 14, 1957), 46-48.
Rideout, Walter B. *The Radical Novel in the United States.*
Rock, Virginia. "Agrarianism as a Theme in Southern Literature:

The Period since 1925," *Georgia Review* XI (Summer 1957), 154-160.

Rouse, Blair. "Time and Place in Southern Fiction," *Southern Renascence*, 126-150.

Schorer, Mark. *The Novelist in the Modern World.*

——————. "Technique as Discovery," *Hudson Review* I (Spring 1948), 80-87.

Scott, W. T. "The Literary Summing-Up: A Personal Winnowing of 1950's Books," *Saturday Review of Literature* XXXIII (Dec 30, 1950), 6-8; 28-29.

"Serials verus Novels," *Dial* LVII (Sept 1, 1914), 125-127.

Shaw, Irwin. "If You Write About the War," *Saturday Review of Literature* XXVIII (Feb 17, 1945), 5-6.

Sherman, Caroline B. "Farm Life Fiction," *South Atlantic Quarterly* XXVII (Jul 1928), 310-324.

Smith, Harrison. " 'Damn the Torpedoes!' " *Saturday Review of Literature* XXXIV (Apr 21, 1951), 22-23.

——————. "Defeatism in Contemporary Literature," *Saturday Review* XXXIX (Dec 29, 1956), 20.

——————. "The Novel & the Facts of Life," *Saturday Review* XXXVI (Jan 3, 1953), 16.

——————. "The Novelist's Dilemma," *Saturday Review* XXXIX (Aug 18, 1956), 20.

——————. "The Power of the Novel," *Saturday Review* XLII (Aug 8, 1959), 22.

——————. "Sizing Up the Comers," *Saturday Review of Literature* XXXII (Feb 12, 1949), 9-11.

——————. "Thirteen Adventurers: A Study of a Year of First Novelists, 1947," *Saturday Review of Literature* XXXI (Feb 14, 1948), 6-8; 30-31.

——————. "Time for a Change," *Saturday Review of Literature* XXXII (Sept 17, 1949), 24.

——————. "Wanted: New Novelists," *Saturday Review* XXXVII (Jul 31, 1954), 22.

——————. "Who Are These People?" *Saturday Review of Literature* XXXIV (Jun 9, 1951), 22-23.

Spencer, Benjamin T. "Wherefore This Southern Fiction?" *Sewanee Review* XLVII (Oct-Dec 1939), 500-513.

Steadman, R. W. "A Critique of Proletarian Literature," *North American Review* 247 (Spring 1939), 142-152.

Stegner, Wallace. "The Anxious Generation," *College English* X (Jan 1949), 183-188.

Stewart, George R. "The Novelists Take Over Poetry," *Saturday Review of Literature* XXIII (Feb 8, 1941), 3-4; 18-19.

Stewart, Randall. "American Literature Between the Wars," *South Atlantic Quarterly* XLIV (Oct 1945), 371-383.

——————. "The Outlook for Southern Writing: Diagnosis and Prognosis," *Virginia Quarterly Review* XXI (Spring 1955), 252-263.

Stone, Edward. "From Henry James to John Balderston: Relativity and the '20's," *Modern Fiction Studies* I (May 1955), 2-11.

Strauch, Carl F. "The Crisis in Modern Literature," *College English* V (May 1944), 423-428.

Strauss, Harold. "The Illiterate American Writer," *Saturday Review of Literature* XXXV (May 17, 1952), 8-9; 39.

——————. "Realism in the Proletarian Novel," *Yale Review* XXVIII (Dec 1938), 360-374.

Swados, Harvey. "The Image in the Mirror," *New World Writing* 12 (1957), 207-228.

Tindall, William York. "The Sociological Best Seller," *College English* IX (Nov 1947), 55-62.

Trilling, Diana. "What Has Happened to our Novels?" *Harper's Magazine* 188 (May 1944), 529-536.

Turner, Katherine C. "American Literature in China," *Colorado Quarterly* VI (Spring 1958), 418-428.

Uzzell, Thomas H. "Mob Reading: Romantic Ingredients of the Super Best Seller," *Saturday Review of Literature* XVII (Nov 20, 1937), 3-4; 16-18.

——————. "Modern Innovations," *College English* VII (Nov 1945), 59-65.

"A Vocal Group: The Jewish Part in Literature," *London Times Literary Supplement*, Nov 6, 1959, xxv.

Wagenknecht, Edward. "The Little Prince Rides the White Deer: Fantasy and Symbolism in Recent Literature," *College English* VII (May 1946), 431-437.

Warfel, Harry R. *American Novelists of Today.*

Webster, Henry Kitchell. "A Brace of Definitions and A Short Code," *The Novel of Tomorrow*, 113-119.

West, Ray B., Jr. "Four Rocky Mountain Novels," *Rocky Mountain Review* X (Autumn 1945), 21-28.

Wharton, Edith. "The Great American Novel," *Yale Review* XVI (Jul 1927), 646-657.

——————. "Tendencies of Modern Fiction," *Saturday Review of Literature* X (Jan 27, 1934), 433-434.

Whicher, George F. "Proletarian Leanings," *The Literature of the American People*, 954-958.

White, William Allen. "Splitting Fiction Three Ways," *The Novel of Tomorrow*, 123-133.

Willcox, Louise C. "The Content of the Modern Novel," *North American Review* 182 (Jun 1906), 919-929.

Williams, Stanley T. "Aspects of the Modern Novel," *Texas Review* VIII (Oct 1922-Jul 1923), 245-256.

Wilson, Edmund. "The All-Star Literary Vaudeville," *A Literary Chronicle*, 76-81.

Wilson, James Southall. "The Novel in the South: 'A Taboo Is No Longer a Red Light,'" *Saturday Review of Literature* XXVI (Jan 23, 1943), 11-12.

Wilson, John W. "Delta Revival," *College English* X (Mar 1949), 299-306.

Wolle, Francis. "Novels of Two World Wars," *Western Humanities Review* V (Summer 1951), 279-296.

Woolf, Virginia. "American Fiction," *Saturday Review of Literature* II (Aug 1, 1925), 1-3.

Wyatt, Edith Franklin. "Dreaming True," *The Novel of Tomorrow*, 137-147.

GENERAL

"American Books," *Dial* XXXIV (Jan 1, 1903), 5-7.

Anderson, Carl. *The Swedish Acceptance of American Literature.*

Angoff, Charles. "Three Notes on American Literature," *North American Review* 247 (Spring 1939), 38-41.

Arnold, Aerol. "The Social Novel as a Best Seller," *University of Kansas City Review* VIII (Oct 1941), 59-64.

——————. "Why Structure in Fiction: A Note to Social Scientists," *American Quarterly* X (Fall 1958), 325-337.

Arvin, Newton. "A Letter on Proletarian Literature," *Partisan Review and Anvil* III (Feb 1936), 12-14.

Atherton, Gertrude. "Why is American Literature Bourgeois?" *North American Review* 178 (May 1904), 771-781.

Bacon, Josephine D. "Is American Literature Bourgeois?" *North American Review* 179 (Jul 1904), 105-117.

Banks, Loy Otis. "The Credible Literary West," *Colorado Quarterly* VIII (Summer 1959), 28-50.

Barnett, James Harwood. *Divorce and the American Divorce Novel 1858-1937.*

Beck, Warren. "Abstract and Chronicle," *College English* XXI (Dec 1959), 117-126.

Becker, Allen W. "Agrarianism as a Theme in Southern Literature: The Period 1865-1925," *Georgia Review* XI (Summer 1957), 150-154.

Bennett, Arnold. "The Future of the American Novel," *North American Review* 195 (Jan 1912), 76-83.

Bernbaum, Ernest. "The Views of the Great Critics on the Historical Novel," *PMLA* XLI (1926), 424-441.

Blackmur, R. P. "The American Literary Expatriate," *The Lion and the Honeycomb*, 61-78.

Blotner, Joseph L. *The Political Novel.*

Bone, Robert A. *The Negro Novel in America.*

Bowen, Edwin W. "Is the Novel Decadent?" *South Atlantic Quarterly* (Jul 1903), 261-266.

Bowling, Lawrence Edward. "What Is the Stream of Consciousness Technique?" *PMLA* LXV (Jun 1950), 333-345.

Bowron, Bernard, Leo Marx, and Arnold Rose. "Literature and Covert Culture," *American Quarterly* IX (Winter 1957), 377-386.

Boynton, Percy H. *America in Contemporary Fiction.*

——————. "The Novel of Puritan Decay: From Mrs. Stowe to John Marquand," *New England Quarterly* XIII (Jun 1940), 626-637.

——————. *The Rediscovery of the Frontier.*

Boys, Richard C. "The American College in Fiction," *College English* VII (Apr 1946), 379-387.

Bracher, Frederick. "California's Literary Regionalism," *American Quarterly* VII (Fall 1955), 275-284.

Bradsher, Earl L. "Some Aspects of the Early American Novel," *Texas Review* III (Oct 1917-Jul 1918), 241-258.

Brawley, Benjamin. "The Negro in American Fiction," *Dial* IX (May 11, 1916), 445-447.

Brodin, Pierre. *Le Roman Régionaliste Américain.*

Brooks, Van Wyck. "Beyond Adolescence," *Atlantic Monthly* CXCI (Apr 1953), 70-76.
——————. *The Confident Years.*
——————. "On Creating a Usable Past," *Dial* LXIV (Apr 11, 1918), 337-341.
——————. *The Writer in America.*
Brown, Herbert Ross. *The Sentimental Novel in America 1789-1860.*
Bryan, William Alfred. *George Washington in American Literature 1775-1865.*
Burns, Wayne. "The Genuine and Counterfeit: A Study in Victorian and Modern Fiction," *College English* XVIII (Dec 1956), 143-150.
Byrd, James W. "Stereotypes of White Characters in Early Negro Novels," *CLA Journal* I (Nov 1957), 28-35.
Cairns, William B. "British Republication of American Writings, 1783-1833," *PMLA* XLIII (1928), 303-310.
Calmer, Alan. "The American Novelists Discover Russia," *Books Abroad* VIII (Apr 1934), 149-151.
Calverton, V. F. "Marxism and American Literature," *Books Abroad* VII (Apr 1933), 131-134.
Canby, Henry Seidel. *Classic Americans.*
——————. *Definitions.*
——————. "Fiction Tells All," *Harpers Magazine* 171 (Aug 1935), 308-315.
Carlisle, Henry. "The Comic Tradition," *American Scholar* XXVIII (Winter 1958-59), 96-108.
Carter, Everett. "The Meaning of, and in, Realism," *Antioch Review* XII (March 1952), 78-94.
Carver, Wayne. "The American Novel—the Short Course," *Antioch Review* XIV (Mar 1954), 109-118.
Chase, Richard. *The American Novel and Its Tradition.*
——————. "Cesare Pavese and the American Novel," *Studi Americani* III (1957), 347-369.
Coad, Oral Sumner. "The Gothic Element in American Literature Before 1835," *Journal of English and Germanic Philology* XXIV (1925), 72-93.
Compton, Charles H. "The Librarian and the Novelist," *South Atlantic Quarterly* XXVI (Oct 1927), 392-403.
Cowie, Alexander. *The Rise of the American Novel.*

Cunliffe, Marcus. *The Literature of the United States.*
Daiches, David. "Problems for Modern Novelists," *Accent* III (Spring 1943), 144-151; (Summer 1943), 231-239.
Davidson, Donald. *Southern Writers in the Modern World.*
Davidson, Levette J. "Folk Elements in Midwestern Literature," *Western Humanities Review* III (Jul 1949), 187-195.
——————. "The Literature of Western America," *Western Humanities Review* V (Spring 1951), 165-173.
Davies, Horton. *A Mirror of the Ministry in Modern Novels.*
Davis, David Brion. *Homicide in American Fiction, 1798-1860.*
DeVoto, Bernard. *The Literary Fallacy.*
——————. "Why Read Dull Novels?" *Harper's Magazine* 204 (Feb 1952), 65-69.
Dickinson, A. T., Jr. *American Historical Fiction.*
Dike, Donald A. "Notes on Local Color and Its Relation to Realism," *College English* XIV (Nov 1952), 81-88.
Donovan, Frank P., Jr. *The Railroad in Literature.*
Dreiser, Theodore, Newton Arvin, Josephine Herbst, Robert Herrick, Matthew Josephson, Kenneth Burke, Waldo Frank, William Troy, William Carlos Williams, Joseph Freeman. "What Is Americanism? A Symposium on Marxism and the American Tradition," *Partisan Review and Anvil* (Apr 1936), 3-16.
Drew, Elizabeth. *The Modern Novel.*
Duffey, Bernard. *The Chicago Renaissance in American Letters.*
Durham, Philip. "Dime Novels: An American Heritage," *Western Humanities Review* IX (Winter 1954-1955), 33-43.
——————. "A General Classification of 1,531 Dime Novels," *Huntington Library Quarterly* XVII (May 1954), 287-291.
Edgar, Pelham. "The Drift of Modern Fiction," *University of Toronto Quarterly* I (Oct 1931), 123-139.
Ehnmark, Anders. "Rebels in American Literature," *Western Review* XXIII (Autumn 1958), 43-56.
Farrar, John. "The Condition of American Writing," *College English* XI (Oct 1949), 1-8.
Farrell, James T. *Reflections at Fifty.*
——————. "Social Themes in American Realism," *Literature and Morality*, 15-25.
Fast, Howard. "American Literature and the Democratic Tradition," *College English* VIII (Mar 1947), 279-284.

Fenn, William Purviance. *Ah Sin and His Brethren in American Literature.*
Fiedler, Leslie A. *The Jew in the American Novel.*
Firkins, O. W. "Undepicted America," *Yale Review* XX (Sept 1930), 140-150.
Flory, Claude Reherd. *Economic Criticism in American Fiction 1792 to 1900.*
Freeman, Joseph. "Mask, Image, and Truth," *Partisan Review* II (Jul-Aug 1935), 3-17.
French, Warren. "The Cowboy in the Dime Novel," *Texas Studies in English* XXX (1951), 219-234.
Geismar, Maxwell. "Naturalism Yesterday and Today," *College English* XV (Jan 1954), 195-200.
Gelfant, Blanche Housman. *The American City Novel.*
Glicksberg, Charles I. "The Furies in Negro Fiction," *Western Review* XIII (Winter 1949), 107-114.
——————. "Negro Fiction in America," *South Atlantic Quarterly* XLV (Oct 1946), 477-488.
Goodrich, Nathaniel L. "Prose Fiction: A Bibliography," *Bulletin of Bibliography* IV, 118-121; 133-136; 153-155; V, 11-13; 38-39; 54-55; 78-79.
Gordon, Caroline. *How to Read a Novel.*
Gross, John J. "The Writer in America: A Search for Community," *Queen's Quarterly* LXIII (Autumn 1956), 375-391.
Gurko, Leo. "American Literature: The Forces Behind Its Growing Up," *College English* VII (Mar 1946), 319-322.
Halsey, Van R. "Fiction and the Businessman: Society Through All Its Literature," *American Quarterly* XI (Fall 1959), 391-402.
Hart, James D. *The Popular Book.*
Hartwick, Harry. *The Foreground of American Fiction.*
Hassan, Ihab H. "The Idea of Adolescence in American Fiction," *American Quarterly* X (Fall 1958), 312-324.
——————. "The Victim: Images of Evil in Recent American Fiction," *College English* XXI (Dec 1959), 140-146.
Haviland, Thomas P. "Precosité Crosses the Atlantic," *PMLA* LIX (Mar 1944), 131-141.
Haycraft, Howard. *Murder for Pleasure.*
Heiney, Donald. "American Naturalism and the New Italian

Writers," *Twentieth Century Literature* III (Oct 1957), 135-141.
Herran, Ima Honaker. *The Small Town in American Literature.*
Herrick, Robert. "The American Novel," *Yale Review* III (Apr 1914), 419-437.
Hicks, Granville. "Fiction and Social Criticism," *College English* XIII (Apr 1952), 355-361.
----------. *The Great Tradition.*
Hinz, John. "Huck and Pluck: 'Bad' Boys in American Fiction," *South Atlantic Quarterly* LI (Jan 1952), 120-129.
Holman, C. Hugh. "Agrarianism as a Theme in Southern Literature: Summary: The Utility of Myth," *Georgia Review* XI (Summer 1957), 161-164.
Howe, Irving. *Politics and the Novel.*
Howells, William Dean. "A Possible Difference in English and American Fiction," *North American Review* 173 (1901), 134-144.
Hubbell, Jay B. *The South in American Literature.*
Humphrey, Robert. " 'Stream of Consciousness': Technique or Genre?" *Philological Quarterly* XXX (Oct 1951), 434-437.
Hutchinson, W. H. "The 'Western Story' as Literature," *Western Humanities Review* III (Jan 1949), 33-37.
Hyman, Stanley Edgar and Ralph Ellison. "The Negro Writer in America: An Exchange," *Partisan Review* XXV (Spring 1958), 197-222.
Kahler, Erich. "The Transformation of Modern Fiction," *Comparative Literature* VII (Spring 1955), 121-128.
Kazin, Alfred. "American Naturalism: Reflections from Another Era," *New Mexico Quarterly* XX (Spring 1950), 50-60.
----------. *On Native Grounds.*
Keiser, Albert. *The Indian in American Literature.*
Kessler, Sidney H. "American Negro Literature: A Bibliographic Guide," *Bulletin of Bibliography* XXI (Sept-Dec 1955), 181-185.
Knight, Grant C. *American Literature and Culture.*
Knox, George. "The Negro Novelist's Sensibility and the Outsider Theme," *Western Humanities Review* XI (Spring 1957), 137-148.
Leach, Joseph. "The Paper-Back Texan: Father of the American

Western Hero," *Western Humanities Review* XI (Summer 1957), 267-275.

Leisy, Ernest E. *The American Historical Novel.*

——————. "Folklore in American Literature," *College English* VIII (Dec 1946), 122-129.

——————. "Folklore in American Prose," *Saturday Review of Literature* XXXIV (Jul 21, 1951), 6-7; 32.

——————. "The Novel in America: Notes for a Survey," *Southwest Review* XXII (Oct 1936), 88-99.

Lesser, Simon. "The Attitude of Fiction," *Modern Fiction Studies* II (May 1956), 47-55.

——————. *Fiction and the Unconscious.*

Levin, Harry. *Symbolism and Fiction.*

Lewis, R. W. B. "The Danger of Innocence: Adam as Hero in American Literature," *Yale Review* XXXIX (Mar 1950), 473-490.

Loggins, Vernon. *The Negro Author.*

MacLeish, Archibald. "The American Writers and the New World," *Yale Review* XXXI (Sept 1941), 61-77.

MacLennan, Hugh. "Fiction in the Age of Science," *Western Humanities Review* VI (Autumn 1952), 325-334.

Marble, Annie Russell. "The Novel of American History," *Dial* XXXII (Jun 1, 1902), 369-372.

Matthews, Brander. "Literature in the New Century," *North American Review* 179 (Oct 1904), 513-525.

McCormick, John O. "The Novel and Society," *Jahrbuch für Amerikastudien* I (1956), 70-75.

Meier, August. "Some Reflections on the Negro Novel," *CLA Journal* II (Mar 1959), 168-177.

Mencken, H. L. "Puritanism as A Literary Force," *A Book of Prefaces*, 197-283.

Mendilow, A. A. *Time and the Novel.*

Michaud, Régis. *The American Novel To-Day.*

Monroe, N. Elizabeth. *The Novel and Society.*

——————. "Toward Significance in the Novel," *College English* II (Mar 1941), 541-551.

Morley, S. Griswold. "Cowboy and Gaucho Fiction," *New Mexico Quarterly* XVI (Autumn 1946), 253-267.

Morris, Ruth. "The Novel as Catharsis," *Psychoanalytic Review* XXXI (Jan 1941), 88-104.

Mott, Frank Luther. *Golden Multitudes.*
Murch, A. E. *The Development of the Detective Novel.*
Myers, Walter L. "The Novel and the Past," *Virginia Quarterly Review* XIV (Autumn 1938), 567-578.
──────────. "The Novel and the Simple Soul," *Virginia Quarterly Review* XIII (Autumn 1937), 501-512.
──────────. "The Novel Dedicate," *Virginia Quarterly Review* VIII (Jul 1932), 410-418.
O'Connor, William Van. "The Novel and the 'Truth' about America," *English Studies* XXXV (Oct 1954), 204-211.
──────────. "The Novel as a Social Document," *American Quarterly* IV (Summer 1952), 169-175.
Orians, G. Harrison. "New England Witchcraft in Fiction," *American Literature* II (Mar 1930), 54-71.
Ormond, John Raper. "Some Recent Products of the New School of Southern Fiction," *South Atlantic Quarterly* III (Jul 1904), 285-289.
Overton, Grant. *An Hour of the American Novel.*
Pattee, Fred Lewis. *The First Century of American Literature.*
Pearson, Edmund. *Dime Novels.*
──────────. *Queer Books.*
Perry, Bliss. "Present Tendencies of American Fiction," *A Study of Prose Fiction*, 335-360.
Peyre, Henri. "American Literature Through French Eyes," *Virginia Quarterly Review* XXIII (Summer 1947), 421-438.
Phelps, Ruth Shepard. "The Lady in Fiction," *North American Review* 205 (May 1917), 766-774.
Phelps, Wallace and Philip Rahv. "Criticism," *Partisan Review* II (Apr-May 1935), 16-31. Discussion by Newton Arvin, Granville Hicks, Obed Brooks.
Praz, Mario. "Racconti Del Sud," *Studi Americani* II (1956), 207-218.
Quinn, Arthur Hobson. *The Literature of the American People.*
Ransom, Ellene. *Utopus Discovers America or Critical Realism in American Utopian Fiction 1798-1900.*
Ransom, John Crowe. "Characters and Character: A Note on Fiction," *American Review* VI (Jan 1936), 271-288.
──────────. "The Content of the Novel: Notes Toward a Critique of Fiction," *American Review* VII (Summer 1936), 301-318.

Rhode, Robert D. "Scenery and Setting: A Note on American Local Color," *College English* XIII (Dec 1951), 142-146.

Rubin, Louis, Jr. "Agrarianism as a Theme in Southern Literature: Introduction," *Georgia Review* XI (Summer 1957), 145-147.

Sanford, Charles L. "Classics of American Reform Literature," *American Quarterly* X (Fall 1958), 295-311.

Scholl, Ralph. "Science Fiction: A Selected Check-List," *Bulletin of Bibliography* XXII (Jan-Apr 1958), 114-115.

Seaver, Edwin. "What Is A Proletarian Novel? Notes Toward a Definition," *Partisan Review* II (Apr-May 1935), 5-15; discussion by Edwin Berry Burgum, Henry Hart, James T. Farrell.

Smith, Bernard. *Forces in American Criticism.*

Smith, C. Alphonso. "The Novel in America," *Sewanee Review* XII (Apr 1904), 158-166.

Smith, Veldren M. "Small Town Life in American Fiction: An Annotated List," *Bulletin of Bibliography* XIII (May-Aug 1928), 113-114; (Sept-Dec 1928), 130-131.

Stern, Philip Van Doren. "Books and Best-Sellers," *Virginia Quarterly Review* XVIII (Winter 1942), 45-55.

Stewart, Randall. *American Literature & Christian Doctrine.*

Stovall, Floyd. *American Idealism.*

Sullivan, Walter. "Southern Novelists and the Civil War," *Southern Renascence,* 112-125.

Sypherd, W. O. " 'Judith' in American Literature," *PMLA* XLV (1930), 336-338.

Thompson, Lawrence. "Bluegrass and Bourbon: The Colonel of Kentucky Fiction," *Georgia Review* VII (Spring 1953), 107-115.

Thorp, Margaret. "The Motion Picture and the Novel," *American Quarterly* III (Fall 1951), 195-203.

Tindall, William York. *The Literary Symbol.*

Trilling, Lionel. "Contemporary American Literature and Its Relation to Ideas," *American Quarterly* I (Fall 1959), 195-208.

————. "Manners, Morals, and the Novel," *The Liberal Imagination;* 205-222.

Turner, H. Arlin. "The Southern Novel," *Southwest Review* XXV (Jan 1940), 205-212.

Van Doren, Carl. *The American Novel 1789-1939.*

————————. "To the Left: To the Subsoil," *Partisan Review and Anvil* III (Feb 1936), 9.
Van Vechten, Carl. "Some 'Literary Ladies' I Have Known," *Yale University Library Gazette* XXVI (Jan 1952), 97-116.
Vollmer, Clement. *The American Novel in Germany 1871-1913.*
Von Abele, Rudolph and Walter Havighurst. "Symbolism and the Student," *College English* XVI (Apr 1955), 424-434.
W., D. G. "Novels by Yale Men," *Yale University Library Gazette* XII (Jan 1938), 63-69.
Wagenknecht, Edward. *Cavalcade of the American Novel.*
Walcutt, Charles Child. *American Literary Naturalism.*
————————. "The Regional Novel and Its Future," *Arizona Quarterly* I (Summer 1945), 17-27.
Wasserstrom, William. "The Lily and the Prairie Flower," *American Quarterly* IX (Winter 1957), 398-411.
Welty, Eudora. "Place in Fiction," *South Atlantic Quarterly* LV (Jan 1956), 57-72.
Westbrook, Max. "The Themes of Western Fiction," *Southwest Review* XLIII (Summer 1958), 232-238.
Widmer, Kingsley. "Timeless Prose," *Twentieth Century Literature* IV (Apr-Jul 1958), 3-8.
Wilbank, Evelyn Rivers. "The Physician in the American Novel, 1870-1955," *Bulletin of Bibliography* XXII (Sept-Dec 1958), 164-168.
Wilder, Amos N. *Theology and Modern Literature.*
Williams, Stanley T. "Spanish Influences in American Fiction: Melville and Others," *New Mexico Quarterly* XXII (Spring 1952), 5-14.
————————. "Who Reads An American Book?" *Virginia Quarterly Review* XXVIII (Autumn 1952), 518-531.
Wilson, James Southall. "The Changing Novel," *Virginia Quarterly Review* X (Jan 1934), 42-52.
Wittke, Carl. "Melting-Pot Literature," *College English* VII (Jan 1946), 189-197.
Wright, Lyle H. "A Statistical Survey of American Fiction, 1774-1850," *Huntington Library Quarterly* II (Apr 1939), 309-318.
Wyman, Margaret. "The Rise of the Fallen Woman," *American Quarterly* III (Summer 1951), 167-177.

BIBLIOGRAPHY

Note: Books which are collections of essays by different authors are indexed by the title of the volume. Titles should be checked in any case in which an entry cannot be found under the name of the author.

BOOKS

Adams, Agatha Boyd. *Thomas Wolfe: Carolina Student. A Brief Biography.* Chapel Hill: University of North Carolina Library, 1950.

Adams, J. Donald. *The Shape of Books to Come.* New York: Viking Press, 1944.

Adams, Lucille. *Huckleberry Finn: A Descriptive Bibliography of the Huckleberry Finn Collection at the Buffalo Public Library.* Buffalo: Buffalo Public Library, 1950.

After the Genteel Tradition: American Writers Since 1910. Edited by Malcolm Cowley. New York: W. W. Norton, 1937.

Åhnebrink, Lars. *The Beginnings of Naturalism in American Fiction: A Study of the Works of Hamlin Garland, Stephen Crane, and Frank Norris, with Special Reference to Some European Influences, 1891-1903* (Essays and Studies on American Language and Literature, IX). Edited by S. B. Liljegren. Upsala: A.-B. Lundequistska Bokhandelin; Cambridge: Harvard University Press, 1950.

——————. *The Influence of Emile Zola on Frank Norris.* Cambridge, Mass.: Harvard University Press, 1947.

Aiken, Conrad. *A Reviewer's A B C: Collected Criticism of Conrad Aiken from 1916 to the Present.* Meridian Books, 1958.

Aldridge, John W. *After the Lost Generation: A Critical Study of the Writers of Two Wars.* New York: McGraw-Hill, 1951.

——————. *In Search of Heresy.* New York: McGraw-Hill, 1956.

All the King's Men: A Symposium. Pittsburg: Carnegie Institute of Technology, 1957.

Allen, Jerry. *The Adventures of Mark Twain.* Boston: Little, Brown, 1954.

American Classics Reconsidered: A Christian Appraisal. Edited by Harold C. Gardiner. New York: Charles Scribner's Sons, 1958.

American Criticism. Edited by William A. Drake. New York: Harcourt, Brace, 1926.

American Radicals: Some Problems and Personalities. Edited by Harvey Goldberg. New York: Monthly Review Press, 1957.

The American Writer and the European Tradtion. Edited by Margaret Denny and William H. Gilman. Minneapolis: University of Minnesota Press, 1950.

American Writing Today: Its Independence and Vigor. Edited by Allan Angoff. New York: New York University Press, 1957.

Anderson, Carl L. *The Swedish Acceptance of American Literature.* Stockholm: Almqvist & Wiksell, 1957.

Anderson, Charles Roberts. *Melville in the South Seas.* New York: Columbia University Press, 1939.

Anderson, Quentin. *The American Henry James.* New Brunswick: Rutgers University Press, 1957.

Anderson, Sherwood. *The Modern Writer.* San Francisco: The Lantern Press, 1925.

Andreas, Osborn. *Henry James and the Expanding Horizon: A Study of the Meaning and Basic Themes of James's Fiction.* Seattle: University of Washington Press, 1948.

Andrews, Kenneth R. *Nook Farm: Mark Twain's Hartford Circle.* Cambridge: Harvard University Press, 1950.

Anthony, Katharine. *Louisa May Alcott.* New York: Alfred A. Knopf, 1938.

The Art of the Novel: Critical Prefaces by Henry James. Edited by Richard P. Blackmur. New York, London: Charles Scribner's Sons, 1934.

Arvin, Newton. *Hawthorne.* Boston: Little, Brown, 1929.

_____. *Herman Melville* (American Men of Letters Series). New York: William Sloane Associates, 1950.

Atkins, John Alfred. *The Art of Ernest Hemingway: His Work and Personality.* London: P. Nevill, 1952.

Auden, W. H. *The Enchafèd Flood: Or The Romantic Iconography of the Sea.* New York: Random House, 1950.

Baird, James. *Ishmael.* Baltimore: Johns Hopkins Press, 1956.

Baker, Carlos. *Hemingway: The Writer as Artist.* Princeton: Princeton University Press, 1956.

Baldwin, Charles C. *The Men Who Make Our Novels.* New York: Dodd, Mead, 1925.

Bamford, Georgia L. *The Mystery of Jack London: Some of His Friends, Also a Few Letters—A Reminiscence.* Oakland: The Author, 1931.

Barnett, James Harwood. *Divorce and the American Divorce Novel 1858-1937: A Study in Literary Reflections of Social Influences.* Philadelphia, 1939.
Barzun, Jacques. *The Energies of Art: Studies of Authors Classic and Modern.* New York: Harper & Brothers, 1956.
Beach, Joseph Warren. *American Fiction: 1920-1940.* New York: Macmillan, 1941.
——————————. *The Method of Henry James.* Philadelphia: Albert Saifer, 1954.
——————————. *The Twentieth Century Novel.* New York and London: Appleton-Century-Crofts, 1932.
Beatty, Richmond Croom. *Bayard Taylor: Laureate of the Gilded Age.* Norman: University of Oklahoma Press, 1936.
Beaty, John O. *John Esten Cooke, Virginian.* New York: Columbia University Press, 1922.
Beer, Thomas. *Hanna, Crane, and the Mauve Decade.* New York: Alfred A. Knopf, 1941.
——————————. *Stephen Crane: A Study in American Letters.* Garden City, N. Y.: Garden City, 1927.
Beers, Henry A. *Four Americans.* New Haven: Yale University Press, 1919.
Bellamy, Gladys Carmen. *Mark Twain as a Literary Artist.* Norman: University of Oklahoma Press, 1950.
Benét, William Rose. *The Prose and Poetry of Elinor Wylie.* Norton: Wheaton College Press, 1934.
Bennett, Mildred R. *The World of Willa Cather.* New York: Dodd, Mead, 1951.
Bernard, Harry. *Le Roman Régionaliste aux Etats-Unis.* Montreal: Fides, 1949.
Berryman, John. *Stephen Crane.* New York: William Sloane, 1950.
Bewley, Marius. *The Complex Fate: Hawthorne, Henry James and Some Other American Writers.* London: Chatto and Windus, 1952.
——————————. *The Eccentric Design: Form in the Classic American Novel.* London: Chatto and Windus, 1959.
Bikle, Lucy Leffingwell Cable. *George W. Cable: His Life and Letters.* New York: Charles Scribner's Sons, 1928.
Bishop, Ferman. *The Sense of the Past in Sarah Orne Jewett.*

University of Wichita Bulletin, University Studies No. 41, XXXIX (Feb 1959).
Bishop, John Peale. *The Collected Essays of John Peale Bishop.* New York: Charles Scribner's Sons, 1948.
Bittner, William. *The Novels of Waldo Frank.* Philadelphia: University of Pennsylvania Press, 1958.
Blackmur, R. P. *The Expense of Greatness.* New York: Arrow Editions, 1940.
―――――――. *The Lion and the Honeycomb: Essays in Solicitude and Critique.* New York: Harcourt, Brace, 1955.
Blotner, Joseph L. *The Political Novel.* Garden City: Doubleday, 1955.
Bluestone, George. *Novels into Film.* Baltimore: Johns Hopkins Press, 1957.
Bogan, Louise. *Selected Criticism.* New York: Noonday Press, 1955.
Bonaparte, Marie. *The Life and Works of Edgar Allan Poe: A Psycho-Analytic Interpretation.* London: Imago, 1949.
Bone, Robert A. *The Negro Novel in America.* New Haven: Yale University Press, 1958.
Bourne, Randolph. *The History of a Literary Radical & Other Papers.* New York: S. A. Russell, 1956.
Bowden, Edwin T. *The Themes of Henry James: A System of Observation Through the Visual Arts.* Yale Studies in English, 132. New Haven: Yale University Press, 1956.
Bowman, Sylvia E. *The Year 2000: A Critical Biography of Edward Bellamy.* New York: Bookman, 1958.
Boynton, Henry Walcott. *James Fenimore Cooper.* New York: Century, 1931.
Boynton, Percy H. *America in Contemporary Fiction.* Chicago: University of Chicago Press, 1940.
―――――――. *More Contemporary Americans.* Chicago: University of Chicago Press, 1927.
―――――――. *The Rediscovery of the Frontier.* Chicago: The University of Chicago Press, 1931.
―――――――. *Some Contemporary Americans.* Chicago: University of Chicago Press, 1924.
Bracher, Frederick. *The Novels of James Gould Cozzens.* New York: Harcourt, Brace, 1959.

Bradford, Gamaliel. *Portraits of American Women*. Boston and New York: Houghton Mifflin, 1919.

Branch, Edgar Marquess. *A Bibliography of James T. Farrell's Writings 1921-1957*. Philadelphia: University of Pennsylvania Press, 1959.

――――――. *The Literary Apprenticeship of Mark Twain: With Selections from His Apprentice Writing*. Urbana: University of Illinois Press, 1950.

Brashear, Minnie M. *Mark Twain, Son of Missouri*. Chapel Hill: University of North Carolina Press, 1934.

Brashear, Minnie M. and Robert M. Rodney (eds.). *The Art, Humor, and Humanity of Mark Twain*. Norman: University of Oklahoma Press, 1959.

Braswell, William. *Melville's Religious Thought: An Essay in Interpretation*. Durham, N. C.: Duke University Press, 1943.

Breit, Harvey. *The Writer Observed*. Cleveland and New York: World, 1956.

Brinnin, John Malcolm. *The Third Rose: Gertrude Stein and Her World*. Boston: Little, Brown, 1959.

Brodin, Pierre. *Le Roman Régionaliste Américain*. Paris: G.-P. Maisonneuve, 1937.

Brooks, Van Wyck. *The Confident Years: 1885-1915*. New York: E. P. Dutton, 1952.

――――――. *The Dream of Arcadia: American Writers and Artists in Italy, 1760-1915*. New York: E. P. Dutton, 1958.

――――――. *Emerson and Others*. New York: E. P. Dutton, 1927.

――――――. *The Flowering of New England 1815-1865*. New York: E. P. Dutton, 1936.

――――――. *Howells: His Life and World*. New York: E. P. Dutton, 1949.

――――――. *New England: Indian Summer 1865-1915*. New York: E. P. Dutton, 1940.

――――――. *The Ordeal of Mark Twain*. New York: E. P. Dutton, 1920.

――――――. *The Pilgrimage of Henry James*. London: Jonathan Cape, 1928.

――――――. *The Times of Melville and Whitman*. New York: E. P. Dutton, 1947.

──────────. *The World of Washington Irving*. New York: E. P. Dutton, 1944.

──────────. *The Writer in America*. New York: E. P. Dutton, 1953.

Brown, E. K. *Willa Cather: A Critical Biography*. Completed by Leon Edel. New York: Alfred A. Knopf, 1953.

Brown, Herbert Ross. *The Sentimental Novel in America 1789-1860*. Durham: Duke University Press, 1940.

Browne, Nina Eliza. *A Bibliography of Nathaniel Hawthorne*. Boston: Houghton Mifflin, 1905.

Brownell, William C. *American Prose Masters*. New York: C. Scribner's Sons, 1909.

Brussel, I. R. *A Bibliography of the Writings of James Branch Cabell: A Revised Bibliography*. Philadelphia: Centaur Book Shop, 1932.

Bryan, William Alfred. *George Washington in American Literature 1775-1865*. New York: Columbia University Press, 1952.

Burdett, Osbert. *Critical Essays*. London: Faber and Gwyer, 1925.

Burgum, Edwin Berry. *The Novel and the World's Dilemma*. New York: Oxford University Press, 1947.

Burke, Kenneth. *The Philosophy of Literary Form: Studies in Symbolic Action*. Baton Rouge: Louisiana State University Press, 1941.

Burr, Anna Robeson. *Weir Mitchell: His Life and Letters*. New York: Duffield, 1929.

Burton, Richard. *Literary Leaders of America*. New York: Charles Scribner's Sons, 1904.

Butcher, Philip. *George W. Cable: The Northhampton Years*. New York: Columbia University Press, 1959.

Cabell, James Branch. *Joseph Hergesheimer: An Essay in Interpretation*. Chicago: Bookfellows, 1921.

──────────. *Some of Us: An Essay in Epitaphs*. New York: Robert M. McBride, 1930.

──────────. *Straws and Prayer-Books: Dizain des Diversions*. New York: Robert McBride, 1924.

Cady, Edwin Harrison. *The Gentleman in America: A Literary Study in American Culture*. Syracuse: Syracuse University Press, 1949.

──────────. *The Realist at War: The Mature Years 1885-1920 of William Dean Howells*. Syracuse: Syracuse University Press, 1958.

——————. *The Road to Realism: The Early Years 1837-1885 of William Dean Howells.* Syracuse: Syracuse University Press, 1956.

Caldwell, Erskine. *Call It Experience: The Years of Learning How to Write.* New York: Duell, Sloan and Pearce, 1951.

Calverton, V. F. *The Newer Spirit: A Sociological Criticism of Literature.* New York: Boni & Liveright, 1925.

Campbell, Harry Modean and Ruel E. Foster. *Elizabeth Madox Roberts.* Norman: University of Oklahoma Press, 1956.

——————. *William Faulkner: A Critical Appraisal.* Norman: University of Oklahoma Press, 1951.

Campbell, Louise. *Letters to Louise: Theodore Dreiser's Letters to Louise Campbell.* Philadelphia: University of Pennsylvania Press, 1959.

Canby, Henry Seidel. *American Estimates.* New York: Harcourt, Brace, 1929.

——————. *Classic Americans: A Study of Eminent American Writers from Irving to Whitman with an Introductory Survey of the Colonial Background of Our National Literature.* New York: Harcourt, Brace, 1931.

——————. *Definitions: Essays in Contemporary Criticism.* New York: Harcourt, Brace, 1922.

——————. *Turn West, Turn East: Mark Twain.* Boston: Houghton Mifflin, 1951.

Cantwell, Robert. *Nathaniel Hawthorne: The American Years.* New York: Rinehart, 1948.

Cardwell, Guy A. *Twins of Genius.* East Lansing: Michigan State College Press, 1953.

Cargill, Oscar. *Intellectual America: Ideas on the March.* New York: Macmillan, 1948.

Carter, Everett. *Howells and the Age of Realism.* Philadelphia and New York: J. B. Lippincott, 1954.

Cary, Elisabeth Luther. *The Novels of Henry James: A Study.* New York: G. P. Putnam's Sons, 1905.

Cary, Richard. *The Genteel Circle: Bayard Taylor and His New York Friends.* Ithaca: Cornell University Press, 1952.

Cathcart, Wallace H. *Bibliography of the Works of Nathaniel Hawthorne.* Cleveland: The Rowfant Club, 1905.

Cather, Willa. *Not Under Forty.* New York: Alfred A. Knopf, 1936.

──────────. *On Writing: Critical Studies on Writing as an Art*. New York: Alfred A. Knopf, 1949.

Chase, Cleveland B. *Sherwood Anderson*. New York: Robert M. McBride, 1927.

Chase, Richard. *The American Novel and Its Tradition*. Garden City, N. Y.: Doubleday, 1957.

──────────. *Herman Melville: A Critical Study*. New York: Macmillan, 1949.

Chislett, William, Jr. *Moderns and Near-Moderns: Essays on Henry James, Stockton, Shaw, and Others*. New York: The Grafton Press, 1928.

Clark, David Lee. *Charles Brockden Brown: Pioneer Voice of America*. Durham: Duke University Press, 1952.

Clark, Emily. *Innocence Abroad*. New York and London: Alfred A. Knopf, 1931.

Clarke, Helen Archibald. *Hawthorne's Country*. Toronto: Musson, 1910.

Clemens, Clara. *My Father Mark Twain*. New York, London: Harper and Brothers, 1931.

Clymer, William Branford Shubrick. *James Fenimore Cooper*. Beacon Biographies. Boston: Small, Maynard, 1900.

Cohn, Louis H. *A Bibliography of the Works of Ernest Hemingway*. New York: Random House, 1931.

College Prose. Edited by Theodore J. Gates and Austin Wright. Boston: D. C. Heath, 1942.

Colum, Padraic. *A Half-Day's Ride*. New York: Macmillan, 1932.

The Coming of Age of a Great Book. New York: Vanguard Press, 1953.

Conrad, Joseph. *Notes on Life and Letters*. Garden City, N. Y.: Doubleday, Page, 1923.

Cooke, Delmar Gross. *William Dean Howells: A Critical Study*. New York: E. P. Dutton, 1922.

Cooper, James Fenimore (ed.). *Correspondence of James Fenimore Cooper*. 2 vols. New Haven: Yale University Press, 1922.

Coughlan, Robert. *The Private World of William Faulkner*. New York: Harper & Brothers, 1954.

Cowie, Alexander. *The Rise of the American Novel*. New York: American Book Co., 1948.

Cowley, Malcolm. *Exile's Return: A Literary Odyssey of the 1920's*. New York: Viking Press, 1951.

──────────────. Introduction, *The Portable Faulkner*. New York: Viking Press, 1946.

──────────────. *The Literary Situation*. New York: Viking Press, 1954.

Crews, Frederick C. *The Tragedy of Manners: Moral Drama in the Later Novels of Henry James*. New Haven: Yale University Press; London: Oxford University Press, 1957.

Critiques and Essays on Modern Fiction, 1920-1951: Representing the Achievement of Modern American and British Critics. Edited by John W. Aldridge. New York: Ronald Press, 1952.

Cunliffe, Marcus. *The Literature of the United States*. London: Penguin Books, 1954.

Cunningham, Scott. *A Bibliography of the Writings of Carl Van Vechten*. Philadelphia: The Centaur Book Shop, 1924.

Currie, Barton. *Booth Tarkington: A Bibliography*. Garden City: Doubleday, Doran, 1932.

Daiches, David. *Willa Cather: A Critical Introduction*. Ithaca: Cornell University Press, 1951.

Daniel, Robert W. *A Catalogue of the Writings of William Faulkner*. New Haven: Yale University Library, 1942.

Davidson, Donald. *Southern Writers in the Modern World*. Athens: University of Georgia Press, 1958.

Davidson, Edward Hutchins. *Hawthorne's Last Phase*. New Haven: Yale University Press, 1949.

──────────────. *Poe: A Critical Study*. Cambridge, Mass.: Harvard University Press, 1957.

Davies, Horton. *A Mirror of the Ministry in Modern Novels*. New York: Oxford University Press, 1959.

Davis, Charles Belmont (ed.). *Adventures and Letters of Richard Harding Davis*. New York: Charles Scribner's Sons, 1917.

Davis, David Brion. *Homicide in American Fiction, 1798-1860: A Study in Social Values*. Ithaca: Cornell University Press, 1957.

Davis, Merrell R. *Melville's Mardi: A Chartless Voyage*. New Haven: Yale University Press, 1952.

Delakas, Daniel L. *Thomas Wolfe, La France et les Romanciers Français*. Paris: Jouve & Cie, Editeurs, 1950.

Dell, Floyd. *Upton Sinclair: A Study in Social Protest*. New York: George H. Doran, 1927.

DeVoto, Bernard. *The Literary Fallacy.* Boston: Little, Brown, 1944.

——————. *Mark Twain at Work.* Cambridge: Harvard University Press, 1942.

——————. *Mark Twain's America.* Boston: Little, Brown, 1932.

Dibble, Roy F. *Albion W. Tourgée.* New York: Lemcke & Buechner, 1921.

Dickinson, A. T., Jr. *American Historical Fiction.* New York: The Scarecrow Press, 1958.

Donovan, Frank P., Jr. *The Railroad in Literature.* Boston: Railway and Locomotive Historical Society, 1940.

Downey, Fairfax. *Richard Harding Davis: His Day.* New York and London: Charles Scribner's Sons, 1933.

Downs, Robert B. *Books That Changed the World.* New York: New American Library, 1956.

Drake, William A. (ed.). *American Criticism 1926.* New York: Harcourt, Brace, 1926.

Dreiser, Helen. *My Life with Dreiser.* Cleveland and New York: World, 1951.

Drew, Elizabeth. *The Modern Novel: Some Aspects of Contemporary Fiction.* London: Jonathan Cape, 1926.

Dudley, Dorothy. *Forgotten Frontiers: Dreiser and the Land of the Free.* New York: Harrison Smith and Robert Haas, 1932.

Duffey, Bernard. *The Chicago Renaissance in American Letters: A Critical History.* East Lansing: Michigan State College Press, 1954.

Dupee, F. W. *Henry James* (American Men of Letters Series). New York: William Sloane, 1951.

Durham, Frank. *DuBose Heyward: The Man Who Wrote Porgy.* Columbia: University of South Carolina Press, 1954.

Earnest, Ernest. *S. Weir Mitchell: Novelist and Physician.* Philadelphia: University of Pennsylvania Press, 1950.

Eastman, Max. *Art and the Life of Action.* New York: Alfred A. Knopf, 1934.

Edel, Leon. *Henry James: The Untried Years, 1843-1870.* Philadelphia and New York: J. B. Lippincott, 1953.

——————. *The Prefaces of Henry James.* Paris: Jouve et Cie, 1931.

──────────. *The Psychological Novel, 1900-1950*. New York and Philadelphia: J. B. Lippincott, 1955.

Edel, Leon and Gordon N. Ray. *Henry James and H. G. Wells: A Record of their Friendship, their Debate on the Art of Fiction, and their Quarrel*. Urbana: University of Illinois Press, 1958.

Edgar, Pelham. *The Art of the Novel From 1700 to the Present Time*. New York: Macmillan, 1933.

──────────. *Henry James: Man and Author*. Boston and New York: Houghton Mifflin, 1927.

Eight American Authors: A Review of Research and Criticism. New York: Modern Language Association, 1956.

Elias, Robert H. *Theodore Dreiser: Apostle of Nature*. New York: Alfred A. Knopf, 1949.

──────────. (ed.). *Letters of Theodore Dreiser: A Selection*. 3 vols. Philadelphia: University of Pennsylvania Press, 1959.

Emberson, Frances Guthrie. *Mark Twain's Vocabulary: A General Survey*. University of Missouri Studies, Vol. X, No. 3. Columbia: University of Missouri, 1935.

Embree, Edwin R. *13 Against the Odds*. New York: Viking Press, 1944.

Ernest Hemingway: The Man and His Work. Edited by John M. McCaffery. Cleveland and New York: World, 1950.

Erskine, John. *The Delight of Great Books*. Indianapolis: Bobbs-Merrill, 1928.

──────────. *Leading American Novelists*. New York: Henry Holt, 1910.

Essays and Studies by Members of the English Association. Vol. V. Collected by Oliver Elton. London: Oxford University Press, 1914.

Essays in Modern Literary Criticism. Edited by Ray B. West, Jr. New York: Rinehart, 1952.

F. Scott Fitzgerald: The Man and His Work. Edited by Alfred Kazin. Cleveland and New York: World, 1951.

Fadiman, Clifton. *Party of One*. New York: World, 1955.

Fagin, Nathan Bryllion. *The Phenomenon of Sherwood Anderson: A Study in American Life and Letters*. Baltimore: Rossi Bryn, 1927.

Fannie Hurst: A Biographical Sketch, Critical Appreciation &

Bibliography. New York and London: Harper & Brothers, 1928.
Farrell, James T. *Literature and Morality.* New York: Vanguard Press, 1947.
——————. *Reflections at Fifty and Other Essays.* New York: Vanguard Press, 1954.
Faust, Bertha. *Hawthorne's Contemporaneous Reputation: A Study of Literary Opinion in America and England 1828-1864.* Philadelphia, 1939.
Feidelson, Charles, Jr. *Symbolism and American Literature.* Chicago: University of Chicago Press, 1953.
Feinberg, Leonard. *Sinclair Lewis as a Satirist.* Urbana: University of Illinois Press, 1946.
Fenn, William Purviance. *Ah Sin and His Brethren in American Literature.* Peking: College of Chinese Studies, 1933.
Fenton, Charles A. *The Apprenticeship of Ernest Hemingway: The Early Years.* New York: Viking Press, 1954.
Ferguson, John De Lancey. *American Literature in Spain.* New York: Columbia University Press, 1916.
Fiedler, Leslie A. *An End to Innocence: Essays on Culture and Politics.* Boston: Beacon Press, n.d.
——————. *The Jew in the American Novel.* New York: Herzl Institute Pamphlet No. 10, 1959.
Fifty Years of the American Novel: A Christian Appraisal. Edited by Harold C. Gardiner, S. J. New York: Charles Scribner's Sons, 1951.
Firkins, Oscar W. *William Dean Howells: A Study.* Cambridge: Harvard University Press, 1924.
Fiske, Horace Spencer. *Provincial Types in American Fiction.* Chautauqua, N. Y.: Chautauqua Press, 1903, 1907.
Fitzgerald, F. Scott. *The Crack-Up . . . And Essays and Poems by Paul Rosenfeld, Glenway Wescott, John Dos Passos, John Peale Bishop and Edmund Wilson.* Edited by Edmund Wilson. New York: New Directions, 1945.
Flitcroft, John E. *The Novelist of Vermont: A Biographical and Critical Study of Daniel Pierce Thompson.* Cambridge: Harvard University Press, 1929.
Floan, Howard R. *The South in Northern Eyes 1831 to 1861.* Austin: University of Texas Press, 1958.

Flory, Claude Reherd. *Economic Criticism in American Fiction 1792 to 1900.* Philadelphia, 1936.

Fogle, Richard Harter. *Hawthorne's Fiction: The Light & the Dark.* Norman: University of Oklahoma Press, 1952.

Foley, Richard Nicholas. *Criticism in American Periodicals of the Works of Henry James.* Washington, D. C.: The Catholic University of America Press, 1944.

Foner, Philip S. (ed.). *Jack London, American Rebel: A Collection of His Social Writings Together with an Extensive Study of the Man and His Times.* New York: Citadel Press, 1947.

——————. *Mark Twain, Social Critic.* New York: International Publishers, 1958.

Ford, Ford Madox. *Portraits from Life.* Boston and New York: Houghton Mifflin, 1937.

Forms of Modern Fiction. Edited by William Van O'Connor. Minneapolis: University of Minnesota Press, 1948.

Forster, E. M. *Aspects of the Novel.* New York: Harcourt, Brace, 1927.

Foster, Charles H. *The Rungless Ladder: Harriet Beecher Stowe and New England Puritanism.* Durham, N. C.: Duke University Press, 1954.

Foster, Edward. *Mary E. Wilkins Freeman.* New York: Hendricks House, 1956.

Fraenkel, Michael. *The Genesis of the 'Tropic of Cancer.'* Berkeley: Packard Press, 1946.

The Fred Newton Scott Anniversary Papers, Contributed by Former Students and Colleagues of Professor Scott. Chicago: University of Chicago Press, 1929.

Frédérix, Pierre. *Herman Melville.* Paris: Gallimard, 1950.

Freeman, John. *Herman Melville.* New York: Macmillan, 1926.

Friedrich, Gerhard. *In Pursuit of Moby Dick.* Wallingford, Penn.: Pendle Hill, 1958.

Frohock, W. M. *The Novel of Violence in America: 1920-1950.* Dallas: Southern Methodist University Press, 1950.

Frost, O. W. *Young Hearn.* Tokyo: Hokuseido Press, 1958.

Fryckstedt, Olov W. *In Quest of America: A Study of Howells' Early Development as a Novelist.* Upsala, 1958.

Fuller, Edmund. *Man in Modern Fiction: Some Minority Opin-*

ions on Contemporary American Writing. New York: Random House, 1958.

Furnas, J. C. *Goodbye to Uncle Tom.* New York: William Sloane, 1956.

Garland, Hamlin. *Roadside Meetings.* New York: Macmillan, 1930.

Gastón, Nilita Vientós. *Introducción a Henry James.* Universidad de Puerto Rico, 1956.

Geismar, Maxwell. *American Moderns: From Rebellion to Conformity.* New York: Hill and Wang, 1958.

——————. *The Last of the Provincials: The American Novel, 1915-1925.* Boston: Houghton Mifflin, 1947.

——————. *Rebels and Ancestors: The American Novel, 1890-1915.* Boston: Houghton Mifflin, 1953.

——————. *Writers in Crisis: The American Novel: 1925-1940.* Boston: Houghton Mifflin, 1942.

Gelfant, Blanche Housman. *The American City Novel.* Norman: University of Oklahoma Press, 1954.

Gibson, W. M. and George Arms. *A Bibliography of William Dean Howells.* New York: New York Public Library, 1948.

Gilbertson, Catherine. *Harriet Beecher Stowe.* New York: D. Appleton-Century, 1937.

Gilman, William H. *Melville's Early Life and Redburn.* New York: New York University Press, 1951.

Glasgow, Ellen. *A Certain Measure: An Interpretation of Prose Fiction.* New York: Harcourt, Brace, 1943.

Gleim, William S. *The Meaning of Moby Dick.* New York: Edmond Byrne Hackett, 1938.

Gohdes, Clarence. *American Literature in Nineteenth-Century England.* New York: Columbia University Press, 1944.

——————. See *Literature of the American People.*

Gordan, John D. *Nathaniel Hawthorne: The Years of Fulfillment 1804-1853: An Exhibition from the Berg Collection First Editions, Manuscripts, Autograph Letters.* New York: New York Public Library, 1954.

Gordon, Caroline. *How to Read a Novel.* New York: Viking Press, 1957.

Great Moral Dilemmas in Literature, Past and Present. Edited by R. M. MacIver. New York: Harper & Brothers, 1956.

Greenslet, Ferris. *The Life of Thomas Bailey Aldrich.* Boston and New York: Houghton Mifflin, 1908.

Griffin, Martin I. J. *Frank R. Stockton: A Critical Biography.* Philadelphia: University of Pennsylvania Press, 1939.

Grossman, James. *James Fenimore Cooper* (American Men of Letters Series). William Sloane, 1949.

Gulliver, Lucile. *Louisa May Alcott: A Bibliography.* Boston: Little, Brown, 1932.

Gurko, Leo. *The Angry Decade.* New York: Dodd, Mead and Co., 1947.

Gwathney, Edward M. *John Pendleton Kennedy.* New York: Thomas Nelson and Sons, 1931.

Gwynn, Frederick L. and Joseph L. Blotner. *The Fiction of J. D. Salinger.* Pittsburgh: University of Pittsburgh Press, 1958.

——————— (eds.). *Faulkner in the University: Class Conferences at the University of Virginia 1957-1958.* Charlottesville: University of Virginia Press, 1959.

Hall, Lawrence Sargent. *Hawthorne, Critic of Society.* New Haven: Yale University Press, 1944.

Hamburger, Philip. *J. P. Marquand Esquire: A Portrait in the Form of a Novel.* Boston: Houghton Mifflin, 1952.

Hamlin Garland Memorial. Federal Writers Program, South Dakota, 1939.

Hansen, Harry. *Midwest Portraits: A Book of Memories and Friendships.* New York: Harcourt, Brace, 1923.

The Happy Rock: A Book About Henry Miller. Printed for Bern Porter. Berkeley: Packard Press, 1945.

Harris, Frank. *Contemporary Portraits,* second series. New York: Published by the author, 1919.

———————. *Contemporary Portraits,* third series. New York: Published by the author, 1920.

———————. *Contemporary Portraits,* fourth series. New York: Bretano's, 1923.

Harrison, Oliver. *Sinclair Lewis.* New York: Harcourt, Brace, 1925.

Hart, James D. *The Popular Book: A History of America's Literary Taste.* New York: Oxford University Press, 1950.

Hartwick, Harry. *The Foreground of American Fiction.* New York: American Book Co., 1934.

Harvey, Alexander. *William Dean Howells: A Study of the Achievement of A Literary Artist.* New York: B. W. Huebsch, 1917.

Hatcher, Harlan. *Creating the Modern American Novel.* New York: Farrar and Rinehart, 1935.

Hawthorne, Julian. *Hawthorne and His Circle.* New York: Harper & Brothers, 1903.
Haycraft, Howard. *Murder for Pleasure: The Life and Times of the Detective Story.* New York: D. Appleton-Century, 1941.
Henderson, Archibald. *Mark Twain.* London: Duckworth, 1911.
Henderson, Philip. *The Novel Today: Studies in Contemporary Attitudes.* London: John Lane, 1936.
Herold, Amos L. *James Kirke Paulding: Versatile American.* New York: Columbia Press, 1926.
Herron, Ima Honaker. *The Small Town in American Literature.* Durham: Duke University Press, 1939.
Hewett-Thayer, Harvey W. *American Literature As Viewed in Germany, 1818-1861.* Chapel Hill: University of North Carolina Press, 1958.
Hicks, Granville. *The Great American Tradition: An Interpretation of American Literature Since the Civil War.* New York: Macmillan, 1933.
Hillway, Tyrus. *Melville and the Whale.* Stonington, Conn.: Stonington, 1950.
Hillway, Tyrus and Luther S. Mansfield. *Moby-Dick Centennial Essays.* Dallas: Southern Methodist University Press, 1953.
Hintz, Howard W. *The Quaker Influence in American Literature.* New York: Fleming H. Revell, 1940.
Hoffman, Charles G. *The Short Novels of Henry James.* New York: Bookman Associates, 1957.
Hoffman, Frederick J. *Freudianism and the Literary Mind.* 2nd ed. Baton Rouge: Louisiana State University Press, 1957.
——————. *The Modern Novel in America, 1900-1950.* Chicago: Henry Regnery, 1951.
——————. *The Twenties: American Writing in the Postwar Decade.* New York: Viking, 1955.
Holt, Guy. *A Bibliography of the Writings of James Branch Cabell.* Philadelphia: Centaur Book Shop, 1924.
Hornstein, Simon. *Mark Twain: La Faillite D'un Idéal.* Paris: Les Editions Renée Lacostre & Cie, 1950.
Howard, Leon. *Herman Melville: A Biography.* Berkeley and Los Angeles: University of California Press, 1951.
Howe, Irving. *Politics and the Novel.* New York: Horizon Press, 1957.
——————. *Sherwood Anderson.* New York: William Sloane, 1951.

──────────. *William Faulkner: A Critical Study*. New York: Random House, 1952.

Howells, Mildred (ed.). *Life in Letters of William Dean Howells*. 2 vols. Garden City: Doubleday, Doran, 1928.

Howells, William Dean. *Heroines of Fiction*. 2 vols. New York and London: Harper & Brothers, 1901.

──────────. *My Mark Twain: Reminiscences and Criticisms*. New York, London: Harper and Brothers, 1910.

──────────. *Prefaces to Contemporaries (1882-1920)*. Gainesville, Florida: Scholars' Facsimiles & Reprints, 1957.

Howgate, George W. *George Santayana*. Philadelphia: University of Pennsylvania Press, 1938.

Hoyt, Nancy. *Elinor Wylie: The Portrait of an Unknown Lady*. Indianapolis, New York: Bobbs-Merrill, 1935.

Hubbell, Jay B. *The South in American Literature, 1607-1900*. Durham: Duke University Press, 1954.

Hueffer, Ford Madox. *Henry James: A Critical Study*. London: Martin Secker, 1913.

Hughes, Babette. *Christopher Morely: Multi ex Uno*. Seattle: University of Washington Chapbooks 12.

Hughes, Carl Milton. *The Negro Novelist: A Discussion of the Writings of American Negro Novelists: 1940-1950*. New York: Citadel Press, 1953.

Humanism and America: Essays on the Outlook of Modern Civilization. Edited by Norman Foerster. New York: Farrar and Rinehart, 1930.

Hume, Robert A. *Runaway Star: An Appreciation of Henry Adams*. Ithaca, N. Y.: Cornell University Press, 1951.

James, C. L. R. *Mariners, Renegades and Castaways*. New York: C.L.R. James, 1953.

James Fenimore Cooper: A Re-Appraisal. Edited by Mary E. Cunningham. *New York History* XXXV. Cooperstown, N. Y.: New York Historical Association, 1954.

James, Henry. *Notes on Novelists: With Some Other Notes*. London: J. M. Dent & Sons Ltd., 1914.

──────────. See *Art of the Novel*.

Jelliffe, Robert A., (ed.). *Faulkner at Nagano*. Tokyo: Kenkyusha Ltd., 1956.

Jessup, Josephine Lurie. *The Faith of Our Feminists: A Study* in the Novels of Edith Wharton, Ellen Glasgow, Willa Cather. New York: Richard R. Smith, 1950.

John Dos Passos: An Appreciation. New York: Prentice-Hall, 1954.

Johnson, Merle. *A Bibliography of the Works of Mark Twain.* New York and London: Harper and Brothers, 1935.

Johnson, Pamela Hansford. *Hungry Gulliver: An English Critical Appraisal of Thomas Wolfe.* New York and London: Charles Scribner's Sons, 1948.

——————. *Thomas Wolfe: A Critical Study.* London and Toronto: William Heinemann, 1947.

Jonas, Klaus W. *Carl Van Vechten: A Bibliography.* New York: Knopf, 1955.

Jones, Howard Mumford and Walter B. Rideout (eds.). *Letters of Sherwood Anderson.* Boston: Little, Brown, 1953.

Josephson, Matthew. *Portrait of the Artist As American.* New York: Harcourt, Brace, 1930.

Karlfeldt, Erik Axel and Sinclair Lewis. *Why Sinclair Lewis Got the Nobel Prize.* New York: Harcourt, Brace, 1930.

Kazin, Alfred. *The Inmost Leaf: A Selection of Essays.* New York: Harcourt, Brace, 1955.

——————. *On Native Grounds: An Interpretation of Modern American Prose Literature.* New York: Reynal & Hitchcock, 1942.

Keiser, Albert. *The Indian in American Literature.* New York: Oxford University Press, 1933.

Kelley, Cornelia Pulsifer. *The Early Development of Henry James.* Chicago: University of Illinois, 1930.

Kenneth Roberts: An American Novelist. New York: Doubleday, Doran, 1938.

Kern, John Dwight. *Constance Fenimore Woolson, Literary Pioneer.* Philadelphia: University of Pennsylvania Press, 1934.

Kirk, Clara and Rudolf. *William Dean Howells: Representative Selections, with Introduction, Bibliography, and Notes* (American Writers Series). New York: American Book, 1950.

Kirkpatrick, John Ervin. *Timothy Flint: Pioneer, Missionary, Author, Editor 1780-1840.* Cleveland: Arthur H. Clark, 1911.

Knight, Grant C. *American Literature and Culture.* New York: Ray Long & Richard R. Smith, 1932.

_____. *The Critical Period in American Literature.* Chapel Hill: University of North Carolina Press, 1951.

_____. *James Lane Allen and the Genteel Tradition.* Chapel Hill: University of North Carolina Press, 1935.

_____. *The Strenuous Age in American Literature.* Chapel Hill: University of North Carolina Press, 1954.

Koch, Vivienne. *Willam Carlos Williams.* Norfolk, Conn.: New Directions, 1950.

Kronhausen, Eberhard and Phyllis. *Pornography and the Law.* New York: Ballantine, 1959.

Lawrence, D. H. *Studies in Classic American Literature.* New York: Doubleday, 1955.

Lawton, Mary. *A Lifetime with Mark Twain: The Memories of Katy Leary, for Thirty Years His Faithful and Devoted Servant.* New York: Harcourt, Brace, 1925.

Leavis, F. R. *The Great Tradition: George Eliot, Henry James, Joseph Conrad.* London: Chatto and Windus, 1948.

LeClair, Robert C. *Young Henry James: 1843-1870.* New York: Bookman, 1955.

Leisy, Ernest E. *The American Historical Novel.* Norman: University of Oklahoma Press, 1950.

Lesser, Simon. *Fiction and the Unconscious.* Boston: Beacon Press, 1957.

Levenson, J. C. *The Mind and Art of Henry Adams.* Boston: Houghton Mifflin Co., 1957.

Levin, Harry. *The Power of Blackness.* New York: Alfred A. Knopf, 1958.

_____. *Symbolism and Fiction.* Charlottesville: University of Virginia Press, 1956.

Levy, Leo B. *Versions of Melodrama: A Study of the Fiction and Drama of Henry James, 1865-1897.* Berkeley and Los Angeles: University of California Press, 1957.

Lewis, Edith. *Willa Cather Living: A Personal Record.* New York: Alfred A. Knopf, 1953.

Lewis, Grace Hegger. *With Love from Gracie: Sinclair Lewis: 1912-1925.* New York: Harcourt, Brace, 1951.

Lewis, R.W.B. *The American Adam: Innocence, Tragedy and Tradition in the Nineteenth Century.* Chicago: University of Chicago Press, 1955.

_____. *The Picaresque Saint: Representative Figures in*

Contemporary Fiction. Philadelphia and New York: J. B. Lippincott, 1959.

Lewis, Wyndham. *Men Without Art.* London: Cassell, 1934.

Linn, James Weber and Houghton Wells Taylor. *A Foreword to Fiction.* New York: D. Appleton-Century, 1935.

Linson, Corwin K. *My Stephen Crane.* Syracuse, N. Y.: Syracuse University Press, 1958.

Lippmann, Walter. *Men of Destiny.* New York: Macmillan, 1927.

Lisca, Peter. *The Wide World of John Steinbeck.* New Brunswick: Rutgers University Press, 1958.

The Literature of the American People: An Historical and Critical Survey. Edited by Arthur Hobson Quinn. New York: Appleton-Century-Crofts, 1951.

Lively, Robert A. *Fiction Fights the Civil War: An Unfinished Chapter in the Literary History of the American People.* Chapel Hill: University of North Carolina Press, 1957.

The Living Novel: A Symposium. Edited by Granville Hicks. New York: Macmillan, 1957.

Loggins, Vernon. *The Hawthornes.* New York: Columbia University Press, 1951.

——————. *The Negro Author: His Development in America.* New York: Columbia University Press, 1931.

Lohf, Kenneth A. and Eugene P. Sheehy. *Frank Norris: A Bibliography.* Los Gatos, Calif.: Talisman Press, 1959.

London, Charmian. *The Book of Jack London.* 2 vols. New York: Century, 1921.

London, Joan. *Jack London and His Times: An Unconventional Biography.* New York: Doubleday, Doran, 1939.

Long, E. Hudson. *Mark Twain Handbook.* New York: Hendricks House, 1957.

Loshe, Lillie Deming. *The Early American Novel.* New York: Columbia University Press, 1907.

Lovett, Robert Morss. *Edith Wharton.* New York: Robert M. McBride, 1925.

Lubbock, Percy. *The Craft of Fiction.* New York: Charles Scribner's Sons, 1921.

——————. *Portrait of Edith Wharton.* New York, London: D. Appleton-Century, 1947.

Lucas, F. L. *Authors Dead & Living.* London: Chatto & Windus, 1926.

Lueders, Edward. *Carl Van Vechten and the Twenties.* Albuquerque: University of New Mexico Press, 1955.

Lundblad, Jane. *Nathaniel Hawthorne and European Literary Tradition.* Upsala: A. B. Lundequistska Bokhandeln, 1947.

----------. *Nathaniel Hawthorne and the Tradition of Gothic Romance.* Upsala: A. B. Lundequistska Bokhandeln, 1946.

Lyde, Marilyn Jones. *Edith Wharton: Convention and Morality in the Work of A Novelist.* Norman: University of Oklahoma Press, 1959.

Lynd, Robert. *Books & Authors.* London: Richard Cobden-Sanderson, 1922.

Lynn, Kenneth S. *The Dream of Success: A Study of the Modern American Imagination.* Boston and Toronto: Little, Brown, 1955.

----------. *Mark Twain and Southwestern Humor.* Boston: Little, Brown, 1959.

Mabie, Hamilton Wright. *Backgrounds of Literature.* New York: Grosset & Dunlap, 1904.

Maclean, Catherine Macdonald. *Mark Rutherford: A Biography of William Hale White.* London: Macdonald, 1955.

Macy, John. *The Spirit of American Literature.* New York: Boni and Liveright, 1912.

Male, Roy R. *Hawthorne's Tragic Vision.* Austin: University of Texas Press, 1957.

Malin, Irving. *William Faulkner: An Interpretation.* Stanford, Calif.: Stanford University Press, 1957.

Mantz, Harold Elmer. *French Criticism of American Literature Before 1850.* New York: Columbia University Press, 1917.

Marble, Annie Russell. *Heralds of American Literature: A Group of Patriot Writers of the Revolutionary and National Periods.* Chicago: University of Chicago Press, 1907.

----------. *A Study of the Modern Novel British and American Since 1900.* New York: D. Appleton, 1930.

Marchand, Ernest. *Frank Norris: A Study.* Stanford, Calif.: Stanford University Press, 1942.

Mark Twain's Huckleberry Finn. Problems in American Civilization. Edited by Barry A. Marks. Boston: D. C. Heath, 1959.

Mary Austin: A Memorial. Edited by Willard Hougland. Santa Fe: Laboratory of Anthropology, 1944.

Mason, Ronald. *The Spirit Above the Dust: A Study of Herman Melville.* London: John Lehmann, 1951.

Masters, Edgar Lee. *Mark Twain: A Portrait.* New York and London: Charles Scribner's Sons, 1938.

Matthews, Brander. *Inquiries and Opinions.* New York: Charles Scribner's Sons, 1908.

Matthiessen, F. O. *American Renaissance: Art and Expression in the Age of Emerson and Whitman.* New York: Oxford University Press, 1949.

——————. *Henry James: The Major Phase.* London: Oxford University Press, 1944.

——————. *The James Family: Including Selections from the Writings of Henry James, Senior, William, Henry, and Alice James.* New York: Alfred A. Knopf, 1947.

——————. *Sarah Orne Jewett.* Boston and New York: Houghton Mifflin, n.d.

——————. *Theodore Dreiser.* New York: William Sloane, 1951.

Maugham, W. Somerset. *Ten Novels and their Authors.* London: William Heinemann, 1954.

Mayes, Herbert R. *Alger: A Biography Without a Hero.* New York: Macy-Masius, 1928.

McCarthy, Harold T. *Henry James: The Creative Process.* New York: Thomas Yoseloff, 1958.

McCole, John C. *Lucifer at Large.* London: Longmans, Green, 1937.

McDonald, Edward D. *A Bibliography of the Writings of Theodore Dreiser.* Philadelphia: Centaur Book Shop, 1928.

McNeill, Warren A. *Cabellian Harmonics.* New York: Random House, 1928.

Meigs, Cornelia. *Invincible Louisa: The Story of the Author of Little Women.* Boston: Little, Brown, 1945.

Mencken, H. L. *A Book of Prefaces.* New York: Alfred A. Knopf, 1920.

——————. *James Branch Cabell.* New York: Robert M. McBride, 1928.

——————. *Prejudices, First Series.* New York: Alfred A. Knopf, 1919.

Mendelson, M. *Soviet Interpretation of Contemporary American Literature*. Washington: Public Affairs Press, 1948.

Mendilow, A. A. *Time and the Novel*. London and New York, British Book Centre, 1952.

Metcalf, Eleanor Melville. *Herman Melville: Cycle and Epicycle*. Cambridge, Mass.: Harvard University Press, 1953.

Michaud, Régis. *The American Novel To-Day: A Social and Psychological Study*. Boston: Little, Brown, 1931.

──────────. *Panorama de la Littérature Américaine Contemoraine*. Paris: Kra, 1926.

Miller, James E., Jr. *The Fictional Technique of Scott Fitzgerald*. The Hague: Martinus Nijhoff, 1957.

Miller, Perry. *The Raven and the Whale: The War of Words and Wits in the Era of Poe and Melville*. New York: Harcourt, Brace, 1956.

Miller, R. N. *A Preliminary Checklist of Books and Articles on Theodore Dreiser*. Western Michigan College Library, 1947.

Miller, Rosalind S. *Gertrude Stein: Form and Intelligibility*. New York: Exposition Press, 1949.

Miner, Ward L. *The World of William Faulkner*. New York: Grove, 1959.

Minnigerode, Meade. *Some Personal Letters of Herman Melville and a Bibliography*. New York: Edmond Byrne Hackett: The Brick Row Book Shop, 1922.

Miron, George Thomas. *The Truth About John Steinbeck and the Migrants*. Los Angeles: Haynes, 1939.

Mizener, Arthur. *The Far Side of Paradise: A Biography of F. Scott Fitzgerald*. Boston: Houghton Mifflin, 1951.

Monroe, N. Elizabeth. *The Novel and Society: A Critical Study of the Modern Novel*. Chapel Hill: University of North Carolina Press, 1941.

Moore, Harry Thornton. *The Novels of John Steinbeck: A First Critical Study*. Chicago: Normandie House, 1939.

Moore, Nicholas. *Henry Miller*. Wigginton, England: Opus Press, 1943.

More, Paul Elmer. *Shelburne Essays. Second Series*. New York and London: G. P. Putnam's Sons, 1909.

Morgan, Arthur E. *Edward Bellamy*. New York: Columbia University Press, 1944.

──────────. *The Philosophy of Edward Bellamy*. New York: King's Crown Press, 1945.

Morris, Lloyd. *Postscript to Yesterday. America: The Last Fifty Years.* New York: Random House, 1947.

Morris, Wright. *The Territory Ahead.* New York: Harcourt, Brace, 1958.

Mott, Frank Luther. *Golden Multitudes: The Story of Best Sellers in the United States.* New York: Macmillan, 1947.

Mueller, William R. *The Prophetic Voice in Modern Fiction.* New York: Association Press, 1959.

Muller, Herbert J. *Thomas Wolfe.* Norfolk, Conn.: New Directions, 1947.

Mumford, Lewis. *The Golden Day: A Study in American Experience and Culture.* New York: Boni and Liveright, 1926; Boston: Beacon Press, 1957.

————————. *Herman Melville.* New York: Harcourt, Brace, 1929.

Munson, Gorham B. *Destinations: A Canvass of American Literature Since 1900.* New York: J. H. Sears, 1928.

Murch, A. E. *The Development of the Detective Novel.* London: Peter Owen, 1958.

Nevius, Blake. *Edith Wharton: A Study of Her Fiction.* Berkeley: University of California Press, 1953.

Newlin, Claude Milton. *The Life and Writings of Hugh Henry Brackenridge.* Princeton: Princeton University Press, 1932.

Nin, Anais. *Preface to Henry Miller's Tropic of Cancer.* New York: Lawrence R. Maxwell, 1947.

Noel, Joseph. *Footloose in Arcadia: A Personal Record of Jack London, George Sterling, Ambrose Bierce.* New York: Carrick & Evans, 1940.

Norwood, Hayden. *The Marble Man's Wife: Thomas Wolfe's Mother.* New York: Charles Scribner's Sons, 1947.

The Novel of Tomorrow and the Scope of Fiction. By Twelve American Novelists. Indianapolis: Bobbs-Merrill, 1922.

Nowell, Elizabeth (ed.). *The Letters of Thomas Wolfe.* New York: Charles Scribner's Sons, 1956.

Nowell-Smith, Simon (ed.). *The Legend of the Master.* London: Constable, 1947.

Oberndorf, Clarence P. *The Psychiatric Novels of Oliver Wendell Holmes.* New York: Columbia University Press, 1946.

O'Connor, Frank. *The Mirror in the Roadway.* New York: Alfred A. Knopf, 1956.

O'Connor, William Van. *The Tangled Fire of William Faulkner*. Minneapolis: University of Minnesota Press, 1954.

――――――. *William Faulkner*. University of Minnesota Pamphlets on American Writers, No. 3. Minneapolis: University of Minnesota Press, 1959.

Of-By-and About Henry Miller. Yonkers, N. Y.: Alicat Bookshop Press, 1947.

Olson, Charles. *Call Me Ishmael*. New York: Reynal & Hitchcock, 1947.

Orton, Vrest. *Dreiserana: A Book About His Books*. New York: Chocorua Bibliographies, 1929.

Orwell, George. *A Collection of Essays*. New York: Doubleday, 1954.

――――――. *Inside the Whale and Other Essays*. London: Victor Gollancz, 1940.

Outland, Ethel R. *The "Effingham" Libels on Cooper: A Documentary History of the Libel Suits of James Fenimore Cooper Centering Around the Three Mile Point Controversy and the Novel Home as Found 1837-1845*. Madison: University of Wisconsin Studies in Language and Literature No. 28, 1929.

Overton, Grant. *An Hour of the American Novel*. Philadelphia: J. B. Lippincott, 1929.

――――――. *When Winter Comes to Main Street*. New York: George H. Doran, 1922.

――――――. *The Women Who Make Our Novels*. New York: Dodd, Mead, 1928.

Page, Rosewell. *Thomas Nelson Page: A Memoir of a Virginia Gentleman*. New York: Scribner's Sons, 1923.

Paine, Albert Bigelow. *A Short Life of Mark Twain*. New York, London: Harper and Brothers, 1920.

Paltsits, Victor Hugo (ed.). *Family Correspondence of Herman Melville 1830-1904 in the Gansevoort-Lansing Collection*. New York: New York Public Library, 1929.

Papashvily, Helen Waite. *All the Happy Endings*. New York: Harper & Brothers, 1956.

Parks, Edd Winfield. *Charles Egbert Craddock*. Chapel Hill: University of North Carolina Press, 1941.

Parrington, Vernon Louis. *Sinclair Lewis: Our Own Diogenes*. Seattle: University of Washington Book Store, 1930.

Pattee, Fred Lewis. *The First Century of American Literature: 1770-1870.* New York, London: D. Appleton-Century, 1935.

——————. *Mark Twain (Samuel Langhorne Clemens): Representative Selections, with Introduction and Bibliography* (American Writers Series). New York: American Book Co., 1935.

——————. *Side-Lights on American Literature.* New York: Century, 1922.

Pearson, Edmund. *Dime Novels; or, Following an Old Trail in Popular Literature.* Boston: Little, Brown, 1929.

——————. *Queer Books.* Garden City: Doubleday, Doran, 1928.

Percival, M. O. *A Reading of Moby-Dick.* Chicago: University of Chicago Press, 1950.

Perlés, Alfred. *My Friend Henry Miller: An Intimate Biography.* New York: John Day, 1956.

Perry, Bliss. *Park-Street Papers.* Boston and New York: Houghton Mifflin, 1908.

——————. *A Study of Prose Fiction,* Rev. Ed. Boston: Houghton Mifflin, 1920.

Phelps, William Lyon. *Essays on Modern Novelists.* New York: Macmillan, 1912.

Phillips, Mary E. *James Fenimore Cooper.* New York and London: John Lane, 1913.

Pollock, Thomas Clark and Oscar Cargill. *Thomas Wolfe at Washington Square.* New York: New York University Press, 1954.

Pommer, Henry F. *Milton and Melville.* Pittsburgh: University of Pittsburgh Press, 1950.

Porter, Katherine Anne. *The Days Before.* New York: Harcourt, Brace, 1952.

Potter, Jack. *A Bibliography of John Dos Passos.* Chicago: Normandie House, 1950.

Pound, Ezra. *Literary Essays,* edited by T. S. Eliot. London: Faber and Faber, 1954.

Powys, John Cowper. *Enjoyment of Literature.* New York: Simon and Schuster, 1938.

Prescott, Orville. *In My Opinion: An Inquiry into the Contemporary Novel.* Indianapolis and New York: Bobbs-Merrill, 1952.

Preston, George R., Jr. *Thomas Wolfe: A Bibilography*. New York: Charles S. Boesen, 1943.

Pugh, Griffith Thompson. *George Washington Cable: A Biographical and Critical Study*. Nashville, Tenn.: Private edition, 1947.

The Question of Henry James: A Collection of Critical Essays. Edited by F. W. Dupee. New York: Henry Holt, 1945.

Quinby, Henry Cole. *Richard Harding Davis: A Bibliography*. New York: E. P. Dutton, 1924.

Quinn, Arthur Hobson. *American Fiction: An Historical and Critical Survey*. New York and London, 1936.

—————————. See *Literature of the American People*.

Quinn, Patrick F. *The French Face of Edgar Poe*. Carbondale, Ill.: Southern Illinois University Press, 1957.

Randell, William Peirce. *Edward Eggleston: Author of 'The Hoosier School-Master'*. New York: King's Crown Press, 1946.

Ransom, Ellene. *Utopus Discovers America or Critical Realism in American Utopian Fiction 1798-1900*. Nashville: Joint University Libraries, 1947.

Rapin, René. *Willa Cather*. New York: Robert McBride & Co., 1930.

Rascoe, Burton. *Theodore Dreiser*. New York: Robert M. McBride, 1925.

Raymond, Thomas L. *Stephen Crane*. Newark, N. J.: Carteret Book Club, 1923.

Read, Herbert. *Collected Essays*. London: Faber and Faber, 1938.

Reid, Alfred S. *The Yellow Ruff & The Scarlet Letter: A Source of Hawthorne's Novel*. Gainesville: University of Florida Press, 1955.

Reid, B. L. *Art by Subtraction: A Dissenting Opinion of Gertrude Stein*. Norman: University of Oklahoma Press, 1958.

Rexroth, Kenneth. *Bird in the Bush: Obvious Essays*. New York: New Directions, 1959.

Richardson, Lyon N. *Henry James: Representative Selections, with Introduction, Bibliography, and Notes* (American Writers Series). New York: American Book Co., 1941.

Rideout, Walter B. *The Radical Novel in the United States*

1900-1954: Some Interrelations of Literature and Society. Cambridge: Harvard University Press, 1956.

Robb, Mary Cooper. *William Faulkner: An Estimate of his Contribution to the American Novel.* Critical Essays in English and American Literature No. 1. Pittsburgh: University of Pittsburgh Press, 1957.

Rogers, W. G. *When This You See, Remember Me: Gertrude Stein in Person.* New York, Toronto: Rinehart, 1948.

Rosenberry, Edward H. *Melville and the Comic Spirit.* Cambridge: Harvard University Press, 1955.

Rosenfeld, Paul. *By Way of Art: Criticisms of Music, Literature, Painting, Sculpture, and the Dance.* New York: Coward-McCann, 1928.

——————. *Men Seen: Twenty-four Modern Authors.* New York: Dial Press, 1925.

——————. *Port of New York: Essays on Fourteen American Moderns.* New York: Harcourt, Brace, 1924.

A Round-Table in Poictesme: A Symposium. Edited by Don Bregenzer and Samuel Loveman. Cleveland, Ohio: Colophon Club, 1924.

Rourke, Constance. *American Humor: A Study of the National Character.* New York: Harcourt, Brace, 1931; Garden City, N. Y.: Doubleday, 1953.

Rouse, Blair (ed.). *Letters of Ellen Glasgow.* New York: Harcourt, Brace, 1958.

Rubin, Louis D., Jr. *No Place on Earth: Ellen Glasgow, James Branch Cabell and Richmond-in-Virginia.* Austin: University of Texas Press, 1959.

——————. *Thomas Wolfe: The Weather of His Youth.* Baton Rouge: Louisiana State University Press, 1955.

Russell, Francis. *Three Studies in Twentieth Century Obscurity.* Aldington: Ashford: Kent: The Hand and Flower Press, 1954.

Russo, Dorothy Ritter and Thelma L. Sullivan. *A Bibliography of Booth Tarkington, 1869-1946.* Indianapolis: Indiana Historical Society, 1949.

Sackville-West, Edward. *Inclinations.* London: Secker and Warburg, 1949.

Sadlier, Michael. *Excursions in Victorian Bibliography.* London: Cox, 1922.

Samuels, Ernest. *Henry Adams: The Middle Years.* Cambridge, Mass.: Harvard University Press, 1958.

Samuels, Lee. *A Hemingway Check List.* New York: Scribner's, 1951.

Schevill, James. *Sherwood Anderson: His Life and Work.* Denver: University of Denver Press, 1951.

Schorer, Mark. *The Novelist in the Modern World.* Riecker Memorial Lecture No. 3. University of Arizona Bulletin Series, Vol. XXVIII, No. 2. Tucson: University of Arizona Press, 1957.

Schubert, Leland. *Hawthorne, the Artist: Fine-Art Devices in Fiction.* Chapel Hill: University of North Carolina Press, 1944.

Sealts, Merton M. *Melville's Reading: A Checklist of Books Owned and Borrowed.* Cambridge, Mass.: Harvard University Press, 1950.

Sedgwick, Henry Dwight. *The New American Type and Other Essays.* Boston and New York: Houghton Mifflin, 1908.

Sedgwick, William Ellery. *Herman Melville: The Tragedy of Mind.* Cambridge, Mass.: Harvard University Press, 1944.

Sergeant, Elizabeth Shepley. *Willa Cather: A Memoir.* Philadelphia and New York: J. B. Lippincott, n.d.

Sherman, Stuart P. *Americans.* New York: Charles Scribner's Sons, 1924.

——————. *Critical Woodcuts.* New York: Charles Scribner's Sons, 1926.

——————. *On Contemporary Literature.* New York: Henry Holt, 1917.

——————. *The Main Stream.* New York: Charles Scribner's Sons, 1927.

——————. *Points of View.* New York, London, 1924.

Shulenberger, Arvid. *Cooper's Theory of Fiction.* Lawrence, Kansas: University of Kansas Publications, Humanistic Studies, No. 32.

Slochower, Harry. *No Voice Is Wholly Lost: Writers and Thinkers in War and Peace.* New York: Creative Age Press, 1945.

Smith, Bernard. *Forces in American Criticism: A Study in the History of American Literary Thought.* New York: Harcourt, Brace, 1939.

Smith, Harrison (ed.). *From Main Street to Stockholm: Letters of Sinclair Lewis, 1919-1930* New York: Harcourt, Brace, 1952.

Smith, Henry Nash. *Virgin Land: The American West as Symbol and Myth.* Cambridge, Mass.: Harvard University Press, 1950; New York: Vintage Books, 1957.

Smith, S. Stephenson. *The Craft of the Critic.* New York: Thomas Y. Crowell, 1931.

Snell, George. *The Shapers of American Fiction, 1798-1947.* New York: E. P. Dutton, 1947.

Southern Renascence: The Literature of the Modern South. Edited by Louis D. Rubin, Jr., and Robert D. Jacobs. Baltimore: Johns Hopkins Press, 1953.

A Southern Vanguard. Edited by Allen Tate. New York: Prentice-Hall, 1947.

Speare, Morris Edmund. *The Political Novel: Its Development in England and in America.* New York: Oxford University Press, 1924.

Spiller, Robert E. *The Cycle of American Literature: An Essay in Historical Criticism.* New York: Macmillan, 1955; New York: New American Library (Mentor), 1957.

_____. *Fenimore Cooper: Critic of his Times.* New York: Minton, Balch, 1931.

Spiller, Robert E. and Philip C. Blackburn. *A Descriptive Bibliography of the Writings of James Fenimore Cooper.* New York: R. R. Bowker, 1934.

Sprigge, Elizabeth. *Gertrude Stein: Her Life and Work.* London: Hamish Hamilton, 1957.

Starke, Aubrey Harrison. *Sidney Lanier: A Biographical and Critical Study.* Chapel Hill: University of North Carolina Press, 1933.

Starrett, Vincent. *Stephen Crane: A Bibliography.* Philadelphia: Centaur Book Shop, 1923.

The Stature of Theodore Dreiser: A Critical Survey of the Man and His Work. Edited by Alfred Kazin and Charles Shapiro. Bloomington: Indiana University Press, 1955.

Stein, Gertrude. *The Autobiography of Alice B. Toklas.* New York: Literary Guild, 1933.

Stein, William Bysshe. *Hawthorne's Faust: A Study of the Devil Archetype.* Gainesville: University of Florida Press, 1953.

Steinbeck and His Critics: A Record of Twenty-Five Years. Edited by E. W. Tedlock, Jr. and C. V. Wicker. Albuquerque: University of New Mexico Press, 1957.

Stern, Madeleine B. *Louisa May Alcott*. Norman: University of Oklahoma Press, 1950.

Stern, Milton R. *The Fine Hammered Steel of Herman Melville*. Urbana: University of Illinois Press, 1957.

Stevenson, Elizabeth. *The Crooked Corridor: A Study of Henry James*. New York: Macmillan, 1949.

——————. *Henry James: A Bibliography*. New York: Macmillan, 1955.

Stewart, Randall. *American Literature & Christian Doctrine*. Baton Rouge: Louisiana State University Press, 1958.

——————. *Nathaniel Hawthorne: A Biography*. New Haven: Yale University Press, 1948.

Stock, Irvin. *William Hale White (Mark Rutherford): A Critical Study*. New York: Columbia University Press, 1956.

Stolper, Benjamin J. R. *Stephen Crane: A List of His Writings and Articles About Him*. Newark, N. J.: Newark Public Library, 1930.

Stone, Geoffrey, *Melville*. New York: Sheed & Ward, 1949.

Stone, Irving. *Sailor on Horseback: The Biography of Jack London*. Cambridge: Houghton Mifflin, 1938.

Stone, Wilfred. *Religion and Art of William Hale White ("Mark Rutherford")*. Stanford University Publications: University Series, Language and Literature, Vol. XII. Stanford: University Press, 1954.

Stovall, Floyd. *American Idealism*. Norman: University of Oklahoma Press, 1943.

Sundermann, K. H. *Herman Melvilles Gedankengut: Ein kritische Untersuchung seiner weltanschaulichen Grundideen*. Berlin: Verlag Arthur Collignon, 1937.

Sutherland, Donald. *Gertrude Stein: A Biography of Her Work*. New Haven: Yale University Press, 1951.

Swan, Michael. *Henry James*. London, New York and Toronto: Longmans, Green, 1950.

——————. *Henry James*. London: Arthur Barker, 1952.

Taylor, Marie Hansen. *On Two Continents: Memories of Half a Century*. New York: Doubleday, Page, 1905.

Taylor, Walter F. *The Economic Novel in America*. Chapel Hill: University of North Carolina Press, 1942.

Terry, John Skally (ed.). *Thomas Wolfe's Letters to His Mother, Julia Elizabeth Wolfe*. New York: Charles Scribner's Sons, 1943.

Theodore Dreiser, America's Foremost Novelist. New York and London: John Lane, n.d.

Thompson, Lawrance. *Melville's Quarrel with God.* Princeton, N. J.: Princeton University Press, 1952.

Thorp, Willard. *Herman Melville: Representative Selections, with Introduction, Bibliography, and Notes* (American Writers Series). New York: American Book Co., 1938.

Tindall, William York. *The Literary Symbol.* New York: Columbia University Press, 1955.

Toulmin, Harry Aubrey, Jr. *Social Historians.* Boston: Richard G. Badger, 1911.

Transitions in American Literary History. Edited by Harry Hayden Clark. Durham: Duke University Press, 1953.

Trilling, Lionel. *The Liberal Imagination: Essays on Literature and Society.* New York: Viking Press, 1950.

──────────. *The Opposing Self: Nine Essays in Criticism.* New York: Viking Press, 1955.

Turner, Arlin. *George W. Cable: A Biography.* Durham, N. C.: Duke University Press.

Twelve Original Essays on Great American Novels. Edited by Charles Shapiro. Detroit: Wayne State University Press, 1958.

Underwood, John Curtis. *Literature and Insurgency: Ten Studies in Racial Evolution.* New York: Mitchell Kennerley, 1914.

Van Doren, Carl. *The American Novel, 1789-1939.* New York: Macmillan, 1940.

──────────. *Contemporary American Novelists: 1900-1920.* New York: Macmillan, 1928.

──────────. *James Branch Cabell.* New York: Literary Guild, 1932.

──────────. *Many Minds.* New York: Alfred A. Knopf, 1926.

──────────. *Sinclair Lewis: A Biographical Sketch.* Garden City: Doubleday, Doran, 1933.

Van Doren, Mark. *Nathaniel Hawthorne.* New York: William Sloane, 1949.

──────────. *The Private Reader: Selected Articles & Reviews.* New York: Henry Holt, 1942.

Vickery, Olga W. *The Novels of William Faulkner: A Critical Interpretation.* Baton Rouge: Louisiana State University Press, 1959.

Vilas, Martin S. *Charles Brockden Brown: A Study of Early American Fiction.* Burlington, Vt.: Free Press Association, 1904.

Vincent, Howard P. *The Trying-Out of Moby-Dick.* Boston: Houghton Mifflin, 1949.

The Vintage Mencken. Edited by Alistair Cooke. New York: Vintage Books, 1956.

Vollmer, Clement. *The American Novel in Germany 1871-1913.* Philadelphia: International Printing, 1918.

Von Abele, Rudolph. *The Death of the Artist: A Study of Hawthorne's Disintegration.* The Hague: Martinus Nijhoff, 1955.

Wagenknecht, Edward. *Cavalcade of the American Novel: From the Birth of the Nation to the Middle of the Twentieth Century.* New York: Henry Holt, 1952.

Waggoner, Hyatt H. *Hawthorne: A Critical Study.* Cambridge: The Belknap Press of Harvard University Press, 1955.

————. *William Faulkner: From Jefferson to the World.* Lexington, Ky.: University of Kentucky Press, 1959.

Walcutt, Charles Child. *American Literary Naturalism, A Divided Stream.* Minneapolis: University of Minnesota Press, 1956.

————. *The Romantic Compromise in the Novels of Winston Churchill.* University of Michigan Contributions in Modern Philology No. 18 (Nov 1951).

Walker, Franklin Dickerson. *Frank Norris: A Biography.* New York: Doubleday, Doran, 1932.

Walpole, Hugh. *The Art of James Branch Cabell.* New York: Robert M. McBride, 1920.

Walser, Richard Gaither. *The Enigma of Thomas Wolfe: Biographical and Critical Selections.* Cambridge: Harvard University Press, 1953.

Waples, Dorothy. *The Whig Myth of James Fenimore Cooper.* New Haven: Yale University Press, 1938.

Warfel, Harry R. *American Novelists of Today.* New York: American Book Co., 1951.

————. *Charles Brockden Brown: American Gothic Novelist.* Gainesville: University of Florida Press, 1949.

Warner, Anna B. *Susan Warner* ("Elizabeth Wetherell"). New York and London: G. P. Putnam's Sons, 1909.

Warren, Austin. *Nathaniel Hawthorne: Representative Selections, with Introduction, Bibliography, and Notes* (American Writers Series). New York: American Book Co., 1934.

——————. *Rage for Order: Essays in Criticism.* Chicago: University of Chicago Press, 1948.

Warren, Robert Penn. *Selected Essays.* New York: Random House, 1958.

Wasserstrom, William. *Heiress of All Ages: Sex and Sentiment in the Genteel Tradition.* Minneapolis: University of Minnesota Press, 1959.

Watkins, Floyd C. *Thomas Wolfe's Characters: Portraits from Life.* Norman: University of Oklahoma Press, 1957.

Weaver, Raymond M. *Herman Melville, Mariner and Mystic.* New York: George H. Doran, 1921.

Weber, Clara and Carl J. *A Bibliography of the Published Writings of Sarah Orne Jewett.* Waterville, Maine: Colby College Press, 1949.

Webster, Samuel Charles (ed.). *Mark Twain: Business Man.* Boston: Little, Brown, 1946.

Wecter, Dixon. *Sam Clemens of Hannibal.* Boston: Houghton Mifflin, 1952.

Wegelin, Christof. *The Image of Europe in Henry James.* Dallas: Southern Methodist University Press, 1958.

West, Anthony. *Principles and Persuasions.* New York: Harcourt, Brace, 1957.

West, Herbert Faulkner. *A Stephen Crane Collection.* Hanover, N. H.: Dartmouth College Library, 1948.

West, Ray B., Jr. and Robert Wooster Stallman. *The Art of Modern Fiction.* New York: Rinehart, 1949.

West, Rebecca. *Henry James.* New York: Henry Holt, 1916.

——————. *The Strange Necessity.* Garden City, N. Y.: Doubleday, Doran, 1928.

Westbrook, Percy D. *Acres of Flint: Writers of Rural New England, 1870-1900.* Washington: Scarecrow Press, 1951.

Whicher, George. See *Literature of the American People.*

Whipple, T. K. *Spokesmen: Modern Writers and American Life.* New York: D. Appleton, 1928.

——————. *Study Out the Land.* Berkeley: University of California Press, 1943.

Wickham, Harvey. *The Impuritans.* New York: Lincoln MacVeagh, 1929.

Wilder, Amos N. *Theology and Modern Literature*. Cambridge: Harvard University Press, 1958.

Wiley, Lulu Rumsey. *The Sources and Influence of the Novels of Charles Brockden Brown*. New York: Vantage Press, 1950.

Willa Cather: A Biographical Sketch, an English Opinion and an Abridged Bibliography. New York: Alfred A. Knopf, 1927.

William Faulkner: Biography and Criticism 1951-1954. Eugene: University of Oregon Library, 1955.

William Faulkner: Two Decades of Criticism. Edited by Frederick J. Hoffman and Olga W. Vickery. East Lansing: Michigan State College Press, 1951.

Williams, Ames W. and Vincent Starrett. *Stephen Crane: A Bibliography*. Glendale, Calif.: John Valentine, 1948.

Wilson, Edmund. *Classics and Commercials: A Literary Chronicle of the Forties*. New York: Farrar, Straus and Company, 1950.

——————. *Eight Essays*. Garden City, N. Y.: Doubleday Anchor Books, 1954.

——————. *A Literary Chronicle: 1920-1950*. Garden City, N. Y.: Doubleday, 1956.

——————. *The Shores of Light: A Literary Chronicle of the Twenties and Thirties*. New York: Farrar, Straus and Young, 1952.

——————. *The Triple Thinkers: Ten Essays on Literature*. New York: Harcourt, Brace, 1938.

——————. *The Wound and the Bow: Seven Studies in Literature*. Cambridge: Houghton Mifflin, 1941.

Wilson, Forrest. *Crusader in Crinoline: The Life of Harriet Beecher Stowe*. Philadelphia: J. B. Lippincott, 1941.

Winters, Yvor. *In Defense of Reason*. New York: Swallow Press & William Morrow, 1947; Alan Swallow [3rd edition], 1960.

——————. *Maule's Curse: Seven Studies in the History of American Obscurantism*. Norfolk, Conn.: New Directions, 1938.

Woodberry, George Edward. *Nathaniel Hawthorne: How to Know Him*. Indianapolis: Bobbs-Merrill, 1918.

Woodress, James. *Booth Tarkington, Gentleman From Indiana*. Philadelphia and New York: J. B. Lippincott, 1954.

——————. *Howells & Italy*. Durham: Duke University Press, 1952.

Worthington, Marjorie. *Miss Alcott of Concord: A Biography.* Garden City, N. Y.: Doubleday, 1958.

Wright, Nathalia. *Melville's Use of the Bible.* Durham, N. C.: Duke University Press, 1949.

Writers at Work: The Paris Review Interviews. Edited by Malcolm Cowley. New York: Viking Press, 1958.

Writers of To-day, Vol. 2. Edited by Denys Val Baker. London: Sidgwick and Jackson, 1948.

Wyatt, Edith. *Great Companions.* New York: D. Appleton, 1917.

Wynn, Dudley Taylor. *A Critical Study of the Writings of Mary Hunter Austin (1868-1934).* New York: New York University, 1941.

Yates, Elizabeth. *Pebble in a Pool: The Widening Circles of Dorothy Canfield Fisher's Life.* E. P. Dutton, Inc., 1958.

Young, Philip. *Ernest Hemingway.* New York: Rinehart, 1952.
──────────────. *Ernest Hemingway.* University of Minnesota Pamphlets on American Writers, No. 1. Minneapolis: University of Minnesota Press, 1959.

Zabel, Morton Dauwen. *Craft and Character: Texts, Method, and Vocation in Modern Fiction.* New York: Viking Press, 1957.

PERIODICALS

Accent
American Imago
American Literature
American Mercury
American Notes and Queries
American Quarterly
American Review
American Scholar
Anglia
Antioch Review
Arizona Quarterly
Atlantic Monthly
Books Abroad
Boston Public Library Quarterly
Boston University Studies in English
Brigham Young University Studies
Bulletin of Bibliography

Bulletin of the New York Public Library
Chimera
CLA Journal
College English
Colorado Quarterly
Commentary
Comparative Literature
Contact
Criterion
Critic
Critique
Dial
discovery
ELH
English Institute Essays
English Studies
Etudes Anglaises
Evergreen Review
Explicator
Faulkner Studies
Georgia Review
Harper's
Harvard Library Bulletin
Hudson Review
Huntington Library Quarterly
Jahrbuch für Amerikastudien
Journal of English and Germanic Philology
Kenyon Review
Library Chronicle of the University of Texas
Mark Twain Journal
Modern Fiction Studies
Modern Language Notes
Modern Language Quarterly
New Mexico Quarterly
New World Writing
Nineteenth-Century Fiction
North American Review
Notes & Queries
Partisan Review
Personalist

Perspective
Philological Quarterly
Prairie Schooner
Princeton University Library Chronicle
Psychoanalytic Review
PMLA
Queen's Quarterly
Rutgers University Library Journal
Saturday Review
Scrutiny
Sewanee Review
South Atlantic Quarterly
Southern Review
Southwest Review
Studi Americani
Studies in Bibliography
Studies in Philology
Tennessee Studies in Literature
Texas Review
Texas Studies in Literature and Language
Trace
Tulane Studies in English
Twentieth Century Literature
University of California Publications in English
University of Kansas City Review
University of Texas Studies in English
University of Toronto Quarterly
University Review
Virginia Quarterly Review
Western Humanities Review
Western Review
Yale Review
Yale University Library Gazette
Zeitschrift für Anglistik und Amerikanistik